S0-AFM-614

A MOMENT OF CRISIS

A MOMENT

Jimmy Carter,
the Power of a Peacemaker,
and North Korea's
Nuclear Ambitions

OF CRISIS

MARION V. CREEKMORE, JR.

PublicAffairs
New York

Copyright © 2006 by Marion V. Creekmore, Jr.

Published in the United States by PublicAffairs™,
a member of the Perseus Books Group.

All rights reserved.
The opinions and characterizations in this book are those of the author, and do
not necessarily represent official positions of the United States Government.
Printed in the United States of America.

No part of this book may be reproduced in any manner whatsoever without written
permission except in the case of brief quotations embodied in critical articles and
reviews. For information, address PublicAffairs, 250 West 57th Street, Suite 1321,
New York, NY 10107.

Public Affairs books are available at special discounts for bulk purchases in the U.S.
by corporations, institutions, and other organizations. For more information, please
contact the Special Markets Department at the Perseus Books Group,
11 Cambridge Center, Cambridge, MA 02142, call (617) 252–5298, or email
special.markets@perseusbooks.com.

Designed by Brent Wilcox

Library of Congress Cataloging-in-Publication Data
Creekmore, Marion V., 1939-
    A moment of crisis : Jimmy Carter, the power of a peacemaker, and North
Korea's nuclear ambitions / Marion V. Creekmore, Jr.
       p.   cm.
    Includes bibliographical references and index.
    ISBN-13: 978-1-58648-414-9 (hardcover : alk. paper)
    ISBN-10: 1-58648-414-1 (hardcover : alk. paper)
    1. United States—Foreign relations—Korea (North)   2. Korea (North)—
Foreign relations—United States.   3. Carter, Jimmy, 1924-   4. Nuclear crisis
control—History—20th century.   5. United States—Foreign relations—
1993–2001.   I. Title.
    E183.8.K7C74   2006
    327.730519309'049—dc22
                                                            2006008251

10 9 8 7 6 5 4 3 2 1

To Linda

CONTENTS

BBC British Broadcasting Company
CIA Central Intelligence Agency
CRP Conflict Resolution Program
CVID complete, verifiable, and irreversible dismantlement
DCM deputy chief of mission
DIA Defense Intelligence Agency
DMZ demilitarized zone
DPRK Democratic People's Republic of Korea
HEU highly enriched uranium
IAEA International Atomic Energy Agency
INN International Negotiating Network
INR Bureau of Intelligence and Research
JCS Joint Chiefs of Staff
KEDO Korean Energy Development Organization
KEDO Korean Peninsula Energy Development Organization
LWRs light water reactors
MAC Military Armistice Commission
MIA missing in action
NGO nongovernmental organization
NPR National Public Radio
NPT Nuclear Non-Proliferation Treaty

NSC National Security Council
OAS Organization of American States
ROKG Republic of Korea Government
UN United Nations
UNDP United Nations Development Program
UNSC United Nations Security Council
USIP United States Institute of Peace

On June 15, 1994, former U.S. President Jimmy Carter faced the heaviest armed frontier in the world. Soon he would step across the demilitarized zone (DMZ) at Panmunjom, South Korea, and enter North Korea, a closed, isolated, and enigmatic land that few Americans had visited and none could claim to fully understand.

The DMZ, the no-man's-land established between North Korea and South Korea at the end of the Korean War in 1953, snaked 150 miles across the middle of the Korean Peninsula. Fences of barbed and razor wire, reinforced with watchtowers, guard posts, and bunkers, stretched along both sides of the heavily mined, two-and-a-half mile strip of land. At the time, North Korea fielded a military force of more than a million troops, about 60 percent more than the combination of South Korean forces and the 37,000 U.S. military personnel based in South Korea. Two-thirds of the North Korean troops and much of its firepower stood deployed along the DMZ, and South Korea's capital city of Seoul, with a population of 13 million, lay only thirty miles away, well within North Korea's artillery range.

The DMZ itself had been the site of forceful, official rhetoric in previous months. In July 1993, President Bill Clinton, clad in a fatigue jacket and wearing a cap emblazoned with "U.S. Forces Korea," had publicly warned North Korean leaders that their development and use of nuclear weapons "would be the end of their country." In April 1994, in a bilateral Korean meeting at the DMZ, the North Korean representative had threatened to turn Seoul into "a sea of fire" if UN sanctions were imposed on his country.

Security in Panmunjom was tight—the equivalent to that provided a standing president. The faces of the soldiers on both sides of the DMZ reflected alertness and intensity. Their eyes scrutinized every movement—of their military opponents, of the reporters and photographers jostling for position, of the government officials who would witness the crossing, of President and Mrs. Carter and their small team of advisers and secret service agents. Reportedly, an unseen rapid reaction force stood armed and ready on the southern side—within one minute's driving distance.

Despite the activity and noise, Jimmy Carter was calm, his mind riveted on his self-appointed mission—to talk directly with the North Korean dictator, Kim Il Sung, the same man who had ordered his troops to invade South Korea forty-four years earlier. Carter hoped to jump-start a negotiating process that would resolve peacefully the increasingly dangerous international crisis over North Korea's nuclear program. Unless he succeeded, he was convinced that a new and even more devastating war would erupt on the Korean Peninsula.

Carter knew fully the obstacles he faced. He lacked strong government support for his initiative from both the United States and South Korea. The Washington administration had acquiesced to his foray into North Korea with considerable reluctance. President Kim Young Sam of South Korea had called President Clinton to complain that Carter's trip was a mistake. Critics inside and outside of the U.S. government were charging that the former president's actions would make the crisis worse and strengthen a regime that understood only force. Carter considered the policy prescriptions of his detractors to be misguided and dangerous. But, to his chagrin, he knew that such views enjoyed wide circulation.

Carter also feared that his intervention would be too late. Because of the inflexibility of the involved governments, he thought his odds of success were low. Nevertheless, the chance to prevent an unnecessary and unwanted war drove him forward.

Carter's concerns about the possibility of war were not his alone. For weeks, the international press had speculated about how North Korea might act should the U.S.-led effort in the United Nations result in sanctions against the Pyongyang regime. As it intensified its diplomatic effort in New York, the Clinton administration had started augmenting its military forces in South Korea.

Tensions had been palpable when Carter arrived in South Korea on June 13, the same day the Seoul government held an exercise to determine the mobilization status of more than 6 million reservists. Reacting to South Korean reporting about the growing threat of war, the South Korean Defense Ministry had been using daily press conferences to try to calm the public, although it had admitted that the North Korean army was at its highest level of readiness of the last four years. Ordinary South Koreans had been stockpiling basic foodstuffs and besieging their legislators with anxious calls. The same day that Carter stood before the DMZ, South Korea engaged in the largest nationwide civil defense exercise in years as air-raid sirens wailed and people raced to protective shelters.

At the DMZ, Colonel Forest Chilton, the U.S. officer coordinating the crossing at Panmunjom, indicated that it was time to move. Carter shook hands with his friend Jim Laney, the U.S. ambassador to South Korea who had urged Carter to go to North Korea, and Laney hugged Mrs. Carter. Picking up his well-worn brown briefcase, Carter took Rosalynn's hand and nodded to Chilton. The three of them, along with the author and the rest of the Carter team, walked briskly toward the DMZ.

As he approached, Carter thought of the DMZ as "evidence of an incredible lack of communication and understanding." He reflected sadly that for "more than forty years, the Koreans and Americans have stared at each other across that armed border with total suspicion and often hatred and fear." As he stepped over that military barrier, for him a "bizarre and disturbing experience," he was also crossing the communications barrier between the United States and North Korea to talk directly with

Kim Il Sung, the man who had ruled his country with an iron hand since its independence in 1948.[1]

The crisis that brought former president Jimmy Carter to the DMZ in 1994 had been brewing for a long time, but developments had become increasingly alarming during the past two years. Following discoveries in 1992 that North Korea possessed more plutonium than it had admitted earlier to the International Atomic Energy Agency (IAEA) and knowing that North Korea was constructing additional nuclear reactors and a reprocessing facility, first the George H. W. Bush administration and then the Bill Clinton administration demanded that Pyongyang open all its facilities to inspection by the IAEA or face strong international action. From early 1993, the Clinton national security team and the North Korean leadership had engaged in a threat and counter-threat scenario interspersed with short-lived initiatives to try to resolve their differences through peaceful negotiations. By the spring of 1994, the United States had mounted a major campaign to get the United Nations Security Council (UNSC) to impose economic sanctions on North Korea if it continued to reject IAEA full-scope safeguards, and North Korean leaders were publicly and privately asserting that they would regard UN sanctions as a declaration of war. Despite the worsening crisis, no U.S. cabinet-level official tried to talk directly with his North Korean counterpart, much less with North Korean President Kim Il Sung.

National image and pride drove both sides, too. President Clinton and his advisers worried about the disparaging attacks from critics in the Congress, the media, and conservative think tanks depicting the administration as being weak and "wimpish" on foreign policy. By the time the crisis reached its peak in June 1994, the United States, with strong South Korean support, was rigidly insisting on a negotiating scenario in which North Korea would first have to give up its nuclear option and only then would the United States consider possible means of improving the bilateral relationship. The North Koreans, rejecting the unilateral and advance surrender of its only effective leverage—its nuclear threat, was demanding instead a package arrangement in which both sides would simultaneously receive benefits and undertake obligations. In May, the North Koreans surprised Washington, the IAEA, and the rest of the world by beginning to discharge from its nuclear reactor spent fuel rods that could be reprocessed into plutonium for making nuclear weapons. By June, the UN sanctions resolution was moving toward the final vote in the Security Council, and the usually caustic North Korean rhetoric was becoming increasingly shrill. Some new approach was needed to change the dynamics and steer the volatile situation away from military confrontation.

Jimmy Carter would provide that approach. He and his nongovernmental organization, The Carter Center, had demonstrated in previous interventions elsewhere that they would deal with odious regimes if doing so would serve the cause of peace. In Carter's mind, one had to try to work with the decisionmakers who could do you harm if you wanted to resolve crises without resorting to war. He did not regard an arrangement in which both sides gained and undertook commitments to be intrinsically bad, even if one of the parties had a disreputable past—as long as the agreement could be structured to ensure that both participants met their obligations. He rejected as well the shibboleth often voiced by hard-liners that such an arrangement would be appeasement or surrender to blackmail. Nor did he accept the argument that for the United States to engage in negotiations after earlier issuing threats would cause an irreparable loss of national credibility. For Jimmy Carter, a long-time leader in the human rights community, war was the ultimate violator of human rights. As he stated in his address upon receiving the Nobel Peace Prize in 2002: "War may sometimes be a necessary evil, but no matter how necessary, it is always evil."[2]

Carter was not alone in expressing concern about the inflexibility of governments dealing with the North Korean nuclear crisis during the first six months of 1994. Several other nongovernmental organizations (NGOs), a few newspaper reporters, and some scholars and retired U.S. government officials urged a more conciliatory approach toward Pyongyang, one that aimed at a settlement with which all sides could live.

Yet they were few, and their influence on U.S. policy was limited. Only Carter had the recognition, media access, and potential political clout that might enable him to influence the North Korean leadership and cause the Washington administration to consider a change in its approach.

The periodic shifts in policies by the South Korean government of President Kim Young Sam compounded the difficulties caused by the lack of unity within the Clinton administration over how to deal with North Korea. Kim harbored understandable antipathy toward the North Korean regime[3] and was strongly influenced by swings in public opinion polls about using force or conciliation in dealing with the North.

———

Such was the context for the historic trip of Jimmy Carter to the North Korean capital of Pyongyang in 1994. The outcome of his talks with Kim Il Sung would be a commitment by the North Koreans to freeze their nuclear program pending the outcome of official talks between their government leaders and those in Washington. Skillful negotiations by Washington and Pyongyang would result in the 1994 Agreed Framework. This agreement halted the reprocessing of spent fuel into bomb-making plutonium in return for the commitment of an international consortium, financed primarily by South Korea and Japan, to replace the existing North Korean graphite-moderated nuclear reactors with two light water nuclear reactors with less proliferation risk. These provisions and others in the agreement, including the gradual normalization of bilateral relations, ended the 1994 crisis. The United States and North Korea remained parties to this agreement until December 2002 when North Korea withdrew amid charges on both sides that the other had violated the eight-year-old pact.

The following pages discuss the intervention of Jimmy Carter and The Carter Center in the nuclear crisis of 1994. It is primarily a study of President Carter and his wife, adviser, and confidant, Rosalynn Carter. But it also mentions the contributions of a number of other persons, some working at The Carter Center at the time and others engaged elsewhere. I was fortunate to have been involved and to have accompanied the Carters across the demilitarized zone (DMZ). This narrative is my version of the events based on what I witnessed and what I learned from others. I am indebted to those who have shared their views with me. I regret any errors and misinterpretations, for which I take sole responsibility.

The book has three main purposes. First, it seeks to tell the story from Carter's viewpoint. This study draws on Carter Center records as well as on conversations with the Carters and entries in President Carter's private diary. It quotes extensively from Carter's own conversations, letters, and notes; from memoranda and letters provided to him by his staff and persons outside The Carter Center; and from my personal notes taken before, during, and after Carter's historic trip.

Second, this book attempts to demonstrate how well Carter was prepared for the intervention he undertook and how astute his understanding of the North Korean mentality was at the time he went to Pyongyang. Many of Carter's critics before and after his trip castigated him as being unknowledgeable about North Korea, naïve, and gullible. I believe that this narrative shows that Carter was neither unknowledgeable nor naïve, but rather had greater understanding of the thinking and priorities of the North Korean leadership than his detractors. Neither was Carter gullible. Even though his domestic critics greeted his June 16, 1994, CNN interview from Pyongyang with derision and incredulity, what Carter stated at the interview to be the commitments of the North Korean dictator was confirmed a few days later in diplomatic channels. Carter's negotiated freeze of the North Korean plutonium-based nuclear weapons program constituted a key component in the 1994 Agreed Framework; and for eight years, until the agreement was scrapped in 2002, the North Korean plutonium program remained frozen and verified by international inspection. With the collapse of this agreement and the expulsion of the international inspectors, Pyongyang regained full control over its plutonium-based nuclear program.

Third, the 1994 experience provided lessons that should be seriously considered by senior officials engaged in international affairs, including those dealing with North Korea. These lessons are discussed in the epilogue.

Two explanations are needed before beginning this narrative. I have often chosen to quote extensively from private and public documents rather than to summarize them for several reasons. Researchers have not previously had access to much of the source material that is used in this study. Additionally, Carter's negotiating style is unique; he is the most astute negotiator with whom I have worked closely during my twenty-eight-year diplomatic career and my four years in the NGO world. A few summary paragraphs cannot illuminate fully the talents and skills he brings to individual negotiations. A more lengthy description of key conversations enables the reader to comprehend more clearly how Carter approaches and conducts key consultations. There are several constants: intensive preparation, an ability and patience to listen attentively and to comprehend in detail the positions of others, a proclivity to grasp quickly the fundamental issues and ensure that marginal questions do not side-track the discussions, a tactical flexibility coupled with a firm view of the substantive outcome he seeks, and a gentle but forceful style of presentation that relies more on his superb memory than on written notes. Finally, much of the story of citizen Carter's intervention in the 1994 nuclear crisis is a story of what Carter was doing and saying and how others, inside and outside of government, were interpreting and reporting on what he did and said. Spelling out the various views and positions in some depth should enhance understanding.

The second explanation relates to semantics. Discussions on the 1994 Korean crisis, as well as many other foreign policy issues, often use value-laden terms such as "hard-liners" and "moderates." I will use these conventions, but I want to define what I mean by them in this study. When I mention "hard-liners," I refer primarily to those experts or observers who believed that North Korea was building a nuclear weapons capacity to deter attack, intimidate its neighbors, and/or sell its products to others. They also believed that North Korea understood only force. For them, threats or actions, such as UN sanctions or the establishment of blockades, were required to convince the North Koreans to dismantle their nuclear weapons program. If such methods did not work, military action might be necessary. Underlying the view of many of the "hard-liners" were two fundamental considerations: first, a belief that the North Korean regime would soon crumble, and nothing must be done to help it survive, and second, an unwillingness to pay for any North Korean constructive action on the nuclear front because that would be "surrendering to blackmail."

The so-called "moderates" (I prefer "bargainers") believed that North Korea's primary purpose for its nuclear program was to use it as a bargaining chip to leverage the United States and others into providing North Korea with political, economic, and security benefits. Although sensitive to the likelihood that without verification the North Koreans would cheat, the "moderates" believed that a negotiated solution should be pursued and that a mutually advantageous outcome could be possible.

The first chapter describes the origins and development of the nuclear crisis up until June 1994, drawing primarily on secondary sources. Chapters 2–13 trace the actions and activities of Jimmy Carter and The Carter Center before, during, and immediately after the crisis. The epilogue focuses on how the experiences of Carter's nongovernmental organization in this specific crisis have relevance to current and future sensitive foreign policy issues.

It has been twelve years since I traveled to Pyongyang, North Korea, to induce President Kim Il Sung to stop his country's nuclear weapons program. As Marion Creekmore's narrative documents, the world in 1994 was marching toward a war that was neither wanted nor necessary. Yet the governments most directly involved—the United States, North Korea, and South Korea—had maneuvered themselves into a diplomatic gridlock from which their respective policies offered no retreat. Threats and counter-threats dominated the diplomatic atmosphere as the situation became increasingly precarious, but no top official in Washington was willing to meet one-on-one with Kim Il Sung, the ruler of North Korea since its independence in 1948 and the only person who could decide what actions his strange and isolated country would take.

In my view, someone had to determine firsthand whether Kim Il Sung wanted conflict or preferred to resolve the serious nuclear crisis diplomatically. I knew that a war would bring devastating consequences to North Korea, and that casualties in and around Seoul, South Korea, might exceed those in the previous Korean War. Since I had a long-standing invitation to visit North Korea and consult with him, I decided to go. I was acutely aware of Washington's reservations and I knew that my failure would bring sharp and enduring condemnation. But I hoped that Kim Il Sung was looking for a way to resolve the crisis peacefully, and believed that his views should be explored before the United States risked a dangerous and costly war. My expectations proved to be correct. Kim Il Sung wanted to deal, and he and I negotiated an agreement that froze the North Korean plutonium-based nuclear program, placed it under continuous international inspection, and promised summit talks between the leaders of North and South Korea. This laid the bases for the official Agreed Framework of October 1994 between the United States and North Korea.

For the next eight years, North Korea did not produce any plutonium. It did not make any nuclear bombs. Its nuclear facilities that existed in 1994 were locked down, and outside experts monitored them twenty-four hours a day, seven days a week. There were later direct talks between the leaders of the two Koreas, for which President Kim Dae Jung of South Korea received the Nobel Prize for peace.

Unfortunately, because of actions by both North Korea and the United States, the Agreed Framework collapsed in December 2002. The international inspectors were expelled, and the North Koreans regained unrestricted access to spent fuel rods from which plutonium could be manufactured. Since then, North Korea has had the capability, which it has probably employed, to reprocess enough plutonium to make a half dozen nuclear weapons. Additionally, it is accumulating more spent fuel each year, and without a change in the current policies of North Korea and the United States, Pyongyang's capacity to manufacture nuclear weapons will significantly increase in the future.

I believed then, as did Bill Clinton and his top national security advisers, that the Agreed Framework of 1994 was a major foreign policy success. It made the United States and the world safer, and its collapse was a tragedy, even for North Korea. This outcome was not inevitable, and the responsibility does not rest on just one country. I hope that the situation has not deteriorated beyond repair, and that it will prove possible, through diplomatic means, to frame a new and perhaps better arrangement than the Agreed Framework. But to achieve this result, all the key players must forego threatening rhetoric and mount a concerted, consistent, and genuine effort to structure a negotiated arrangement that embraces the fundamental interests of all the parties, including those of North Korea.

My intervention into the North Korean nuclear crisis of 1994 reflected my basic beliefs about existing and potential conflicts and how third party mediation can sometimes help prevent or resolve such confrontations. Violent conflicts represent one of the most serious challenges facing the international community. They cause enormous suffering, and often feed on deep-rooted antagonisms. They usually involve each side demonizing the other, which tends to preclude objective thinking and makes it extremely difficult to find a mutually acceptable compromise.

In many conflicts, the antagonists have not reached the point where they perceive a negotiated settlement to be preferable to starting or continuing military action based on the hope for greater gains for their side and greater losses for the other. But on those occasions, where both sides see—or can be helped to see—real value in avoiding or ending violent confrontation but do not know how to achieve this goal, then an outside mediator may be able to help them break through their own intolerance and ignorance of the other's views, create an atmosphere of mutual respect, and frame a final settlement that protects the fundamental interests of each.

I underwent a trial by fire in conflict mediation while serving as president of the United States. For thirteen days in October 1978, I cajoled and pressed Prime Minister Menachem Begin of Israel and President Anwar Sadat of Egypt to end their confrontation and negotiate a peaceful resolution of their three-decade-long state of war. Since the two disputants could not constructively engage in face-to-face consultations, I went back and forth between the two leaders and their advisers, seeking first to understand fully their countries' basic interests and then to draft and sell them on compromise language that preserved the interests of both sides. I think Begin and Sadat understood that I respected each of them, that I was committed to helping them frame a mutually acceptable settlement, and that I attached great importance to the subject since I gave it my primary attention, despite other world demands, for almost two weeks. As a result of the 1978 Camp David Accord and the peace treaty that followed between the two countries, Israel withdrew from the occupied Sinai, and the two countries established diplomatic relations. Not a word of this peace treaty has been violated since then.

As we were establishing the Conflict Resolution Program at The Carter Center in 1985, I studied what scholars and practitioners said about mediation as a means of preventing or ending war, and improved my own techniques. I realized that, even though I was no longer president, I might still use the approach that had been successful at Camp David. When The Carter Center intervenes in a conflict, obviously with the approval of the protagonists, I seek first to build confidence in my fairness, my neutrality, and my unwavering commitment to help them resolve their dispute peacefully. As a mediator, I will sometimes meet with the disputants in the same room, serving as moderator and facilitator of their discussions. On other occasions, I use shuttle diplomacy, as I did with Begin and Sadat, moving back and forth between the groups in different locations, and helping each of them focus on their own bottom-line interests and then on understanding the legitimate needs and interests of their opponents. If only one person or group is the key to resolving a problem, as was Kim Il Sung, then my efforts are more easily concentrated.

Regardless of the meeting arrangements, once I understand the key issues involved and have a good idea of the necessary elements for a peaceful settlement, I usually draft a single document that I think meets the basic requirements of each side. Then I work with them, revising the document as necessary, to get the acceptance of all involved. In the North Korean case, I wrote down prior to leaving the United States the main elements that I thought must comprise an agreement that would be mutually acceptable to the United States and North Korea and also obtain the acquiescence of South Korea. I was fortunate to have been trained in nuclear technology as a young submarine officer, so I was familiar with the key issue. The arrangement on which Kim Il Sung and I agreed several days later was quite similar to what I had earlier drafted.

A keen understanding of the issues and a proven mediating procedure are essential tools for a successful mediator. But there is something more important. The mediator—or for that matter, the direct negotiator—should project respect and a desire to accommodate the interests of the individuals with whom he is negotiating. I have sometimes been criticized for dealing with "tyrants" and accused of coddling "miscreants." To the question of whether to negotiate with such a person, my answer is simple. We live in an imperfect world. If that person holds the power to do harm or to prevent it, I would seriously negotiate with him, not out of fear or naïveté, but from conviction that such an approach will maximize the chances of alleviating or preventing the problem.

Isolation, public insults, or threats will seldom resolve a crisis and will often exacerbate a serious situation. Economic sanctions, as imposed by the United States on Cuba, quite often injure and alienate people who are already suffering, and tend to strengthen domestic and international support for a leader who is the target of our displeasure. The military option is always available, particularly for a country as powerful as the United States. But as we are relearning in Iraq, an armed attack or invasion is not cost-free and its long-term consequences are not certain. Whether we are constrained by pragmatic consequences or moral standards, a peaceful resolution of disputes is usually best. War should be the last alternative, even when dealing with tyrants.

In addition to showing respect for adversaries, a mediator or a negotiator must also try to understand their frames of reference, their motivations, and the pressures on them. This is very difficult for Americans, who take the economic, military, and cultural preeminence of our nation for granted and rarely consider it necessary to understand or accommodate contrary views from other people. More than we realize, these "foreigners" often fear or distrust us, are alienated, and sometimes react with hatred.

When pride or other constraints make it impossible for a government to deal directly with those considered to be troublemakers, then alternative approaches must be used to resolve a serious threat or problem. Leaders of other nations can fill this role, or perhaps unofficial intermediaries.

I often reflect back on my trip to North Korea in 1994, on my two lengthy meetings with Kim Il Sung, on what we achieved, and how it formed the basis for the peaceful resolution of the nuclear crisis of the time. I believe what happened then demonstrated the validity of some of the principles I have discussed above. I believe as well that they showed why sincere negotiations should almost always precede the use of military force to advance our national objectives of security, democracy, freedom, and human rights.

Marion Creekmore was uniquely qualified to write about The Carter Center's intervention in the North Korean nuclear crisis of 1994. As the program director of the Center from 1993–1996, he coordinated many of my international initiatives, joining Rosalynn and me as principal adviser for the North Korean initiative and going with us to Pyongyang. His narrative draws heavily on our shared experiences, our respective notes, and voluminous Carter Center files—most of which have never been perused by researchers. As a former U.S. diplomat whose career included an ambassadorial assignment before coming to The Carter Center, Marion understood and captured in his book the bureaucratic and political maneuvering within which The Carter Center initiative took place.

Marion's manuscript is the most comprehensive treatment of my role in resolving the 1994 nuclear crisis that has yet been written. Its final chapter relates the lessons we learned more than a decade ago to the current nuclear imbroglio with North Korea. His advocacy of serious, sustained, and genuine negotiations with North Korea mirrors my own.

THE CRISIS DEVELOPS
Part I

CHAPTER 1

Toward Diplomatic Gridlock

The precarious situation on the Korean Peninsula in 1994 grew out of a series of developments that stretched back two decades. From the mid-1970s to the mid-1990s, North Korea accelerated its nuclear activities as it confronted increasing economic difficulties and declining political clout. In the mid-1970s, South Korea began pulling away economically from its northern neighbor; by the 1990s, South Korea's economy was from fifteen to twenty times larger than that of North Korea.[1] In the late 1980s, Pyongyang's principal political allies, the Soviet Union and China, no longer deferred to North Korea in their dealings with South Korea. Both countries sent teams to the Olympic Games in Seoul in 1988, against the wishes of North Korea, and established diplomatic relations with South Korea in 1990 and 1991, respectively. Because of the implosion of the Soviet Union a short time later and China's increasing commitment to market economics, North Korea lost the subsidized imports of oil and other critical products as well as the guaranteed markets in Eastern Europe[2] that had helped its leaders hide from its people—and, to some extent, from the world—the sad state of their economy and their growing political isolation.

Throughout its independent history, North Korea had relied on a large military to protect its security, back its political leadership, and worry its neighbors, particularly South Korea.[3] At some point, probably in the late 1970s,[4] North Korea decided to augment its military force with a nuclear weapons program. It built a 2 MWe (megawatt) research reactor that went into operation in 1965. At Moscow's insistence, North Korea placed this reactor under the safeguards of the International Atomic Energy Agency (IAEA) in 1977. Two years later, North Korea began to develop indigenously a 5 MWe[5] research reactor fueled by natural uranium and moderated by graphite, minerals available locally; this reactor became operational in 1986. A year earlier, Pyongyang had obtained a commitment from the Soviet Union to provide North Korea with one light water nuclear reactor[6] to help alleviate the country's growing electric power shortage, and, as a condition for this deal, placed its indigenous 5 MWe reactor under IAEA safeguards and signed the Nuclear Non-Proliferation Treaty (NPT). The Soviets subsequently reneged on their commitment and did not—probably because of the USSR's own economic problems—provide the promised reactor. Nevertheless, North Korea did not withdraw from the NPT, but its negotiations with the IAEA dragged on until early 1992, when Pyongyang finally signed a safeguard agreement with the Vienna agency.[7]

The same year that North Korea joined the NPT, 1985, it started constructing a new and larger graphite-moderated reactor (50 MWe) and, subsequently, a third, even larger, 200 MWe reactor. In 1991, U.S. satellites identified a large building under construction that was later identified as a reprocessing facility for converting spent fuel into weapons-grade plutonium. Once this facility and the two reactors became operational, North Korea would have the technical capacity to produce enough plutonium for approximately thirty nuclear bombs a year. U.S. intelligence sources projected that unless North Korea changed its nuclear policies, it might be able to produce atomic bombs by the mid-1990s.[8]

The administration of George H. W. Bush viewed the North Korean nuclear program as a serious potential threat to South Korea and Japan, and to international stability in general. It initially decided to deal with this problem through engagement with Pyongyang while maintaining the strong U.S. military support for, and presence in, South Korea. In trying to encourage the North Korean leadership to terminate its nuclear weapons efforts, the Bush government offered various inducements: It permitted more than $1 billion of goods, mostly food and medical supplies, to be sold to North Korea; it allowed North Koreans to visit the United States for educational, social, and athletic exchanges; and, with Pyongyang's concurrence, it established a formal channel for diplomatic contact between the embassies of the United States and North Korea in Beijing.[9] Then, in September 1991, President Bush announced his decision to redeploy to the United States all tactical nuclear warheads based on land and on board U.S. ships (with the exception of air-delivered arms in Europe); and in December, President Roh Tae Woo of South Korea stated publicly that there were no nuclear weapons in South Korea, and he reaffirmed the willingness of South Korea, in consultations with the United States, to undergo nuclear inspections if North Korea did the same.[10] These pronouncements undercut the Pyongyang line that it could not accept intrusive IAEA nuclear inspections in its country while being threatened by nuclear weapons in South Korea. In the same time frame, North Korea adopted a more conciliatory policy toward South Korea and the United States.[11] After Pyongyang proposed new inter-Korean talks in 1990, officials from the two Koreas undertook serious bilateral negotiations, the result being the initialing of a bilateral agreement on reconciliation, nonaggression, and cooperation in December 1991 and a bilateral agreement pledging not to "test, manufacture, produce, receive, store, deploy or use nuclear weapons" and "not to possess nuclear reprocessing and uranium enrichment facilities" in January 1992. The latter agreement, officially called the Declaration on the Denuclearization of the Korean Peninsula, also contained provisions for reciprocal inspections by a joint nuclear control commission established by the agreement.[12]

These positive developments on the Korean peninsula led the Bush administration to break precedent and, in January 1992, hold its own bilateral consultations with North Korea. (The United States had not held high-level diplomatic talks with North Korea since the end of the Korean War.)[13] However, many within the administration had strong reservations about talking officially and at a high level with North Korea. They held that to do so before Pyongyang had permitted full IAEA inspections and terminated its nuclear weapons program would be to succumb to North Korean nuclear blackmail. As a result of the bureaucratic battle in preparing for the talks, the leader of the U.S. delegation, Under Secretary of State Arnold Kanter, took with him to New York rigid negotiating instructions. They demanded that North Korea accept IAEA inspection of all its nuclear facilities and give up its nuclear weapons options; only after compliance would the United States discuss what it might be able to offer in return. Kanter could not even agree to a second round of talks unless U.S. demands were fully met. Not surprising, the meeting was short and unproductive.[14] Nevertheless, despite its disappointment that the United States refused to schedule follow-on discussions, the North Korean leadership signed the long-delayed safeguard agreement with the IAEA on January 30, 1992, and the North Korean parliament ratified the agreement early in April.[15] In May 1992, Pyongyang provided the IAEA with an extensive inventory of its nuclear program, including confirmation that a reprocessing plant was being constructed. During the agency's inspection later in the month, North Korean officials told the Vienna inspectors that their nuclear experts had reprocessed 90 grams of plutonium from partially irradiated fuel rods during the shutdown of its 5 MWe reactor in 1990.[16] The IAEA subsequently decided that more plutonium had been produced than had been revealed by the North Koreans.[17]

The momentum in the bilateral Korean talks about fulfilling their two new agreements slowed during the summer and fall. In October 1992, the United States and South Korea announced the resumption of the annual Team Spirit joint military exercises, to be held in 1993.[18] North Korea responded by canceling most of its bilateral contacts with South Korea. It also refused to disclose additional information about the status of its nuclear program to the IAEA, and it specifically rejected the Vienna agency's request to examine two sites that the North Koreans had not declared as nuclear-related in the inventory provided earlier to the IAEA.[19] The IAEA (and United States) thought that such an examination would reveal the amount of plutonium that North Korea possessed. These developments, though fueling the ire of hard-liners in the United States and South Korea, did not get sustained attention in either government since both were engaged in the last phase of presidential elections.[20]

The North Korean nuclear issue forced itself on the Clinton administration within weeks of its taking office—well before the new government had organized itself to deal with this matter. The IAEA, intelligence information from U.S. satellites in hand, demanded formally in February that North Korea submit to "special inspections" of the two undeclared nuclear sites by March 16. The Vienna agency simultaneously notified the United Nations Security Council (UNSC) that it would have to enforce this demand if North Korea failed to comply. Pyongyang took an equally firm position. On March 12, threatening to be the first NPT member to renounce the treaty, North Korea gave the required ninety days notice for withdrawing from the NPT. In early March, the previously scheduled Team Spirit military exercise commenced, labeled publicly by Pyongyang as a "nuclear war test aimed at a surprise, preemptive strike at the northern half of the country."[21]

As Don Oberdorfer recorded, the North Korean nuclear question "leaped to the top of the international agenda."[22] Some politicians, much of the media, and many think tank representatives pressured the Clinton team to take forceful action against Pyongyang. Many of those demanding that the United States not negotiate with Pyongyang believed that North Korea, one of the few remaining Communist countries and one that had previously engaged in terrorism, was teetering toward political collapse. They opposed any U.S. government action that might help the rulers of North Korea stay in power.

Early criticized as "wimpish" in international affairs, the Clinton team, closely attuned to public reaction and polls, hesitated to appear

weak in dealing with North Korea. As it struggled to decide how to respond, the foreign minister of the new South Korean government of
Kim Young Sam came to Washington with a proposed strategy. Han
Sung Joo saw great danger in the current situation: He feared that developments were leading to North Korean possession of nuclear
weapons, an outbreak of war on the peninsula, and/or an arms race in
which South Korea and Japan would go nuclear. He argued for a
"stick-and-carrot" approach to influence North Korea to remain in the
NPT. The "stick" would be the threat of UN sanctions ranging from
diplomatic isolation to military action, and the "carrot" would include
the cancellation of the Team Spirit exercise, provision of security guarantees for North Korea, and promises to Pyongyang of increased trade
and other inducements. Confronted simultaneously with castigations
from hard-liners in the United States and South Korea, counterpres-
sure from China for direct U.S.-North Korean negotiations, and what
was thought to be the South Korean government's support for the suggested "stick-and-carrot" approach, the Clinton administration decided to talk bilaterally with North Korea, but to restrict the
consultations to nuclear issues.[23]

Intensive U.S.-North Korean talks took place in New York in June
1993. The two sides issued a joint statement at the conclusion of the
talks in which North Korea agreed to suspend its withdrawal from the
NPT and accept "the impartial application of full-scope safeguards"
while unilaterally asserting that it was no longer required to undergo the
full panoply of IAEA inspections.[24] The statement, using language
drawn largely from the UN Charter, also contained assurances against
the threat and use of force and for a nuclear-free Korean Peninsula as
well as respect for each other's sovereignty and for noninterference in
each other's internal affairs. Even though the language was unexcep-
tional, the statement drew sharp rebuke from hawks, such as Lally
Weymouth of the *Washington Post*, because the United States had never
before been party to a joint statement with North Korea.[25] Then, in interviews with the BBC and the *New York Times*, President Kim Young
Sam of South Korea criticized the joint statement and claimed that

North Korea was buying time to advance its nuclear program. His comments not only shocked the U.S. officials, who believed they had initiated bilateral talks at the behest of the South Korean government, but set off a frenetic set of diplomatic exchanges aimed at reconciling the public positions of Washington and Seoul. This occasion would not be the last time that the Kim Young Sam government would send mixed signals to Washington.[26]

As agreed in June, the United States and North Korea met again in July in Geneva.[27] These talks made no progress on the issue of "special inspections," although North Korea said that it would consult with the IAEA on "outstanding safeguards and other issues." But the North Koreans raised another issue that more than a year later would form the basis for a bilateral agreement between the United States and the Democratic People's Republic of Korea (DPRK). Announcing that he had "bold, new instructions," the North Korean negotiator, First Vice Foreign Minister Kang Sok Ju, asserted that North Korea would be willing, with financial assistance from abroad, to replace its graphite moderated nuclear reactors with light water reactors (LWRs). When the new reactors were in place, Pyongyang would "reaffirm its commitment to the NPT."[28] Over lunch, Kang Sok Ju stressed to Assistant Secretary of State Robert Gallucci, the U.S. negotiator, that the proposal represented a major change in policy for North Korea and had been approved by President Kim Il Sung, who reportedly wanted better relations with the United States. After reviewing the proposal, Washington instructed its delegation in Geneva not to make a commitment to the North Koreans. U.S. law prohibited the United States from selling nuclear reactors to North Korea. Because the costs of such reactors would run into billions of dollars, the administration assumed that Congress would reject any U.S. financial involvement in supplying the North Koreans with nuclear technology from third countries.[29] Nevertheless, the U.S. statement at the end of the talks said that the United States would "support the introduction of light water reactors" in North Korea. Both countries' statements indicated that the bilateral talks would resume in two months; but the U.S. statement added the condition that the "third round" of consultations must be preceded by separate, serious discussions by North Korea with the IAEA and with South Korea.[30]

During the fall, as North Korea and the IAEA failed to agree on the extent of future inspections[31] and North-South talks stymied, the Clinton administration took an increasingly tough public line toward North Korea, though still falling short of the hard-liners' demands. In November, Defense Secretary Les Aspin briefed the press about the forward deployment of North Korean troops near the demilitarized zone (DMZ), omitting that this development had been going on for some years. The resulting press stories, which suggested incorrectly that the North Koreans were adopting a more aggressive military posture, stimulated a war scare that lasted for several weeks.[32] The same month, President Clinton, probably reacting to mounting criticism of U.S. actions in Somalia and Haiti, told *Meet the Press* that North Korea could not be allowed to develop a nuclear bomb, and he did not suggest the use of negotiations to stop them. The United States took a forward position in pushing critical resolutions in the IAEA against North Korea when Pyongyang's talks with the Vienna agency failed to make progress. The United States postponed the third round of bilateral talks with North Korea.[33]

Despite the externally tough position, U.S. officials found it difficult to agree internally on "sticks" that might be used to force North Korean compliance. The notion of sanctions had been under consideration since before the Clinton administration came to power. But when this issue was examined again in the fall and winter of 1993–1994, U.S. analysts concluded that sanctions would not likely cause North Korea to reverse course. Moreover, this approach could set off a chain reaction: "Dialogue would end, Pyongyang would accelerate its nuclear program, and Washington would face enormous pressure to use military force. In those circumstances, fear of a U.S. strike might cause North Korea to launch a preemptive attack." Moreover, China made clear to the United States its lack of support for sanctions, and Japan and South Korea advised that diplomacy should be exhausted before sanctions were pursued.[34]

Within the administration, Gallucci and others sought to develop a new negotiating position that built on the June and July talks and could be sold to their superiors. Encouraged by Foreign Minister Han of South Korea as well as appeals by the North Koreans and the successful October 1993 trip of Congressman Gary Ackerman to Pyongyang, they fashioned a new approach that called for a comprehensive "package agreement" providing simultaneous quid-pro-quos that met the minimum requirements of both countries as well as those of South Korea.[35] The interagency Deputies Committee in October recommended this comprehensive approach to the Principals Committee, whose members, including President Clinton, endorsed it in mid-November despite reservations by some participants. A few days later, however, the administration back-pedaled when Kim Young Sam came to Washington. Ignoring that his subordinates had concurred in the package concept, the South Korean president attacked the "comprehensive approach." He insisted that the U.S.-North Korean talks should occur and Team Spirit be cancelled only after a North Korean envoy had visited Seoul and engaged in "serious discussions" on North-South issues. Clinton accepted Kim's revisions.[36] Whereas a "thorough and broad" approach, the new descriptive language adopted during the visit of President Kim, sounded similar to a "comprehensive" or a "package" approach, it differed fundamentally in that it returned to the older idea of insisting that North Korea had to meet certain preconditions before other elements could come into play. When informed, the North Koreans reacted negatively. They privately complained to U.S. officials that the new formula gave South Korea control over the timing of the "third round" of U.S.-North Korean talks and publicly criticized the United States for trying to pressure North Korea.[37]

On February 15, 1994, Deputy Assistant Secretary Thomas Hubbard (who had been Gallucci's deputy in the 1993 negotiations with North Korea in New York and Geneva), supported by Ken Quinones and Gary Samore, took up discussions in New York with the North Korean deputy ambassador, Ho Jong, and his colleagues in an attempt to restart the Gallucci-Kang Sok Ju talks. By February 26, 1994, they seemed to

have succeeded. They planned for the U.S. and North Korean governments to announce that agreement had been reached to hold a third
round of U.S.-North Korean talks, suspend the Team Spirit exercises,
initiate new IAEA inspections of North Korea's declared nuclear facilities, and undertake an exchange of envoys by the two Koreas. However,
the United States insisted that the matter of timing on envoys had to be
resolved between the two Koreas.[38] During the following days, the
Clinton administration said that the IAEA inspections and the exchange of envoys between the two Koreas had to be completed before
the U.S.-North Korean talks could be held and the Team Spirit exercises officially suspended. On March 3, North Korea announced that,
contrary to the expressed views by Washington and Seoul, the New
York agreement contained no preconditions requiring an envoy exchange.[39] The carefully crafted compromise fell apart.

The failure of this initiative hinted at the continuing policy struggle
going on within the Clinton national security team on how to deal with
North Korea. The State Department, focused primarily on protecting the
nuclear nonproliferation regime and learning definitively about Pyongyang's nuclear past, insisted that North Korea must rejoin the NPT and
permit full-scope nuclear safeguards, including special inspections. After
these actions had been taken, the United States would begin a "careful
process" to address North Korea's principal concerns. The Defense Department gave a much higher priority to stopping North Korean plutonium production, and it was willing to offer early incentives to achieve
that goal. Although in mid-March the Principals Committee agreed, as a
fallback position, that special inspections would not have to be implemented immediately,[40] those insisting that North Korea had to give up its
nuclear weapons program without a commitment in advance by the
United States of what it might be willing to offer in return held the upper
hand. Many advocating this view also insisted that should North Korea
continue to reject this scenario, it must be confronted with UNSC economic sanctions that would progressively become more stringent.

Two developments in January and February 1994 reflected the growing strength of those favoring the more forceful approach. The Rev-

erend Billy Graham, who had been invited to visit North Korea in late January to speak and conduct worship services, asked whether the administration wished him to convey a message to Kim Il Sung, with whom he was scheduled to meet. A short, rather blunt, message from President Clinton was given to the evangelist. It told the North Korean leader that his country must "cooperate" on the nuclear issue before relations could improve. President Kim Il Sung's reported response: The "language of threats" could "drive the situation to catastrophe."[41] In early February, James Woolsey, the director of the CIA, went public in a speech with the charge that during the 1989–1991 period, North Korea had reprocessed and hidden enough plutonium to make two nuclear weapons. The media reports headlined that North Korea *possessed* nuclear weapons, implying that tough counteraction was imperative. It was lost in the static that Woolsey's "worst-case scenario" was highly disputed within the intelligence community, and that many of his administration colleagues sharply, but privately, rebuked him. Nevertheless, the administration's critics used Woolsey's speech as proof of the failure of the Clinton team to prevent North Korea from developing nuclear weapons.[42]

From his post in Seoul, the U.S. ambassador, James T. Laney, grew increasingly alarmed at what he perceived to be a dangerous spiral toward potential conflict. He flew to Washington in February to lobby for a senior administration official to be placed in charge of developing and implementing a coherent strategy toward the Korean Peninsula. Laney was enraged by Woolsey's public statement because he knew that its contents were disputed and that public disclosure had not been discussed. Laney complained that the administration's "overheated rhetoric and brinksmanship" were pushing North Korea toward violent action—a view, he emphasized, that was shared by General Gary Luck, the commander of U.S. forces in South Korea who also had operational control in wartime over the South Korean forces. Shortly after the ambassador left a White House meeting with senior administration officials, Assistant Secretary Bob Gallucci was named overall coordinator for dealing with North Korea and given the title of ambassador; his deputy in the State Department's Political/Military Bureau assumed Gallucci's non-Korean responsibilities.[43] Laney's visit, however, did not cause the administration to change its sanctions strategy or to urge a less public and less confrontational approach by the IAEA.

Events outside Washington added to the drumbeat for a more forceful response to perceived North Korean recalcitrance. On March 15, the IAEA withdrew its inspectors from North Korea because the North Koreans had refused to give permission on the spot for a procedure to which they had not agreed prior to the inspectors' arrival—to allow them to take smears of a hot cell for handling spent nuclear fuel. The Vienna agency thought these smears would enable it to ascertain how much plutonium North Korea had accumulated in the past. However, the inspectors left North Korea convinced by their completed tests that Pyongyang had not conducted any reprocessing since their last visit in August 1993. Nevertheless, shortly thereafter, the IAEA sent the North Korean nuclear issue to the UN Security Council. The United States formally cancelled the third round of talks with Pyongyang.[44]

A few days later, the bilateral Korean talks collapsed. In a vitriolic exchange at a meeting on the DMZ, the head of the South Korean delegation threatened UN sanctions against North Korea, and his North Korean counterpart answered that Pyongyang would respond with an "eye for an eye and a war for a war." The North Korean delegate went further: "If war breaks out, Seoul will turn into a sea of fire," he declared. The South Korean government quickly released the tape of this part of the talks, recorded on closed-circuit television, to public television stations. As expected, the public reaction against North Korea was immediate and hostile. Then Kim Young Sam's government approved deployment to South Korea of U.S. Patriot missiles, which reportedly "inflamed the leadership and military circles in North Korea." Washington, for its part, decided to reschedule Team Spirit, send the Patriot antimissile batteries to South Korea, and start working on a UN resolution for economic sanctions against North Korea. The South Korean defense minister surprised Washington when he revealed publicly that the joint U.S.-South Korean military strategy for dealing with potential attacks had been shifted from its earlier defensive approach to offensive maneuvers.[45]

Laney's misgivings in February proved prescient. Faced with IAEA demands for UN Security Council action against North Korea, along with the U.S. and South Korean campaign for sanctions, their rescheduling of the Team Spirit exercises, and the strengthening of their military capacities, Pyongyang threatened publicly as well as privately that it would regard UN sanctions as a declaration of war against North Korea. And it did more than threaten. It acted. In early May, Pyongyang surprised the world by announcing its intention to remove immediately the spent fuel rods from its 5 MWe reactor. It invited IAEA inspectors to observe the defueling process, but it refused the request of the Vienna agency to segregate for subsequent analysis a cross section of three hundred rods from the more than 8,000 to be removed.[46] The agency sent its inspectors to North Korea, but its director general, Hans Blix, implying the need for early international action, advised the UN Security Council in writing that the North Korean refusal to isolate the three hundred rods would permanently destroy the record of the past extraction of plutonium. President Kim Il Sung told the visiting Cambodian chief of state, Norodom Sihanouk, that his country would "rather accept a war" than let its military secrets be exposed. On June 5, Pyongyang issued a public statement declaring that "sanctions mean war, and there is no mercy in war."[47]

Laney, his senior officers at the embassy, and U.S. military leaders based in South Korea took the North Korean public threats seriously, in part because they reinforced private assertions being made by North Korean military officers stationed on the DMZ to their American counterparts. These officers stressed that Pyongyang would not let the United States augment its forces on the Korean Peninsula as it had done in the Persian Gulf before the launching of Operation Desert Storm in January 1991. Additionally, North Korea stepped up exercises of offensive and defensive troops, tested its secure communications network used in national emergencies, and mobilized its population.

Subsequently, the senior U.S. Air Force officer in Korea at the time confided that although he and the other American commanders did not say so out loud, "inside we all thought we were going to war." Some Washington officials apparently shared their anxiety. Bob Gallucci reportedly saw unfortunate parallels between the spring of 1994 and those last days before the outbreak of World War I when "misunderstanding, cross-purposes, and inadvertence" led to military conflict.[48]

For months, even as his administration moved toward UN sanctions and the possibility of war, President Clinton had insisted that the U.S. strategy should allow a face-saving way out for the North Koreans.[49] But none had been built into the sanctions approach. When he was briefed on May 19 by General Luck, back from Seoul to discuss war plans should the North Koreans carry out their threats in the event of UN sanctions, the president grew cautious. The general advised Clinton that the cost of a second Korean war would be "52,000 U.S. casualties, killed or wounded; 490,000 South Korean military casualties in the first 90 days, plus an enormous number of North Korean and civilian lives, at a financial outlay exceeding $61 billion, very little of which could be recouped from U.S. allies."[50] The next day, Clinton told his foreign policy advisers to place emphasis on the diplomatic strategy. On May 23, U.S. working-level officials informed their North Korean counterparts that the United States was prepared to convene the third round of bilateral talks despite the refueling. But when the IAEA announced publicly on June 2 that the removal of the fuel rods destroyed its ability to verify the historical record, the United States pulled back its offer for bilateral talks and concentrated on getting support for UN sanctions against Pyongyang—even though administration officials conceded that "sanctions were unlikely to force North Korea to reverse course" because it was "relatively invulnerable to outside pressures."[51]

The administration, while believing that it would be able to line up the votes for UN sanctions, faced reluctance on the part of Japan, Russia, and China, the last two of which enjoyed veto power within the Security Council. Japanese officials feared serious internal protests by longtime pro-Pyongyang Korean residents living in Japan if the sanctions required them to stop sending remittances home.[52] Moscow urged that an international conference be held to deal with the North Korean issue before a sanctions resolution was adopted, a proposal that the United States repeatedly tried to deflect. China, North Korea's major source of energy and food imports, consistently insisted on negotiations, calculating that sanctions, and potentially war, would destabilize the region and stimulate a flood of North Korean refugees into China.[53] At the same time, China pressed North Korea to accommodate world opinion on the nuclear issue, suggesting, perhaps, that China might be reluctant to cast a veto in the face of strong international sentiment favoring sanctions.[54]

Neither North Korea's public statements nor its actions suggested that Pyongyang was cowed. It repeatedly threatened to regard sanctions as an act of war and to respond accordingly.[55]

While the U.S. diplomats worked the Security Council corridors, the Pentagon focused on how to defeat the North Korean military should that prove necessary. Secretary of Defense Bill Perry, who had replaced Aspin in 1994, later said that the Air Force had developed contingency plans for bombing North Korea's nuclear facilities in Yongbyon, and it had assured him that it possessed the "technical ability to take them out quickly and effectively without spreading radiation far and wide."[56] The administration privately consulted Japan and China about a preemptive attack on Yongbyon, but both nations opposed such action.[57] In any event, Perry ruled out this option because he feared it would start a general war.[58]

Instead, the Pentagon looked at possibilities for augmenting further U.S. forces in and around South Korea. By mid-June, Secretary Perry and the Joint Chiefs of Staff (JCS) had three staffed-out options ready for President Clinton's consideration. Option one called for the "immediate dispatch to Korea of 2000 additional troops needed for the rapid deployment of larger forces later." Option Two, favored by Perry and the Joint Chiefs, "added squadrons of frontline tactical aircraft to Korea; deployment of several battalions of combat U.S. ground troops; and stationing of a second aircraft carrier battle group in the area." The third option called for the further deployment of additional tens of thousands of ground troops from the army and the Marine Corps, and for more combat aircraft.[59]

Perry thought that more deployments could either cause Pyongyang to launch a preemptive attack or to back down in the face of this demonstration of U.S. seriousness and determination.[60] "We did not know enough about the Korean mentality to know how to gauge the negative aspects vs. the positive aspects of the signal we were sending," he later said. "Therefore, I chose in my own thinking to set that signal aside, not knowing how to assess it, and recognizing that we could have either of these possibilities."[61] This admission revealed the degree to which administration officials were operating in the dark with regard to North Korean intentions and reactions as they took decisions that could have led to war.

General Luck was given only a few hours notice that the Pentagon would ask President Clinton to authorize the build-up of U.S. forces in South Korea. He called Laney, and they met quickly and secretly at Laney's residence; both were concerned that should North Korea interpret the new American move as a U.S. decision to destroy the Kim Il Sung regime, North Korea would attack preemptively. Despite Laney's and Luck's past prodding, Washington had not ordered the evacuation of the 80,000 American dependents and other civilians living in South Korea. The two men drafted a firm message to Washington arguing that evacuation must precede a major augmentation of troops and equipment. Laney also told his visiting daughter and grandchildren to shorten their planned stay and leave Seoul by Sunday, three days later.[62]

As the administration intensified its diplomatic campaign in the UN and the U.S. military planned for strengthening U.S. forces in East Asia, most U.S. media, correspondents, and think-tank officials advocated a forceful and uncompromising position toward North Korea. Two of the top foreign policy experts in the previous Bush administration, Brent Scowcroft, the former national security adviser, and Arnold Kanter, the former Department of State counselor, urged in a *Washington Post* op-ed a surgical strike at Yongbyon unless North Korea signaled willingness to submit to the continuous and unfettered monitoring of its nuclear facilities. The two former officials admitted that war might result, though they thought this possibility unlikely.[63] A poll by *Time* and CBS reported that 51 percent of the American public favored military action against North Korea to destroy its nuclear facilities if Pyongyang continued to refuse international inspections, and 48 percent said it was "worth risking war to prevent North Korea from manufacturing nuclear weapons."[64]

As the situation spiraled toward possible war, few people, whether inside or outside the U.S. administration, showed concern that senior American officials had not talked recently to their North Korean counterparts. Except for the one senior-level session during the Bush administration in 1992, and the two during the Clinton administration in 1993, all contacts between the United States and North Korea had been conducted by lower-policy-level officials with North Korean diplomats assigned to the North Korean mission in New York. Toward the end of May, at the urging of Ambassador Laney, the administration asked Senators Sam Nunn (Democrat) and Richard Lugar (Republican) to go to Pyongyang to talk with senior North Korean leaders; but North Korea denied them visas. No contact or communication at the presidential level was attempted, and none at the level of secretary of state or foreign minister, either. Yet virtually everyone with knowledge of the Koreas knew that the decision in North Korea as to whether or not to go to war would be made by that nation's dictator, Kim Il Sung, or by him in concert with his son and chosen heir, Kim Jong Il.

CHAPTER 2

Jimmy Carter
Watches and Worries

Jimmy Carter was uniquely qualified for the role he assumed in 1994. A nuclear engineer by training and a former U.S. president who had sought to reduce nuclear weapons on a global basis, Carter understood the potential dangers associated with a North Korean nuclear program that was not under effective IAEA safeguards. As a politician and a strategic planner, he appreciated that some in the United States and South Korea, in their efforts to achieve other political objectives, would likely exaggerate the North Korean nuclear threat; he also understood that North Korean leaders would seek to leverage their nuclear program for security and other concessions—given their country's economic difficulties and diplomatic isolation. Because Carter was a former U.S. head of state, the Pyongyang leadership viewed his trip to North Korea as a high-level American gesture of respect for their country and for their leader, Kim Il Sung.

Carter's involvement with the Korean Peninsula did not begin in 1994. It started more than four decades earlier. As a graduate of the U.S. Naval Academy, Carter entered into active duty in the U.S. Navy in 1946 in the expectation of pursuing a naval career. He went to East Asia for the first time in 1949 as a naval officer aboard the submarine USS *Pomfret*. When the Korean War broke out a year later, many of Carter's friends and professional acquaintances were killed by North Korean troops.[1] Neither his deep religious views nor his sense of humanity caused him to question his conviction that the North Korean military machine and its leadership should be defeated and, if possible, destroyed. Decades later, he recalled that at the time he hated Kim Il Sung for starting the war and hoped for the dictator's death.

The Korean Peninsula received much attention in Jimmy Carter's White House. According to Don Oberdorfer, Carter tried unsuccessfully to force a reluctant Washington bureaucracy and the Seoul government to accept a significant reduction in the level of U.S. troops and nuclear weapons in South Korea—a promise he had made during his presidential campaign.[2] In 1979, he contemplated proposing a summit initiative to bring together the presidents of South Korea and North Korea to talk about starting a peace process; he viewed the successful Camp David talks with Israel and Egypt the previous year as a possible model for this Korean consultation. He mentioned his idea to Deng Xiaoping during the Chinese leader's visit to Washington in 1979 and urged him to use his influence with North Korea to encourage direct bilateral Korean talks. Deng said that he supported the concept, but he declined involvement, his explanation being that Beijing would lose its limited influence on Pyongyang if it were perceived as trying to pressure North Korea. Carter's senior advisers convinced the president not to raise the summit idea during his South Korean visit two months later. They predicted that if he did so, both Korean leaders would reject his proposal and thereby embarrass his administration.[3] Carter shelved the notion of helping to arrange a Korean summit meeting at the time, but he did not discard the concept. Nor did he forget what Deng had said about China's reluctance to press the North Koreans on sensitive policy issues.

In his White House involvement with Korean affairs, Carter also exchanged communications with the North Korean president, Kim Il Sung, a ruthless dictator who nevertheless enjoyed the respect of his country's populace, which referred to him as its "Great Leader." Carter's call for a sharp reduction in U.S. troops in South Korea pleased the North Korean leader, who had long sought the removal of U.S. troops as a way to strengthen his country vis-à-vis South Korea. Using Pakistani channels, Kim Il Sung sent President-Elect Carter a personal letter asking for direct contact between the two governments, and he restrained the normally virulent North Korean public rhetoric against the United States at the time of Carter's inauguration. During the new administration's first month in office, the North Koreans expressed a desire to avoid confrontation, to seek peaceful reunification with South Korea, and to open bilateral peace talks. The United States responded favorably to the proposed talks, but insisted that South Korea must be included as a full participant. Pyongyang rejected South Korean involvement. During the next two years, Kim Il Sung wrote to Carter three more times urging bilateral talks, but Carter remained firm in calling for trilateral consultations. He did try to signal a more receptive attitude toward North Korea by lifting the ban that prevented American citizens from traveling to that country and by permitting the North Korean representatives at the United Nations to be invited to an official U.S. reception. In July 1977, when a U.S. helicopter strayed onto the North Korean side of the DMZ and was shot down, Carter played down the incident; he said the flight had been a mistake, and North Korea returned the bodies of the dead Americans much more quickly than had been expected. Nevertheless, as Carter modified his original troop reduction plan, Kim Il Sung became increasingly critical of the American president when talking to foreign visitors to North Korea. His attempts to communicate with Carter stopped.[4]

A few months after leaving the White House, the Carters traveled to China as guests of the Chinese government.[5] High-level Chinese leaders virtually duplicated the protocol of an official state visit. The Carters consulted with most of China's senior leaders, including Party Chairman Deng Xiaoping and Prime Minister Zhao Ziyang. Years later, Jimmy and Rosalynn Carter spoke enthusiastically about this trip, the warmth of their reception, and the insight of Chinese officials, particularly on topics related to East Asia. Since the trip, Carter has maintained ties with the Chinese leadership: He exchanges views periodically by letter, in conversations with the various Chinese ambassadors posted to Washington, and, in recent years, during trips to China connected with The Carter Center's health programs and monitoring of Chinese village elections. Carter communicated with Chinese contacts about North Korean attitudes before, during, and after the 1994 nuclear crisis.[6]

In 1982, Jimmy and Rosalynn Carter created The Carter Center in conjunction with Emory University. Carter decided early on that a principal focus of the new institution would be conflict resolution. The Conflict Resolution Program (CRP) was established in 1985 with Dayle Powell, a federal prosecutor from Birmingham, Alabama, as the program's first director.[7] In 1987, Carter and the CRP created the International Negotiating Network as a nongovernmental vehicle of distinguished international personalities, such as Javier Perez de Cuellar, the former UN secretary general, and Cyrus Vance, the former U.S. secretary of state, and scholars who were prepared to engage in mediation when requested by disputing parties or governments. The same year, Carter invited the secretary generals of the UN, the Organization of American States (OAS), and the British Commonwealth to The Carter Center to discuss intrastate conflicts. This group concluded that most intergovernmental organizations had limited ability to deal with such conflicts and that nongovernmental organizations (NGOs) should become more active in this area. The CRP took this charge as its action agenda and began to monitor approximately twenty-five conflicts, or potential conflicts, around the world, including the strained relations between the two Koreas. Carter and his associates searched for ways that the Center might encourage the eventual peaceful reunification between South and North Korea.[8]

As North Korea in 1990–1991 sought to improve relations with South Korea and to open dialogues with Japan and the United States, Pyongyang took the initiative and contacted Carter. In July 1990, the North Korean head of a delegation to a conference organized by the Center for International Security and Arms Control of Stanford University asked the Center's codirector, John W. Lewis, to question the former president about visiting North Korea. Lewis wrote and urged Carter to consider a trip to both North and South Korea so that he could take advantage of North Korea's reaching out to the United States and South Korea. Suggesting that South Korea would view arms control as being in its interest and that arms control might "prove crucial to moving Pyongyang to bring its Yongbyon nuclear facilities under the IAEA safeguards," Lewis thought that a Carter trip would allow the exploration of ideas that United States officials could not yet propose.[9]

Carter called Lewis and said that he would be interested in pursuing the proposal if he received "separate but firm" invitations from the leaders of the two Koreas and agreement from both that he could "cross the border between visits to their capitals."[10] Carter also told Lewis that he would emphasize the "pre-mediation" character of his visit. These points were an integral part of Carter's approach to conflict resolution. He would not undertake mediation unless all relevant parties invited him to assist. He appreciated that although mediation and negotiation by an NGO—often called Track II diplomacy—could sometimes facilitate the peaceful resolution of an explosive dispute, such mediation must be followed by official negotiations between the involved governments (or between a government and a group competing for power within the same country)—Track I diplomacy—to reach a viable and durable settlement. Although Lewis reportedly considered Carter's response as "exciting and reasonable,"[11] this particular initiative was not endorsed by either Pyongyang or Seoul. The North Koreans refused to permit Carter to cross the DMZ, and the South Koreans did not issue an invitation to Carter to visit Seoul.

After his exchange with Lewis, Carter instructed the CRP to develop a briefing paper tracing the history of the two Koreas, their relations with each other and with third countries, and the status of North Korea's nuclear weapons programs. Among other things, it pointed out that satellite photos suggested that North Korea was trying to develop a nuclear weapons capability, but that experts predicted that Pyongyang was "at least five years away" from achieving that goal.[12] Subsequent memos kept Carter apprised of ongoing developments on the Korean Peninsula.[13]

In early 1991, Carter received a more direct approach from Pyong-yang. This time, Charles A. Wickman of the William Carey International University, a Baptist institution in Pasadena, California, advised Carter that the North Korean government would welcome a visit by him. A small delegation from the university had traveled to North Korea in November 1990 and had met Han Shi Hai, the former North Korean ambassador to the United Nations (observer status)[14] and at the time vice chairman of North Korea's national reunification committee. Han had intimated to the Americans that a visit from Carter was desirable; he would not have raised this matter without official instructions. Subsequently, Dr. Han came to the United States at the invitation of the Carey International University and, along with Wickman, traveled to Atlanta to meet with Carter.[15] Han told Carter that North Korea would like to have serious talks with the United States, but admitted that there were nuclear problems, particularly—from the North Korean viewpoint—the possible use of nuclear weapons by the United States against North Korea. Carter told Han that North Korea's development of nuclear explosives would be regarded by the United States as gravely destabilizing. Han replied that Pyongyang had offered to discuss this matter with the United States, but Washington had insisted that all sixteen nations that had participated in the Korean War should take part. According to Carter's notes of the meeting, Han told him that the North Korean government wanted Carter to "play an important role in seeking agreement with SK [South Korea] and in promoting serious US-NK [U.S.-North Korean] talks." Carter showed an interest in possibly taking a mediating role and in visiting Pyongyang, but said he would insist on visiting Seoul during the same trip. He also reminded Han that he was a private citizen and that when he communicated with the U.S. government, he did so unofficially.[16] When Han said that his government wanted a positive indication from Carter before formally issuing its invitation, Carter said that before he could make a decision about the trip he would need evidence of North Korea's sincerity and flexibility on key issues. He suggested that "his choice of proof" would be permission for him to cross the DMZ. Han answered that this would never be permitted, but Carter insisted. Han promised to discuss the matter at home with Kim Il Sung and then reply to Carter.[17]

Three months later, Carter received an official invitation from the North Korean government. While on a Carter Center fund-raising trip in New York, Carter met with Kim Yong Nam, the North Korean foreign minister, who was attending the UN General Assembly's opening session. The foreign minister told Carter that in its negotiations with South Korea, North Korea was seeking a nonaggression pact, the confederation of the two Koreas, and the free movement of people and goods in a unified nation.[18] He handed Carter a letter from Song Ho Kyong, the director of the North Korean Institute for Disarmament and Peace, that officially invited the former president to visit North Korea and informed him that he could cross the DMZ in doing so.[19] Carter still needed a South Korean invitation before he would travel to the Korean Peninsula.

In Washington two months earlier, Dayle Spencer had met with Ambassador Hyun Hong Choo of South Korea. Spencer told him about the North Korean overtures to Carter and said that the former president was inclined to accept but wanted Seoul's counsel before making a final decision. The ambassador promised to consult his capital for a formal response, but did express his "personal view," namely, that the Pyongyang government would use a Carter visit to gain greater legitimacy while preventing Carter from seeing the true state of affairs in North Korea. But should a visit materialize, he saw no problem with Carter's crossing the DMZ; Korean participants in bilateral talks occasionally took that route. He also told Carter to make substantive talks with Kim Il Sung a precondition for his going to Pyongyang. Previously, some foreign visitors had been promised a meeting with the North Korean leader but were passed off to lower-level diplomats once they arrived.[20] Carter accepted that advice.

In September, the South Korean ambassador communicated his government's official response to Dayle Spencer: It hoped Carter would postpone his trip to the Korean Peninsula because the North Koreans had suspended prime minister–level talks scheduled for August and were dragging their feet on signing the agreement with the IAEA that Pyongyang had earlier initialed. The ambassador said that an early visit by Carter would cause Pyongyang to "underestimate the importance of the inter-Korean dialogue."[21]

Within a month, for reasons unknown, the South Korean government changed its mind. An embassy official informed Spencer that the Seoul government was prepared to receive Carter and would welcome a Carter Center advance team to help plan for the Carter visit.[22]

Before authorizing a reply to the South Korean embassy, Carter spoke with Larry Eagleburger, the first Bush administration's deputy secretary of state, and subsequently to Assistant Secretary Richard Solomon. Solomon told Carter that the prime ministers of the two Koreas would meet on October 23 and that the U.S. position had been to let the two Koreas reach their own decisions without outside intervention. He intimated that although a nonofficial intervention might be useful later, it was currently premature. Carter said he would delay his decision until after the meeting of the prime ministers. The result of this and subsequent prime minister–level meetings led to the bilateral nonaggression agreement (December 1991) that defined areas of reconciliation and cooperation between the two Koreas and the bilateral nuclear agreement (January 1992) under which both Koreas promised not to acquire nuclear weapons or possess nuclear reprocessing or uranium enrichment facilities. Citing this progress, Secretary of State Jim Baker discouraged Carter from traveling to the Korean Peninsula, and Carter decided not to go.[23]

The International Negotiating Network (INN) held its annual meeting at the Center in January 1992. One of its discussion groups focused on the relationship of the two Koreas. The current ambassadors to the United Nations of South Korea and North Korea participated in this study group, as did other diplomats from the two countries, Korean scholars, NGO representatives, and a leading member of the opposition party in the South Korean National Assembly. The group recommended that President Carter and the INN travel to the Korean Peninsula to encourage more direct dialogue between North Korea and South Korea, but it did not advocate that Carter and the INN offer to serve as third-party mediators between the two Koreas. The representatives from South Korea and North Korea agreed on one issue—that NGOs should not try to influence discussions between the IAEA and either Korean government. Such matters, they insisted, must remain the provenance of governments.[24]

The opposition member in the South Korean National Assembly requested a private meeting with Carter to pass on an appeal from Kim Dae Jung, his party's leader. Kim Dae Jung, earlier a dissident whose death sentence Carter, when president, had helped have commuted, suggested that Carter and the INN bring to both Koreas nuclear scientists who could carry out nuclear inspections additional to those of the IAEA.[25] Sensitive to the concerns of the Washington and Seoul administrations, Carter wrote Kim Dae Jung after the INN meeting and told him that he had no early plans to visit the peninsula. He said that The Carter Center took care not to interfere with or duplicate the efforts of the two Korean governments and those of the U.S. government. But he assured Kim Dae Jung that the INN was "committed to help when needed."[26]

Following the January INN conference, Carter focused principally on other Carter Center activities, but he periodically received signals from Pyongyang encouraging him to visit. The hoped-for improvement in inter-Korean relations gradually turned to disillusionment with the failure of the bilateral Korean talks to make progress by mid-year. In July 1992, Carter received a Chinese delegation at his home in Plains, Georgia. The visitors expressed concern about Pyongyang's nuclear development, but said they were convinced that North Korea would launch a devastating attack on Seoul if it were forced into a corner. Carter confided later that their opinion made a "lasting impression" on him.[27]

The same month, Carter decided to send Dayle Spencer and her husband, Bill, to the two Koreas to assess whether Carter and the INN could play a constructive role by traveling to the peninsula. During the two-week trip, they visited both Korean capitals, talked with government officials, and consulted with Korean scholars attending a conference in Kyoto, Japan. Their reporting memo to Carter discussed the history of the peninsula since World War II, outlined the main disagreements between the two Korean states, and explained the attitudes of neighboring countries and the United States toward South Korea and North Korea. It described such relevant elements of Confucian philosophy as the primary importance attached to order and harmony, the role of leaders in upholding these values within their society, and the equal importance of form and substance. This perceptive memo cautioned that philosophically Asians, including Koreans, viewed conflict differently from the way it was viewed in the West. In the Asian context, conflicts did not have distinct beginnings and endings; instead, they were perceived as cycles that could be transformed over time with the right interpersonal relationships between those involved. These relationships were more important than contractual or legal obligations. As people became weary of conflict, they could decide to submerge their differences, at least for a time, when reconciliation seemed mutually preferable to hostility.[28]

The Spencer report recommended a Carter trip, one that would initiate a process designed to create an environment conducive for future progress. It said that Carter could have valuable discussions with leaders in Seoul and Pyongyang about how to advance the North-South dialogue, defuse the nuclear issue, and open the door for future involvement by The Carter Center and other NGOs on issues tangentially related to reunification. They urged Carter to travel to the peninsula in the October-November timeframe, well ahead of the South Korean presidential election in December 1992.[29]

Carter initially responded that his schedule was too crowded for a trip in 1992, but he changed his mind when the bilateral Korean talks moved toward gridlock. He again consulted with Secretary of State Baker, who continued to oppose Carter's travel to the peninsula. Carter reluctantly shelved plans for a trip in 1992.[30]

In mid-November 1992, Carter received a letter from the North Korean foreign minister, Kim Yong Nam, urging the "earliest possible visit" as a follow-up to the trip of his advance team. (Earlier in November 1992, Bill Clinton would defeat the incumbent, George H. W. Bush, and the next month, Kim Young Sam, the candidate of the ruling National Liberal Party, would defeat the opposition leader, Kim Dae Jung, to become the president of South Korea.) The foreign minister said that

Carter would meet with Kim Il Sung and that their conversation would "make a major breakthrough in resolving the pending issues between our country and the United States and improving bilateral relations." He reaffirmed that Carter would be permitted to cross the DMZ.[31]

Korea was not a group topic at the INN annual meeting at The Carter Center in February 1993, but the issue figured prominently in the press reporting of the event. Carter met with reporters, most of whose questions focused on whether and how Carter and the INN would relate to the new Clinton administration in Washington. Carter told the reporters that he saw a role for the INN, but one that would not interfere with U.S. foreign policy or duplicate the work of the UN and other international organizations. He mentioned several areas where he would like to become engaged, including the Korean Peninsula, and said that he would discuss these matters with the new secretary of state, Warren Christopher, when he met him in Washington in March. Carter revealed for the first time publicly that he had invitations to visit both Koreas. He also said that both countries had asked for his help the previous year, but that the Bush administration's State Department had requested that he not be involved. He noted that the Koreans had renewed their request for his engagement during the past week. (Carter was referring here to North Korean appeals, which he received regularly, but he did not make this distinction in his statement.)[32]

Subsequent press reports on Friday, February 19, heralding that Carter had been invited to "enter negotiations between North and South Korea," and that the Bush administration had earlier asked him not to become involved,[33] set off a mild firestorm. The Korean consul general, on instructions, met with Dayle Spencer and told her of his government's concern about Korean press stories that interpreted Carter's statements as meaning that he intended to play a mediation role in Korean reconciliation and nuclear issues. The Seoul government had issued a statement denying it had asked for Carter's mediation in inter-Korean affairs. A Carter visit—not related to mediation—would still be welcomed, but Seoul strongly hoped that the former president's trip would be delayed until the North Korean dispute with the IAEA (over "special inspections") had been resolved. The State Department weighed in as well to urge a delay of several months for any trip to the peninsula.[34] Carter heeded the advice of his friend James T. Laney, the president of Emory University and a person with long experience in Korea, to tamp down quickly the agitation.[35] He wrote to the two Korean presidents and issued a press statement affirming his and The Carter Center's support for the inter-Korean dialogue and stating that any role of the Center would be "totally nonofficial" and would honor the "diplomatic proprieties expected of invited guests who represent an academic institution." He expressed his appreciation for the invitations to visit both countries and wished the two countries' leaders "success in [their] efforts to resolve differences through direct and official talks."[36]

Carter often consulted Laney about Korea and other issues. The two men had enjoyed a long and mutually productive relationship. Laney served as president of Emory University from 1977 to 1993, and previously as dean of the Emory School of Theology. With a $105 million grant in 1979 from the Woodruff Foundation, the largest donation made to an American university until that time, Laney had led the effort that transformed Emory from a good regional institution of higher learning to a nationally ranked research university. An ordained Methodist minister, Laney had taught for several years in Yonsei University in South Korea in the early 1960s; earlier, before the Korean War, he had served in the U.S. military counterintelligence in Korea. Laney arranged for Carter to be appointed as Distinguished Emory Professor in 1982 when The Carter Center was established, initially on the Emory campus, and he and Carter collaborated on various projects. Laney was a major Carter adviser on Korea in the late 1980s and early 1990s; he would have accompanied Carter had the former U.S. president traveled to the Korean Peninsula in 1992. In 1993, President Clinton named Laney U.S. ambassador to South Korea, an appointment for which former president Carter and Senator Sam Nunn of Georgia lobbied strongly.

Carter left for Washington a few days later for his first meetings with officials of the Clinton administration. He was treated with respect; he was praised for the work of The Atlanta Project, a private-government part-

nership to improve conditions for the poor;[37] and he was given the opportunity to explain the international initiatives of the Center. Secretary of
State Warren Christopher and his State Department associates expressed
appreciation for his offer for the Center to be helpful wherever the new
administration thought would be useful. But they made no commitment,
nor did they suggest an area in which the Center might play a role.[38]

Carter left Washington profoundly disappointed. He had expected
the new Democratic administration to want to use him and The Carter
Center in difficult international situations with which he had knowledge, experience, and personal relations with some of the parties involved, and where a nonofficial intervention might prove useful.
Instead, he encountered what he interpreted as a stiff-arm by Christopher, the first of several encounters that Carter would perceive as slights
at the hands of officials in the Clinton administration. Carter, proud of
the achievements The Carter Center had chalked up during the past
decade and believing he could help the new Democratic regime, did not
fully grasp either the inclinations or the politics that led administrative
officials, including some who had held important positions in his administration, to hold him at bay.

At the time, I was serving as diplomat-in-residence at The Carter
Center and, although still in the employ of the State Department, I
considered Carter my superior, the person to whom I owed primary loyalty. Even though I did not accompany the former president to Washington, I presumed that some key officials wanted to keep distance
between the new Clinton administration and Carter because of Republican charges during the 1992 campaign that a Clinton government
would be a clone of the earlier "unsuccessful" Carter administration. I
also guessed that many on the Clinton team who had worked with
Carter in the past worried that, with his strong sense of self-confidence
and independence, he would not be constrained by policy guidelines in
initiatives he might undertake officially. Rather, they thought that he
might operate as a "loose cannon," and that could prove embarrassing.[39]

Carter would be repeatedly disappointed when his suggestions for involvement were deflected. At first privately, and then publicly, he would

say that previous Republican administrations had been more willing to collaborate with The Carter Center than the current Democratic one. For the most part, Carter directed his ire at the State Department and its officials rather than toward the White House.[40] Carter tried to avoid criticizing President Clinton publicly, believing him more willing to call on him and the Center than most of his subordinates. The exception was Vice President Al Gore, whom Carter considered as the person within the administration with whom he could work most easily.

In my view, various administrations made mistakes in not using Carter more often. Having been a career diplomat for twenty-eight years before retiring and joining The Carter Center staff in October 1993, I could understand the concern of government officials about the involvement of "outsiders" in sensitive foreign policy matters. Management of the policy process on a delicate issue is always difficult because of the inevitable bureaucratic infighting in Washington and the differences of views among allies and opponents abroad. Consequently, the policymakers and implementers are disinclined to encourage intervention by others, particularly those not subject to policy discipline. But on occasion, this view could be myopic. What is important is to achieve the objectives that a policy embraces, not to pursue a rigid tactical course. Sometimes nonofficial actors, such as The Carter Center, can be useful even if they are not fully controllable. They may well have access to or experience with parties to a dispute that a government cannot, or does not want to, duplicate. Unlike governments, NGOs do not commit the conflicting parties and outside governments to a specific action. But on occasion, their relative neutrality and strong interest in helping frame a peaceful settlement can make a critical difference. Moreover, an administration can always define its relationship to the NGO's intervention, including labeling it a "private" initiative. If it succeeds, the administration can take part or all of the credit; if it fails, the blame can be placed on the NGO, the administration saying that it raised concerns before the intervention.

In the months following his exchanges in Washington, Carter pursued a hectic schedule. He became directly involved in pre-mediation efforts in Sudan and Somalia, and he visited several African countries where the Center was conducting health and agricultural programs. He spent considerable time working with Center experts and outside contractors to develop a pilot project in Guyana by which the various local stakeholders would formulate an indigenous national strategy for the economic development of their country and for negotiating with bilateral and multilateral aid donors. He directed much energy toward The Atlanta Project.

But Carter did not forget the Korean Peninsula. He obtained information from private sources, particularly current and past Chinese officials, Japanese supporters of The Carter Center, and his friend and Korean adviser, Jim Laney. The Conflict Resolution Program, now temporarily headed by me—I would subsequently become Director of Programs at the Center—drew on a wider group of sources within government and nongovernmental circles and so increased the quantity and comprehensiveness of its Korean memos. As early as April 1993, Peter Goldmark, head of the Rockefeller Foundation, contacted Carter and offered to fund a Carter Center trip to the two Koreas if Carter thought such a trip would be useful. Tom Graham, a former U.S. government official who at the time ran the Foundation's nonproliferation program, feared that the Washington and Seoul governments were pursuing policies that could lead to an unnecessary war with North Korea. Carter told Goldmark that he shared his view of the seriousness of the situation, expressed appreciation for the offer of funding, and said that he would consider making the trip if he became convinced that he could help defuse the crisis and advance the cause of peace.[41]

During the U.S.-North Korean discussions in New York and Geneva during the summer of 1993, when North Korea suspended its withdrawal from the NPT and said that it was willing to replace its graphite-moderated nuclear reactor with light water ones, the former president avoided action that might adversely influence the deliberations or cause problems for the U.S. negotiators. The North Korean deputy ambassador to the United Nations, Ho Jong, sought in July, before the Geneva talks were completed, to schedule a meeting with

Carter for August. Carter did not agree to the appointment because he wanted the State Department's assessment of the July talks before talking with the North Korean diplomat. Two months after these talks, which both governments had characterized as generally constructive, Carter accepted a call from Ho Jong. Ho said that the North Korean government still wanted Carter to visit Pyongyang and that the visit would deal with substantive issues and help "resolve the remaining problems." Carter told Ho that his interest remained keen, but that he "would follow the advice of the State Department."[42]

As I discussed in chapter 1, the tense situation, temporarily ameliorated by the bilateral talks in June and July, rapidly turned sour as the fall wore on, and the Carter Center followed developments closely. The North Korean negotiator at Geneva, Kang Sok Ju, announced publicly that North Korea would allow nuclear inspections of some of its nuclear-related facilities if the United States would cancel its Team Spirit exercises for 1994. According to a report by R. Jeffrey Smith in the *Washington Post,* State favored accepting the proposal, but the Joint Chiefs and the Defense Department opposed. Smith also noted that Hans Blix, the IAEA director general, had said in a recent speech that because his agency had not been permitted to inspect North Korean facilities in the fall, it could not verify that work was not taking place on new nuclear weapons. Unnamed U.S. officials reportedly said that the entire IAEA inspection system could be undermined within a couple of months.[43]

Sue Palmer, a member of The Carter Center's Conflict Resolution Program, spoke with Ken Quinones, the desk officer for North Korea in the State Department's Office of Korean Affairs, about this article and related developments. Knowing that the information would be passed to Carter, Quinones confirmed confidentially the article's accuracy. He also advised that senior administration officials were meeting that day to discuss the Korean problem, and if the impasse continued, the senior officials might consider encouraging Carter to travel to the Korean Peninsula in December to engage in informal discussions with officials there. Three days later, Ken told Sue that the administration planned to make a counterproposal to the North Koreans: if Pyongyang would accept the inspections deemed necessary by the IAEA and exchange envoys with South Korea, the United States would not hold Team Spirit exercises in 1994 and would agree to a third round of bilateral U.S.-North Korean talks. The Center was asked to hold this information closely because the administration did not intend to mention this proposal to North Korea until after it had been discussed with the South Korean president, Kim Young Sam, during his official visit to Washington a few days later.[44]

On November 19, the same day Carter first received the information about the administration's possible counterproposal, he accepted another call from the North Korean deputy ambassador, Ho Jong. The ambassador's purpose was to reiterate the public message of the North Korean negotiator Kang Sok Ju—that North Korea desired to negotiate a package deal on all outstanding issues with the United States. Not divulging the offer the administration intended to make to the North Koreans, Carter replied that neither the U.S. government nor the general American public had "clear information on the North Korean position concerning nuclear inspections, the fear of U.S.-South Korean military exercises, direct peace talks between the two Koreas, or the desire of Pyongyang to resolve all these issues in a comprehensive way." The ambassador agreed. He also expressed concern about recent public statements by President Clinton and Secretary of State Christopher that North Korea would not be allowed to develop a nuclear bomb, characterizing them as "abusive ultimatums."[45] As was typical, Ho Jong ignored that the North Korean propaganda machine frequently castigated U.S. leaders and their policies.

Carter also raised with Ambassador Ho the idea of CNN's going to North Korea and providing a "fair and balanced report in the U.S. and around the world" on his country and its people.[46] Ho recalled his previous conversation with CNN's CEO, Tom Johnson, on this subject and said he would raise the CNN trip again with his leaders. Carter urged him to tell Pyongyang that CNN should be given maximum access to top spokespersons and to sites around the country so that its reports could be comprehensive.[47] A few days later, Ambassador Ho advised that North Korea could not accommodate a CNN trip in 1993, but a future visit might be possible.[48]

In late November-early December, Tom Graham of the Rockefeller Foundation, Professor Han Park of the University of Georgia—a scholar of Korean origin who had traveled to North Korea several times, including twice during the past year—and Ambassador Ho Jong petitioned Carter to open a "high-level, non-official dialogue with North Korea" because they perceived the official talks to be stalemated. They believed that "constant pressure on North Korea without talk would be counterproductive."[49]

In reporting these appeals to Carter, the Conflict Resolution Program included a copy of a draft op-ed piece written by Professor Park. Park described the mindset of the leaders and populace of "this most isolated nation." Sanctions would not cause North Korea to surrender, as many U.S. hard-liners insisted. Even though North Korea's economy was deteriorating and its population suffering, there was no evidence of an internal challenge to the regime. Most North Koreans attributed their economic difficulties to adversarial powers abroad, not to the North Korean government. The masses would not rise against the regime if deprived of basic economic needs. In fact, economic sanctions would have only a marginal effect on the North Korean economy because it was already independent of most external supplies with the exception of those provided by China and the Korean residents of Japan. It would be difficult to persuade China and Japan to agree to UN sanctions; and if that occurred, implementation of the sanctions would be extremely difficult. Park argued against the assumption that North Korean leaders were rational decisionmakers. Their ideological extremism was comparable to Islamic fundamentalism. A preemptive military attack by the United States would carry much risk because North Korea could retaliate against South Korea "with devastating consequence." In Park's view, a negotiated settlement would be the best alternative, and some concessions might have to be made to get North Korea to stop developing weapons that they considered necessary for their survival. His suggested deal: North Korea would abandon its nuclear weapons program, the Team Spirit exercises would be terminated, the armistice treaty ending the Korean War would be gradually converted into a peace treaty, the economic embargo would be gradually lifted, and over time efforts would be made to normalize diplomatic relations between the United States and North Korea. Park concluded: "A deal might work out if we package it right. The alternatives could be catastrophic."[50] Carter wrote on his copy that he agreed with this analysis.

During this same period, Ken Quinones told us again that a visit to the peninsula by Carter would not be useful "at this time." He said that more than a dozen people, including Han Park, had approached various persons within the administration about serving as an emissary, and each offer had been turned down.[51] Carter agreed that the CRP should inform the Rockefeller Foundation and Professor Park that although the Center was following the situation closely, the former president did not expect to travel to the Koreas at an early date. However, Carter revealed his growing unease with inaction—his cryptic, handwritten comment on the returned memo: "If it's not just a continuing delay."[52]

In mid-December, I went to Washington to talk with David Brown, the director of State's Office of Korean Affairs, and Ken Quinones, about the U.S.-North Korean talks in New York. I reported subsequently to Carter that State officials had told the North Korean diplomats that the administration had two preconditions for canceling Team Spirit for 1994 and beginning the third round of bilateral talks—IAEA inspection of all North Korean declared nuclear sites and exchange of special envoys between North and South Korea. They also told them that if the nuclear issue was resolved and Pyongyang remained in the NPT, the U.S. would be prepared to take the following three actions desired by the North Koreans: provide "negative security assurances," that is, a legal guarantee against an attack on North Korea; assist North Korea with economic development; and move in steps toward full diplomatic recognition of North Korea by the United States.

I reported to Carter that bureaucratic differences continued to plague the administration's approach to North Korea, although the State Department thought its view was gaining ascendancy at the expense of the hawks, particularly in the Department of Defense. State officials believed that the continued international isolation of Pyongyang could be counterproductive and that carefully modulated pressure was producing results. They confided that the United States had not detected an increase in North Korean military preparations for several months. Finally, the State contacts told me that if the New York consultations did not lead to a new round of U.S.-North Korean talks, they thought the administration might turn to Carter for assistance.[53]

Whether the periodic suggestion of a Carter role represented the thinking of the supervisors of our State working-level contacts or a ploy to dissuade Carter from contemplating a trip to the peninsula in early 1994 could not be definitively determined. Because our sources were friends with whom I had worked earlier, I presumed the former and communicated this view to Carter. But as the months wore on, the former president leaned increasingly toward the interpretation that these suggestions were a delaying tactic to forestall whatever initiative he might be inclined to take. I consistently urged my State interlocutors to "think of ways that [Carter's] talents could be used before everything else was stalemated."[54]

The same day that Carter got this report from me, he received advice from Jim Laney, then the U.S. ambassador in South Korea, about how to respond to a request from Kim Dae Jung to serve as an honorary member on the advisory board of Kim's new Peace Foundation. Kim had established the foundation to promote democracy and peace after he had lost the 1992 presidential election and announced his retirement from politics. He sought a tie with The Carter Center and indicated that he might be able to help the Center find funding in South Korea for its work. Jim Brasher, who headed the Center's fund-raising efforts, traveled to Seoul to talk with Kim Dae Jung and some of his associates. In their conversations, Kim Dae Jung told Brasher that his Peace Foundation would have a program on Korean reunification that would promote his "sunshine approach" of seeking more cooperative relations with North Korea. Following the Brasher visit, Kim Dae Jung wrote a letter to Carter asking him to join the advisory board and expressing the hope of seeing him in Atlanta on his next trip to the United States.[55]

Carter asked John Hardman, the executive director of The Carter Center since late 1992,[56] to call Laney and seek his advice about whether Carter should join Kim Dae Jung's board. Laney advised the former president to decline, pointing out that despite Kim Dae Jung's announcement that he had left politics, he remained the head of the opposition party bent on bringing down the government of Kim Young Sam. Kim Young Sam would interpret Carter's joining the Peace Foundation's advisory board as his aligning himself with Kim Dae Jung, an action that would destroy the trust Carter needed with the current South Korean president to contribute to the inter-Korean dialogue. Laney told Hardman that he and his deputy, the career diplomat Charles Kartman,[57] believed Carter could be a "key individual" in dealing with the North-South process and play a "definitive role in the peace initiative." Laney said that he had urged Carter's participation in his personal messages to the State Department, but admitted that the decision on this matter would be made either by Clinton or Christopher. Based on Laney's advice, Carter had Hardman inform Kim Dae Jung's associates that he would not be able to accept.[58]

During the first two months of 1994, the CRP kept Carter apprised of U.S.-North Korean consultations. Carter learned on February 16 that the United States had decided to put on hold the deployment of a Patriot missile battery to South Korea, had not scheduled Team Spirit exercises for 1994, had assessed that there was no need to change the state of readiness of U.S. and South Korean troops, and intended to meet with South Korea and Japan on February 17 to plan for the third round of U.S.-North Korean talks tentatively scheduled for March 21.[59] Unfortunately, the tentative U.S.-North Korean agreement fell apart shortly after March 3, when implementation was supposed to begin. North Korea blamed South Korea and the United States for its failure, and they, in turn, blamed Pyongyang.

The situation spiraled downward. The North Koreans refused to let the IAEA complete all aspects of its inspection and walked out of the North-South talks. The IAEA sent the matter to the UN Security Council, and the United States called off the third round of talks with North Korea.

Carter worried that the situation would spin out of control. He did take advantage of opportunities to encourage others to pressure the White House to use him, but avoided being linked directly to such appeals. He knew the administration would react negatively to a campaign on his part to force his involvement.

In mid-April, David Brown passed through Atlanta and stopped at The Carter Center to update my colleagues and me (and through us, President Carter) on the recent developments related to the North Korean nuclear issue. He first explained that in early December 1993, the National Security Council (NSC) had taken over the policy leadership on the North Korean nuclear issue because of its concerns about press leaks and how the U.S. position was being portrayed. During the past months, the regional and nonproliferation experts within the administration had continued to promote divergent views. Because the Defense Department had been largely cut out of policy formulation, it periodically made bellicose public statements. Deputy Secretary Strobe Talbott had recently persuaded the NSC to return the management of Korean issues to State, and Bob Gallucci had been appointed the special U.S. representative who would focus on Korean matters. One of Gallucci's early tasks would be to reengage Defense and to ensure a consistent public administration posture.[60]

Brown said that Washington knew that North Korea had tried to develop nuclear weapons, but it did not know whether Pyongyang had been successful. Some intelligence agencies believed that North Korea had one or two nuclear weapons, but State's Bureau of Intelligence and Research (INR) judged the evidence inconclusive. The entire intelligence community did agree that North Korea had no effective means of delivering a nuclear weapon to a target, and that it had not engaged in

reprocessing since 1992. Within the administration, the debate continued about whether to try to persuade or to force Pyongyang to refrain
from further nuclear activity; State strongly preferred persuasion. The
administration was insisting that North-South talks be restarted before
new U.S.-North Korean consultations took place; an overriding concern
of South Korea was that North Korea would open a formal dialogue
with Washington independent of Seoul. He said China had advised the
United States that it would not consider UN sanctions on North Korea
"at this time," but Washington thought China was leaning on North
Korea without telling the United States. Brown also said that Washington was surprised when, in March, the North Koreans refused to let the
IAEA complete all the inspections necessary to confirm that there had
been no reprocessing during the previous months. Hans Blix would report to the UNSC during the first half of May on his discussions with
the North Koreans about completing the IAEA inspections.[61]

The briefing then turned to U.S.-North Korean talks. Brown said
that little progress was expected until after Kim Il Sung's birthday celebrations on April 15. Some consideration was being given to the idea of
a special envoy, but even if this option was chosen, a later decision
would be required as to whether the envoy would merely be a "message
carrier" or would be authorized to negotiate.[62]

Additional information was passed to Carter a couple of weeks later.
The United States had presented new proposals to the North Korean
diplomats in New York on April 29 suggesting that bilateral talks be
restarted in mid-May. The administration source said that the examination of the spent fuel rods could be done as they were removed—which
the IAEA preferred—or subsequently, as long as the rods remained
under IAEA safeguards.[63] Our contact stated that the United States
now had more room for maneuver because the South Korean government had dropped its previous insistence that Seoul and Pyongyang
must exchange envoys before the third round of U.S.-North Korean
talks commenced. Referring to a recent public statement by Secretary of
Defense William Perry that North Korea might try to refuel its reactor
without IAEA monitoring, the official acknowledged that within the

administration there was a serious debate going on as to the advisability of preemptory air strikes to prevent Pyongyang from causing significant quantities of plutonium "to disappear" by discharging the fuel rods or refueling the reactor without IAEA inspectors on the scene.[64]

Carter was told that if the third round of talks commenced, Gallucci preferred to present a "package of arrangements" that the United States would be willing progressively to put in place once the nuclear issue was resolved. These arrangements could include economic assistance to North Korea, the termination of U.S.-South Korean military exercises, and, ultimately, U.S.-North Korean diplomatic relations.[65]

From The Carter Center's perspective, the Clinton administration's approach toward North Korea could have unwitting but dangerous consequences. On the one hand, the Clinton team had developed a package proposal. But this negotiated approach might never be tried because, in its diplomatic efforts in capitals and at the UN, the administration was urging the use of UN sanctions. Carter, deeply distrustful of the sanctions strategy, rejected the administration's rationale that threats would make Pyongyang more reasonable. In his view, because the North Korean leaders viewed their nuclear program as their only bargaining leverage, the politics of confrontation would leave them without a face-saving way to retreat. Their reaction could be explosive; it could lead to war.

This conviction, coupled with his increasing anxiety about developments and his growing belief that Washington would not likely call on his services, led Carter to question his self-imposed guideline not to undertake sensitive international missions without at least the acquiescence of the administration in power. Because of this guideline, he had already turned down three invitations to visit North Korea since 1991. But throughout the spring of 1994, he would ask himself repeatedly whether this constraint should be revised. Specifically, he pondered what course of action he should follow if he became convinced that war was likely and that he might have a chance of preventing it.

CHAPTER 3

Carter Chooses Involvement

By early May, Jimmy Carter's concern about Korean developments had grown to alarm. He feared that the situation might plunge the United States, the two Koreas, and perhaps others, into devastating war. To him, it appeared that none of the involved governments were looking for a mutually acceptable solution. With the South Korean government waving them on, the United States and North Korean governments seemed locked into diplomatic maneuvering and public posturing—not unlike the deadly adolescent game of "chicken" whereby two drivers race their automobiles toward each other and bet that the other will swerve first to avoid the head-on collision. But what if neither gave way? Carter knew that the cost of a new Korean War, should it erupt, would be large. He would learn later from the U.S. general who commanded the American and South Korean troops just how astronomical official U.S. projections of casualties were.

Carter believed that there must be an alternative way, and in the period from May 1 to June 6, 1994, he became convinced that he knew what it was. His new approach did not change the administration's policy objectives: prevent the emergence of a nuclear-armed North Korea, improve stability on the peninsula, maintain strong U.S.-South Korean ties, and support the global nonproliferation effort. It offered instead a better chance of achieving them, but it required two significant changes in tactics—actions that had been debated within the administration but had not been adopted and consistently applied. First, as the quid pro quo for North Korea's halting and dismantling its nuclear weapons program, submitting its nuclear energy program to more rigorous international inspection, and returning to the Nuclear Non-Proliferation Treaty (NPT) as a fully participating member, Pyongyang leaders should receive assurances against an American attack, for economic assistance, and for a transition process that could lead eventually to normalized relations with the United States. All these elements needed to be wrapped into one "package," each side taking actions and receiving benefits simultaneously rather than demanding that North Korea alone make the initial concessions.

The second tactical modification called for a senior American leader to speak and deal directly with the North Korean leadership, specifically with the founder and president of North Korea, Kim Il Sung. Ideally, this person should be a senior member of the Clinton team, such as the secretary of state, but Washington had apparently ruled out this idea—presumably fearing either that the North Korean leader would try to exploit senior-level communication in order to weaken international support for sanctions, or that hard-liners at home would condemn it as demonstrating the administration's weakness and indecisiveness. Under these circumstances, some prestigious person outside of government, such as Carter himself, might be able to fill the role. But this person would have to be able to convince Washington and Pyongyang to accept the same deal. To accomplish the outcome he sought, Carter knew that in approaching Kim Il Sung, he would have to build a personal relationship involving trust. With the Clinton administration, he would have to overcome suspicion regarding his motives, resentment by some that he was treading on their policy turf and undercutting a strategy that they believed would eventually work, and concern about being roasted by its foreign policy critics.

Consequently, in five weeks, Carter's own priorities shifted—from intervening abroad only if he had administration acquiescence to the possibility of acting on his own if he thought he might be able to prevent a war. Once he had made his decision, his sense of certainty coupled with some stubbornness—traits he had repeatedly exhibited in his life—would drive him to focus on how to achieve his goals. He would not waste his time on second-guessing his decision even though he knew that his historical reputation might well be at stake. Reinforced by his faith, Carter would act.

At the beginning of May, Don Oberdorfer wrote a lengthy story in the *Washington Post*[1] that accurately summarized the history and state of play of the North Korean nuclear problem prior to North Korea's removal of the spent fuel rods from its existing reactor. Oberdorfer suggested that the Clinton administration seemed ill-prepared to deal with the complex issues involved. He ended his article with a series of worrisome conclusions:

- The Clinton administration would see thousands of Americans die if war broke out and the rest of its domestic and foreign agenda in tatters. Yet it was not devoting "sufficient energy" to this issue.
- Clinton often received "diametrically opposite analyses" on North Korea because of disagreement in Washington and elsewhere about whether North Korea views its nuclear weapons program as a bargaining card or as a serious effort to obtain nuclear weapons to "prevent attack and insure survival of the regime."
- North Korea was increasingly isolated and under siege with its "inexplicable shifts on nuclear inspections."
- If North Korea removed the fuel rods without IAEA supervision, Washington had warned repeatedly that it would break off negotiations, and the United States was "at the top of North Korea's political and economic wish list."
- If the North Korean economy continued to deteriorate, more and more refugees would cross into China, and Seoul and China were just beginning to grapple with this issue and its potential impact on regional stability.[2]

Carter's analysis coincided in many ways with Oberdorfer's. He sent a copy of the article to Ambassador Jim Laney "in case you [Laney] haven't seen Don's article."[3]

Carter's own assessment, however, included a critically important element not developed in the Oberdorfer article. He was convinced that North Korea would retaliate militarily if the UNSC imposed economic sanctions on it. He believed that the North Korean leadership and populace would interpret UN sanctions as a calculated snub by the United States and others designed to denigrate their country as a "pariah nation" and to condemn their president—revered almost as a deity throughout his nation—as an "international outlaw." Such perceived outrage and injustice would unite the isolated North Korean nation to avenge these insults with the only weapon it had—its military. In Carter's view, North Korea must have a face-saving way out. Years later, information would emerge that showed President Clinton shared some of the same worries as Carter in these critical weeks.[4]

Carter had three meetings between May 3 and June 5 that reinforced his views. The first was with President Clinton on May 3 when he came to Atlanta to deliver an address, televised from the Carter Center, to the annual CNN World Report Conference for its international reporters.[5] The second was a meeting on May 4 with Ambassador Jim Laney, who had returned to Atlanta to receive an honorary degree at Emory University's commencement ceremonies. The third was a briefing given to Carter by Ambassador Robert Gallucci at the Carter home in Plains, Georgia, on June 5.

Before he made his remarks to the CNN conference, President Clinton met alone with President Carter in the latter's office. Carter emphasized his concerns about the Korean situation, and Clinton reported that his advisors were providing him conflicting advice. Carter mentioned the persistent invitations he had received from the North Koreans to visit their country. He urged Clinton to develop a "comprehensive approach" for dealing with North Korea.[6]

The following day, Ambassador Laney came to The Carter Center to talk with his former Emory colleague and friend, Jimmy Carter. Unlike some politically appointed ambassadors, Laney possessed impressive credentials for his job. He had lived for several years in South Korea, and he had followed closely Korean developments for more than forty years. Laney and his wife, Berta, had many Korean friends, some of whom they had known for decades, when they arrived in Seoul in 1993. Consequently, the Korean experts whom Laney encountered in Washington before leaving for his ambassadorial assignment in Seoul did not awe him. Years later, he would express dissatisfaction about the briefings he received before he departed to his post—he described one as "atrocious" and bearing little resemblance to the Korea he knew. Laney confided that some of Washington's intelligence experts tended to speculate widely about the meanings of the charts they read; indeed, these experts showed little interest in trying to discern the minds of the North Korean leaders, whom they tended to demonize. Laney noted parenthetically that to demonize someone destroyed all efforts to accomplish objectivity.[7]

According to Laney, when he was first approached about becoming an ambassador, he entertained hopes that the two Koreas could move toward reunification and that he could contribute to the process. By the time he left for Seoul, he no longer expected movement in this direction. Instead, he had a strong sense that things on the peninsula were "ominous." He did not believe Kim Il Sung's explanation that his country's nuclear energy efforts were directed solely toward securing needed electricity for its economic development. But he found interesting Gallucci's description of the North Korean proposal of July 1993 to replace its graphite reactors with light water reactors (LWRs). Laney left their luncheon discussion with the impression that Gallucci thought the exchange was feasible, though complex.[8]

Not cowed by bureaucratic discipline, Laney was prepared to act independently when he thought it necessary. He called issues as he saw them, and he conveyed his views forcefully, even when he knew his superiors would not welcome them. He would first try to deal with matters about which he felt strongly through normal bureaucratic channels. But when stymied, he would go outside channels to pursue the results he thought the situation demanded. He knew he served at the president's discretion, but as long as he held the position of ambassador, he intended to use his best judgment in promoting what he considered key U.S. interests—even if doing so shortened his time in government.

Soon after Laney arrived in Seoul in October 1993, Defense Secretary Les Aspin visited to attend the U.S.-South Korean Joint Security Meeting. During the secretary's stay at the ambassadorial residence, Laney tried to alert him to his mounting concern about the growing tensions on the peninsula, the need for the United States to try to tamp down rather than fuel the existing frictions, and his skepticism of U.S. intelligence. In later years, the ambassador would assess wryly that he had failed to convince the secretary: Aspin's press briefing on his plane returning to Washington exaggerated North Korean military activities, which media reporting turned into a major war scare.[9] Laney thought Aspin's departure from the administration a short time later was a good thing.[10]

The ambassador returned to Washington for the visit of the South Korean president, Kim Young Sam, in November. He used his meetings with senior administration officials to express his concern about the lack of policy clarity on Korea and to complain about the absence of a senior-level coordinator for policy concerning the peninsula. According to Laney, Assistant Secretary of State Winston Lord turned down his suggestion that Deputy Assistant Secretary Tom Hubbard be charged full-time with the Korean responsibility, reportedly saying that Hubbard's broader responsibilities prevented his being able to focus solely on Korea. They would have to do the best they could with the current structure. Laney's reply: "That would not cut it." Sitting next to Hillary Clinton at the White House dinner for the South Korean president, Laney confided his frustrations. He told her that unless someone in Washington took hold of the Korean issue, tragedy could result. Laney left Washington suffering greater anxiety than when he arrived.[11]

As he thought about the situation, Laney became convinced that U.S. Korean policy should simultaneously pursue two primary objectives: to maintain peace and stability on the peninsula and to get rid of the North's nuclear program. But the achievement of either alone while sacrificing the other would be "at best a Pyrrhic victory." On his instructions, Laney's embassy officers quickly produced a document elaborating this concept and dispatched it to Washington.

"Reflections on the Korean Situation," did not carry the kind of high security classification that is typically used on memoranda prepared by the State Department and other agencies dealing with national security issues. Instead, this embassy report was labeled "For Official Use Only," which allowed it to be shared at the discretion of the ambassador and its authors. The paper began by stating its basic premise: that U.S. policy must simultaneously pursue—not choose between them—the maintenance of peace on the peninsula and the prevention of the proliferation of nuclear weapons. U.S. strategy "must avoid at all cost a miscalculation that could have catastrophic consequences for our allies, our interests, and our world leadership," it held. "Our task is to persuade the North that abandoning the nuclear 'card' will serve its best interests whereas pursuing it would jeopardize the Regime's prospects for survival."[12]

According to this analysis, the nuclear problem was rooted in the "profound changes" of the previous two decades. South Korea had emerged as "one of the strongest economic engines in East Asia" and a model "to the third world showing the harmony between economic and democratic development." In contrast, North Korea, which in the 1970s had economic parity with South Korea and a stronger military, had since then suffered enormous losses in economic vitality and international political support. Earlier, North Korea had expected to absorb the South; currently, its "paramount fear" was the reverse. Consequently, the United States, in seeking to deal with the North Korean nuclear problem, should appreciate that North Korea was weak overall—despite its military strength— but also should realize that it was imbued with the "Asian cultural compulsion to mask weakness with intransigence and bluster." Moreover, "each year of prosperity in the South and atrophy in the North brings closer the prospect of unification on ROK [Republic of Korea—South Korea] terms." If the South Koreans seemed to be less alarmed about the

North's nuclear and conventional threat than Westerners, it was because they had a "justifiable sense of certainty" that they would prevail, an appropriate sense of confidence in their strength, and a determination that, "in the end game," they did not intend to put at risk all that their nation had managed to achieve. In short, the South Koreans were "convinced that time [was] on their side."

The paper insisted that the U.S. government must assess the North Korean nuclear situation objectively and realistically, not just aggregate worst-case hypotheses. The "preservation of the system and the regime" was the top priority of the Pyongyang leadership. Although the North Korean "military posture remains threatening," the South Korean and U.S. forces were superior. Whatever nuclear material North Korea possessed ("the statistical maximum is judged to be up to two bombs worth") it obtained it before mid-1992, and there was no credible evidence to suggest that it had a parallel nuclear program outside Yongbyon. "As long as the operation in Yongbyon is frozen, we are not racing to beat a crash North Korean effort to build nuclear capacity."[13]

Consequently, the U.S. goal should be "to modify North Korean behavior at an acceptable cost and without significant risk," for which diplomacy, with "incentives and checks," is the best instrument. "Few credible observers claim that tightening the vice [with sanctions] would force North Korea to disgorge its nuclear secrets." Instead, an effective U.S. approach requires cultural realism and insight that takes into account North Korea's obsession with "face" and its proclivity toward "brinkmanship." The paper concluded that, "The U.S. stake in the stability and prosperity of Northeast Asia demands that we apply patience, persuasion, and objectivity to this task."[14]

When Senators Sam Nunn (Democratic chairman of the Senate Armed Services Committee) and Richard Lugar (Republican minority leader of the Senate Foreign Relations Committee) visited Seoul in early January 1994, Laney argued that Washington was handling Korea in a "disjointed way." Laney stressed that U.S. policy to remove the North's nuclear program was subordinating all other important considerations concerning the peninsula. He shared the recently prepared policy paper with the two senators, who reportedly found its arguments and conclusions persuasive.[15]

When Laney sent a copy of the paper to President Carter on January 26, 1994, he said that it attempted to "bring some coherence to our understanding of the Korean situation." He told Carter that it had been sent to the State Department, and that Nunn and Lugar had used much of it for their report on their trip. He mentioned that he planned to be back in Atlanta in May and hoped to see Carter at that time.[16] Carter replied that he looked forward to seeing Laney in May or sooner and that he found the paper to be "incisive and helpful." Expressing his admiration, he told Laney that he was "increasingly grateful" that Laney was in Korea because "the situation require[d] sound judgment and statesmanship."[17]

During the next weeks, Laney's dismay mounted. He found it outrageous that James Woolsey, the CIA director, in a February 8 speech in Omaha went public with internally disputed intelligence that the North Koreans might have enough plutonium to make one or two nuclear bombs. When Laney returned to Washington later that month, he did not mince his words. "Woolsey was speaking out of turn," Laney complained to the White House. "Most people think the D.C.I. [Director of Central Intelligence] knows more than he says. This guy was saying more than he knows." [18] Laney's main purpose was to try again to have appointed a high-level official with the Korean mandate and to urge greater policy coherence. He made the rounds at State, Defense, and the NSC, reporting that the South Korean government worried more about the "overheated rhetoric and brinksmanship in Washington than about a potential nuclear threat from North Korea." He made clear his anxiety that an accidental war could break out on the peninsula, and he said that General Gary Luck agreed with him.[19] With White House chief of staff, Thomas (Mack) McLarty, and the White House adviser, David Gergen, Laney reiterated his worry that the United States would stumble into war. He described the bureaucratic situation as a "terrible mess." He said there was no senior-level official whose primary responsibility was the Korean Peninsula and who could talk authoritatively about policy toward both North and South Korea. McLarty, at one point in the conversation, said that creating a special senior position within the administration would be difficult—presumably because it would be interpreted by political hard-liners as elevating the status and importance of North Korea. Laney countered that 50,000 body bags resulting from an unnecessary war would also be a difficult political issue. After the meeting, McLarty called Secretary of State Christopher and told him to appoint someone immediately to be in charge of Korea; Christopher called Gallucci and told him to turn his other responsibilities over to his deputy and assume the Korea job full-time with the rank of ambassador. But at the time Laney did not know of these developments. He returned to Seoul thinking he had accomplished little.[20]

That said, Laney was pleased with the Gallucci appointment. He considered the new Korea point man to be smart and understanding of nuance. He was an expert on nuclear matters. He had little experience with East Asia and the Korean Peninsula, but he was a fast learner. Laney later commended Gallucci on the way he took charge. But unfortunately, according to Laney, Gallucci did not have the bureaucratic clout to control how Tony Lake, the national security adviser; Warren Christopher, the secretary of state; and William Perry, the new secretary of defense, would come out on Korean-related issues.[21] In Laney's view, the administration continued to move toward sanctions without adequately exploring other options. It ignored or discounted Kim Il Sung's repeated private and public statements that sanctions would mean war. Laney said that the North Koreans would not sit by passively if the United States tried to strengthen its forces on the peninsula as it did in the Gulf region before launching Operation Desert Storm in 1991.[22]

Laney flew to Atlanta in early May. At that time, the UN Security Council (UNSC) had the North Korean nuclear question under consideration, the North Korean negotiator in the bilateral Korean talks had already issued his "sea of fire" threat, and the United States, moving toward a sanctions initiative, continued to reject North Korea's entreaties to hold a third round of bilateral talks.[23]

In Carter's spacious office with its large windows displaying the luxuriant Japanese garden molded into the gentle hillside on which the Carter Center sat, the two friends discussed their shared worries that the situation on the peninsula was fast deteriorating and that the administration was locked into an inflexible and dangerous policy warp. Laney told Carter that the United States faced a "first-class political problem." Washington had no way of communicating directly with the North Korean leadership. Serious mistakes could be made if either side misread the signals the other was trying to send.[24] He told Carter that the United States might attack preemptively because of a misunderstanding—the same way World War I had started. Someone had to establish what the signals really were to ensure that the United States did not inadvertently stumble into war.[25]

Carter expressed his own anxieties, reinforced by Laney's description of the lack of effective communication channels between leaders in Washington and Pyongyang. He told Laney that he was convinced that Kim Il Sung and the North Korean populace would react violently if the UNSC levied economic sanctions on them. The damage such sanctions might do to the North Korean economy was not the issue. This economy, though deteriorating, derived little from the economies of others with the exception of China, and China did not view economic collapse in North Korea as serving Beijing's interest. The real issue with UN sanctions was that the North Koreans would view them as an unforgivable insult to their revered leader and proud country, and they would react—most probably with their military. Threats of sanctions would not force them to back away from their nuclear efforts but rather would likely have the opposite effect. Carter emphasized the need to deal directly with Kim Il Sung, the only person who could make decisions in North Korea, and he thought any top-level American could take on this mission. Laney concurred.

Laney told Carter about his efforts to persuade the administration to send Senators Nunn and Lugar as emissaries to North Korea. After

considerable internal discussion, this idea was adopted, and the two senators made preparations to go. Inexplicably, the North Koreans denied
them visas. Talking about these events years later, Laney said that the administration would have found a Nunn-Lugar trip easier to live with, but
it was best that Carter went. Apparently, Kim Il Sung attached a great deal
of importance to Carter's status as a former U.S. president.

Carter reviewed North Korea's three-year effort to get him to visit
Pyongyang. He brought Laney up-to-date on recent appeals by North
Korea's deputy ambassador, Ho Jung, and NGO leaders for him to become involved in trying to resolve the crisis. He also told Laney that the
administration had deflected his many appeals to assist.

Carter and Laney agreed that Carter should try to go to North
Korea. The former president said he would check with the North Koreans to confirm that his invitation remained valid. The two men
promised to stay in close touch after Laney returned to Seoul.[26]

Shortly thereafter, Kim Dae Jung visited the United States, spending
most of his time in Washington. Because he did not travel to Atlanta on
this trip, President Carter called him on May 11 to discuss the situation
on the peninsula. Kim Dae Jung summarized what he intended to say
to the National Press Club the next day. Subsequently, he sent Carter
the text of his remarks and a copy of his working paper.[27]

Carter studied closely Kim Dae Jung's remarks to the National Press
Club, which discussed two major, closely connected topics: "The Way to
Resolve the North Korean Nuclear Problem" and "Understand[ing] the
Sensibility of Asians." Kim began his presentation by saying he believed
it possible to resolve the North Korean nuclear problem. North Korea's
goal in developing nuclear weapons was to realize "its number one foreign policy objective—normalization of diplomatic relations with the
United States." Kim Il Sung "desperately" hoped to escape from the
country's serious economic situation and its international isolation
through diplomatic relations and economic cooperation with Western
countries. Kim Dae Jung said that North Korea would have to give up
development of nuclear weapons to achieve these goals.[28]

Faced with the collapse of the Soviet Union and developments in Eastern Europe, North Korea had recently made shifts in policy. In 1991, it made "three concessions to the West": joint entry of the two Koreas into the UN; acceptance of countries diplomatically recognizing both Koreas; and recognition of the South Korean government "as a legitimate entity, by signing a North-South agreement in December 1991." Kim Il Sung expected as a quid pro quo diplomatic and economic cooperation with the West and the cancellation of the annual Team Spirit joint military exercises. When these expectations remained unfulfilled, the hard-liners in Pyongyang gained the upper hand, resulting in the North's announcement of its intention to pull out of the NPT. In Kim Dae Jung's view, the North Korean hard-liners would analyze the situation as follows: "If we are given no way out but to ruin, we might as well go down fighting to the end."

Kim Dae Jung said that shortly after North Korea announced its decision to leave the NPT, he proposed a "two-pronged approach to this problem: a package of simultaneous give and take, together with cooperation from China." His package would include North Korea's giving up its nuclear ambitions and guaranteeing the security of South Korea; the United States would reciprocate with "diplomatic normalization leading to economic cooperation and North Korea's security assurance including the cancellation of the annual Team Spirit exercise." Before agreeing to such a package, the United States should get China's cooperation because China did not want North Korea to possess nuclear weapons. Then, if North Korea accepted the "package," everyone would benefit; if it rejected it, China would "have no choice but to support economic sanctions unless of course it [was] willing to endure international criticism and lose face."

Kim Dae Jung then discussed Asian sensitivities, to which Carter was much more attentive than Washington policymakers appeared to be. He said that to an Asian, "face-saving is as important as saving his life." An East Asian does not practice the "give and take method of the West." If he "feels he is treated with dignity, [he] may cheerfully give two for one," Kim instructed. "On the other hand, if he is displeased, he

might reject the deal altogether, no matter how advantageous to him."
To deal successfully with Asians, insisted Kim Dae Jung, one must understand and practice these sensitivities. Face-saving is particularly important in dealing with North Korea. "Kim Il Sung's face cannot be
compromised no matter what might be offered in return." Kim Dae
Jung said that Kim Il Sung had recently shown signs of being willing to
make concessions; he had even said he would like to visit the United
States. Kim Dae Jung then proposed that President Clinton—after
consulting with the government of South Korea—send an internationally respected elder statesman, a person "trusted by the Chinese and
North Koreans and sharing the views of President Clinton," first to
China and then to North Korea to consult directly with Kim Il Sung.[29]

During the question-and-answer period, one questioner asked Kim
Dae Jung who he thought would be the appropriate person to be President Clinton's emissary to China and North Korea. The future president of South Korea answered that "President Carter would be the
most qualified."[30]

During that critical month of May, Carter became increasingly convinced that an accidental war could break out, that such an outcome
would be an unnecessary catastrophe, and that Kim Il Sung must be
given a face-saving means of retreat if hostilities were to be avoided.
Carter shared his concerns and his view of the urgency of the situation
with his chief adviser, Rosalynn Carter, but either he did not confide the
intensity of his growing anxiety to his staff during those critical days or
we did not appreciate adequately what he told us. For instance, I was
not then fully cognizant of the substance of his conversations with President Clinton and Ambassador Laney, nor of the letter described above
from Kim Dae Jung. Carter normally spent only about one week a
month in The Carter Center; the rest of the time he traveled or worked
out of his home, two-and-a-half hours away by road, in Plains, Georgia.
When he needed specific information from his subordinates, or they
wished to convey information or views to him, this exchange took place
via courier—if the information needed to be treated confidentially or

was lengthy—or facsimile machine. As a result, those of us working at the Center on Korea perceived only later his mounting worries.

On June 1, Carter called President Clinton to express his view that the situation on the Korean Peninsula was becoming extremely precarious and that the U.S. push for UN economic sanctions against North Korea could lead to war. Clinton, about to leave for Europe for the fiftieth anniversary of the Normandy invasion of 1944, heard out the former president, but made no commitment. He did offer to send a senior administration official to brief Carter at his home in Plains, leaving open the possibility of subsequent discussions upon his return.

Carter instructed me to work with the NSC on arrangements. I spoke with Dan Poneman, the special assistant to the president and the senior director for nonproliferation and export controls in the NSC, who told me that he had been asked to brief Carter. Washington commitments prevented Dan's traveling until the weekend, although he said he preferred to fly to Atlanta on Monday because his wife had just given birth and he would like to be with his family during the weekend. Operating behind the curve on Carter's sense of alarm, and knowing the importance the former president attached to family, I told Poneman that Monday should be fine. I then notified Faye Dill, Carter's personal and executive assistant,[31] who passed the message to Carter.

Carter apparently received this information with considerable irritation. He interpreted his conversation with Clinton to mean that a senior-level briefer would come to Plains immediately—not five days later. (Carter frequently told staff members that when he was president, he would quickly dispatch government officials to brief former presidents on critical issues, often acting on his own initiative.) Feeling rebuffed and angry, Carter called Mack McLarty, the White House chief of staff, and told him that a late briefing by someone who seemed too young to be a senior official was inconsistent with Clinton's promise to him. He added that he was furious. McLarty promised to check into the matter and get back to him quickly. He did. He advised Carter that Ambassador Robert Gallucci, the administration's point person on Korea, would fly to Plains as quickly as his schedule would permit, which would probably be the weekend.[32] Gallucci offered to come to Plains either on Saturday afternoon, but late, after meetings that could not be postponed, or on Sunday morning. Carter selected Sunday morning.

On the morning of June 5, Gallucci arrived at the Hartsfield Airport in Atlanta. His instructions were to explain the administration's policy, make the case for why this policy was being pursued, and seek to gain Carter's support for it.[33] I met him and drove him to Plains, Georgia. During the two-and-a-half-hour trip, Gallucci and I talked extensively. I explained Carter's heightened concern—which I now fully appreciated—and told Gallucci that, in my personal opinion, Carter intended to become involved. I suggested that the administration should try to use Carter. If he were successful, the administration could claim credit; if he failed—and Carter was not afraid to fail—the administration could distance itself from his initiative. Gallucci explained the complex situation in Washington. He said that the policymakers from the various departments were at odds over the appropriate approach to North Korea. He stressed the pressure being exerted on the administration by the hard-liners on Capitol Hill, in think tanks, and among former Bush foreign policy experts with their charges that the Clinton team was "wimpish" and was undermining the credibility of American leadership and power.

Jimmy and Rosalynn Carter received Bob Gallucci graciously in their comfortable but unpretentious ranch-style home that stood on property which had been in the Carter family for several generations. Gallucci had reservations for a return flight that would have required him to depart Plains after a couple of hours. But when Carter asked how long he would be able to talk, Gallucci said he would stay as long as Carter wished him to. As it turned out, the conversation lasted more than three hours, and Gallucci had to rearrange his return flight plans when he arrived back at the Atlanta airport. After about an hour of discussion, Mrs. Carter slipped away to the kitchen close by and made ham sandwiches for the three men and herself. She worked quietly, following intently the conversation as she prepared the lunch.

The conversation flowed easily. Gallucci, deferential to the former U.S. president and seemingly impressed with Carter's knowledge and interest, provided a detailed briefing, which Carter assessed as superb. The former president listened thoughtfully, made notes, interjected questions periodically, and explained his concerns. The two men covered a lot of territory, and when they had finished, each seemed to have a high regard for the other. That mutual respect would be revealed on several occasions in the weeks that followed.

Carter considered their discussion that afternoon highly important to his understanding of the issues and to his final decision to intervene personally in the North Korean nuclear crisis. For these reasons, this conversation is extensively described below. I have drawn largely from Carter's handwritten notes.

Following his usual approach, Carter opened the conversation by demonstrating his interest and involvement in the issue at hand. He outlined the previous invitations he had received from North Korea and the one from South Korea, mentioned the trip to the peninsula of the Carter advance team in 1992, and said that he had refrained from traveling himself because each time he had asked to go, the State Department had asserted that bilateral talks "were going great" and his involvement "was not needed."[34] When the North Koreans subsequently contacted Carter, they said that Kim Il Sung needed a way to talk about resolving North Korea's problems with the United States in a definitive way.[35]

Gallucci's briefing then commenced. He said that the North Korean nuclear program consisted of a zero-power reactor under IAEA inspection; a nuclear fabricating facility; a 5 MWe graphite-moderated reactor; a radiation chemical laboratory of which the reprocessing capacity was being doubled; and a 200 MWt thermal reactor (50 MWe) to be completed in 1995 or 1996. North Korea's nuclear program was self-sufficient, from its uranium mines to its finished fuel rods. Gallucci further said that the bilateral denuclearization declaration by the two Koreas contained provisions for no reprocessing, mutual inspections, and the formation of a joint nuclear control commission, but it might not have been officially signed and was not currently being honored—although it remained a "potential for the future."[36]

Gallucci expressed his "personal view" that North Korea wanted to make a deal. He thought that Kim Il Sung wanted enough investment to strengthen the economy and so protect the country during the political transition from his rule to that of his son.[37]

Gallucci said that the two undeclared North Korean nuclear sites needed to be inspected to ascertain what had been done in the past. But Hans Blix, reacting to criticism that the IAEA was too lax in Iraq, was being more aggressive and inflexible than Washington would prefer.

When North Korea refused inspection of the two disputed sites in early 1993 and then threatened to withdraw from the NPT, the United States suggested a meeting in New York. To induce North Korean flexibility on the special inspections issue, the United States had been prepared at the June 1993 meeting to offer mutual inspections of sites in South Korea as well as in North Korea, but it never put this proposal on the table. Instead the two sides agreed on a joint statement. Shortly thereafter, North Korea surprised the United States with its unprecedented claim to "special status" under the NPT, asserting that it had suspended but not withdrawn its threat to leave the NPT. The United States followed with a unilateral announcement of what would be necessary for future talks to take place: continuity of safeguards, no reprocessing, continued North Korean membership in the NPT, and IAEA observance of fuel rod discharge from the North Korean reactor. At the July meeting in Geneva, Kang Sok Ju surprised the U.S. delegation again—offering to alleviate most of the reprocessing concerns by replacing graphite reactors with light water reactors. Gallucci said that except for this announcement, the meeting was "otherwise not productive." Then during IAEA inspections in August 1993, there was an "altercation" between the inspectors and the North Koreans who, in reaction, turned off the lights and refused to let the IAEA experts continue their work.

Gallucci then described the developments that led to the increasing tensions in recent months, including the cancellation of a third round of

U.S.-North Korea talks. That March, Gallucci met with PRC leaders in Beijing; they agreed to urge North Korea to comply with IAEA inspections, but Gallucci did not know whether they had done so. On March 31, after the IAEA had taken the issue of North Korean intransigence to the UN, the Security Council issued a strong statement instructing Pyongyang to accede to IAEA inspections. In April, Seoul changed its position that North-South talks be a prerequisite to the U.S.-North Korean talks, and the United States communicated to Pyongyang that it would participate in the third round of talks if the North Koreans would permit inspections.[38] In May, IAEA inspectors took the appropriate wipes and gamma scans in the North's nuclear facilities and found them to be "o.k." The United States indicated that it was prepared to hold new talks with North Korea in Geneva. But then the next issue arose: The North Koreans had been told they should not remove their fuel rods from the 5 MWe reactor unless IAEA inspectors were present and had the authority to segregate a "representative sample of specific rods, about 300 out of 8010." The North Koreans said that the fuel rods had to be discharged, an event that was long overdue; they agreed that the IAEA could observe this discharge, but rejected segregation of the spent rods as demanded by the IAEA. Gallucci said that the United States became "very flexible" at this point, in part because Secretary of Defense William Perry, after reviewing the surgical strike option and its possible adverse consequences, favored a negotiated settlement. Washington told the North Koreans that the third round of talks could commence if they would either stop discharging the rods or only remove them very slowly. Another North Korean surprise: Pyongyang said no, and the accelerated removal of the rods continued, which was the "present status."[39] North Korea did suggest an alternative method for dealing with the fuel rods, but the IAEA found it inadequate because Pyongyang's plan reportedly did not ensure that the correct rods would be segregated.[40]

Gallucci then compared the military forces on the Korean Peninsula. He said that North Korea's army of 1 million persons was mobilized and possessed formidable artillery, with 10,000 artillery pieces deployed near the demilitarized zone. He added that North Korea had the largest contingent of special forces in the world. Its Do Dung missiles, with a 1,000 km range, could reach all of South Korea. It was developing Tapo Dung missiles, which had much greater range, but they were inaccurate. The United States and South Korea were dominant in the air. North Korea would have major problems in coordinating its forces and with geography, which favored air power over tank power. In South Korea, the United States had 36,000 troops; in addition, there were 80,000 civilian Americans who would have to be evacuated in time of war. Seoul's 13 million inhabitants were within North Korea's artillery range. Gallucci repeated General Luck's assessment: "I can win, but not right away." He added that not trying to reach a negotiated settlement would be "insane." Gallucci said that in the event of war, Seoul might be taken before the North Korean forces are stopped.[41]

Gallucci summarized for Carter the current basic position of the South Korean and Chinese governments: Seoul: "Be flexible, but firm"; Beijing: "We don't want a nuclear arsenal in North Korea, nor do we want a war. Don't push them too hard."

Gallucci then turned to the subject that caused Carter the most concern—UN sanctions. He said that President Clinton had repeatedly promised sanctions and was now under pressure to deliver on his promises. Washington's thinking was to ratchet up sanctions as necessary to force North Korea's compliance, admitting at one point that North Korea might perceive sanctions as provocative. As "early sanctions," the United States would suggest to the UN the following: no nuclear cooperation; an end to foreign aid, mostly from the United Nations Development Program (UNDP); no scheduled air flights; a freeze on North Korean financial assets; the termination of remittances from North Koreans living in Japan; and the prevention of North Korean trade in weaponry. Carter expressed doubts that the Chinese would approve UN sanctions that could lead to war. He also said that such sanctions, particularly on the remittances from Japan, would place great pressure on Tokyo. Gallucci recognized that sanctions would be a "tough choice" for the Chinese, but he assured Carter that Japan and

South Korea had told Washington that they would support UN sanctions if they passed in the Security Council.[42]

Gallucci shifted to an assessment of the North Korean leadership. He said that Kim Il Sung was active and, in fact, seemed quite vigorous, as depicted recently on CNN.[43] He still made the major decisions. His son, Kim Jong Il, was "in charge on a daily basis," but he stayed in the background as was customary in North Korean families. The son may have been the one to make the last-minute decision that caused the North Korean-IAEA deadlock. Gallucci suggested that the North Korean military was loyal to the country's political leadership. The country's primary concern was "the impending transition from father to son," along with maintaining political stability and improving the economy.

Gallucci said that a crucial question under debate within the administration was the relative importance of past North Korean nuclear transgressions and its future behavior. He said that the hawks and some others held that the North Korean-IAEA issue of past reprocessing must be resolved in favor of the IAEA, including its inspection of the disputed sites; backing down on this issue would signal U.S. weakness and cause a loss of national respect. Others within the administration held that preventing major plutonium production in the future, which would be the outcome of a North Korean permanent pullout from the NPT, was far more significant than what had happened up to the present. If they developed them, the North Koreans could sell nuclear missiles to countries such as Iran, Libya, and Iraq. According to Gallucci, Defense Secretary Perry and General Luck supported the latter position; Secretary of State Christopher and sometimes National Security Adviser Lake, "along with the hawks," subscribed to the former view. Gallucci noted the statement made by First Vice Foreign Minister Kang Sok Ju: "We can settle the future on nuclear and other matters, if the U.S. drops its infatuation with the past."

Carter emphasized his strong view about how to deal with Kim Il Sung. He said that despite Washington's understandably negative view of him and his record, Kim Il Sung must be treated with respect and honored as a senior statesman if the crisis was to be resolved peacefully. Unfortunately, the administration had moved in the opposite direction. It was proposing sanctions that, even if not implemented, would be a "tangible and official branding of him [Kim Il Sung] as a criminal and outlaw." He insisted that the passage of a sanctions resolution by the United Nations Security Council would likely cause North Korea to leave the NPT permanently. The act of imposing sanctions, whether done in one or more stages, would be for North Korea "an act of war."

Gallucci admitted that Washington did not have a reliable communications channel with North Korea. He defined it aptly as a "tube problem." The North Korean mission in New York was the official point of contact for communications, the mouth of the "tube." The administration had no assurance that what it put in the tube was what actually came out at the other end; nor did it know who got the message and what was done with it. According to Gallucci, in January consideration was given to having Ron Dellums (the Democratic chairman of the House Armed Services Committee) go to Pyongyang. And, of course, the administration approved a trip by Senators Sam Nunn and Richard Lugar that did not happen. Gallucci said that so far, there had not been and was not contemplated any sure communication with North Korea's top leaders.

Gallucci's final point related to U.S.-South Korean relations. He said that North Korea's insistence on dealing directly with the United States was aimed at separating the United States from South Korea. The best friend of the United States in the Kim Young Sam government was Foreign Minister Han Sung Joo, who viewed U.S.-South Korean harmony as crucial. Yet South Korean leaders could not appear to be dependent or subservient to the United States.

The Carter-Gallucci conversation concluded with Carter saying that he was assessing what would be the downside of his going to Pyongyang, either as a private citizen representing the Carter Center, or, if requested, as an emissary.

Neither the Carters nor I remember (or recorded in our notes) a discussion in Plains with Gallucci about whether or not North Korea could reprocess its spent fuel rods under IAEA safeguards as permitted in the NPT. Gallucci, on the other hand, recalls such a discussion.[44] This matter would come up later. Carter warmly thanked Gallucci, expressed his appreciation for the excellent briefing and candid discussion, and hinted broadly that the conversation had convinced him of the need for some American of stature to talk directly with Kim Il Sung.

Gallucci did not mention to Carter one attempt that he had recently made to convey to the North Koreans the Clinton administration's desire to resume bilateral negotiations. Gallucci was in Beijing when he learned that Mike Chinoy, a CNN correspondent based in China, had been given permission by Pyongyang to attend and report on Kim Il Sung's eighty-second birthday celebration on April 13, 1994. Gallucci contacted Chinoy. According to Chinoy, Gallucci said that, although he was not asking him to transmit a specific message to the North Koreans, it was important that Pyongyang understand the American position. The United States wanted to resume bilateral discussions and was looking for ways to get back to the negotiating table. The United States was not trying to bring down the North Korean regime and was seeking to "get the nuclear issue behind us." Chinoy reportedly passed this message to Kim Yong Sun, the influential secretary of the country's ruling party, shortly after he arrived in Pyongyang.[45]

On the drive back to Atlanta, I inferred that Gallucci would support Carter's involvement. Years later, Gallucci confirmed my suspicion. Discussing his briefing of Carter, Gallucci said that at the time he believed that if the North Koreans wanted to have a showdown, no one would be able to prevent it; but if they wanted to back away from that outcome, Carter might be able to provide them a graceful way to do so.[46] On our return trip to Atlanta, Gallucci cautioned that he would not be the policymaker in the Clinton administration who would make the final decision on Carter's intervention or on any other major issue on the Korean question. Such decisions would be taken in NSC-chaired meetings, usually led by Tony Lake, the NSC adviser; the top officials of State, Defense, NSC, and other attendees often disagreed. I emphasized again the importance of direct communication with the North Korean leadership. I urged that Carter be used to establish this communication tie if senior Washington officials continued to believe that it was inappropriate for them to do so. After arriving in Washington, Gallucci called Sandy Berger, the deputy national security adviser, and told him that he thought Carter wanted to go to North Korea.[47]

That evening, Carter typed his notes on his conversation with Gallucci, conferred with Rosalynn, and decided that he would go to North Korea. He still hoped for administration approval or, at least, acquiescence. But for the first time in his postpresidential years, he had decided that if Washington objected, he would go anyway and involve himself directly in a major international dispute to which the United States government was a party. Firmly believing that the situation was leading to war—even though none of the participants wanted that outcome—he determined that the pursuit of a peaceful resolution of the nuclear crisis had a higher priority than his belief that former presidents should not cause international problems or embarrassment for their successors. He knew he would be criticized. He knew the odds of his succeeding were small. He knew that his historical reputation could suffer. But he believed that this war was not necessary and should be avoided—regardless of the potential cost to him.

CHAPTER 4

The Countdown:
Phase One

Having made his decision to intervene in the North Korean nuclear crisis, Jimmy Carter, the trained engineer, shifted into high gear in preparing for his trip. He immediately laid out his plans for the next few days and then efficiently executed them. First, he needed to communicate his intention to President Clinton, and he wrote a letter to him a few hours after Gallucci departed. The letter below was faxed to the White House the next day, Monday, June 6.

To President Bill Clinton

Repetitively during the past three years, the North Korean leaders have asked me to visit Pyongyang so that they could explain their position and attempt to resolve existing issues harmoniously. On one occasion in 1992, with the tacit understanding of President Bush and his State Department, I even sent an advance team over to prepare for my prospective trip to Seoul and Pyongyang. In a scenario with which you are thoroughly familiar, an oscillating wave of successes and failures was occurring, and when it seemed at the time that official channels would achieve a reasonable solution of the

problems among North and South Korea and the United States, I re-
frained from going.

Now, the North Koreans have renewed their invitation for me to meet
with their top leaders. This time I have accepted, and am making
arrangements for an early trip, using private transportation available
to me. My current plan is to go as a private citizen, representing The
Carter Center. However, if you would like for me to represent you in
any capacity, official or unofficial, I would be glad to do so. As a result
of our conversation shortly before you departed for Europe, I have been
brought up-to-date on the latest developments, but further briefing
would be helpful. This would be particularly helpful on the nuclear
question.

My goal would be to explore the outstanding issues with the North Ko-
reans, hoping to comprehend as accurately as possible the concerns and
proposals of Kim Il-sung and other leaders. I understand from them
that they cannot yield to the public pressure being brought on them, pri-
marily from Washington, but would like to see the existing deadlock on
both the nuclear issue and North-South relations broken in a peaceful
and mutually respectful way. According to them, this opportunity may
be closed if official sanctions are voted by the Security Council, in effect
branding North Korea as an outlaw nation and their leaders as crimi-
nals. I realize that, on the other hand, you are committed to proceed
with a vote on sanctions.

If I go as an unofficial visitor, I will be very careful not to adopt the role
of a negotiator or attempt to speak on behalf of our country. But I will, of
course, relay any messages to you or others that might be forthcoming.

Sincerely,

Jimmy Carter (signed)[1]

Carter called early Monday morning and instructed me to confirm
with the North Korean mission in New York that his earlier invitation re-

mained valid. I told Minister Counselor Han Song Ryol that Carter was seriously considering a trip to his country if the invitation was still open. The North Korean diplomat promised to send an immediate message to Pyongyang and advise as soon as a reply was received.[2] The next day, Tuesday, June 7, Minister Counselor Han advised that the invitation remained valid, that Carter would be allowed to enter North Korea by crossing the DMZ, and that he would be able to meet Kim Il Sung.

President Clinton being in Europe, Vice President Al Gore received Carter's letter. Gore called the former president and urged him to change the language in his letter from saying that he had accepted the North Korean invitation to saying that he was inclined to accept. With that change, the vice president said he would urge President Clinton to approve Carter's traveling to Pyongyang as a private citizen representing The Carter Center. Carter agreed, revised his earlier letter as suggested,[3] and had the new version faxed to Washington.

Carter's letter set off an intense discussion among Clinton's senior national security advisers. They found it difficult to say no to the former president, but thought it risky to say yes. These officials believed the North Korean regime "so insular that there was no clear sense that an accurate picture of reality—or the dire straits it faced—was fully conveyed to the North Korean leaders," the same concern Gallucci had mentioned to Carter on June 5. According to Bob Gallucci and Dan Poneman, who attended the meeting, some within the administration worried that although the United States might convince the international community to increase pressure on Pyongyang by acting collectively against North Korea, this pressure might not lead North Korea to comply fully with global nonproliferation norms. They reasoned that a Carter visit might help North Korea "climb back from the precipice." On the other hand, other senior officials, particularly among those who had worked with Carter in the past, believed that Carter would "free lance" when he found himself at odds with U.S. policy, and thereby undermine the administration's strategy. Gore reportedly came out in favor of the Carter trip, whereas Christopher "thought it a bad idea." Gore called Air Force One, which was bringing the presidential party back from Europe, and spoke with Tony Lake, who agreed that Carter should go. Lake spoke with the president, and Clinton approved the trip.[4]

Carter had not waited for Gore's confirmation before scheduling briefing sessions for the trip. On June 8, he had a lengthy discussion with Weston M. Stacey, an expert in nuclear engineering at Georgia Tech University, about nuclear technology. In reviewing the technical aspects of the plutonium production rate of graphite-moderated and light water reactors, Stacey discussed how and why the graphite-moderated reactors produced more weapons-grade plutonium than light water reactors and how spent fuel in the rods removed in previous shutdowns of the North Korean reactor could have been reprocessed into weapons-grade plutonium. Stacey thought that it would be difficult to determine how much plutonium had been produced earlier without knowing the location in the fuel core of the rods currently being discharged by North Korean nuclear experts into the cooling pond.[5]

The next day, the Carters, joined by the Center's executive director, John Hardman, and me, met with Tom Johnson, CNN's chief executive officer, and Eason Jordan, the president of CNN Newsgathering, over lunch at The Carter Center. The purpose was to learn about and discuss the insights the CNN officials had gained in preparing for and covering Kim Il Sung's birthday celebrations in North Korea less than two months earlier. Jordan had traveled to North Korea as part of a delegation of the Washington-based Summit Council, a group affiliated with the Unification Church, whose officials periodically visited Pyongyang. For the first two days of his weeklong trip, he had pleaded with North Korean authorities to permit Mike Chinoy and his crew to travel from Beijing to Pyongyang so that on-the-ground reports could be filed on CNN's worldwide network. When permission was ultimately given, Jordan was told that Kim Jong Il had made the decision.[6]

Jordan explained that Kim Il Sung was always referred to by his subordinates as the "Great Leader." At one point during the birthday festivities, Kim Il Sung had assembled a small group of dignitaries and journalists for talks and lunch in his presidential palace. Jordan described the North Korean dictator as "remarkably healthy for a man of his age" and "feisty, quick-witted and very much in command."

Kim Il Sung told Jordan and the other guests that North Korea had no nuclear weapons and did not want them. He admitted that North Korea built military hardware for export because it needed the money. What he and North Korea demanded was respect, not threats. He lamented that no one dealt with North Korea with respect.

The elder Kim expressed confidence in his son. He insisted that Kim Jong Il, whom Jordan did not meet, played an important role in the life of the country and in his own life, but said that his son "must stand on his own legs." The father also said that Kim Jong Il helped keep him informed about domestic and international developments by personally recording audiotapes and sending them to him when he was absent from the office.

Two incidents that occurred during the interview shed additional light on Kim Il Sung's authority. According to Jordan, when the "Great Leader" spoke, a rose-colored spotlight descended from the ceiling to shine on him; it would silently retract when Kim Il Sung ended his remarks.[7] Less bizarre but still notable, whenever he asked a subordinate a question, that person would rise quickly to his feet, snap to attention, and give the answer.[8] (The Carter team would witness the same obeisance in its formal meeting with Kim Il Sung.)

The North Korean leader said he was living an active life and described with relish his hunting and fishing, activities in which he participated regularly. He boasted of having recently bagged the biggest bear of his career. He admitted with a smile, however, that the kill had been an easy one because North Korean soldiers had earlier captured the bear, fattened it, and released it within shooting distance of him.

Jordan's notes further depicted the personality cult created by Kim Il Sung and the effort to embrace his son in it:

The bizarre "paradise" of the Great Leader is unlike any place on earth. Kim Il-Sung is everywhere. All North Koreans wear Kim Il-Sung lapel pins. Every residence and office prominently features framed photos of the Great Leader and his son, Dear Leader Kim Jong-Il. North Korean TV features seemingly incessant images of at least one of the two Kims, with accompanying martial music (North Koreans rarely hear the voices of their leaders).

Songs praising the Great One and the Dear One can be heard virtually everywhere—in the streets, in hotels and aboard North Korean airliners.[9]

After Jordan had described Kim Il Sung's forceful demeanor, the authority with which he spoke, and the veneration in which he was held, he told Carter that he was convinced Kim Il Sung made the key policy decisions for North Korea.[10] Despite his expectation of finding a nation "hunkered down for war," he saw no signs of preparation for an impending conflict when he arrived or during his visit, nor did he sense tension. Contrasting what he saw and heard in North Korea with what he had encountered in war zones and would-be hot spots elsewhere, Jordan left convinced that a new Korean conflict was "far from imminent."

Jordan concluded that, according to what he had seen and heard, there were separate camps of advisers around Kim Il Sung and Kim Jong Il. His dealings with Kim Yong Sun, the secretary of the ruling Workers' Party, led him to believe that this person was close to both the father and the son.[11]

Jordan's description of Pyongyang read:

> Pyongyang is a peculiar yet phenomenal city—scenic, spotless and safe. The North Korean capital probably has more spectacular monuments (most honoring the Great Leader) per square mile than any city in the world. The city's many skyscrapers are dwarfed by a 105-story pyramid-shaped hotel, which is fully formed yet still under construction. The metro is among the world's finest. Few cars are in the streets. Many people appear to run to work in their business clothes. People exercise outside with their work groups. Children are dressed smartly in school uniforms. I saw thousands of North Koreans in both staged and unstaged environments. All appeared to be well fed. Most people appeared to be in good spirits.[12]

Jordan commented favorably on the way the CNN crew was treated, but this would have been expected because North Korea would want CNN to file positive reports. Good interpreters were provided as well as two cars for a round trip visit to Panmunjom. Jordan and his colleagues assumed that their rooms and cars were bugged, as would any visiting diplomat. Their escorts were polite. They found that despite the country's self-imposed isolation, North Korean ministries, government institutions, and the ruling party bosses monitored CNN International closely.[13]

Tom Johnson then summarized the discussions he and Jordan had had with officials in Washington before the latter's trip to North Korea. They were told that since the 1950s the North Koreans had placed underground all critical military facilities, including artillery, and that big earthen bins stood in front of these tunnels. North Korea devoted from 30 to 50 percent of the country's budget to the military. The Washington experts said that North Korean officials did not believe U.S. announcements that there were no nuclear weapons in South Korea. North Korea could probably produce from two to four nuclear weapons within six to eight months because allegedly it had access to Russian and Chinese nuclear scientists.[14] Nuclear weapons would give the North Koreans "great clout" because they already possessed aircraft that could deliver nuclear weapons to Japan and South Korea. The North Korean intention was "to get respect," whereas the United States wanted "fully intrusive inspections" of the two undeclared nuclear sites because they would "reveal what bombs the North Koreans already have."[15]

The officials providing the briefing insisted that the political succession process in North Korea was complete, that Kim Jong Il was in charge. (Johnson reaffirmed that the CNN assessment differed.) The Washington experts then castigated the character and activities of Kim Jong Il along lines that I would later hear with additional embellishment from South Korean sources. They said that the son, who adulated his father, was not crazy, even though some reports suggested he was, nor was he charismatic; he might be narcissistic. He liked to give and attend large drinking parties. The military really did not like him. Having made those points, the Washington experts admitted that they really had no solid information on Kim Jong Il. He seldom traveled outside the country. Foreign embassies in Pyongyang were segregated from the Korean people and society, and their officers had little, if any, access to North Korean leaders. China provided 75 percent of the aid received by North Korea, and as North Korea's primary oil supplier, Beijing had a strong lever over Pyongyang.

As the luncheon concluded, Jordan told Carter that he believed CNN would be permitted to enter the country to cover his trip. Carter, though skeptical, said he would be pleased if that happened. Johnson told the former president that the CNN bureaus in South Korea and Beijing would be notified about Carter's travels, which CNN would cover extensively.[16]

After the luncheon, I called the Korea Desk of the State Department to request assistance in arranging for a Korean interpreter to accompany us to North Korea. Carter and I had discussed earlier the need for such an individual in addition to the interpreters the North Koreans would provide. We wanted our own interpreter for two reasons: to check that the Carter exchanges with North Korean officials were correctly conveyed to both parties by the North Korean interpreter, and to be able to know what was being said if the North Korean officials sought to converse among themselves in Korean during sessions with Carter. The latter would occur with some regularity, and Carter would learn almost immediately from our interpreter what was being said. We initially sought an interpreter who was not on the U.S. government payroll; Carter was suspicious about having a State Department official on our delegation. Nevertheless, with the trip only days away, Carter accepted the State Department offer to provide the services of Richard (Dick) Christenson, the U.S. consul general in Okinawa, Japan, who was fluent in Korean and had served previously in Seoul.

Christenson performed superbly, providing invaluable assistance to the Carters. Dick was equally pleased to have been selected for the Carter team. The one slightly tense moment occurred on the Tuesday morning the day after we arrived in Seoul: Christenson and I were talking in Jim Laney's living room. Laney brought Carter over to introduce Dick to him. Carter looked straight and unblinking into his eyes. "Dick," said the former president, "are you working for me or the State Department on this trip?" After a moment, Dick responded, "I don't imagine there will be any conflict of interest. I intend to support you the best that I can."[17] He did.

Carter sought out other persons who had visited North Korea recently to hear their views on that country and its leadership and their advice on how to approach his North Korean interlocutors once he was in Pyongyang.

Carter spoke by phone with the Reverend Billy Graham about the latter's trip to North Korea five months earlier. Graham had no doubt that Kim Il Sung was totally in charge. He stressed the importance of treating

Kim Il Sung as a friend and with respect. He mentioned that he had carried a message from President Clinton, but that it had been short and unhelpful; it had said that relations could improve only after North Korea cooperated on the nuclear issue. The evangelist and his aide, Stephen Linton, who with his missionary parents had lived for several years in South Korea, had served in Korea while in the U.S. Army, and had focused on Korea while obtaining his doctorate at Columbia, reportedly tried to add polite explanations to the message, but the letter aroused Kim Il Sung's ire. He told Graham: "Pressure and threat cannot work on us."[18]

Graham subsequently sent Carter copies of the speeches he had given in North Korea; he included a perceptive paper, written by Steve Linton, on negotiating with North Koreans, which Carter read and found useful. In his three public declarations—airport arrival, welcome banquet, and address at the Kim Il Sung University—Graham had stressed friendship between the United States and North Korea and the necessity of overcoming current mistrust and of working together for peace. He had called on the two nations to climb "the mountain of challenges" as friends, not struggle against each other as enemies. Frequently using a garden analogy, he said he had come to try to prevent the "seeds of friendship" earlier planted between North Korea and the United States [referring to the period from late 1991 through mid-1992] from being damaged by an "unseasonable frost," to "cultivate this friendship and pray for a good harvest." He said that President Clinton and most Americans wanted to put the remaining element of the Cold War, including tensions with North Korea, behind them. "I have known President Clinton for many years personally, and I know that he is committed to peace," he noted. He also made favorable references to Kim Il Sung, calling him a "wise leader," an interesting person, and an instant friend.[19]

The Linton paper's advice on negotiating tactics contrasted sharply with the views of those demanding a stern and inflexible posture when dealing with North Korean officials. According to Linton, the Graham team made gestures that "did not surrender principle or high moral ground," yet allowed the North Koreans to see that this American group was not hostile. As a result, the North Korean interlocutors became much more open than the Americans had expected. Although acknowledging that North Korea is "probably the greatest negotiating challenge on the planet," the Graham group had learned that a "steady, friendly and determined approach can meet with some success." In their two years of negotiating with senior North Korean officials, Linton said he and the others had deduced three general principles.[20]

The first was that personal relationships had to be "cemented before anything concrete can be done." Because of North Korea's isolation, solid personal relationships were even more important in dealing with Pyongyang than with other Asian societies. Linton believed that "warm and cordial relationships between leaders can move mountains." But when personal relationships are negative and when hostility is expressed verbally toward the leadership, even simple and reasonable tasks "become almost impossible to negotiate." Linton drew four implications from this principle: First, problems should be depicted as "annoying obstacles to what is most important: friendship between the highest levels of leadership." In effect, "to ask a favor as a friend has far more impact than an offer to 'make a deal.'" Second, negotiations should focus on people, not problems: "Korean sensibilities are often offended by excessively goal-oriented negotiations." Third, "North Korean diplomacy has a much stronger personal dimension and a much weaker legal dimension than is customary in most diplomatic exchanges." Fourth, the best way to achieve progress in negotiations is through "exchanges of personal envoys at the highest levels of leadership."

The second principle was that negotiators must avoid threats to North Korea's national existence and social cohesion. One implication was that a "personal and confidential relationship is possible only in a bilateral context" and "attempts to include third parties in the negotiating process almost guarantee failure." North Koreans "will not risk vulnerability in an open forum," particularly when someone connected with South Korea is involved. Neither Korean state recognized the other's legitimacy; indeed, "diplomacy on the Korean peninsula is a zero-sum game." Yet an outside nation could have good relations with both Koreas as long as the bilateral relations were kept "sufficiently compartmentalized."

The third general principle dealt with "face" and "philosophy." Linton's explanation was consistent with that of Kim Dae Jung and several others who communicated with The Carter Center, but provided more depth.

He pointed out that North Koreans were "extremely sensitive if they perceive what they interpret to be an attempt to humiliate them publicly." They expressed their feelings in strong language, and because "they feel insecure in their national existence, they are also easily offended." The positive side of this equation was that they responded positively in negotiations to symbolic gestures that "affirm legitimacy and express respect." Because of their *Juche* philosophy, which holds that North Korea can achieve its own destiny through the self-reliant efforts of its people, North Korean leaders believe they are at the center of world affairs, not a "peripheral communist state as they are often depicted in the Western press." Consequently, negotiators should conduct their discussions in an atmosphere that "shows respect (if not agreement) with this [North Korean] perspective." A willingness to travel to Pyongyang for negotiations was "a very important symbolic gesture that will make a deep impression." Linton suggested three corollaries to this principle: (1) North Koreans preferred informal, secret negotiations: "Public encounters should be held only when all the details have been worked out in advance." (2) North Koreans did not believe the media was a "forum for meaningful debate"; for them, public discussion of foreign relations was either speeches that "celebrate a relationship" or "rhetoric designed to humiliate, criticize and/or 'de-legitimize' the other party." In public remarks, leaders of countries dealing with North Korea should exercise "friendly restraint," leaving criticism to lower-ranking officials. (3) Despite Western skepticism, public opinion did play a role in North Korea. If the North Korean government decided on a change in policy, it must be able to explain the shift in a palatable way to the population. This process must be managed particularly carefully if the change involved the United States because for half a century the North Korean people have been bombarded with anti-American propaganda. Yet, if carefully handled, the North Korean media "can be a valuable instrument for building a positive image of the relationship."

Carter also read papers sent to him by Tom Graham of the Rockefeller Foundation; Tony Namkung, Korean-born scholar who traveled frequently to both Koreas; Dayle Spencer, former director of The Carter Center's Conflict Resolution Program; and Richard Solomon, president of the United States Institute of Peace.

One person Carter did not consult was Selig Harrison of the Carnegie Endowment for International Peace, who was in Pyongyang a week before the Carter trip. Harrison met with Kim Il Sung and later said that the North Korean leader had indicated willingness to freeze his country's nuclear program if he received a binding commitment for the delivery and financing of light water reactors. Neither Carter nor I heard about Harrison's trip until we returned from the Korean Peninsula. Had Carter known, he would have tried to talk with Harrison before entering North Korea.

The more Carter listened to people who had actually visited North Korea and dealt with its senior leadership, the more convinced he became that it was essential to treat his North Korean interlocutors with respect and appreciate the importance they placed on "face." For years Carter had held that in trying to settle an international crisis, one must deal with the people who have the power to agree to a settlement and make it stick—even if those people had previously done despicable things. Often the best way, sometimes the only way, to deal with them was to accord them respect. In Carter's mind, such an approach in no way lessened his commitment to human rights, particularly because he believed that unnecessary war was one of the worst of human rights abuses. Despite occasional criticism by human rights groups that Carter coddled disreputable people, the former president heard his own drummer on this issue, strengthened by the knowledge that few, if any, world political leaders had done more than he to advance human rights worldwide.

On Thursday evening and early Friday morning, Carter reflected on what he had been told, what he knew, and what additional information he would need to be fully prepared for his meetings in Pyongyang. In standard Carter fashion, he compiled a list of specific questions whose answers would help fill in knowledge gaps and/or test information he had already received. He sent these questions to Tony Lake and Bob Gallucci at 7:41 A.M. on Friday morning with instructions that they were some of the issues he would like to address in his Washington discussions that afternoon.[21]

Carter had intended to advise the South Koreans of his trip to Pyongyang and request permission to visit South Korea for consultations before crossing to the North. But he wanted to avoid a duplication of the events of February 1993 when South Korea had reacted negatively and publicly to press reports that he might soon travel to the peninsula. Consequently, he decided to wait until he had Clinton's approval before informing the South Korean officials. After the Gore confirmation call on Wednesday, June 8, we agreed that I would call the South Korean consul general in Atlanta on Thursday morning and ask him to visit the Center later that day to discuss a Carter trip to the region. At that time I would share whatever information we had on our evolving itinerary, request meetings in Seoul before going North, and ask him to inform us of the response from his government as soon as possible.

The plans changed on Thursday morning. Carter received an early call from Tony Lake, who said that a member of the Washington press corps had gotten wind of Carter's trip, which was not supposed to be made public until his departure. They agreed that press guidance, cleared by The Carter Center and the White House, should be released that afternoon. The Center quickly produced a draft press release and faxed it to Washington, but it did not receive word that the text had fully run the clearance gamut in Washington until about 4:00 P.M. Thirty minutes later, the Center issued the following press announcement in the former president's name:

My wife Rosalynn and I will be visiting North Korea and South Korea next week. We will be going as private citizens, representing The Carter Center. The initiative for this trip has been from Korea, not Washington, and I will have no official status relating to the U.S. government. Since 1991, I have received numerous invitations to make this visit, and on one occasion sent a Carter Center advance team to both countries to prepare for my prospective trip. As is the case with other international issues since leaving the White House, I have attempted to stay adequately briefed on the Korean situation. My hope is to discuss some of the important issues of the day with the leaders in the area.[22]

Before the press statement was issued, I phoned the South Korean consul general, Kwon Young Min, in Atlanta to alert him to the impending announcement. I apologized that his government had not been informed sooner, explaining that the North Korean invitation and

Washington approval of the trip had occurred only shortly before, and that the press statement was being issued to avoid press speculation. I read him the text of the statement, which he took down verbatim so that he could send it immediately to Seoul. I agreed to brief him in detail about the events leading up to the trip the next morning.

The media quickly reported the Carter trip. Three major press services, AP, UPI, and Reuters, as well as CNN, published stories drawn largely from the Center's press release. Reuters said an administration official had stressed that Carter was making his trip as a private citizen and would not be representing the U.S. government, but he had already received briefings from government officials and would be briefed further in Washington before his departure. The press reports placed the trip in context, emphasizing that pressure was building to impose sanctions on North Korea. Agence France Presse linked the Carter announcement with its report of a rather grueling session Bob Gallucci had endured the day before when he testified on the administration's policy on North Korea before the Asian subcommittee of the House Foreign Affairs Committee. Gallucci reportedly told the open meeting that the United States hoped China would support sanctions in the UN Security Council, but he was unable to predict Beijing's vote; he expected Japan to respect a sanctions resolution voted by the UNSC; and he characterized Russia's position as similar to that of the United States. According to Reuters, the subcommittee members were not impressed. Chairman Gary Ackerman, a New York Democrat, called the administration's policy "shaky." Thomas Lantos, a California Democrat, said the administration's approach had a "profoundly Alice in Wonderland quality." Republican Congressman Jim Leach of Iowa called for punishment, saying that the administration was acting as if it were trying to stop a crime from being committed when in fact the crime was already underway. The press also reported that U.S. and South Korean troops were accelerating defense preparedness for a military showdown, which might follow the imposition of sanctions, and that the IAEA was preparing to suspend nonmedical aid to North Korea because of its refusal to comply with the agency's inspection demands.[23]

For those working on Korea at The Carter Center, Friday, June 10, started early and ended late. President Carter met his scheduled morning appointments dealing with other subjects, as did Mrs. Carter, but he used any spare time to study information on Korea that was flowing into the Center.

I focused exclusively on the trip. I had a lengthy meeting in my office with Consul General Kwon of South Korea. As expected, Kwon voiced his consternation at not being consulted earlier about the possibility of a Carter trip—reminding me that he had always responded immediately to Center requests in the past. I understood his frustration. I had no doubt that the response to his cable to Seoul the previous evening had contained a sharp reprimand because he had failed to provide an earlier warning of the Carter trip. I explained again how the report of a press leak in Washington had forced the premature announcement of the trip, and I stressed that our intention had been to communicate with his government through him and his embassy in Washington well before the matter became public.[24]

Kwon then provided the guidance he had received. He said that even though it was a "sensitive time" because of the nuclear issue, his government wanted to help make the Carter visit useful. It was important that it be "handled properly." His government hoped that President Carter would convey directly to Kim Il Sung the "serious concern of the international community" and the consequences North Korea would face if it did not meet its "duties and responsibilities." Continuing, Kwon said there was no alternative at this time to sanctions, and they should be "effective, swift, and gradual."[25] I knew Carter's approach to the North Koreans would be more nuanced.

I told the consul general that Carter would fly to Washington around noon for administration briefings that we expected to last most of the afternoon. I asked whether it would be possible for the Carters to talk with the South Korean ambassador following those briefings. Kwon promised to check as soon as he returned to his office, and he called back shortly, inviting the Carters and me to have dinner with Ambassador Han Seung Soo and his wife that evening. Even though the ambassador would be hosting a reception at the embassy, he and his wife would slip away when the Carters arrived.[26]

After the consul general left the Center, David Brown called me from the State Department with two items of information. He repeated Ambassador Han's invitation for dinner and said that the ambassador's deputy, Minister Ban Ki Moon, would also participate. Then he advised that President Kim Young Sam of South Korea was very upset about the Carter trip. Kim was highly skeptical that anything positive could come out of it. But the main reason for his irritation was that Kim Dae Jung, his political rival, was trumpeting to the South Korean press that his speech at the National Press Club in Washington and his conversation with Carter had convinced Carter to travel to North Korea. According to Brown, the South Korean press was having a heyday with the news. Peter Tarnoff, the political under secretary of state for political affairs, had been besieged in Tokyo by South Korean and Japanese reporters.[27]

Shortly before noon, the Carters and I drove from the Center to the airport, where we boarded the Delta flight to Washington. In the car I reported on my meeting with the South Korean consul general and conversation with David Brown. Before takeoff, Carter, as was his custom, strolled through the aisles of the plane to speak and shake hands with fellow passengers. As always, he seemed to enjoy the recognition and brief conversations and picture taking; a consummate politician, Jimmy Carter conveys to the person with whom he is speaking that he is genuinely interested in what he or she has to say—even if the chat lasts only a few seconds. The quick up-and-down-the-aisle ritual also ensured that he was given more privacy during the actual flight.

As the Carters relaxed during the short flight to Washington, the former president could look back with satisfaction on the first phase of his countdown to departure for the Korean Peninsula. He had ticked off several items on the mental checklist he had composed on the Sunday evening after the Gallucci visit. Yet he knew that the second and final phase of the countdown—his half day in Washington dealing with administration officials, most of whom would have preferred that his trip not take place, and his last day in Plains, where he would frame his strategy for his meetings with the leaders from both Koreas—would be difficult. Even for this inveterate workaholic, the next thirty-six hours seemed almost overwhelming.

CHAPTER 5

The Countdown: Phase Two

By the time the plane landed in Washington, D.C., Carter had re-viewed and virtually memorized his list of questions.[1] He had thought about how to try to orchestrate the upcoming meetings to gain the maximum amount of new information and insights. He regretted that his impending trip did not have the level of support within the administration that he would have liked, but he knew that any deal he might be able to negotiate with the North Korean leadership would have to gain subsequent Washington endorsement. Consequently, he hoped he would be able to use the meetings with American officials to demonstrate that he and they had the same objectives.

As soon as we deplaned, shortly after 3:00 P.M., the briefings started in a small room in the Delta lounge, where Tony Lake, Bob Gallucci, and Dan Poneman were waiting. This venue had been chosen because Lake would fly out of Washington after the meeting.

Three hours earlier, Lake and his two colleagues had participated in a meeting of top foreign policy officials to discuss Carter's impending trip. Even though President Clinton told his foreign policy team that Carter had never violated an understanding with him, the principals reportedly agreed unanimously that Carter should *not* be an official emissary. They thought that even acting as an official emissary would not restrain him from straying from policy guidelines, which in turn would send North Korea mixed signals "when clarity and consistency were of vital importance." Yet, despite the reservations of many of them, all the participants knew that they could not stop Carter's travel to Korea. Consequently, they sought to frame for him a useful and confined position as a message carrier and fact finder. They reasoned that Carter might be able to give Kim Il Sung and the other North Korean leaders a clear reading of the U.S. position, and, upon his return, provide Washington with a better sense of the North Korean leader's thinking. Some even suggested that his visit might also provide the opportunity for a face-saving retreat for North Korea, a strong and persistent concern for President Clinton. To impress on Carter what the administration thought he should do, the principals decided on a two-step process: a small meeting for him with Tony Lake, who was thought to have the best relationship with Carter, followed by a larger briefing involving key officials responsible for relations with North and South Korea.[2]

Lake opened the airport meeting by telling Carter what President Clinton and his senior foreign policy advisers hoped his trip could accomplish.[3] It would be useful for Carter—as a private citizen, not as an official channel—to explain clearly to Kim Il Sung the administration's position and that of the international community on North Korea's nuclear actions; Washington did not know whether Pyongyang understood U.S. views and actions. Lake also asked Carter to emphasize to Kim Il Sung that President Clinton wanted a "peaceful resolution to the nuclear problem" and to assure the North Korean leader that Washington was serious about being willing to improve economic and political relations if the nuclear issue could be solved. Reflecting administration concern that the North Koreans might react with force when the United States augmented its military capacities on the peninsula, Lake told Carter that it was "vitally important" for the North Koreans to understand that measures taken to reinforce U.S. troops in the South would be strictly defensive and would not be done in a provocative manner. President Clinton would want the former president to share with him his judgment of North Korea's aims upon his return.[4]

Turning to logistical issues, Lake informed Carter that President Kim Young Sam planned to host a dinner for him on Tuesday, June 14, and that he and Foreign Minister Han would like to meet with Carter after he left North Korea and before he returned to the United States. Lake said Washington was still working on the communications problem; earlier, Carter had asked whether he would be able to communicate in a secure manner with Washington while in North Korea. (In the end, no arrangement could be made for secure communications within North Korea. Important calls had to occur over open telephone lines, the participants knowing that the North Koreans were listening.) Lake also told Carter that Dick Christenson, the Korean-speaking diplomat who would accompany us to North Korea, would fly to Seoul from Japan and meet us there.

Carter then raised several issues. He asked whether the administration was prepared to share with North Korea light water reactor nuclear technology as part of an overall settlement. Lake responded that the United States could not commit to providing the reactors because of legal restrictions, but the administration would not stand in the way of others making such technology available to North Korea. Gallucci said that the real benefit of light water reactors was that they required enriched uranium, which was not available internally in North Korea. He added that the fuel rods then being unloaded from the North Korean graphite-moderated reactors had to be reprocessed within a year.

Carter asked about the Team Spirit military exercises and the administration's position on U.S. and South Korean military facilities in South Korea by North Koreans in return for similar bilateral inspections in the North. Lake said that Team Spirit was scheduled for the fall; given the current situation and timing, the administration intended to keep that option in play. It was a "neuralgic point" for the South Koreans. Carter did not receive a direct answer about reciprocal nuclear inspections; instead he was told that a final U.S.-North Korean agreement could include a reference to President Bush's decision in 1991 to withdraw most tactical nuclear weapons from outside the continental United States, and the subsequent public announcement by the South Korean president, Roh Tae Woo, that there were no nuclear weapons in South Korea.

Next Carter asked how much support the United States had in the UN Security Council for the sanctions resolution. Lake said that the South Koreans were enthusiastic about sanctions. Japan would go along with a sanctions resolution passed by the Security Council despite Japanese press reports to the contrary. He admitted, however, that the Japanese had reservations about including in the sanctions a provision freezing the funds North Koreans living in Japan regularly sent back to North Korea. Because the North Korean organization in Japan, Chosen Soren, did good work, the Japanese government would prefer to keep the issue of remittances from Japan out of a final resolution. Lake said that recent talks with China had been encouraging. China had never said it would veto the resolution if it came to a vote in the Security Council; its public statements could be interpreted both as supporting and as opposing sanctions. The administration knew that the Chinese leadership was frustrated by North Korea. China had abstained on the recent statement by the UNSC president calling on North Korea to comply with IAEA demands and on the IAEA vote (taken on June 10) on denying technical assistance to North Korea.

Carter asked about the Russian proposal, floated in April, for an international conference to try to solve the North Korean crisis prior to the Security Council voting on a sanctions resolution. Lake said that the U.S government viewed this Russian move as a needless diversion from bringing pressure on North Korea. Moscow wanted to increase its role in dealing with the nuclear crisis. I thought that the Russian initiative probably reflected as much its determination to demonstrate internationally its continued great-power role despite the 1991 implosion of the Soviet Union as its desire to find a negotiated solution to the crisis involving its previous ally, North Korea. According to Lake, on May 30, despite earlier U.S. pressure to drop the proposal, Foreign Minister Andrei Kozyrev had told Secretary of State Christopher that Russia intended to push its proposal, and it subsequently had put forward a resolution to that effect in the Security Council. Whereas China and North Korea seemed lukewarm to negative on the conference idea, South Korea outright opposed it. President Kim Young Sam of South Korea had recently visited Moscow and urged President Boris Yeltsin to support sanctions and forget about the conference idea. He thought he had Yeltsin's agreement not to oppose sanctions, but he failed to secure a commitment to drop the conference proposal.[5] In an attempt to mollify the Russians, Clinton had told Yeltsin that such a conference might be useful at some point and that the United States was prepared to accept some reference to it in the Security Council resolution on sanctions. Lake said that Christopher had been charged with working out the timing of the conference with Kozyrev.

Carter asked about the possibility of direct bilateral talks between the U.S. secretary of state and the North Korean foreign minister. He was told that such a meeting would be possible but only after progress had been made on the nuclear issue. The administration understood that a time would come when a broad and thorough dialogue would be needed. Lake said that the United States could talk with North Korea on issues concerning bilateral relations, such as nuclear questions and trade, but that Seoul would have to be involved in any discussions regarding the future of the Korean peninsula.

Carter's last question looked to the future. He asked that if the nuclear issues could be resolved and good faith talks could be held, would the United States be prepared to establish diplomatic relations with North Korea? Lake told him that diplomatic relations were on the menu, but the administration viewed them as something to be achieved over the long-term.

Lake ended the meeting so that he could make his flight connections. He assured Carter that Gallucci, Poneman, and others would provide the former president with a full briefing of the problems with North Korea and the administration's positions. We agreed to reassemble in Gallucci's office in the State Department.

A strong briefing team awaited us. It included, in addition to Gallucci and Poneman, John Deutch, the deputy secretary of defense, later the director of the Central Intelligence Agency (CIA); a representative from the Joint Chief of Staff (JCS); Winston Lord, the former ambassador to China and currently assistant secretary for East Asia and the Pacific; one of Lord's deputies, Tom Hubbard, who would be named ambassador to South Korea several years later; David Brown, the director of the Korean Office, along with his deputy, Lynn Turk, and the North Korean desk officer, Ken Quinones; Bob Carlin, long-time observer of North Korea in the Intelligence and Research Bureau of the State Department; and the representatives from the CIA and the Defense Intelligence Agency (DIA).[6]

Gallucci quickly summarized for his colleagues the main points that had been covered at the airport. He asked Poneman to elaborate on the Japanese position on sanctions. Poneman said that, despite Japanese press predictions that Japan would not support sanctions, Japanese officials were firmly on board with the process that was "moving down the Security Council track."[7]

Carter observed that the toughest burden would fall on Japan—if sanctions required that Japan freeze the annual remittances that Koreans in Japan sent annually to North Korea. Carter said that such a freeze would probably subject the Japanese government to outspoken domestic criticism and possibly disruptive behavior by the North Korean community in Japan as well as to political contretemps from Pyongyang. Assistant Secretary Lord repeated that Japan's support for sanctions was solid. If necessary, the Japanese would cut off remittances; they understood the importance of security and of not appearing weak in support of the treaty alliance. Further, they wanted to avoid a new round of criticism such as Japan received for its less-than-enthusiastic support of the Gulf War in 1991.[8]

Deutch discussed the technical issues involving the North Korean nuclear program. He said that North Korea had a complete fuel cycle. The North Koreans mined uranium within their country. They processed the uranium in their own processing plant. They had a 25 MWt (5 MWe) reactor,[9] which is fueled by about 8,000 fuel rods. They were building a reprocessing facility that would convert spent uranium fuel into plutonium. Finally, they were developing a weapons program. In short, the North Koreans had all it took to make bombs. On the other hand, should North Korea acquire light water reactors, they would have to acquire enriched uranium from abroad; they had no uranium enrichment facility. The deal they proposed earlier was for the United States to arrange for them to get the light water reactors, provide the fuel, and take away the spent fuel. Lord said that the North Koreans had mentioned more than once their willingness to adopt a different type of reactor, and Hubbard said that in July 1993 the North Koreans had told the American delegation in Geneva that they were willing to convert all their graphite reactors to light water reactors and to dismantle the others. Their requirement: that the United States accept a package deal that would include diplomatic relations and provide the light water reactors. He added that the United States must know what Pyongyang would plan to do with its spent fuel if they shifted to light water reactors.

Deutch continued, saying that in addition to its current 25 MWt (5 MWe) reactor, the North Koreans were constructing a 200 MWt (50 MWe) reactor that should go critical within two years.[10] He asserted that the uncompleted reprocessing plant is the "real concern." The current conflict, however, revolved around how much plutonium the North Koreans had reprocessed from their existing 25 MWt (5MWe) reactor. In 1986, the North Koreans put the fuel rods in the reactor and started it operating. They admitted that they shut the reactor down for seventy-one days in 1989 and took out eighty-eight rods, their explanation being that they had reprocessed a portion of the spent fuel only once. The United States suspected additional reprocessing. U.S. experts needed to do an analysis of the rods to determine whether the burn-up was uniform or whether new fuel rods had been added over time.

Deutch said that the North Koreans were claiming that the reactor's history had not been lost with the discharge of the fuel rods from the reactor into the storage ponds. They said that they would give the IAEA a list of where the rods came from; the IAEA could then reconstruct where the rods had been located in the fuel core. However, the IAEA would not trust a list provided solely by the North Koreans. The North Koreans further claimed that by analyzing the liquid waste, the IAEA could estimate how much plutonium had been reprocessed. They claimed that they had reprocessed 70 grams of plutonium, but the United States feared that more had been reprocessed.[11] The United States and IAEA could determine accurately the amount of plutonium reprocessed by inspecting the two special ("undeclared") sites that the North Koreans had consistently refused to let the Vienna agency examine—claiming they were within military facilities.

Carter then asked a question that would reveal a significant disagreement of view within the administration: He asked what would happen if the North Koreans continued preventing the two undeclared sites from being inspected.

At first, Deutch did not answer the question directly. He said that to help induce the North Koreans to permit special inspections, the United

States was prepared to work out a mutual inspection of each other's military facilities.[12] He then took on Carter's question directly. He said that the United States knew that the spent fuel being removed from the 25 MWt (5 MWe) reactor could produce, when reprocessed, 6 kilograms of plutonium a year. The 200 MWt (50 MWe) reactor under construction would be able to produce many more kilograms of plutonium.

Deutch also said that the U.S. objective was to persuade Pyongyang to give up its plutonium. His personal position, shared by the Defense Department, was that if North Korea agreed to shut down all plutonium production in the future, the United States should be prepared to "give up the past." Gallucci immediately exclaimed: "Absolutely not." He said that the United States had never overlooked the violation of NPT commitments by a country that was a member to the treaty. It would be impossible for a South Korean government to accept the position Deutch had stated. Hubbard interjected that the South Korean government could live with ambiguity, and Gallucci softened by saying that engagement could take place without resolving the ambiguity.[13]

Deutch seemed to sense that, because he was briefing non-administration officials, he had gone too far. He quickly said that the problem had both past and future elements, and that both must be dealt with. Lord raised the political issue of U.S. credibility. He said that President Clinton had climbed up the hill (in demanding special inspections) and could not be seen as going down again. On the other hand, the United States would "give absolution" to the North Koreans for past behavior if they would confess to what they had really done. Gallucci added that he had told Kang Sok Ju that the United States would not take political advantage of a North Korean declaration revising the amount of plutonium it had reprocessed.

Deutch resumed his description of the North Korean nuclear program: "We don't know what they have done with the plutonium they possess. They could have constructed 2 bombs. But we have no evidence that they have a weapon that could deliver the bomb." To Carter's question, Deutch said that North Korea would be in violation of the NPT if it possessed any plutonium that it had not declared to the IAEA and had not put under safeguards.

Deutch said that North Korea would likely try to reload the 25 MWt reactor and that it could do so within one month. The spent fuel could stay in the storage pond for up to one year, but within that twelve-month period something would have to be done to it.[14] From the unloaded fuel, Deutch estimated that the North Koreans could produce from 20 to 30 kilograms of plutonium, or five bombs.

Carter asked what the U.S. reaction would be if the North Koreans said that as a matter of principle, they were not willing to permit inspections of the two undeclared sites to take place but would turn over all rods in the pond to the IAEA and buy light water reactors. Gallucci said that such a proposal would be an interesting development, but at some point the United States and IAEA would need to establish an accurate accounting of the amount of plutonium in North Korea's possession. Gallucci also said that Carter's hypothetical did not accord with current reality. The North Koreans were asking the IAEA inspectors to leave North Korea. If such a development occurred, the United States and IAEA would not know in real time when and whether reprocessing was underway.

Carter asked about the so-called "special status" claimed by North Korea. Gallucci said that North Korea and the IAEA had agreed (in June 1993) to stop the ninety-day clock that would have terminated North Korean membership in the NPT. North Korea insisted that this mutual action gave it "special status," which Pyongyang defined as North Korea's not having to comply with full-scope safeguards even though it would permit monitoring to ensure that material was not being diverted. In effect, the North Koreans were asserting that past violations were not subject to NPT standards, a position taken by no other member country. Hubbard added that North Korea was also contending that it had no obligation to maintain a continuity of safeguards. Poneman said that eighty-nine of the ninety days had expired before North Korea and the IAEA had stopped the clock. The United States did not know whether, should the clock start running again, it would need to run for another ninety days, or only one day, before North Korea would make good its threat to withdraw from the nonproliferation treaty. However, a decision would not turn on a day or two. Hubbard said that the North Koreans had made it clear that they had taken the actions to halt the clock to please the United States, not because of what they regarded as binding IAEA obligations.

Carter asked whether he should express concern to the North Koreans about the IAEA inspectors. Gallucci said that the IAEA had voted to cut off technical assistance to North Korea the preceding day. He recommended that Carter ignore that point unless the North Koreans raised it with him. Hubbard pointed out that the North Koreans had a strong animus against the IAEA; it would be preferable to keep Carter separated from the IAEA-North Korean imbroglio.[15]

Gallucci then called on the intelligence experts to brief Carter on the status of the North Korean military, and he added additional information to their presentations. Knowing that the Carter team had the appropriate security clearances, these officials talked in specific terms about the size of North Korea's special operations forces and their means of rapid deployment in the event of war; the size and quality of its troops, their deployment, and their state of readiness; its artillery systems and its tanks and their location; its SCUD missiles; its chemical and biological weapons capacities; and its tunneling expertise.

The briefers said that even though the United States believed that the North Korean preferred option for fighting a new war would be a sudden attack to the south, no premobilization actions had been detected. They did not believe that the North had made a decision to attack. On the other hand, it had launched a war preparation campaign to prepare the masses and soldiers for the armed reunification of the peninsula, and this theme of psychological readiness was new. North Korean leaders would give the military option high consideration if they were convinced that the regime could not survive otherwise. In fact, they might even think they could win. North Korean propaganda was currently criticizing the U.S. administration, attacking Kim Young Sam and his government, and warning Japan that it "would not fail to suffer consequences" of a military reaction to sanctions.

The JCS representative said that the U.S. military would reinforce its capabilities in terms of people, aircraft, and antiaircraft batteries if the sanctions resolution were passed. They would also take actions to evacuate noncombatants. These actions should be taken concurrently.[16]

Carter emphasized his belief that the North Koreans would interpret the adoption of sanctions as a declaration of war. He hoped that his trip would create new conditions that would make sanctions unnecessary. Gallucci said that President Clinton had met today with his advisers on the sanctions question and agreed on specified sanctions to be taken with the adoption of the UNSC resolution.[17]

Bob Carlin of INR, supported by his CIA and DIA colleagues, then provided an analysis of the internal conditions in North Korea. They admitted that most of the government's sources were travelers, North Koreans who had left the country, and South Korean intelligence. North Korea faced serious problems. Yet the situation was not as desperate as non-government sources were reporting. The North Koreans thought the world had always been hostile to them. They felt abandoned by their former allies and did not trust them. Respect and toughness were important to the North Koreans. They were not interested in love.

Carlin labeled Kim Il Sung an "ultimate survivor." He did not panic. He was not an ideologue. He was tough but engaging. His most important principles were "independence, national dignity, and pride." He was determined not to let foreigners control North Korea.

Carter intervened, contrasting what Carlin had said were the principal motivations of Kim Il Sung with the current U.S. policy of publicly scorning North Korea. North Korea wanted respect, Carter said, but the U.S. strategy sought to use UN sanctions to force North Korea through "abject surrender" to accede to IAEA inspection of the two undeclared sites.

Carlin said that the North Koreans had not tried to defend rationally some of their decisions. Emotions were important to them. Nevertheless, North Korean leaders could be highly pragmatic even while using ideology to control their people and their country. Their philosophy of *Juche* was malleable; it could be refined as needed.

The intelligence experts said that the political succession had already occurred in North Korea. The son, Kim Jong Il, was already in charge in most areas. Only the symbolic transfer of power had not yet taken place. But they also said, somewhat inconsistently, that there were two lines of authority in North Korea, presumably one to Kim Il Sung and one to Kim Jong Il.

Unknown to the administration officials in the room, Carter's skepticism about the accuracy of U.S. intelligence concerning North Korean officials and their intentions was mounting. The intelligence experts seemed to be saying that Kim Il Sung was no longer the key decisionmaker on major issues. Carter had just been told that the Washington analysis was based in part on the views of travelers to North Korea, but in his own conversations with recent travelers to North Korea he had been given a dramatically different view—that on fundamental questions, particularly those related to war and peace, Kim Il Sung was the ultimate authority. This view had most recently been communicated to Carter by Eason Jordan, Billy Graham, and through the reports of experts who had spent time in North Korea in recent years. Carter had also received similar information about Kim Il Sung's decisionmaking authority from private Chinese contacts and from a couple of Japanese sources with close ties to North Korea. He appreciated that these visitors had been in North Korea for only a short time and that they could possibly have been misled. But he found very disturbing the certainty with which the intelligence experts downplayed Kim Il Sung's role as well as their failure to offer much analysis to support their assertions.

Carter asked the intelligence experts who made the decision to refuse to open the undeclared sites to IAEA inspectors. They answered, "The son made the decision." "Who" Carter asked, "made the North Korean decision to threaten Japan?" "The son," was the reply, followed by elaboration: Kim Il Sung had some good days and he gave good interviews. But he was not involved in the day-to-day decisionmaking. At this point, Carter's quick temper showed. He asked then—and would come back to the point later—what solid intelligence they had to support their proposition that Kim Il Sung no longer made the major policy decisions. How many of them had visited North Korea or talked directly with North Korean policymakers? His skepticism was clear. Carlin admitted that a key problem for dealing with North Korea for the Clinton or any previous administration was that personnel from the Executive Branch were seldom allowed to go to North Korea.[18] He and the other intelligence experts, facing Carter's persistent prodding, confirmed that much of their information came from the South Korean government, whose analyses might not always be unbiased. Carter carried away deep reservations about U.S. intelligence regarding Kim Il Sung, which reinforced his belief that U.S. strategy was seriously flawed.[19]

Carlin said that some analysts believed that the son was irrational, but that was not the view of INR. It thought Kim Jong Il was probably quite savvy. If he were mentally unbalanced, that would have shown up by now. He was fifty-one or fifty-two years old, and he had been groomed for leadership for thirty years or more. Yet because of Korean custom, Kim Jong Il must take care not to upstage his father.[20]

Carlin said that there had been differences within the North Korean leadership for years about major issues. Some of these, particularly about Russia and China, were aired in publications in the 1980s, although Washington could not always identify people and positions. The son could have misinterpreted news that he supplied his father.

Carlin said that Kim Jong Il identified with the pragmatists in the North Korean policy ranks. Although they were tough and cautious about opening to the outside and to the United States, the pragmatists understood that their country must accommodate realities and loosen somewhat their economy. Their influence led to the decision to establish a free-trade port area.[21]

The intelligence experts held that, although the North Korean economy had contracted significantly since 1989, it had not collapsed. Light industry had recovered somewhat, and trade with China had increased. The leadership had been putting a lot of effort into this area, but it had considerable trouble with adequate follow-through. In the past few years, harvests had been poor, but there had been less starvation than reports suggested.

After a discussion about reunification in which Carter told the group that the North Koreans had told him that they intended to talk about the issue, Carter asked whether South Korea would accept U.S.-North Korean diplomatic relations if the nuclear differences could be worked out. That question was not answered directly. One of the participating officials explained that the South Koreans insisted that a permanent peace treaty must be worked out on a bilateral Korean basis. Moreover, the South Koreans believed time was on their side. They feared that the Carter trip could change the security position on the peninsula without their being directly involved.

Following a discussion prompted by Carter about how the experts on South Korea expected the country to look in five years, Carter asked how he could deal most productively with President Kim Young Sam. He was told that he should make Kim Young Sam feel that he was being fully briefed. Kim Young Sam attached considerable importance to being informed, and he was highly sensitive to public opinion and needed to show that the United States was not dealing with North Korea over his head. The sanctions resolution was receiving good press. Yet, particularly because neither he nor the South Korean people wanted war, Kim Young Sam was not sure what to do after the adoption of a sanctions resolution.

Gallucci asked Ken Quinones to inform Carter on logistical matters that he might encounter. Quinones said that U.S. military officers would escort Carter to the DMZ, where he would be received by the North Korean military officers. The Carter party would probably be escorted into the "Unification Hut," constructed on the North Korean side in 1953, for refreshments, and then escorted to Mercedes limousines for the drive to Pyongyang. During the trip, the North Korean escorts would pump the Carter team for information to pass on to their superiors. The expressway to Pyongyang, 120 kilometers long, to a city of 2.5 million people, would have virtually no traffic on it. The Carter group would be provided huge rooms in cabinet-level accommodations. Quinones advised Carter to see as many North Korean officials as possible. He recommended a meeting with Kim Il Sung early in the visit and toward the end of his stay. He told Carter that Kim Jong Il had never met Westerners. Quinones expected Carter to be introduced to Kim Young Chol, a major North Korean general; Pak Young Nam, who headed the Ministry of Atomic Affairs; and Kim Yong Nam, the foreign minister. Quinones suggested that Carter visit cultural sites as well as department stores, confirmed that it was okay to carry cameras and take pictures,[22] and said the lights would go out in Pyongyang at 8:00 P.M.

Carter told the group that CNN hoped to be permitted into North Korea to cover the visit.[23] In turn, he was told that he would be exposed to the press and expected to hold press conferences in both South and North Korea. All his remarks would be reported.

Toward the end of the briefing, Carter turned the conversation to the ultimate bargain the United States was willing to accept if, as part of that deal, North Korea stood down on its nuclear program. Most participants indicated either support for or no objection to a package approach: This would entail North Korea's stopping the development of its nuclear weapons program and permitting the continuation of IAEA inspections with some eventual resolution of the disputed plutonium issue; in return, the United States would lift economic sanctions against Pyongyang and begin the process of normalizing bilateral relations, negotiations that could lead in the future to full diplomatic ties. The administration representatives stressed that South Korea had to be brought along in the process so that it would support the package deal, or at least acquiesce to it. (More than one State officer confided to me that the South Korean policy had flip-flopped several times in the past months. In recent days, the Seoul government had become much more concerned about the possibility of war; therefore, it was being less recalcitrant toward suggestions about seeking a diplomatic way out of the impasse with the North.)

Carter said that he was going to North Korea as a private citizen representing The Carter Center. He understood that he had no authorization to speak for the administration. However, it was important that he understood the U.S. position clearly so that he did not mislead the North Koreans. He reiterated his view that he believed Kim Il Sung was the appropriate decisionmaker on the nuclear issue and on issues of war and peace. He further thought that the North Korean dictator wanted to strike a deal that would avoid war and improve relations with the United States. Carter expressed his conviction that such a deal could be struck without weakening U.S.-South Korean relations.

The meeting ended, and President and Mrs. Carter left for the South Korean embassy. I remained behind to work with David Brown and Ken Quinones in preparing and sending a message from Carter to Kim Il Sung via the North Korean mission in New York. This message said that Carter considered his impending visit to be "very important and very significant." He asked to meet President Kim Il Sung shortly after his arrival on Wednesday afternoon and again toward the end of his visit. He also requested meetings with other senior North Korean officials and asked to attend cultural events and visit department stores; the Pyongyang subway; the tomb of Tangun, the legendary founder of the first Korean kingdom in 2333 B.C.; and a farm.

When the Carters arrived at the South Korean residence, Ambassador Han Seung Soo and his wife slipped away from the reception they were hosting and invited the Carters into a private dining area. Following cocktails, they, along with Ban Ki Moon, the South Korean deputy chief of mission (DCM), sat down to dinner. By the time I arrived, they were into serious conversation.

The ambassador told Carter that his government welcomed his efforts, but his comments underlined that the Kim Young Sam government lacked enthusiasm for the Carter mission. The ambassador's primary message: The North Koreans were skilled at propaganda, and they would try to turn the Carter visit into a propaganda coup. The ambassador's advice to the former U.S. president: Be wary. Ambassador Han insisted that international pressure on North Korea was growing. The IAEA had just suspended technical assistance to Pyongyang by a vote of 24–4–1; the Chinese representative had raised objections, but abstained when the vote was called.[24]

Carter explained that the North Koreans took the initiative in approaching The Carter Center. Knowing that the ambassador would report his remarks to Seoul, Carter said that in his personal view, North Korea wanted to be recognized as a legitimate entity. It felt the pressure of isolation. The North Korean people held Kim Il Sung in reverence, and their leaders resented the refusal of the United States to open direct communications with them. He was convinced that the Pyongyang leadership was looking for a way to save face, and he had mentioned to President Clinton that the United States should show flexibility. In North Korea's view, should there be a UN vote approving sanctions, a vigorous response would be necessary. Carter admitted that many in the U.S. government disagreed with his analysis.

The South Korean ambassador concurred that the North Koreans needed to be shown that others were "not trying to straggle them" and that they would be welcomed into the international community once the nuclear issue was solved. Countering the Carter analysis, Ambassador Han said that Seoul believed that the UN's voting of sanctions would "inflict a small amount of pain" on Pyongyang, but the action would open the door for negotiations. He asserted that members of the Security Council agreed with this view.

As the dinner meeting drew to a close, Carter and Ambassador Han agreed that they would not talk to the press about their meeting. Around 9:00 P.M., the Carter party left the ambassador's residence to meet its Delta flight back to Atlanta. Once there, the Carters continued by car to Plains, and I drove to my Atlanta home.

The next morning, Carter, always an early riser, got up at around 5:30 A.M.. As he exercised on the Nordic Track in his study, he reflected on what he had heard and read. Once at his desk, he studied his notes from the previous day and the official answers (then classified confidential) that had been provided to the questions he had sent to Lake and Gallucci. The information in the answers tracked closely his briefings of the day before, and sometimes elaborated on them. The substance of these answers is contained in Appendix A.

Carter then wrote out the talking points that he planned to use with Kim Il Sung.[25] Later that day, he called Bob Gallucci and read the talking points to him. According to Carter, Gallucci did not ask him to modify any of the points. Carter took that to be an informal Washington clearance of the talking points.[26]

Carter was convinced that the points in his paper coincided with U.S. policy positions, and I agreed.[27] Carter adhered closely to them during his conversations in North Korea. Subsequently his critics incorrectly charged that he had misrepresented the administration's view. His talking-point paper in its entirety is found in Appendix B.

For his own use, Carter also wrote out what he titled "Optimum Commitment of North Korea—Prepared in Advance of Trip." This paper would serve as his guideline for what he hoped to achieve in his talks in Pyongyang. He would later add to it the North Korean commitment to allow the IAEA inspectors to remain in the country and continue their work after he learned before crossing the DMZ that North

Korea had announced that it was expelling the IAEA inspectors. The text Carter prepared on June 10 is found in Appendix C.

Additional preparation included Carter's drafting two lists of questions, one for which he would seek answers from his South Korean interlocutors before crossing the DMZ, and a second for information he would hope to obtain through his own observations and in his talks with North Korean leaders. By the time he left South Korea on June 15, and North Korea on June 18, he had answers to most of his questions. Both sets of questions are in Appendix D.

When Carter left Plains, Georgia, early Sunday morning, June 12, 1994, he had accomplished most of the tasks he had set for himself after deciding to make the trip. He had studied carefully information about the two Koreas, the background and current status of the nuclear crisis, the technical aspects of North Korea's nuclear technology, the military balance across the DMZ, explanations from various sources about the North Korean leaders and their motives, and the appropriate way to approach these leaders to maximize chances for a peaceful resolution of the nuclear crisis. He was well briefed; he understood the big picture and the nitty-gritty details. Unlike most government officials on important negotiating missions, his brief also included the views and analyses of many non-governmental organizations and personalities, many of whom had had direct contact and experience with the North Korean leaders.

Jimmy Carter knew that he was placing his reputation on the line. He gave small odds to the possibility of success. He feared the crisis had gone too far to be turned back before military hostilities ensued—something he felt certain would happen if the UN Security Council adopted sanctions against North Korea. Yet as long as there was a hope that his efforts could lead to a peaceful outcome, that consideration would outweigh all others. So forward he went.

CITIZEN JIMMY CARTER INTERVENES
Part II

CHAPTER 6

The Journey Begins

Almost three years after Jimmy Carter received his first invitation to visit North Korea, he finally set off. Although the Clinton administration had given its reluctant acquiescence, it worried that the Carter trip might make its campaign to line up the sanctions votes in the UN Security Council more difficult.[1] The South Korean president expected the North Korean government to turn the Carter venture into a major propaganda coup that would weaken international pressures against Pyongyang and work to Seoul's detriment in the zero-sum diplomacy that characterized the foreign policies of both Koreas toward each other.

From Carter's perspective, 1994 differed fundamentally from earlier occasions when Washington administrations had persuaded him not to travel to Korea. Carter knew that some Washington officials, while pressing for UN sanctions, were privately suggesting possible parallels between the current situation and the unplanned and unwanted plunge into the hostilities that had opened World War I. With his trip, he hoped to help fashion a negotiated solution for the nuclear crisis that would avoid the use of sanctions.

At 6:45 A.M. on Sunday, June 12, 1994, President and Mrs. Carter departed Plains for Atlanta, where they would board the Delta flight to Seoul. A short time later, my wife, Linda, drove me to the Carter Center. After we said goodbye, she drove to Athens, Alabama, where her parents lived.[2] I put together the papers I would need for the trip, and Phil Wise[3] took me to the airport, where I met Nancy Konigsmark,[4] Carter's long-time appointments secretary, at the security guard station outside the terminal. When the small Carter motorcade arrived, Nancy and I jumped in and rode with President and Mrs. Carter across the tarmac to the plane. President Carter would later write: "We left home on Sunday, June 12, as well briefed as possible but without any clear instructions or official endorsement. In effect, we were on our own."[5]

During the long flight, the Carters read, watched movies, and slept. When awake, I reviewed briefing notes, reread some of the material sent to the Carter Center about North Korea, and skimmed a short history of Korea that Carter passed to me on the plane. Nancy, indefatigable as usual, spent much of her time juggling Carter's future schedule, trying to fit into his tightly packed agenda the appointments scrubbed for this unanticipated trip. Carter had to be in Nicaragua the following week, and on several times during the ensuing days he made clear to his North Korean hosts and to me that his schedule could not be changed. I had the distinct impression that he would leave North Korea on Saturday morning even if all the work had not been completed. I found this strange. In most of my negotiating experiences as a diplomat, the participants had engaged in long periods of hard positions and bluffs and, if they succeeded, either they reached last-minute "breakthroughs" or, more likely, an extension of talks beyond the original deadlines until agreements could finally be hammered out. Consequently, I was surprised when Carter insisted on keeping to his schedule when the issue was war or peace. I learned then, and would have it reinforced subsequently, that Carter would usually make clear to his interlocutors at the outset when he intended to depart, and then he would stick to his decision. For Carter, that procedure forced the negotiators to reveal rather quickly whether their intention was to reach an early agreement or merely to drag out the process.

Nancy shared some of President Carter's resoluteness about having a trip go as planned. Minister Counselor Han at the North Korean mission to the UN initially rejected her statement that Carter would be accompanied by his own secret service personnel. Han insisted that North Korea was fully capable of providing for the president's personal security and that his government would not permit Carter to be accompanied by "CIA agents." Konigsmark responded with equal firmness: Carter would indeed be accompanied by secret service agents; they were not CIA personnel; and they would work closely with the North Korean security service while in North Korea. Later, a State Department official told Nancy that North Korea would never permit the entry of three teams of secret service agents: one advance team to prepare for the visit, one to accompany Carter during the day, and a third to cover the guest quarters during the evening. Nancy replied, "They will if they want him to go." And she was right. Han acceded to her request without debate.[6]

The flight arrived at South Korea's Kimpo Airport around 4:30 P.M. Monday afternoon (Seoul time—thirteen hours ahead of Atlanta time). Carter knew what he wanted to accomplish in Seoul. First, he wanted to use his conversations with senior South Korean officials to expand his knowledge about the North Korean leadership. Second, and more important, he wanted to determine what bottom line requirements the South Korean leaders would insist on in a future U.S.-North Korean nuclear agreement.

Ambassador Laney met the Carter party planeside and then drove the Carters to his official residence. Jim Pierce, the embassy's control officer for the visit with whom I had worked in the State Department in the past, accompanied Konigsmark and me in another vehicle.

Shortly after arriving at Laney's residence, Carter received a call from Secretary of State Christopher. He said that Pyongyang had officially announced its intention to withdraw from the IAEA and to expel the IAEA inspectors from its country in reaction to the IAEA's decision to terminate its technical assistance to North Korea. Christopher told Carter that "the outcome of the whole crisis could depend on what happen[ed] to the inspectors."[7] How quickly things change. Three days earlier, State Department officials had advised Carter not to discuss IAEA inspections with the North Koreans unless they raised the subject. Three days after the Christopher phone call to Seoul, when Carter

would announce on CNN in Pyongyang that North Korea had withdrawn the expulsion threat, Washington officials would assert that
nothing new had been achieved.

After chatting with Chuck Kartman, the embassy's deputy chief of
mission (DCM), who subsequently would become deputy assistant secretary for Northeast Asia, the Carter group enjoyed a quiet dinner with
Jim and Berta Laney. Then its members retired early—hoping to sleep
a few hours before jet lag set in.

We had arrived in Seoul at a time of high tension. The international
and South Korean media reported widely on the growing international
crisis and speculated about possible war. The South Korean government
sought simultaneously to reassure the jittery public, prepare it for whatever might happen, and avoid provoking the North Koreans into military action. The Defense Ministry was conducting daily press briefings
to calm citizens by pointing out that the North so far had refrained
from belligerent acts. But it admitted that the North Korean army was
at its highest level of readiness in four years. The public reacted pre-
dictably. With rumors of shortages floating widely, constituents deluged
members of the South Korean National Assembly with phone calls asking whether they should stockpile basic foodstuff. Most acted without
advice, cramming into stores to buy quantities of dried noodles, rice,
and candles. The Seoul stock market plunged 25 percent between June
13–15. The day Carter arrived, the government held an exercise to determine the mobilization status of more than 6 million reservists. Two
days later, the same day he crossed the DMZ, South Korea held an un-
usually large nation-wide civil defense exercise involving an air-raid
drill and all civil defense corps members who organized evacuations and
provided first aid to air-raid victims.[8]

Early Tuesday morning, Carter and Laney went to General Gary
Luck's residence for a breakfast meeting. Luck had served two tours
with special forces in Vietnam and as a senior commander in the Persian Gulf during Operation Desert Storm.[9]

Luck and Laney had wrestled with a difficult dilemma for months.
Although many in Washington considered the Pyongyang threat to

treat UN sanctions as a declaration of war to be a bluff, Luck and Laney continued to think it might accurately reflect the intentions of that country's leaders. From Luck's position, if war were possible, then the United States and South Korea must move more combat and logistical personnel into or near the Korean Peninsula. It also meant bringing in more firepower and new weapon systems, such as the Patriot missiles that had begun arriving in April.[10] But such actions could not be undertaken without the knowledge of North Korea, whose leaders had been suspicious for years that the United States would invade their country to destroy the Pyongyang regime and reunite the two Koreas under South Korean leadership. North Korean military officials had bluntly told their U.S. interlocutors on the DMZ that North Korea, having studied Desert Storm, would not let the United States build up its forces in South Korea to strike their country as it had Iraq.

In the months preceding June 1994, Luck had urged Washington to add troops and equipment, but to do so in the least threatening way possible. As had Laney, he had appealed for policymakers to focus on a diplomatic route out of the imbroglio. But Luck and Laney had failed to persuade their superiors. Unknown to Luck and Laney on June 14, two days later President Clinton and his senior national security officials were scheduled to meet to decide on further increases of troops and equipment. They had implemented a full-court press in the UNSC for sanctions.

Despite their repeated petitions, the U.S. ambassador and U.S. commander had also failed to convince Washington that evacuation of U.S. civilians in South Korea, numbering between 80,000 and 100,000, should take place before the adoption of sanctions. The embassy's emergency evacuation plan had been updated, but the massive movement of people to airports and seaports that it required would be greatly hampered by the onslaught of hostilities. Another fear was that alarming news might cause an unauthorized and uncoordinated evacuation that would result in chaos and might encourage a preemptive move by the North.[11]

Carter understood but rejected the realpolitik argument—that North Korea would not follow through on its threats; that when faced with international determination and a willingness if necessary to use force, it would back down. And if it did not? Some hard-liners would respond that it would be better to use military force to end the life of the odious North Korean regime before it acquired nuclear weapons, which would also free the North Korean people from their repressive government and demonstrate to other rogue regimes that they would not be allowed to develop and possibly use nuclear weapons. These hard-liners seldom mentioned, if indeed they thought about, the likely cost of such an adventure.

The cost of a new military engagement on the Korean Peninsula occupied much of the breakfast discussion of Carter, Laney, and Luck. Luck told Carter that the North Korean military possessed awesome firepower, much of which was located on or near the North's side of the DMZ. Pyongyang had the capacity to rain fire on Seoul, particularly with a surprise attack. Luck had no doubt that the United States and South Korea would win a military confrontation with North Korea; their combined firepower, mobility, command and control, and communications would ensure their victory, but the consequences would be horrendous. Luck calculated that a new Korean war set off by a surprise attack from the North would result in the deaths of more than 50,000 American soldiers (more than in the 1950–1953 Korean War); from 200,000 to 300,000 South Korean troops would be killed, and more than double that number of North Korean troops would be left dead. He estimated that the overall economic damage to the region could reach $1 trillion. Asserting that he had given President Clinton a similar estimate at a previous meeting in Washington (as mentioned in an earlier chapter), Luck said that new military hostilities on the Korean Peninsula would make the 1991 Gulf War look like a "kindergarten." The general's estimates did not include casualty figures for the American civilians in South Korea, many of whom lived in Seoul. Luck also feared that key military decisions were being made in Washington without including his views and the views of Ambassador Laney.[12]

Carter also told me, when he later briefed me on the breakfast meeting, that Laney was acting on his own concerns. Jim and Berta Laney were scheduled to fly the following week to Scotland, where Jim would receive an honorary degree from St. Andrews University. His daughter, son-in-law, and grandchildren were visiting while we were there, and they had planned to stay behind in Seoul for a week or so after Jim and Berta departed; but Jim insisted that they change their plans and fly back to the United States before he left South Korea.[13]

Shortly after the breakfast meeting, Laney and Carter, accompanied by the Carter team, which now included Consul General Dick Christenson, who had flown in from Okinawa, Japan, the previous day, left for the embassy. We went directly to the secure conference room for a briefing by the country team, which lasted about ninety minutes.[14] Although embassy officials often think Washington is less sensitive to local conditions than they, I found striking the greater concern about the possibility of war exhibited by the embassy officers in comparison with the Washington officials with whom we had talked a few days earlier.

Laney stressed the importance of the Carter mission and urged his officers to speak candidly to the former president. He encouraged President Carter to interject questions or comments whenever he wished—a gracious but unneeded gesture. Carter would not hesitate to speak up; he still had unanswered questions, and he was determined to get answers before he crossed the DMZ the next day.

The briefing increased Carter's understanding of the domestic political situation and the motivations of the Seoul government. He was told that the U.S. and South Korean governments had different priorities; Washington's primary concern was North Korea's nuclear intentions, whereas Seoul's top interest was to control how the United States and other countries dealt with North Korea. The South Korean government placed a high premium on avoiding any appearance of powerlessness.[15] But the South Korean people were becoming increasingly apprehensive about the current crisis. Bill Maurer, the public affairs officer, said that the South Korean press, which previously had speculated about an unstable North Korean regime, now emphasized that Kim Il Sung would not be thrown out of power and that any solution to the current crisis required giving the North Korean dictator a chance to save face. Chuck

Kartman said that the Blue House, the office of the president of South Korea, currently operated on different assumptions. It strongly favored sanctions. It believed that the North Korean government would capitulate, and it was seeking to build public support for toughness. Yet the Seoul government had no specific plan for dealing with such a capitulation should it actually happen. During the past months, South Korea had followed an inconsistent policy toward the North, periodically "moving the line around" as to how much pressure to put on North Korea. Kim Young Sam watched polls closely, and changing public perceptions affected his policies.

When the conversation shifted to South Korean-North Korean relations, one of the embassy officers said that since prime minister–level talks had been held earlier, a summit meeting would be the next logical step. President Kim Young Sam had been ambiguous on this matter. He had called for summit consultations in his inaugural address, but had done nothing since to push for them. Little progress had been made on reunification. North Korea wanted to preserve its system, and South Korea, now that reunification was imaginable, was worried about the cost—with the huge expense of German reunification firmly in the minds of its leaders. Carter asked about Seoul's preconditions for diplomatic relations between the two Koreas. One officer said flatly that Seoul would reject such ties, but another said it would be relatively easy to raise the two countries' "liaison offices" at Panmunjom to "interest offices" as a first step toward diplomatic relations. There was no disagreement on one point—that outside mediation of inter-Korean issues was anathema to both sides.

Carter asked how the South Korean government would react if the United States and North Korea established diplomatic ties. "That would be their worst nightmare," replied Danny Russel, the officer in the political section who followed North-South Korean relations most closely.[16] He said that South Korean leaders worried that the United States over time would begin treating the two Koreas equally and that North Korea, with ties to the United States, would ignore South Korea.

Turning to Korean psychology, Kartman, the DCM, characterized the Korean "mindset" in both the North and the South as follows: If one's opponent is down, one should press his foot firmly on the opponent's neck. Russel chimed in that the Korean reaction to gaining an advantage over the other side was to harden—not soften—its position: "Kick 'em while they are down."

Carter asked how the sensitivity of the South Korean government to his visit could be alleviated. Kartman said that it galled Kim Young Sam that his critic and political rival, Kim Dae Jung, was getting favorable publicity with his claim that he had stimulated Carter to travel to the peninsula. Carter explained that his relationship with Kim Dae Jung had begun two decades earlier when he had helped prevent the South Korean's execution. Kim Dae Jung met him periodically in Atlanta, but neither Carter nor his staff had advance notice about Kim's proposal to the Washington Press Club regarding Carter.[17] Carter noted as well that Kim Young Sam had previously visited him in Atlanta.

Danny Russel summarized for Carter the contents of a personal paper he had written and, with the approval of Laney, made the paper available to Carter. Its underlying theme was that the respective views and posturing of the United States and North Korea were making it increasingly difficult to resolve the nuclear dispute peacefully. (Some of the paper's more telling passages appear in Appendix E.)

After the country-team briefing, Carter met with the entire embassy staff of Americans and South Koreans. He explained briefly why he had come on the trip, praised Jim Laney, introduced the members of his team, and lauded the embassy staff for their excellent work.

Almost immediately, Carter began a series of meetings with South Korean officials. The foreign minister invited the Carter team and Ambassador Laney to a luncheon in a downtown hotel; the president invited them for dinner in the Blue House; and the unification minister presided over a breakfast meeting the next day. During each meeting, Carter explained how he became involved, why he thought the UN sanctions approach was likely to lead to war, and what he hoped to achieve in Pyongyang. He stated explicitly that he knew South Korea had concerns about his trip to North Korea, and he hoped he could alleviate those concerns during their talks. Many of the same substantive issues were covered at all the meetings, though with different forcefulness depending on the official involved. In describing the respective meetings, I have focused on the issues given most attention by the Korean official involved or on which he and Carter had the most intense exchange.

In general, the president and the foreign minister were cordial but cool. Their demeanor hinted at their frustrations that Carter had involved himself in a problem that they believed should be handled by Seoul in collaboration with Washington. The unification minister, although not completely in agreement with the former U.S. president, seemed much more sympathetic to the Carter mission.

In their wide-ranging and generally friendly conversation, Carter and Foreign Minister Han Sung Joo engaged in one rather heated dispute. Carter said that he intended to tell the North Korean leaders that they should keep the IAEA inspectors on the job and comply with the IAEA rules, but he was still uncertain about how to handle in Pyongyang the distinctions between past and present North Korean nuclear activities. Han said it was "absolutely necessary to have access to past activities." Carter wondered whether it would be possible to remain "interested in" but "not probe" the two waste sites; Han stated firmly that it would be unacceptable to postpone resolving the issue of the two waste sites until the distant future.

"Are we willing to accept the possibility of war over a small amount of plutonium?" Carter asked bluntly. He did not believe that the IAEA should be allowed to determine the bottom line for resolving the international crisis. The issue of the past had been talked about for a long time. The North probably had hidden some plutonium and did not want to be caught in a lie.

Han countered that "with their threats and lies," Pyongyang was trying to create an artificial choice between war and plutonium. With defense deterrence, South Korea and the United States would prevent such a choice from having to be made. According to Han, knuckling under to North Korean threats would lead to the "slippery slope."

Pyongyang succeeded each time it threatened war, and it would continue to use this strategy. Its reckless talk was a "scare tactic."

Carter persisted. What if they agreed to keep all the rods under inspection, and to allow complete safeguards in the future? If they did so, it would be more practical to let them keep their plutonium than to take the consequences of exposing publicly their eighty-two-year-old leader as a liar. Carter said that some in the United States were willing to "attack" North Korea if it continued to refuse inspection of its waste sites. No one knew what Kim Il Sung would do. Carter told Han that he would try to help the IAEA obtain information all the way back to 1989, but in any event he would return to South Korea after visiting the North to share information and opinions. He said that the unpredictable nature of the North Korean regime was frightening.

Han held firm to his position that the past sites could be neither forgotten nor forgiven. He emphasized that something had to be done even if it was not 100 percent of what the IAEA wanted. Knowledge of the past was important for the sake of peace and security on the Korean Peninsula; forgetting about the past would be politically unacceptable for the U.S. and South Korean governments.

Seeking a common position, Carter suggested that this issue could be kept on the agenda for future discussions. Han, also seeking to bridge their differences, responded that discussions might yield ways for using technical advancements to deal with the issue of waste sites other than through full inspections. But he insisted that the honor of the IAEA must be protected.

I found it interesting that despite the foreign minister's advocacy of toughness to make North Korea back down, he took a more nuanced view when discussing China's role vis-à-vis North Korea. He told Carter and Laney that Beijing had assured Seoul that it was leaning on Pyongyang but not expressing explicitly disapproval of North Korea's actions, which the Chinese said would be counterproductive. Later, when Carter asked him whether the Chinese had chastised Pyongyang for unloading its reactor, the foreign minister did not answer directly. Instead, he said that the North Koreans felt so desperate that they might become nihilistic; the door for a dialogue must be kept open.

Laney insisted that to avoid war Kim Il Sung had to have a face-saving way out. Carter repeated his oft-stated position that the North Korean people would not accept their revered leader's being branded a criminal, but he also pointed out that without some new condition, President Clinton would not call off the sanctions campaign. He suggested, however, that within the framework of a comprehensive settlement, both sides could make concessions.

During the course of the meeting Han Sung Joo also explained the South Korean views on several key issues. He admitted that the South Korean leaders did not know the real intentions of North Korea—whether it wanted to negotiate or to press ahead with its nuclear program. Seoul had tried but failed to convince the "proud North Koreans" that it did not want to absorb their country or cause the collapse of their regime. The South Koreans would like to see the nuclear problem solved and for Pyongyang to have more contact with the outside world. The foreign minister said a decision on the Team Spirit military exercises for 1994 would depend on whether future bilateral Korean talks and new U.S.-North Korean talks took place, and whether progress was made in them. He also said that South Korea had proposed a meeting of the presidents of the two Koreas the previous year, but it did not intend to make another proposal or renew the previous one.

In the late afternoon, the Carter contingent and Ambassador Laney met with President Kim Young Sam in the Blue House. The president ushered us into a luxuriously appointed receiving room dominated by large cushioned chairs and sofas. He placed Carter close to him, with Laney nearby. About an hour later, the participants moved to another room for ginseng tea, and then to the dining room, where the conversation continued over dinner.

President Kim began by praising Ambassador Laney and commenting favorably on General Luck's operational leadership over the combined South Korea-U.S. forces. But he made clear that, as South Korean president, he held the ultimate position of command.

Carter explained that his trip had resulted from a North Korean initiative but was being made "with the approval of President Clinton." After he returned from North Korea, he would report to President Kim or his designee.[18] President Kim said he would meet Carter on his return.

The South Korean president said he wanted to explain the South's concerns about Carter's trip, which related to its experience with the North. He then proceeded with his main objective—by hammering Kim Il Sung, to convince Carter that a viable deal could not be struck with the North Koreans. He said the Pyongyang leaders "lacked sincerity" and would try to exploit the Carter trip to advance their own interests. Kim Il Sung would claim that Carter had come to North Korea to pay respect to him. The eighty-two-year-old dictator did not appreciate the strength of world public opinion about such things as human rights, conflict resolution, and poverty. Kim Young Sam insisted that Kim Il Sung's regime was "the most corrupt in the world"; it executed its critics, held 200,000 people in concentration camps, kept 20 million citizens on a "watch list," and segregated its handicapped.[19] The North Korean government faced a growing number of serious problems, such as insufficient electricity for the country's factories and a scarcity of food so severe that it limited people to one meal a day. It even forced the North Korean people to forego consuming seaweed so that it could be exported to Japan. But this did not affect Kim Il Sung's lavish spending; he had twenty-three palaces, and his son also had one. Again accusing Kim Il Sung of "insincerity," his diplomatic rendition of "lying," Kim Young Sam said that the North Korean leader's recent public assertion that his country did not make nuclear bombs contradicted his statements to the United States that North Korea would stop pursuing a nuclear option if it got light water reactors. Kim Il Sung was also "untrustworthy," stressed Kim Young Sam, which echoed the foreign minister's earlier characterization.[20] Shortly after assuming office, he had permitted an incarcerated North Korean war correspondent, Lee In Mo, to be repatriated as a signal to the North that he wished to improve bilateral relations. But Kim Il Sung did not reciprocate his gesture of good will.[21] On another occasion, Kim Il Sung had responded positively to Kim Young Sam's proposal in his inaugural address for a summit meeting of the two Korean presidents, but his negotiators had prevented real movement on this matter.[22] Then, demonstrating that Kim Il Sung did not want a summit meeting after all, the North Korean delegation head had made his threat to turn Seoul into a "sea of fire."

Carter listened intently to Kim Young Sam's charges, but said he hoped nonetheless to be able to resolve some of the differences North Korea had with the outside world. Things were at an impasse. The former U.S. president assured the current South Korean president that he was not naïve about international diplomacy. He could be tough. He could detect subterfuge and efforts to use his visit for propaganda purposes. Moreover, the global public would listen to his assessment. After reporting to President Clinton, he reserved the right to go to the news media and condemn North Korea if he thought it was not acting in good faith. His public criticism could significantly damage Kim Il Sung.

He returned to the summit idea, asking Kim Young Sam whether the two Korean presidents could meet but forego preparatory sessions. Kim Young Sam responded affirmatively, but at the same time evinced skepticism that the North Korean leader would attend. He said that from 65 to 70 percent of South Koreans supported trying to solve the bilateral problems between the two Koreas. Carter asked whether Kim Young Sam could envisage a future relationship with North Korea that would lead South Korea to favor the withdrawal of U.S. troops. His response: Seoul had secret documents that proved Kim Il Sung started the Korean War, and the presence of American troops on the peninsula remained the "key to peace in Korea and in Northeast Asia."

Responding to other Carter questions, Kim Young Sam said that Kim Il Sung had made a substantial effort to transfer power to his son, but he faced difficulty because Kim Jong Il was not popular. He said he would withhold comment as to whether South Korea would support providing light water reactors to North Korea until after the bilateral Korean dialogue had been restarted. South Korea's basic policy was not to let North Korea "acquire even half a bomb." He emphasized that North Korea faced a revolution at home—and cited the testimony of a recently arrested North Korean infiltrator. This South Korean intelligence claim, like several others made to the Carter delegation, proved to be false, as did Kim Young Sam's assertion that Carter would see not trees but only red soil on his way to Pyongyang because the impoverished North Korean people had to cut down trees for fuel. Pyongyang had refused the South's "sincere offer" to give North Korea 5 million bushels of surplus rice. South Korea would welcome trade with the North; it would even agree to sell its products at substantially less than their value, buy North Korean cement that did not stick well, and, if Pyongyang had a "face-saving" problem, repack its rice in Hong Kong for delivery to North Korea.

After Kim Young Sam berated the North Korean proposal for reunification, Carter said he seemed to be suggesting that there was no issue about which the North and South could talk productively. The South Korean president demurred. He said that if North Korea collapsed, huge numbers of refugees would stream into the South and into China. Therefore, to avoid such a prospect, the two sides should talk first about "peaceful coexistence" and later about a "peaceful unification." A basis for communication must precede unification. A way must be found to pursue the economic cooperation and mutual inspection of each other's military facilities as agreed in the 1991 Basic Agreement between the two countries. Once these goals were realized, South Korean businesses would find ways to assist North Korea.

Carter asked whether Kim Young Sam wanted him to carry any messages to Kim Il Sung. Not surprisingly, the South Korean president's response was not helpful. He told Carter to tell the North Korean leader that although South Korea had no intention of trying to absorb the North, its continued nuclear development would lead to its destruction. He also admonished North Korea for talking with the United States while simultaneously advocating *Juche*. The two Koreas should talk together, not with the United States. South Korea was prepared to help North Korea economically. It had the "will and power to do so."

Carter asked whether the South Korean president was suggesting that the United States should not hold discussions with North Korea. Kim Young Sam responded that North Korea should talk with South Korea and the United States, but the two Koreas should be the main negotiating partners. Kim Young Sam said that North Korea's announcement that it would withdraw from the IAEA had been timed to the Carter visit; Pyongyang thought this action would enhance its bargaining position. When Carter said he did not see the connection, Kim Young Sam admitted that he was speculating, but stressed that North Korea would not be relieved of its NPT obligations by withdrawing from the IAEA.

Knowing that the next day would be difficult, Carter moved to end the discussion. He told Kim Young Sam that his comments had been helpful, and President Kim affirmed that he would look forward to receiving Carter's impressions after his trip. They agreed, at Kim Young Sam's suggestion, that neither would reveal the substance of their discussion to the press. Then the dinner meeting ended and the embassy vehicles returned Ambassador Laney and the Carter contingent to the ambassador's residence. Since our bodies still had not accommodated the thirteen hours time difference with the United States, we visitors quickly excused ourselves and headed to our respective bedrooms. We anticipated long days and nights ahead—though not as long or as grueling as they turned out to be.

Although we had had little time to read them, most South Korean newspapers featured long articles and editorials on the Carter visit to North Korea in their Tuesday, June 14, editions. The editorial in the conservative *Choson Ilbo* warned the former U.S. president not to be "dragged into Kim Il-sung's deceitful tactics."[23]

Carter had his most useful discussion with a South Korean official over breakfast on Wednesday morning when he met with the deputy prime minister and minister for unification, Lee Hong Koo (an Emory University graduate who would later serve as South Korea's ambassador to the United States). However, the meeting got off to a rocky start when South Korean intelligence officials handed Carter a paper containing three questions. They insisted that Kim Il Sung intended to pose these questions to Carter with the intent of embarrassing him and undermining his mission. The first one asked why the United States, which purported to "love peace" and "hate" those who invade other countries, was trying to arouse public opinion against North Korea and was threatening it not only with an economic blockade but also a preemptive military attack. The second said that in the event of a preemptive U.S. military strike, every North Korean would stand and fight, and then it asked Carter, as a faithful Christian, whether he had ever thought about the millions who would be victimized by this U.S. aggression, about why his country was determined to conduct this war, and about what he expected to hear from his God about this matter. The final question asked why the United States, which had remained silent as countries such as India, Pakistan, and Israel developed nuclear weapons, threatened a "ruthless attack under the banner of the United Nations" against North Korea, which has no nuclear weapons and does not intend to develop them.[24]

None of Carter's interlocutors in North Korea broached any of these subjects, which raised in Carter's mind further questions about how much South Korean intelligence had really penetrated the North. The South Koreans traditionally insisted that since they knew the North Koreans better than anyone else, and that since their intelligence was superior to that of others, they should call the shots in dealing with Pyongyang. They did not prove their case in this instance. In fact, they apparently had little, if any, information about what the North Koreans had in mind for the Carter visit.

The remainder of the breakfast was more worthwhile. As is sometimes his wont, Carter avoided diplomatic niceties and jumped right to his concern. He told Minister Lee that he worried about the hard-line position of his government. He had received no signal in his earlier conversations as to how he could be helpful.[25]

Minister Lee explained South Korea's relations with North Korea, its view on the nuclear issue, and its attitude toward Carter's trip. He said that South Korea wanted coexistence and unification with North Korea.

It regretted the food shortage and other adverse conditions suffered by the North Korean people. It did not want North Korea to collapse.

Both countries had proposed unification concepts. The North's "confederal" proposal envisioned the relatively quick establishment of new high-level political institutions. The South's "confederation" proposal focused first on bringing the people of the two countries together, improving their general welfare, and building economic and social communities. Only after a viable common management system was in place, which would probably take at least six years, could a political arrangement, involving councils of presidents, ministers, and parliaments with equal representation from both countries, be established. To build such a commonwealth, North Korea would have to change, and it would find such change difficult given its Stalinist structure. South Korea understood that the collaboration needed to take place in such a way that would not cause the North Koreans to lose face. In the interim, the South Korean government could support liaison offices, but it could not open formal diplomatic relations with North Korea; it could not acknowledge two separate nations.

Turning to the nuclear question, Lee said that nuclear weapons were a serious issue for South Korea. Korean workers were the second largest group of people killed by the atomic bomb that destroyed Hiroshima in 1945. South Korea's principal security objective was to maintain the North/South strategic balance, which one nuclear bomb on the peninsula would dramatically change. South Korea had foresworn building its own nuclear arsenal, but its internal political consensus would break down if North Korea was permitted to keep the plutonium it possessed or if it undertook reprocessing. Such action would also agitate Japanese nationalists, which in turn would agitate the Chinese.

The North Koreans were using the fear of war as a ransom. If they carried out its threat, South Korea would not remain passive. It would not jeopardize its economic and democratic achievements even though its people opposed war. However, the nuclear issue did not have to be solved by sanctions; it could be resolved by negotiations that put whatever plutonium North Korea possessed under international management, preferably by the IAEA. Lee knew that Kim Il Sung faced a difficult choice because North Korea had hard-liners and moderates. The minister said he hoped Carter would be able to convince Kim Il Sung to change his current policy so that sanctions could be avoided.

Carter said he operated on three presumptions. First, Kim Il Sung was intelligent, not stupid. He understood the changes in the world and knew that he must accommodate them while preserving his nation. But he would not let his people see him exposed internationally as a liar. Second, he believed that all he wanted and had worked for was in danger. He had said that he had 70 grams of plutonium, but he probably had more. He did not want to be labeled a liar, but also he did not want to take actions that would be counterproductive to North Korea. Third, he had no way to communicate with leaders of the West. He may see the Carter visit as a way to explain his dilemma and help him resolve it without embarrassment. Carter said he believed Kim Il Sung wanted security and trade for his country and a denuclearized Korean peninsula.

Carter said he knew South Korean leaders feared that North Korea would turn his visit into a propaganda exercise. He assured Lee, as he had Kim Young Sam, that he would publicly condemn North Korea if it did not comply with the nuclear requirements of the international community. He did not think Kim Il Sung wanted that to happen. He also noted that Kim Il Sung had a different interpretation of the NPT from that of the United States and South Korea. The North Korean leader drew a distinction between what had happened before 1990 and after 1990. No one outside of North Korea knew how much plutonium that country had; the key consideration, therefore, should be to ensure that the fuel rods currently being unloaded and future rods were kept under strict safeguards. The debate over what happened in 1989 could continue, but "the future must be frozen." He hoped the North Koreans could be persuaded to shift to light water reactors because they would then have to buy the fuel for the reactors from abroad and return the spent rods to that outside supplier for reprocessing.

Lee said he respected the purpose of Carter's trip. His only concern related to his statement about the amount of plutonium that the North Koreans might possess.

Carter clarified that he, like the South Korean and U.S. governments, sought total accountability with the entire North Korean nuclear program placed under safeguards. But there had been no allegation of reprocessing since 1989. The North claimed it had reprocessed 70 grams, and no one could prove that it had done more. Carter intended to put pressure on Kim Il Sung, but the North Korean leader must have a face-saving way out. That was the reason he had traveled to the peninsula.

Carter told Minister Lee that their discussion had been worth his visit to Seoul. The Carter group left the breakfast meeting more optimistic about South Korean attitudes. We found it encouraging that Minister Lee, who had significant influence in the Kim Young Sam government, seemed genuinely hopeful that the Carter mission would succeed.

We returned to Ambassador Laney's residence, picked up our suitcases, mounted the diplomatic vehicles, and rode forty-five minutes to the DMZ. Approaching Panmunjom, where the American and South Korean troops guarded the border, we entered a military bastion. It was 10:10 A.M., Korean time, as we alighted at the southern side of the most heavily armed border in the world. Upon arrival, Carter, wearing a dark grey suit, and Mrs. Carter, wearing a light blue skirt, matching jacket, and white blouse, got out of the official Cadillac and stopped near the DMZ, their faces etched with emotion. Press reports recorded that Carter and his associates would be the first persons to go to the North via Panmunjom and return to Seoul the same way.[26]

Carter was met by Colonel Forest Chilton, the U.S. officer coordinating the crossing of the DMZ. Carter and Chilton formally reviewed the troops, and then the Carters chatted informally with some of the soldiers before Ambassador Laney and Colonel Chilton ushered them into the multistoried "Peace House" on the southern side of the border. Inside the Military Armistice Commission (MAC) conference room, Chilton told Carter of how the U.S. and South Korean troops faced off against the North Korean soldiers each day, and how the levels of tension rose and fell with the political attitudes in the respective capitals and with international developments. Chilton briefed Carter on past efforts to recover the bodies of American military personnel killed during the Korean War and buried in the North. He told Carter that since many of those killed met their deaths when the Chinese poured across the Yalu River and drove the U.S.-led UN contingents south of the DMZ, the U.S. government had a good idea about where most of the American bodies were buried. In the past, the North Koreans had only been willing to search for the remains of the U.S. soldiers on their own, and they demanded payment for each set of remains delivered—including some whose nationalities were questionable. Most of the missing Americans could be accounted for if U.S. and North Korean teams could investigate the sites together. Chilton's comments reinforced Carter's intention to raise the missing in action (MIA) question with North Korean leaders. (Before Carter left the United States, several American family members of persons missing in action in Korea had appealed to him to do so.)

After about thirty minutes, Colonel Chilton looked at his watch and advised Carter that they should go. Accompanied by Chilton and Laney, Carter and his associates left the building and walked toward the DMZ. The time for debate, study, and briefings had ended. It was now time to test Carter's conviction that he would be able to persuade the North Korean leaders to take constructive actions toward ending the nuclear crisis, making UN sanctions unnecessary and perhaps preventing a new war on the Korean Peninsula.

CHAPTER 7

Into the
"Hermit Kingdom"

I felt strange and apprehensive as we descended the steps of the "Peace House" and walked toward the DMZ. We were about to enter the "Hermit Kingdom," that isolated country of North Korea into which few Americans had ventured since the Korean War ended in 1953. Only a small number of U.S. citizens, usually associated with programs sponsored by a handful of U.S. nongovernmental organizations, often connected to American educational institutions or churches, had traveled there to meet with their North Korean counterparts. Some European and Asian countries had diplomats there, but their movement outside of Pyongyang and association with North Korean people were severely limited. To outsiders, what was happening within the power structure of that country was never clear, though it was subject to constant speculation. Official North Korean statements and press releases were studied scrupulously by Korean experts and intelligence analysts, but the information gleaned was at best opaque. North Korea was far less understood than the Soviet Union had been even during its most mysterious and enigmatic periods. Hence, the "Hermit Kingdom": alone, aloof, unknown, almost unknowable.

We passed the bank of reporters and photographers from many countries who were waiting in a specially roped-off area, pens scribbling furiously and cameras rolling, and filed through a corridor formed by armed U.S. and South Korean military personnel. About fifty yards away, North Korean soldiers stood stock still on their side of the DMZ. Beyond them, North Korean diplomats waited to greet us, their own reporters and photographers jostling for position.

The walkway across the DMZ—square concrete stones abutting each other—stretched about twenty feet between blue buildings, long and low, erected at right angles to the DMZ itself. The line of demarcation cut through these buildings at their exact center so that half their length lay on the southern side and the other half on the northern side. Inside these structures, where meetings between officials of the two Koreas were periodically held, long tables were located so that they, too, precisely straddled the DMZ.

After a pause for photographs, Colonel Chilton and President and Mrs. Carter and their party walked methodically toward the DMZ. At the DMZ, Colonel Chilton stopped to address his North Korean counterpart, Pak Im Su, the deputy chief liaison officer for North Korea, and two of his colleagues.

At that solemn moment, Nancy Konigsmark, prompted by Mrs. Carter, raised her camera to take a picture for the historical record. To get the view she wanted, Nancy stepped forward and twisted to her left. Unknown to her she was now standing—without authorization—on the North Korean side of the DMZ. As she pushed the shutter on her camera, she suddenly felt strong hands gripping her under her armpits; she was lifted silently back across the concrete markers, and set down firmly on South Korean soil. The female secret service agent, eyes staring forward, whispered almost without moving her lips, "Keep quiet and don't move!" Nancy, realizing what had just happened, stared straight ahead, pleased with her picture and choking back her laughter. Later, Mrs. Carter would relish telling the story of Konigsmark's preemptive step into history.[1]

Chilton, ramrod straight and stern—ignoring the indiscipline of the Carter delegation—addressed Pak Im Su. He told him that President and Mrs. Carter, very distinguished Americans, and their associates were being delivered by him to the safe keeping of the North Koreans. He charged Pak to take good care of the American group and to return it safe and unharmed to the same point on Saturday morning. The North Korean colonel accepted responsibility for our safety. We crossed the line; the Carters shook hands with the three North Korean military escorts and then walked with them to meet the waiting Pyongyang civilian officials.

The group of five hundred or so correspondents watched from the south side as the Carter entourage stepped across the DMZ. The only Western media documenting the happenings from the northern side was CNN, which had been granted exclusive permission to cover the Carter visit.[2] The small CNN contingent led by Eason Jordan from Atlanta, and including Mike Chinoy, Mitch Farkas, and Tim Schwarz from Beijing, would be nearby throughout the Carter visit. The CNN crew waved and grinned at their ABC, NBC, CBS, and other competitors trapped on the southern side of the DMZ.[3] Jordan enjoyed recalling later how many of these media colleagues gave the finger to the CNN team.

Vice Foreign Minister Song Ho Kyong moved forward to greet the Carters and escort them up the steps and into the North Korean "Unification Hut." Sipping tea, Carter and Minister Song engaged in pleasantries—too many pleasantries for Carter's taste; he was ready to go to work. After Carter had told his North Korean host how pleased he was to be in North Korea, and had responded to Song's question by cataloguing his meetings in South Korea without mentioning the substance of his discussions there, he asked the deputy foreign minister what they would do next. The somewhat abashed Song asked whether, if they had finished their tea, the members of the Carter team would like to "use the facilities." His old campaign grin in full flare, Carter said, with a touch of impatience, that they had done so on the other side. Shortly thereafter, the protocol requirements having been met, Song escorted us from the building to the waiting caravan of Mercedes.

The drive from the DMZ to Pyongyang lasted approximately two hours. The deputy foreign minister, Carter, and an interpreter rode in the first car. Mrs. Carter, Nancy Konigsmark, and a female officer from the North Korean Foreign Ministry, Choe Sonhee, who served throughout the trip as Mrs. Carter's female interpreter, rode in the second car. Dick Christenson, the North Korean desk officer for the United States, Li Gun, and I rode in the third car. In our vehicle we made attempts to carry on a conversation for the first part of the trip, but the monotony of the straight road and the effects of jet lag had me nodding out for much of the way.

That was not so with President and Mrs. Carter, who kept up steady conversations in their cars and observed the passing landscape. Our vehicles sped along a virtually traffic-free four-lane speedway. During the first hour, our group passed one vehicle on the highway, a bus. On a road that ran through a nearby field, Mrs. Carter observed an animal-drawn wagon and a few trucks. Halfway to Pyongyang, we stopped at a rest-house, a structure built on girders that stretched above and across the four-lane highway. The vice foreign minister told the Carters that North Korea produced no luxury vehicles, only trucks, buses, trains, and subways.[4] That explained why we could drink tea and eat cookies suspended above an expressway undisturbed by the sound of traffic.

After our rest stop, we continued the ride to Pyongyang. We first passed lush fields of cabbage, corn, and rice; these utilized extensive irrigation. Because much of the country was mountainous, cultivated fields were tucked into the steep hillsides; trees had been planted along the way to try to reduce erosion. The next area was a desolate stretch with low-growing green bushes scattered on the mountains. Few people could be seen. Occasionally, clusters of rudimentary concrete houses—box-like, two or three stories high, appearing to be newly constructed—swept by. As the caravan approached the country's capital city, more trees, including an orchard of fruit trees, swept into view.

Mrs. Carter's summary of the scenery en route: "Overall the country-side was beautiful, with mostly rich-looking crops (some poor-looking corn), trees, rivers, and mountains."[5] (I reflected on President Kim Young Sam's confident prediction that we would not see trees after we crossed the DMZ.)

As we entered Pyongyang, the roadway was lined with unending rows of concrete apartment houses; these reminded Mrs. Carter of Russia, although she thought their appearance in the North Korean capital was less grim. The heart of the city featured massive and beautiful buildings, sculptures, parks, and water fountains. Flowers seemed to be everywhere—"roses in full bloom, on bushes along the streets and trailing over fences along the sidewalks . . . stretches of hollyhocks . . . ginkgo trees and weeping willow . . . [a]nd along the banks of the Taedong River that runs through the city, more roses, daises, and weeping willow." Although we arrived shortly after midday, few people were on the streets. Then we saw the most famous landmark of the city, a gigantic monument of a man with one arm outstretched—Kim Il Sung, the "Great Leader" to his countrymen.[6]

Three days is far too short a time to make definitive judgments. But never have I experienced the sense of awe and reverence of people toward an individual as I observed in Pyongyang. Virtually all those we encountered, from government officials to people in the streets—and we would see many when the offices closed in late afternoon—wore lapel buttons emblazoned with Kim Il Sung's picture. The country's accomplishments were all attributed to the "Great Leader," often with some commendation as well to the "Dear Leader," Kim Jong Il. All artistic performances started with a pledge of allegiance to Kim Il Sung, and most finales featured waving national flags, marching people, stirring music, and mammoth pictures of a beneficent and smiling "Great Leader" looking down on and inspiring his people to achievement and sacrifice. We witnessed a human being treated almost as a god. I left that country with an eerie feeling that whatever Kim Il Sung told his fellow citizens to do, they would comply without regard for the consequences.[7]

The motorcade drove Carter and his delegation to the Mansudae Assembly Hall, where Foreign Minister Kim Yong Nam was waiting to greet us. He gave us a quick tour of the large building complex, including its main chamber, where the Supreme People's Assembly met. Built in 1985, the assembly hall seated 2,000 people. At the front of the room, a marble statue of the "Great Leader," forty feet high, looked out over the hall. The foreign minister told Carter that the People's Assembly had 678 members; they represented all parts of the country and they met for two or three days, twice a year. Mrs. Carter wryly observed in her trip report that "Jimmy thought this would be a wonderful relationship between a president and a congress."

The foreign minister then ushered his guests into a large rectangular hall, which could easily have served as a reception room for hundreds of people. Large paintings depicting mountains, waterfalls, and trees with autumn-colored leaves hung above the upholstered seats that lined both sides of the long walls. The foreign minister moved to a seat near the center of the room on one side and motioned for Carter to sit next to him. A North Korean interpreter stood behind the two men. Mrs. Carter and the foreign minister's wife sat a few chairs away, where they engaged in a separate conversation interpreted by Choe Sonhee. Dick Christenson sat next to Carter so that he could hear as much as possible the translations provided by the interpreter, and Nancy and I took the next two seats beyond Dick. A North Korean official sat to the left of the foreign minister. The other North Korean officials sat along the wall opposite us. It was an unusual scene. Eight people sitting on one side of the cavernous room; three, on the other side, at least thirty feet away; and most of us straining to hear the words of the two principals and the interpreter.

Not that there was much of historic import to hear. Since this session constituted the official welcome of the Carters to North Korea, the foreign minister studiously avoided substantive discussion, despite Carter's efforts to begin work right away. Kim Yong Nam complemented Carter for his understanding of the Korean problem when he was president and since then. He complained that the international media often reported inaccurately on conditions in North Korea. He said he understood that Carter was currently studying how unification of the peninsula might be achieved. The foreign minister assured Carter that he enjoyed respect among the North Korean people.

Picking up on the unification point, Carter indicated that as U.S. president, he had urged three-party talks among North Korea, South Korea, and the United States, but now he saw an opportunity for bilateral talks between Washington and Pyongyang, which he hoped his visit would facilitate. He described the circumstances leading up to his visit and defined his role as that of a private citizen who had come to North Korea with the knowledge and support of the U.S. government. He mentioned that he had talked personally with President Clinton in recent weeks about the developing crisis with North Korea. Carter said that he hoped to discuss the nuclear crisis and a range of other issues. He said further that if the nuclear issue could be resolved, he would be able to discuss future government-to-government talks that could lead to increased trade and perhaps even diplomatic relations. Carter shared his belief that considerable misunderstanding existed about North Korea's position on the nuclear issue. He understood that President Kim Il Sung had stated that North Korea did not have a nuclear weapons program, would permit full transparency, and would remain a party to the NPT. He needed to find out from Kim Il Sung whether these views correctly reflected his position. He also would like to discuss matters related to future issues, such as security and friendship between North Korea and the United States. Carter offered his hope—that he would gain a better understanding of the North Korean position on the nuclear issue and that when he shared it with the administration in Washington, the subject of sanctions could be put aside. Finally, he said he would make an immediate report to President Clinton upon his return to the United States.

The foreign minister assured Carter that he would have the opportunity to talk fully about nuclear and all other issues with many North Korean officials, and particularly with President Kim Il Sung. But now, after traveling such a long way, President Carter and his party should have lunch and a rest. At 4:30 P.M., three and a half hours later, the two delegations could begin their substantive discussions. Kim Yong Nam told the Carters that he would host a dinner for them and their associates that evening. He also said that arrangements were being made for the guests to visit various places in the city and surrounding area and to attend cultural programs.

The Carter team was then driven to the government guest quarters. Since few vehicles were on the streets, the trip took only ten minutes even though we passed through a main part of the city. Our North Korean interpreters told us that most North Koreans travel to work by bus or bicycle, and that few people would be on the sidewalks and streets during the working part of the day—other than the street cleaners we observed as we passed by. The streets and sidewalks were immaculate. We were informed that in North Korea all adults worked eight hours a day, six days a week. Women were allowed to stay home for six weeks after giving birth, but then they had to return to work. The state provided day-care services. Our interpreters said that after the offices and factories closed for the day, at about 5:30 or 6:00 P.M., the streets would teem with people.[8]

The Carter delegation pulled up to a massive and lavish government guesthouse. Imposing and stately on the outside, the guesthouse was also extravagant on the inside: The long halls featured gigantic walls displaying large, idyllic paintings of smiling people in beautiful natural settings. Light streamed through the towering windows and slashed bright streaks across the spacious rooms richly appointed with an abundance of upholstered chairs and sofas. The guest quarters sat on large manicured grounds that were replete with a lake, cascading fountains, and a stream meandering beneath the small suspended bridges that decorated pleasant walkways. Large rose gardens displaying brilliant red and pink blossoms tastefully dotted the rolling green lawns.[9]

The rooms of the guesthouse were large, comfortable, and modern. Plants and flowers decorated the rooms, and the bathrooms featured ornate fixtures. My only complaint: The television carried but one channel, and its news reports focused almost entirely on domestic events, including extensive footage showing the "Great Leader" and "Dear Leader" at building sites, in government meetings, and conferring with ordinary citizens. The accompanying narrative always praised the country's accomplishments and the virtues of its *Juche* philosophy. Not surprisingly, the Carter visit got prime time coverage.[10]

Surveying the guest house and gardens, I thought about the money spent on public buildings and the growing economic plight of the citizens of North Korea, about which we had been reading. The first of what would prove to be a series of droughts, floods, and famines hit North Korea in 1994, but the effects were not readily visible to us as we followed our restricted itinerary. Within a couple of years, as conditions worsened, the regime would admit to the world that its economy was suffering and that international assistance was urgently needed. But in June 1994, the North Korean leadership was keeping a stiff upper lip and internally and externally lauding the superiority of its economic and political systems.

At 4:30 P.M., we assembled in one of the conference rooms in the guesthouse. This room was small enough that the two delegations sitting at each of the two covered tables could converse easily. When the meeting began, CNN cameras, along with the North Korean media, filmed the two leaders making complementary remarks to each other. Shortly thereafter, a North Korean official waved the reporters and photographers out of the room and shut the door behind them. The time for business had arrived.

Following a brief mention of his visit to The Carter Center in 1991, Foreign Minister Kim Yong Nam read (with translation) a seventy-five-minute speech that spelled out, in a taxing and repetitive manner, the hard-line position of his country. Though polite, his words and body language said that North Korea, the aggrieved party on all issues, was united, strong, and determined. Others, not North Korea, had the responsibility to resolve the nuclear crisis.

As usual for North Korean diplomats, his presentation started with lavish praise for Kim Il Sung and Kim Jong Il and the glorification of their country and its *Juche* philosophy. North Korea's national unity was built upon the mutual trust between "Great Leader" Kim Il Sung and the North Korean people. The latter also had great confidence in the "Dear Leader," Kim Jong Il, to whom they "entrust their destiny." Guided by *Juche*, North Korea can "resolve all problems" by its "own efforts"; it can remain independent through a "self-supporting national economy." The North Korean people enjoyed their political, economic, and cultural lives. Education and medical treatment were free of charge. No one was unemployed; no one lacked shelter and clothing. They were convinced that they had the best social system in the world.[11]

Turning to the issue of unification, the foreign minister said that neither Korea could impose its system and ideology on the other. North Korea had proposed a formula for confederation, namely, "one nation and one state, two systems and two governments." This confederation, he said, would not be the satellite of a foreign government; it would not join a military bloc. (North Korea regularly charged that South Korea was a U.S. satellite.)

Kim Yong Nam emphasized that North Korea sought improved relations with the United States—despite the long history of hostility. They could become friendly once the United States "adopts a farsighted vision"; the Carters' trip could help.

He described North Korea's nuclear policy as peaceful. His country had neither the capacity nor intention to manufacture nuclear weapons, the fictitious allegations of Washington and Seoul to the contrary. The West suspected North Korea might have from one to two nuclear bombs; it would "be laughable to think we could with such weapons counter the United States, which has 10,000 nuclear weapons." The nuclear issue should be resolved through "dialogue and negotiation" between North Korea and the United States. He said that the concerns could have been addressed earlier if the United States had responded positively to the "package arrangement" that North Korea proposed in late 1993. Instead, the Americans continued to insist that North Korea must make the initial concessions with the United States taking subsequent action—"a relationship and dialogue based on suspicion." Under current circumstances, the nuclear issue could be resolved only through the acceptance of North Korea's "unique status" (regarding the NPT) and by the IAEA's treating it impartially (i.e., subjecting it only to inspection requirements imposed on all other NPT members—not "special inspections"). North Korea had withdrawn from the IAEA because it passed an "unjust resolution" against it.

The foreign minister concluded: "If the U.S. is politically ready to improve relations, the nuclear issues will be resolved. There is no need to have a complicated nuclear issue with us in the future. The U.S. will decide whether or not there will be progress."

After patiently listening to Foreign Minister Kim's presentation, President Carter responded, using as notes the talking points he had shared with Gallucci. He took much less time than had Kim Yong Nam. As would be true throughout his trip, Carter's words and actions focused on achieving four major strategic goals: to persuade the North Korean leadership to keep the IAEA inspectors in place, to stop North Korean actions that could lead to nuclear weapons development, to facilitate U.S.-North Korean negotiations to resolve the outstanding nuclear issues, and to make the imposition of UN sanctions unnecessary. He would play to the sensitivities of his various North Korean interlocutors and project the image of a trusted neutral seeking to help the North Koreans and the United States find a peaceful and mutually productive resolution of their differences.

Carter started by painting a broad picture of U.S. global responsibilities, its willingness to accept former enemies as friends, and its desire to improve relations with North Korea. The United States was a "great and powerful nation with many responsibilities in Asia and around the world"; its basic goals were "to promote peace, freedom, human rights, and independence." Despite World War II, the United States had developed superb relations with postwar Germany, Japan, and Italy; normalized relations with China; and developed friendly ties with Russia. It was exploring possibilities for travel, commerce, and other contacts with Vietnam that could later lead to normal diplomatic relations. For twenty years, the United States had encouraged Korean reunification and sought better relations with North Korea. Washington attached high priority to resolving its differences with Pyongyang. Carter said, "We respect the unity of your people and their commitment to independence and self-reliance. We felt our two nations were making good progress until a number of issues became an important area of misunderstanding." He had listened to statements of President Kim Il Sung and the foreign minister about not developing nuclear weapons and about willingness to account for the plutonium that their country possessed. He knew that about forty other nations did not belong to the IAEA yet remained committed to the NPT, as North Korea was saying was its intention. Carter noted, "There is a crisis now in world opinion about your intentions: whether you intend to retain the IAEA inspectors, what you are doing with the spent fuel rods, whether you will permit the integrity of the surveillance equipment to be maintained—a crucial point for the NPT." He hoped to obtain answers to these questions that would "be compatible" with what the foreign minister and his president had said.

Carter then told the foreign minister that he was authorized to say that if the nuclear issues could be resolved, the United States would be prepared to begin substantive talks on the entire package of issues. Recognizing North Korea's concern with security, he could assure North Korea that "there [were] no tactical nuclear weapons in South Korea or in the seas surrounding the peninsula." The United States was prepared to negotiate an agreement "guaranteeing the denuclearization of the whole region." Under this agreement, North Korea would be able to inspect any military base in South Korea. The United States would be prepared for direct talks with North Korea's highest leaders. On a mutual basis, restraints to free trade could be removed and high-level talks could lead over time to full diplomatic relations between the United States and North Korea. Most of these matters could be negotiated bilaterally, but South Korea would need to be involved on matters related to the entire peninsula. If bilateral Korean talks resumed, military exercises could be suspended and, perhaps as "part of a broad and thorough dialogue, the exercises might be suspended permanently." With his nuclear and reactor training, he appreciated the advantages of light water reactors. The U.S. government would support North Korea's replacing its old reactors with light water reactors by obtaining them from non-U.S. sources.

Carter concluded by saying that all the issues in North Korea's "package proposal" could be resolved between the United States and North Korea. But the critical issue at the moment was for North Korea to provide assurances on the nuclear issue. Action on the UN sanctions was imminent. North Korea needed to "fulfill the policies that you have already announced for your country." Then Carter offered a suggestion: On its own, North Korea could seize the initiative and make a proposal to the United Nations that would lead to a termination of the discussion of UN sanctions.

The foreign minister stopped Carter from elaborating this point further by saying that the banquet honoring the Carters would commence soon. He did, however, want to respond to the proposal that North Korea take an initiative in the United Nations, which he then rejected out of hand. He stressed that the nuclear issue was between the Democratic People's Republic of Korea and the United States, not the IAEA. The United Sates had caused the nuclear problem, and this problem must be dealt with bilaterally between Washington and Pyongyang. North Korea had joined the NPT in 1985 hoping to eliminate the nuclear threat to its country, but all it got from the treaty membership was "vexation, and no benefits." He dismissed the economic impact of sanctions on his country, saying that North Korea had long lived under a U.S. blockade and economic sanctions. "Sanctions may sound novel to you, but they are old hat to us, and our people are not afraid." Then, self-righteously: "All we want is a dialogue with the U.S. in which we hope the U.S. will drop its policy of hostility, renounce its nuclear threat against us, and support our switch to a light water reactor system."

Carter said that the IAEA, not the United States, had brought the issue to the UN Security Council. North Korea would have to decide whether to go to the Security Council, but another possibility might be a joint statement by North Korea and the United States that could remove the issue from the Council's consideration. The foreign minister did not comment.

Carter next probed for possible North Korean flexibility on the IAEA inspectors, whose expulsion had been announced the day before. He asked whether North Korea intended to maintain IAEA surveillance and keep its inspectors on the site where spent fuel rods were being removed from the nuclear reactor—pending bilateral talks with the United States. The foreign minister asserted that the North Korean statement was clear:

> We cannot permit inappropriate inspections until it has been decided whether the Democratic People's Republic of Korea [DPRK—North Korea] will return to the NPT or withdraw from the treaty entirely. Thus the inspectors have nothing further to do in our country. *We strongly reaffirm that any sanctions enacted by the UN Security Council would be seen as a declaration of war* [author's emphasis]. So far we have permitted inspections for the continuity of safeguards. We can no longer do this as it has been done.

With his belligerent point made, he then said the stance on nuclear inspections could be moderated if early talks with the United States could be arranged. He said North Korea would maintain the operation of the surveillance cameras and remain "fully committed to transparency" to show that there is "no diversion of nuclear material." In the third round talks with the United States, North Korea could "guarantee informal and formal inspections."

He then turned to the issue that had caused the IAEA to send the North Korean nuclear issue to the Security Council and the United States to reject third-round talks—Pyongyang's refusal to segregate specific spent fuel rods being discharged from the reactor for later measurement. He said that, before unloading the spent fuel, North Korea had sent the IAEA and the United States its own proposal for measuring the fuel rods. Although its procedure differed from that of the IAEA, it would have produced the needed information. Yet neither responded. Instead, the IAEA took the issue to the UN Security Council and then called for the inspection of two North Korean military sites (the "undeclared sites," where the United States and IAEA thought the nuclear waste that would answer the reprocessing question was stored). Then, with emphasis, Kim Yong Nam said: "The nuclear issue is not just technical. It is political." However, "all things could be discussed in the context of a package solution" in talks with the United States. "We can discuss ending our unique NPT status and permitting the IAEA to undertake ad hoc and routine inspections. If the third round takes place while the fuel rods are still being discharged, they can still preserve the technical possibility for the IAEA to select and segregate a representative sample for future verification."

The foreign minister closed his briefing papers, signaling that the meeting was over. Carter pressed on, asking whether he could talk with the IAEA inspectors (they had not yet left the country) and tell CNN that North Korea intended to continue surveillance of the fuel rods. Kim Yong Nam said he would check about the inspectors but Carter should wait until he talked the next day with North Korea's nuclear experts before saying anything about continued surveillance. Then, all smiles, he said they should conclude and get ready for the banquet, which he hoped the Carters would enjoy. Many high-ranking government and party officials and their spouses would attend. Carter said he was sure he would find the affair delightful, and he looked forward to continuing their talks over dinner. (The foreign minister would avoid substantive issues at the formal dinner; he parried Carter's varying attempts to deal with such matters by insisting that the banquet was a time for friendship and conviviality.)

As the afternoon's meeting had progressed, Carter had become convinced that, if the foreign minister's positions represented the firm view of his government, he was facing a stone wall unless he could persuade the Americans to agree to early bilateral talks. On his notepad he wrote that the North Koreans were "fixed on the 3rd Round of talks (US-NK)—as a prerequisite." He also wrote that he might be able to get Pyongyang's concurrence to let the surveillance cameras remain in place and for the IAEA inspectors to remain in country should North Korea subsequently decide to let them resume actual inspections. (John Ritch, the U.S. ambassador to the IAEA, had urged Carter in a cable sent to Seoul the day before to try to obtain North Korean agreement on these two actions.) In his precise script, he wrote: "Tell Wash. sanctions will have *no* effect here ["no" underlined twice] except as an insult to an aging deity. Advise Gallucci schedule 3rd Round, maybe in Panmunjom *now* ["now" underlined once]. It's a society like the religious group at Waco." Carter's last sentence would prey on his mind for the next hours: "To whom [in the Clinton administration] should I send msg [message]?"[12]

After we left the meeting room, Carter told Christenson and me about his concern at the foreign minister's tone and intransigence. He asked us to prepare a memorandum of the conversation after the formal dinner and slide it under his door so that he could review it when he rose. I did not know then how early that would prove to be. As I walked quickly to my room, the CNN crew approached and asked me whether I could tell them anything. I said no. If anything were to be said publicly, Carter should say it.

The formal dinner honoring the Carters was held at the spacious and brightly lit Moknan House. As promised, many senior North Korean foreign office, military, and party officials attended. At the dinner, I was introduced to Ambassador Ho Jong, who had dealt with Carter and the Center during his tour at the North Korean Mission to the UN. Unusual for a North Korean diplomat, he had established a relatively wide range of contacts in the U.S. government (primarily at the working level), the media, and in the NGO world while serving in New York. Even though our conversation was brief, I was pleased to see him. It had been rumored that Ho Jong had been recalled from New York and put through a "reeducation" program because of his perceived closeness to Americans.

We were served a succulent and lavish meal of many courses on tables beautifully set with full silverware and silver chopsticks. As with all our formal meals in North Korea, we were provided three wine glasses, one filled with beer, a second with a sweet red wine, and the third with ginseng liquor, as well as the traditional small bowl of kimchie—spicy cold Chinese cabbage in an orange-colored herb juice. We were told that rice and kimchie comprised the diet of ordinary citizens;[13] clearly, our fare was beyond the reach—and probably the imagination—of ordinary citizens.

The foreign minister and the Carters sat at the head table of a large room filled with numerous round tables, each seating from ten to twelve persons. At the appropriate time, the foreign minister rose and walked to a standing microphone where, relaxed and smiling—in contrast to his combativeness a short time earlier—he read a lengthy toast. He praised Carter as a distinguished guest who had a "noble desire for peace" and who had "set out on a long and heavy travel to call on us as our welcome guest." He said it was significant that he had the opportunity of receiving Carter "not in the United States or in any other Western country, but precisely here in Pyongyang." He said the "visit would serve as a good sign that the continued mistrust and feelings of hostility between the two countries will gradually give way to the good-neighbor relations of friendship based on mutual respect." He said that his country wished that the "warm feelings of friendliness and harmony that prevail[ed]" in Pyongyang that evening "would lead to the improvement of the currently unsavory relations between the Democratic People's Republic of Korea and the United States." This goal could be achieved if the two sides would "often meet with each other and engage in candid dialogue to resolve our misunderstanding in our step-by-step movement forward." The people of the two nations wanted to replace "currently hostile relations" with "normal relations"; hostilities were not inevitable. If the United States treated North Korea as an equal, all outstanding problems could be solved.

The foreign minister said he was sure that President Carter, when crossing the DMZ, had perceived the "heart-breaking pains" of the "homogeneous Korean nation" because of the "artificial partition" imposed on it five decades earlier. The North Korean people "cherish an ardent desire for Korea's reunification and want a genuine peace." Then came the obligatory references to the unity that allegedly embraced the ordinary citizens, the country's top leaders, and North Korea's special system: "Our people, holding in high esteem the great leader Comrade KIM IL SUNG, and closely rallied in the single-hearted unity around the dear leader Comrade KIM JONG IL, who is exercising a wise leadership over the Party, State, and military affairs, are successfully building the *juche*-oriented socialism, which they have chosen by themselves." He asked Carter to convey to the American people and the world community "a true picture about the peace-loving position of the Democratic People's Republic of Korea." Then, appealing directly to Carter's own views, and perhaps as well to his ego, Kim Yong Nam said, "There is nothing impossible to do, once a human being is firmly determined to do something. I think this step, that you have taken on the basis of your good self's determination, will lead to a thaw in the relations of the two countries and to a peaceful environment." He then proposed a toast to the good health and long life of Kim Il Sung, to Kim Jong Il, to the good health of the Honorable Jimmy Carter and Mrs. Rosalynn Carter, to the health of the American guests and "those present here," and "to the friendship and peace among the people."[14]

After witnessing the foreign minister's afternoon performance and now his toast, I asked myself what might be the DPRK's bottom line. Certainly, it was to deal only with the United States on the nuclear issue through bilateral talks. There was no hint that North Korea would do anything to stop the downward spiral toward confrontation in advance of those talks. Yet with such talks, perhaps major problems could be dealt with and resolved.

As the foreign minister returned to his seat, Carter, without notes, moved briskly to the microphone. He spoke of how he had wanted to visit North Korea for many years and how pleased he was finally to have the opportunity to do so. He thanked the foreign minister and the government of North Korea for their hospitality, and he expressed his pleasure at having the opportunity to talk directly with Kim Il Sung the next day. Carter briefly mentioned the themes he would repeat in various renditions throughout his visit: that he believed it served the interests of the United States and North Korea for the relations between the two countries to improve; that he hoped to contribute to that process; that he was deeply concerned about the current international nuclear crisis, which could deteriorate to the detriment of all; and that he hoped he and Kim Il Sung would be able to find a mutually satisfactory solution to this thorny problem, including full transparency on nuclear matters, that would be consistent with the dignity of all parties involved. In his toast calling for closer ties between the countries and people of North Korea and the United States, the resolution of the nuclear issue, and the hope for peace and stability on the Korean Peninsula, Carter made specific mention of the need for improvement of human rights. His remarks drew warm applause.[15]

After the toasts, coffee and dessert were served. Then a female rock band, its members dressed in frilly skirts, strummed electric guitars and entertained the guests with their renditions of American folk songs, among them "Oh Susannah" and "My Darling Clementine." When this surreal entertainment ended, the foreign minister rose and said goodnight to the Carters. All the guests immediately departed. The entire evening had been carefully choreographed so that there was little time for anything but the most perfunctory exchanges between the Carter delegation and North Korean officials.

Exhausted, we returned to the guest quarters, but sleep had to wait. Dick Christenson and I began drafting the report of Carter's meeting with the foreign minister, but soon Dick suggested that I retire and let him produce the first draft. When he had finished, he woke me to review the report. We passed it to Carter around 1:00 A.M. I fell back into bed, too tired to contemplate the events of the day that would soon dawn, the one for which this whole trip had been undertaken.

Less than two hours later, I was awakened by a loud knock. I struggled out of bed and unlocked the door. Carter stood there half-dressed. "Put something on," he said. "We need to talk—in the garden." He returned to his room. I slipped into trousers and a shirt, threw a light jacket over my arm, and walked down the hall to the

Carter suite. The secret service officers notified the Carters that I was there and shortly thereafter guided President Carter, Mrs. Carter, and me out to the garden. While the officers kept watch, the three of us conversed as we strolled the flower-lined walkways—out of earshot of likely electronic bugs.

In the intervening hours since the meeting with the foreign minister, Carter's concern about the fate of his mission had grown significantly—and our report reinforced his anxiety. He found deeply disturbing the foreign minister's inflexible presentation, his reticence about considering any of Carter's points, his intransigent position on expelling the IAEA inspectors, his firm refutation of any fear about international sanctions, and his insistence that no progress could be made without an early reconvening of the third round of U.S.-North Korean talks. Carter had traveled to North Korea for two reasons: his fear that war could erupt if the two sides continued to pursue their current courses of action, and his belief that the North Korean leadership wanted to find a way out of the crisis without losing face. The foreign minister's posture suggested no inclination toward compromise.

Carter had agonized that he had no formal authority to do anything other than listen in his talks with Kim Il Sung. He thought that his negotiating package proposal, which he had read to Gallucci before departure, would be acceptable to the U.S. government. At one time or another, U.S. government officials had discussed and accepted all elements of the package. Carter's fear was that if he could not tell Kim Il Sung the next morning that the United States was prepared for an early resumption of the bilateral talks, the North Korean leader might actually throw out the IAEA inspectors, batten down the hatches, and move onto a wartime footing.

I shared Carter's concern, but worried about the skepticism with which his trip was being viewed in Washington. The hard-liners on Capitol Hill and in the think tanks wanted forceful action against North Korea. The Clinton administration faced a crescendo of castigation about its "wimpishness." From my conversations with Bob Gallucci to and from Plains, Georgia, on June 5, and with other State Department friends before and after that date, I had drawn the conclusion that the Clinton team believed it had to appear tough. For the administration, a retreat from forceful action in North Korea, unless Pyongyang backed down, would be politically devastating. Yet Jimmy Carter, the former president the right wing loved to hate, was in Pyongyang trying to find a compromise that did not involve truculent inflexibility on either side.

I felt reasonably certain that if Carter sent a message to Washington asking for authority to indicate U.S. willingness to begin the third round of talks without first having obtained concessions from North Korea, the administration would react negatively. To accept Carter's proposal would represent a sharp reversal of the administration posture of linking a new round of talks to specific prior actions by Pyongyang and provide its critics with new ammunition to fire against it. Most foreign policy officials in the government, and pundits outside the administration, did not share Carter's belief that war was near. Many expected the North Koreans to back down in the face of strong pressure; some were prepared, if Pyongyang remained inflexible, to preempt with a military strike on North Korea's nuclear facilities—even though no one knew where North Korea, if indeed it had more plutonium than it had reported to the IAEA, had hidden this plutonium.

As we walked in the garden, President Carter, Mrs. Carter, and I discussed the various issues and aired our views and concerns. We talked for almost two hours and walked for several miles. By 5:00 A.M. we had agreed on a course of action, and President Carter had made his decision. None of us doubted that the administration's position of driving for sanctions in the United Nations could inadvertently lead to war. We concurred that, despite the criticality of soon reopening the U.S.-North Korean talks, a Carter message urging them would probably not be received favorably in Washington. Moreover, it would not be tactically wise to go to Washington before Carter had spoken directly with Kim Il Sung, the man who would make the ultimate decisions for North Korea on the nuclear crisis. There was always the possibility that the foreign minister's role was to play the tough guy, to test Carter's resolve and flexibility, with Kim Il Sung subsequently taking a more moderate line if, as Carter believed, the North Korean dictator really wanted to find a peaceful way out of the current impasse. Should Kim Il Sung repeat Kim Yong Nam's intransigent line, the case would be stronger for a message to Washington for a possible last-minute review of its position.

A critical timing issue remained. Carter's meeting with Kim Il Sung was scheduled for 10:00 A.M. and would probably last at least two hours. Since the only way to get a secure message through to Washington was to have someone drive back to Panmunjom to the U.S. military facility, a two-hour trip, it was unlikely, even with the time difference between Korea and Washington, that a message sent out that afternoon would get a Washington response in time to try to arrange a second meeting with Kim Il Sung. Carter decided that I should leave as soon as possible for Panmunjom with a letter he would prepare for President Clinton. But I would not send the message until I was instructed to do so. Carter and the remainder of his delegation would hold the meeting with Kim Il Sung. Afterwards, Dick Christenson would call me. If the meeting with the North Korean dictator went well, he would tell me not to send the message and return to Pyongyang. If the meeting went poorly, he would convey Carter's instruction to send his letter immediately to President Clinton.

While I cleaned up and dressed, Carter put his letter to Clinton into final form. He gave me the letter to read, which I did, and then put it in my coat pocket. He reiterated his instruction not to send the letter without specific instruction from him. I wished him luck with Kim Il Sung; we shook hands, and I walked outside to meet the car Nancy Konigsmark had arranged for me. At six o'clock in the morning, June 16, a North Korean vehicle, with a puzzled Li Gun seated on the back seat, pulled up at the guest house. I climbed in, and we were off.

Li tried to find out why I was returning to Panmunjom. I said that President Carter wanted me to consult with Washington. Despite his many questions, I refused to elaborate. I answered that nothing was wrong, just that I was carrying out President Carter's instructions to consult with officials back home. After a period of diplomatic thrust and parry, we sat back for the ride, neither of us trying to make social conversation. In fact, I used the opportunity to try to catch up on some sleep—dozing fitfully for much of the trip.

I would not look at the letter again until I was on the southern side of the DMZ. But the substance, if not the exact language, played in my mind as I rode and dozed on the two-hour trip.

Dear President Clinton

I have had direct talks with North Korean leaders. Briefly, here are my assessments. The practical effect of even substantial sanctions on North Korea will be nil, repeat nil. Moreover, they will be considered an insult to an aging deity that could not be accepted. This is literally a unique society, with only one ultimate voice and a degree of reverence that exceeds anything I have ever seen.

I have pressed them to assure me that they will permit the IAEA inspectors to remain on the site and maintain continued surveillance of the recently removed fuel rods. They respond that the U.S. is the direct cause of the nuclear issue, and therefore they must discuss it directly with the U.S. Their repetitive response is that all they want is a dialogue with the U.S. They are fixated on the quote Third Round unquote.

When I remind them that the issue is already in the Security Council as a result of the IAEA report, and ask if the DPRK would maintain surveillance of the fuel rods and keep the inspectors on the reactor site, the foreign minister replied, (a verbatim quote). "We cannot permit inappropriate inspections until it has been decided whether the DPRK will return to the NPT or withdraw from the treaty entirely. Thus the inspectors have nothing further to do in our country. We strongly reaffirm that any sanctions enacted by the UNSC would be seen as a declaration of war. So far we have permitted inspections for the continuity of safeguards. We can no longer do this as it has been done."

They have agreed to maintain the operation of the surveillance cameras for the time being, but insist on the Third Round of talks, in which they can "guarantee informal or formal inspections and discuss all things in the context of a package solution." They went on to say "We can discuss with the U.S. ending our unique NPT status and permitting the IAEA to undertake ad hoc and routine inspections. If the third round takes place while the fuel rods are still being discharged, they can still preserve the technical possibility for the IAEA to select and segregate a representative sample for future verification." They emphasize that the nuclear issue is not just technical, but political.

I am following the suggestions received yesterday from Ambassador Ritch in Vienna, but see no evidence that the North Koreans will agree to either of the two major steps. I have tried to convince them that my discussions should be a substitute for the third round of talks with Gallucci, but without success. What I need is immediate advice on whether I can use agreement for a third round of talks as an inducement for possibly resolving this problem before the chain of surveillance is broken. Other than both we and they backing down somewhat on previous statements, I see no real down side to this proposal.

I suggest that we prepare for an early holding of the "third round," perhaps by immediately sending Bob Gallucci to Seoul for direct talks at Panmunjom. This can be done without publicity. I believe the situation is extremely serious and that the only resolution lies in this direct exchange. The North Koreans may be bluffing about withdrawing altogether from the NPT, but I do not believe it is worth the risk of testing them.[16]

Upon my arrival at the North Korean side of the DMZ, a North Korean military officer escorted me into one of the conference buildings that straddled the DMZ. After a few moments, an American military official appeared and directed me out of the building on the South Korean side of the DMZ. The U.S. embassy had been alerted of my return, and Political Officer Danny Russel had flown by helicopter to the DMZ to meet me. We went to the secure bunker of the U.S. colonel on the UN Military Affairs Committee, where I would await the call from Christenson.[17]

I was not surprised that Russel expressed strong reservations about sending the Carter letter to Washington when I briefed him on its contents. He raised many of the points the Carters and I had discussed, and perhaps others. I also had a secure telephone conversation with Ambassador Laney. I explained the situation to Jim and read him the text of the Carter letter to President Clinton. The ambassador said that for weeks the U.S. administration had turned a deaf ear to the North Korean appeal for a third round of talks, insisting that North Korean concessions must precede any new talks. He stressed that it would be a mistake to send the letter and said that Washington at this point was not putting much weight on the inspectors and the continuity of safeguards. These two points were important symbolically, but, according to the ambassador, the administration would "not pay a dime for them." Washington would view the Carter letter as asking for a U.S. concession with nothing having been given by the North Koreans; it would respond negatively. Laney elaborated. Clinton was under considerable pressure from his critics. He had to have "tangible results" before halting the course the administration was on. Laney added that there was a "short time fuse" for the augmentation of the U.S. military forces, which would be seen by North Korea as provocative. Laney said, "We are heading toward catastrophe. Carter must persuade the North Koreans to make a tangible gesture of good faith to save Clinton's face. Kim Il Sung has to decide on a bold new initiative."

Laney's mention of military augmentation reflected his immediate anxiety. A few hours earlier over breakfast, General Luck had advised the ambassador about a meeting that would take place in Washington several hours later. (It would be 10:00 A.M. Washington time but 11:00 P.M. Korean time.) Laney told me that at that meeting, over which President Clinton would preside, the administration would decide whether and by how much to increase American troops and equipment in and around South Korea as a precaution against a possible military thrust by North Korea. Laney and Luck had fired off a strong rejoinder against increasing the U.S. military presence in South Korea at this time, urging Washington to postpone a decision on this issue. But they did not expect their recommendation to be accepted by Washington policymakers.

Laney urged me to convey to Carter that absent new commitments from Kim Il Sung, Washington would not authorize the next round of talks. Both of us and Russel hoped Carter's meeting with Kim Il Sung, which was then taking place, would make the sending of the former president's letter unnecessary.

CHAPTER 8

The Breakthrough

While Ambassador Laney, Political Officer Russel, and I agonized about the need for a breakthrough in South Korea, Jimmy Carter was achieving one up north.

At 10:00 A.M., President Carter, Mrs. Carter, Dick Christenson, and Nancy Konigsmark, accompanied by Carter's secret service agents, entered Pyongyang's Kumsusan Palace. There they met a smiling Kim Il Sung, who, after greeting his guests, ushered them into an enormous reception room. First, he and President Carter, then the two of them and Mrs. Carter, and finally the Carter team and the North Korean president, Foreign Minister Kim Yong Nam, and First Vice Foreign Minister Kang Sok Ju posed for photographs. Their backdrop: a gigantic wall mural of craggy, snow-capped mountains slashed by a gleaming waterfall that plunged and disappeared behind trees draped with brightly colored autumn leaves.

Kim Il Sung then led the participants into a large conference room and nodded for them to take the center seats on the respective sides of a large, highly polished wooden table that stretched almost the length of the room. The North Korean president took his seat at the center of the table; Foreign Minister Kim and Vice Foreign Minister Song sat down to his left and First Vice Foreign Minister Kang Sok Ju (Gallucci's counterpart at the two sets of bilateral talks in 1993) and the interpreter, Kim

Hyok Chul, to his right. The other participants left an empty seat between them and their "Great Leader." With the photographers filming, Carter and President Kim chatted amiably while members of their two delegations smiled. Then the signal was given, and the media representatives filed out of the room. The delegates, now serious, opened their briefing material and prepared to record what their two principals said. The historic meeting began.

Carter and Kim Il Sung had not met before, but they knew a great deal about one another. Carter recognized that Kim Il Sung had created his own legend in his lifetime: as a fearless leader for national independence in the 1940s against the Japanese imperialists; as an astute and ruthless politician who had seized power as the Japanese departed, and, allied with the Soviets, had neutralized or destroyed his internal rivals; as a determined dictator who had launched a sneak, but ultimately unsuccessful, military attack to unite the Korean Peninsula in 1950 and caused a massive loss of life and enormous property destruction; as the father of his country and its authoritarian ruler for almost fifty years who had through persuasion and brutality achieved a deity-like status over the 22 million people he was ruling in 1994. Unflinching in applying force, even terror,[1] to achieve his purposes, Kim Il Sung could also be jovial, witty, and convivial, as we learned on our trip.[2] He also tolerated the Christian religion because his parents had regularly attended Presbyterian services and, as a young man, he had been close to the Reverend Sohn Jong-do, a Methodist clergyman and Korean independence leader.[3] He allowed North Korean citizens to practice Christianity as long as they did not let their religious beliefs conflict with the country's Communist ideology reinforced by *Juche*. Hence, it was not as surprising as many Americans would have thought that the Reverend Billy Graham was permitted to visit North Korea.

Despite Kim's eighty-two years, the president's appearance and demeanor impressed Carter: "We found him to be vigorous, alert, intelligent, and remarkably familiar with the issues," he wrote in his trip report. "He consulted frequently with his advisers, each of whom bounced up and stood erect while speaking to 'The Great Leader.'" The other members of the group attending this meeting confirmed Carter's opinion: "There was no doubt that Kim Il Sung was in full command and could make the final decisions."[4]

In welcoming Carter, the North Korean dictator said that he had invited the former U.S. president to visit North Korea many times, often using other international figures, such as Marshall Tito of Yugoslavia and Anwar Sadat of Egypt, to convey the invitations. He was pleased that Carter had now come and that he had crossed the DMZ—the second American to do so.[5] Kim noted that this was his and Carter's first direct meeting, "but upon meeting again we will soon become old friends." Then he stated a theme that would be often repeated during our visit. He looked directly at Carter and said, "What is important is that we both have trust in each other. So this meeting is the start of our trust in each other, and as we meet in the future, our trust will grow stronger."[6]

Carter responded that he had arrived in Pyongyang three years after Foreign Minister Kim Yong Nam and Ambassador Ho Jong had delivered Kim Il Sung's message to him. For twenty years, he had been deeply interested in Korean reunification and in improving relations between the United States and North Korea. During his visit they had an opportunity to address some of the "misunderstandings" between their two countries. Having conferred with President Clinton and other senior administration officials before departing the United States, he had come to North Korea "as a private citizen, not as a government official, but with the knowledge and support of [his] government." He had stopped en route in Seoul, and the South Korean president, Kim Young Sam, was "aware of [his] visit and approve[d] it." But Carter emphasized that his message was from his "own country only." That message:

The U.S. desires to live in peace and harmony with North Korea. We don't believe our different government systems should be an obstacle to full cooperation and friendship. This friendship can include mutual respect for each other's politics and culture, and the possibility of trade and commerce. It can include direct personal meetings between the U.S. and North Korean leaders. We hope mutual understanding between us can lead to full, normal diplomatic relations.

As Carter spoke, President Kim listened intently. He lit a cigarette and began slowly to puff on it.[7] But his attention remained glued on Carter.

Carter then raised the matter that brought him to Pyongyang. In a soft but firm voice, looking directly at Kim Il Sung, he said, "The issue that confronts us is that the U.S. and other nations, including North Korea, need to find a way to guarantee the integrity of the Non-Proliferation Treaty. In all countries there must be full compliance with the NPT. I have read your statement that North Korea has no intention, and never has, to develop nuclear weapons." During the last few days North Korea had announced its intention to withdraw from the IAEA, but at the same time reaffirmed its commitments to the NPT. Of the 140 nations that had signed the NPT, forty were not members of the IAEA, yet they were still in compliance with the NPT. (Kim Il Sung remained intently interested in Carter's presentation, alertly turning his head from Carter to the interpreter and back again.) Carter continued, "Part of what the IAEA requires is that international inspectors and equipment be permitted to maintain constant and unbroken surveillance of nuclear waste and fuel rods. The purpose is to ensure that all nations will prevent diversion of used fuel rods to the manufacture of explosive material, and guarantee the transparency of all nuclear programs."

Carter then said that reprocessing as done by North Korea was "not itself prohibited, but must be subject to inspections." In making this point, the former president was correct with regards to NPT requirements, but unknowingly he was stating a position that was inconsistent with U.S. government policy. To keep facilities that could be used in nuclear weapons programs off the Korean Peninsula, the United States had firmly opposed South Korea's building a reprocessing facility or obtaining one from others. Consequently, it would also strongly oppose reprocessing in North Korea even if it were done under IAEA inspection; to do otherwise would likely stimulate new pressures in South Korea to develop its own reprocessing capability. When Carter repeated the point on reprocessing in his afternoon meeting with Kang Sok Ju and the North Korean nuclear experts, Christenson whispered to him that the U.S. government would not accept North Korean reprocessing and briefly explained why. Carter did not mention again that North Korea could reprocess if it were done in the presence of international inspectors.

Since the reprocessing issue would later cause considerable acrimony between Carter and the Clinton administration, some clarification is appropriate. Carter, his wife, and I do not think that the subject of whether North Korea could reprocess under safeguards was discussed during the administration briefings in Plains, Washington, and Seoul, and our notes of these conversations include no references to this issue. On the other hand, Bob Gallucci has a different recollection. The book he co-authored, *Going Critical: The First North Korean Nuclear Crisis of 1994,* has two paragraphs related to this subject in describing his meeting with Carter in Plains. It stated that Carter had suggested that reprocessing was permitted under the NPT if done under IAEA safeguards; Gallucci had responded that reprocessing was prohibited by the Nuclear Non-Proliferation Declaration negotiated by the two Koreas in 1991. Gallucci is also reported to have reminded Carter that under his administration the United States had begun a policy, which had been continued, of discouraging reprocessing by even advanced industrialized countries and stopping "such activities by states of proliferation concern—including North Korea—whether they were NPT members or not."[8] If the subject of reprocessing did arise, it must have been passed over quickly. That the United States government's policy did not accord with that of the NPT certainly did not register with Carter or with me. In fact, when Carter drafted his talking points to use with Kim Il Sung the day before he left for the Korean Peninsula, he included a sentence stating that reprocessing was not prohibited but had to be subject to IAEA inspection.[9] Later that day, Carter read the points over the phone to Gallucci; Bob did not take issue with this point, nor did he with any of the other points.

The former U.S. president pointed out that "there is misunderstanding over whether North Korea is committed to permitting constant, uninterrupted inspections as required" in the United States, in other countries, and in the United Nations. "The result, tragically, is that the IAEA has brought to the UN Security Council a report saying that North Korea has violated its agreements, and recommending that sanctions be adopted." Kim Il Sung nodded abruptly. Expressing his personal view, Carter said, "I think this sanctions effort is a serious mistake." Carter also thought that this comment would prove tactically advantageous since Kim Il Sung had earlier insisted on building trust. Kim simply continued to eye Carter intently.

Carter then pressed for the North Koreans to clear up the "misunderstanding," taking care to modulate his words so as not to rile Kim Il Sung into making threats against sanctions as his foreign minister had done on the previous day. Carter said, "I know that sanctions would not in themselves harm the self-sufficient North Korea, but adoption of sanctions by the UN Security Council would drive a wedge between North Korea and other nations that would be hard to remove." The North Korean dictator nodded.

> I came here [Carter said] because I believe this problem is a result of misunderstandings, and the misunderstandings arise because we do not have any easy way to communicate. So far there have been two successful talks between the U.S. and North Korea. When the third round was considered, the South Korean government objected. This delayed the third round until South Korea withdrew its objection this spring.

Kim turned to his staff and in Korean asked whether the South Korean government now assented to the third round of U.S.-North Korean bilateral talks, which was affirmed to him. Carter pressed on: "Then a major problem occurred in April when you, surprisingly, began to rapidly remove fuel rods from your 5 MWe reactor, which led the

IAEA to determine that it could not properly monitor the North Korean nuclear program."[10] Again Kim sought and received clarification from his staff and then turned back to Carter, listening intently. Carter went on, "The IAEA inspectors reported that North Korea had violated the terms of the NPT, with the result that the third round of talks was not held. Now this problem is on the UN Security Council's agenda." Kim asked his staff for clarification. (Christenson, understanding the discussion in Korean, recorded in his notes that Kim did not know the current status of sanctions, and his staff explained it to him.) After this discussion, Carter resumed: "I have come to talk to you and to find out how I can explain the DPRK position to Washington and the UN."

Until this point, Carter had been talking with little reference to his notes. During the next section of his presentation, he looked down periodically at the talking points he had read to Gallucci on the phone. Carter said, "I was asked by President Clinton to assure you that the U.S. has no nuclear weapons in South Korea, and no nuclear weapons in ships off Korea's coast." Kim nodded deeply. "As part of a broad agreement with North Korea, the U.S. is prepared to enter into a process aimed at ensuring that the Korean peninsula and surrounding area is made free of nuclear explosives." Kim said, "That is good." Carter continued, "I am also authorized to affirm that the United States is prepared to permit the inspection of any U.S. or other military base in South Korea. This would be in accord with the 1991 South-North Non-nuclear Declaration." Again Kim nodded his head. "If the nuclear issue can be resolved, then the U.S. is prepared to enter into immediate high-level bilateral talks with North Korea, with the understanding that with regard to issues that are peninsular in nature, South Korea would be included as a discussion partner." Carter said that he and First Vice Foreign Minister Kang could discuss the nuclear issues in greater detail in their afternoon meeting. Kim assented. Carter concluded, "I hope to continue working on this to assist in my small way to foster fully peaceful relations between North Korea[11] and the U.S."

Kim spoke about his country's nuclear program and its history. (Christenson recorded that the North Korean leader discussed the nuclear issue with "considerable conceptual clarity," although he needed Vice Foreign Minister Kang's help in discussing some specifics about the 5 MWe graphite reactor.) He said that he appreciated Carter's efforts to spur friendship between their countries:

> The central problem is that we lack trust, and creating trust is our most important task. The distrust comes from the lack of contacts between us. On the occasion of my birthday in April, I told CNN that we have no need for nuclear weapons, and no capability to manufacture them. All we have is a 5 MWe graphite reactor . . . and its technology is already outdated. Some say we are extracting plutonium, but we have no need and no way of using plutonium to make nuclear weapons. I have clarified this to a number of American visitors, including Congressman Ackerman, Billy Graham, Bill Taylor, and recently Selig Harrison.[12] Because I am this country's president, what I say should be believed, but they don't seem to believe.[13]

The North Korean leader said that North Korea had told the United States at the July 1993 talks that its 5 MWe graphite reactor was outdated and needed to be replaced by a light water reactor. "If the U.S. had helped us acquire a light water capability, even if from a third country, we could have avoided the current problem, and we would have reached a point of greater confidence, and we would now enjoy improved relations. If the U.S. would agree to hold a third round of talks, and to help us get light water reactors, then there will be no problems." Reiterating that the crisis could be resolved, he said, "We announced that we are withdrawing from the IAEA, but we have not withdrawn completely from the NPT; if we get light water technology, we can take care of these things."

President Kim Il Sung insisted that his country needed additional electricity to achieve its economic development goals. He stated that his nation relied on coal-fired plants and hydroelectric power to meet most of its electricity needs. He said that in 1985 he reached an agreement with Konstantin Chernenko for the Soviet Union to furnish North

Korea with a 2-million-kilowatt light water reactor, but the project was abandoned when the USSR collapsed. Now North Korea had "no choice but to have [its] own small reactor."[14] Again he pressed for better relations with the United States: "We need to build confidence, so your country can help us get light water reactors, and then *we could do away with our existing reactor*" (author's emphasis).

At this point, Kim Il Sung articulated his bottom line: "If we can solve this problem, we intend to return fully to the NPT regime. *If a commitment is made to furnish us a light water reactor, then we will immediately freeze all our nuclear activities* [author's emphasis]. Also we will delay our withdrawal from the NPT until we have the light water reactor. Thus the problem of our withdrawal from the NPT can be solved if we get a light water reactor." Looking to the future, he said: "Then our two nations, despite our different systems, can overcome our problems and improve our relationship. I hope that you [Carter] will advise the U.S. government that our two countries can overcome this problem without the IAEA."

Carter moved quickly to nail down the elements he thought would make possible the negotiation of a mutually acceptable agreement and resolve peacefully the nuclear crisis. He said he would convey Kim's ideas to Washington, but first he needed a question answered: "Will you permit the IAEA inspectors and the surveillance equipment to remain in place until I can get this message to Washington?" After conferring with Kang Sok Ju, Kim said they could stay in place. (Carter had the strong impression that Kim Il Sung had not known of the expulsion of the IAEA inspectors and reversed on the spot the earlier decision of his subordinates.)[15] Carter clarified that the United States could "not directly supply a light water reactor" but could "support North Korea's getting the reactor from another country, or other agency." Kim, after a moment of thought, said that if both the United States and North Korea could agree on the approach Carter had mentioned, North Korea would postpone its withdrawal from the NPT until the light water reactor was delivered. He asked Carter whether the real problem was the complete withdrawal of North Korea from the NPT.

Carter responded that there were other problems as well. He asked what was meant by North Korea's claim that it had "unique NPT status." Kim Il Sung asked his advisers in Korean what this phrase meant. The foreign minister and First Vice Minister Kang discussed the matter with their president with some animation. The interpreter finally said: "The special status also means that North Korea is not subject to the full range of IAEA inspections, which the U.S. has already recognized."

Carter set the record straight. He said, "North Korea articulated this special status concept at the end of the second round of talks [July 1993], and Assistant Secretary Gallucci was surprised by it. It is not clear that the U.S. recognizes this special status." In the abbreviated handwritten notes he was taking during the meeting, Carter had ticked off the points Kim Il Sung had mentioned about the light water reactor, about keeping North Korea in the NPT, about committing to an immediate freeze on all North Korean nuclear activities, and about the removal of all problems between the United States and North Korea. After the discussion on North Korea's presumed "unique NPT status," Carter recorded that the "unique status—can be removed." He then wrote "agreement!"—meaning that, in his mind, all the necessary elements were there.[16]

Carter said he would advise Washington that the IAEA inspectors and equipment to monitor the 5 MWe reactor would remain in place. He would also "confirm to the USG [U.S. Government] that it needs to support North Korea's effort to acquire a light water reactor," and he added that it is "important to go ahead with the third round of talks, so the issues of transparency and other outstanding issues can be discussed and more clearly understood." Kim responded that if the issues could be resolved bilaterally, transparency would not be a problem. He suggested that Carter should be involved in the further discussions in an official capacity, but Carter demurred, knowing that neither Washington nor Seoul would support his having an "official role." He said instead that he wanted to stay involved informally to be sure that problems did not arise because of a "lack of communication."

Kim shifted the conversation to North Korea's dealings with South Korea and the reunification of the Korean Peninsula. Recalling Carter's words that South Korea would have to be included in discussions involving the peninsula, he said that South Korea had expressed a wish not to be involved in such talks, a stance going back twenty years to when South Korea had refused the proposal of then President Carter for three-power talks [the United States, South Korea, and North Korea] and President Kim Il Sung's subsequent proposal for four-power talks, which would have also included China. South Korea, he said, could be involved in talks if Seoul would cease obstructing the progress of such talks, as it does whenever the subject of Korean reunification comes up. Carter asked whether Kim Il Sung meant that South Korea could participate in the third round of talks between North Korea and the United States on the nuclear issue. The North Korean leader said no, but that the South could be part of talks dealing with reunification. According to the North Korean leader, South Korea's President Kim Young Sam had proposed reunification talks during his inauguration, but then South Korea had resisted the North's proposal to exchange special envoys to work on this subject. South Korea always stopped the progress the United States and North Korea were making on the nuclear issues by demanding its participation. The South Korean president had made the task more difficult by saying that "until the nuclear issue is solved we won't even shake hands with you." President Kim Il Sung then repeated the standard North Korea formulation for reunification: "North and South can become one through a confederation formula in which there is one state and one people with two separate systems and two separate governments." He then said (alluding to Carter's earlier comments about the North-South Joint Non-Nuclear Declaration), "Let's move ahead to de-nuclearize the peninsula. Then there will no longer be a need to dispute nuclear issues, and no longer a need for you to doubt us."

Carter said the United States wanted to conclude an agreement among countries in the region to ensure that the area and seas around the peninsula would be free of nuclear weapons. Kim nodded vigorously and said, "Good, that is what we want, too." Carter reiterated that he would call Gallucci to tell him about the results of their conversation so that Gallucci could talk with President Clinton. Kim thanked Carter for understanding the North Koreans and for his good efforts. He said the two of them should meet again before Carter left North Korea, as Carter had requested in his message to the North Korean leader after his June 10 Washington meeting.

As the meeting ended, the participants seemed relieved. The breakthrough had been achieved. There was now a chance—a good chance—that the crisis would be averted, that the world would not, after all, go over the precipice. The task ahead was to keep the agreement from coming unstuck.

CNN was waiting when President Carter left the conference room. As his colleague filmed, Eason Jordan asked Carter whether he had any news to report. Carter stated that he and President Kim Il Sung had had a long discussion about the nuclear issue and other matters of common interest between the United States and North Korea. He found the North Korean president thoroughly familiar with all the issues including reactor design and comparisons of different types of reactors. He confirmed that he would have additional discussions with Kim Il Sung the following day. He declined to share more details of the conversation. But as he was walking away, Carter quipped to Jordan that CNN probably should not leave North Korea yet. Jordan assured him that he and his colleagues would not depart until after Carter himself had left the country.[17]

President and Mrs. Carter then proceeded to a luncheon for the two delegations hosted by President Kim and his wife, Kim Song Ae. Foreign Minister Kim Yong Nam's wife joined her husband for the luncheon, as did the secretary of the Party Central Committee, Hwang Chang Yop, and his wife; Secretary Kim Yong Sun and his wife; and First Vice Foreign Minister Kang Sok Ju. After the luncheon, the Carters and Christenson conferred about the afternoon meeting with the North Korean nuclear experts, and Carter instructed Christenson to call me at Panmunjom and tell me not to send the Carter letter to President Clinton. Instead, I should return to Pyongyang immediately for the Kang Sok Ju meeting.[18]

I notified Ambassador Laney that Carter had apparently concluded a successful meeting with Kim Il Sung because I had been told to return to North Korea without sending the letter to President Clinton. I crossed again the DMZ where I found a North Korean car waiting for me. The meeting with Kang Sok Ju was underway when I arrived.

Key North Korean officials responsible for nuclear questions participated in this Thursday afternoon meeting. Sitting to the left and right of Kang Sok Ju at a long table on one side of the room were Choi U Jin, the vice foreign minister for nuclear issues; Kim Kye Gwan, the ambassador-at-large for nuclear issues; Li Hyong Chol, the director of the American Affairs Bureau in the Ministry of Foreign Affairs; Li Yong Ho, a Foreign Ministry specialist in disarmament issues, and three relatively junior persons identified as notetakers. Across the room, Carter and his team sat behind a second table parallel to the one occupied by the North Korean officials.

Kang Sok Ju rivaled Foreign Minister Kim Yong Nam with the length and histrionics of his opening presentation. He rehearsed the evolution of the nuclear issues from the North Korean perspective; stressed that North Korea, while rejecting the IAEA's proposal for preserving the record of the spent fuel rods, had proposed an "equally valid method," which had been ignored by the IAEA and the U.S. government; and tried periodically to scale back some of the concessions Kim Il Sung had made during the morning meeting. Carter listened closely, often jotting down notes. His purpose: to understand where U.S. and North Korean interpretations on the nuclear questions differed, to correct North Korean false perceptions about U.S. policies, and to force the retraction of any North Korean assertion that varied with that put forward earlier by Kim Il Sung. When he corrected Kang, or asked him whether he was intentionally revising his "Great Leader's positions,"

Kang, with a hint of a grin, backtracked. He reversed most statements without missing a beat.

This experience, following so closely the meeting with the foreign minister the day before, reinforced for the Carter delegation two fundamental principles of North Korean diplomacy. First, North Korean diplomats quickly present themselves as the aggrieved party and then try to wring every possible concession out of the situation, often becoming loud and hyperbolic in their interventions. One must patiently let them go through their performance because their remarks are designed as much to prove their credibility to their colleagues as to win concessions from their negotiating opponents. At the same time, one must remain firm on positions already agreed, or on essential points.[19] Second, in 1994 there was only one final decisionmaker—Kim Il Sung. Reminding the North Koreans what he had already agreed to proved to be a sure way to prevent a bargain from unraveling. Even after his death, North Korean officials, including his son, Kim Jong Il, would not try to reverse what Kim Il Sung had accepted—if his imprimatur could be established.

Kang said that Kim Il Sung had been pleased with his discussions with Carter during their "historic" morning meeting. The friendly and cooperative atmosphere of that session contrasted with the tensions being generated elsewhere by the nuclear problem. He asked Carter how he would like to proceed.[20]

Carter quickly explained the background for his trip to Kang Sok Ju's colleagues because most of them had not attended his earlier meetings. He said he decided to accept Kim Il Sung's invitation to visit because he was concerned about a lack of communication between the leaders of the United States and North Korea. President Clinton had approved his trip. He found his talk with the foreign minister disturbing, but he had been gratified by his discussions with President Kim Il Sung, who was knowledgeable and willing to discuss the present crisis candidly. His personal view was that a UN declaration of sanctions against North

Korea would be a "tragic mistake" in view of Kim Il Sung's public commitment that North Korea lacked the capacity and intention to develop nuclear weapons. The problem was that a "number of countries lack confidence in North Korea's willingness to permit surveillance of the unloaded fuel rods and its uncertain status as a signatory to the NPT."

Kang said the Kim Il Sung-Carter agreement could solve the key nuclear problems. Playing more to his colleagues than to Carter, he reviewed the history of the crisis from the North Korean perspective, repeatedly asserting that North Korea had been wronged by the IAEA, the United States, and others. But then he laid down the new policy for his associates. He announced that President Kim Il Sung had made a "bold decision" to keep the IAEA inspectors and equipment in place, overruling the earlier North Korean intention to force the inspectors to leave the country and to dismantle the surveillance equipment. Kang said Carter's meeting with Kim Il Sung brought about that policy change. Then, alluding to what he earlier characterized as confusion in various government agencies, Kang said: "Since our President gave his commitment to keep the inspectors and the equipment in place, I am sure our concerned agencies will ensure that the inspectors and equipment remain in place." This occasion would not be the only time Kang would hint to us that he had his hands full keeping his competing bureaucratic colleagues in line.

Then Kang began to try to create leverage for walking back some of Kim Il Sung's other commitments. He said that after the morning meeting, he had checked the international situation and found it to be "terrible." Ambassador Gallucci and Ambassador Albright (Madeleine Albright, the U.S. permanent representative to the United Nations and the future secretary of state) had been up all night working on the sanctions resolution to present to the UNSC. (The United States was indeed intensifying its campaign to win UN Security Council approval of sanctions during the week Carter was on the Korean peninsula; the day before it had begun circulating in New York the draft text of a resolution calling for phased sanctions.)[21] Kang said, "All of our people in the country, and in the military, are gearing up now to respond to those sanctions." If sanctions pass, he said, glaring at Carter, "all the work you have tried to do here will go down the drain."

Carter said that he would try to contact Washington to explain the agreement he had reached with President Kim Il Sung and, after doing so, he intended to give an interview to CNN—suggesting that Kang or another North Korean official join him in the interview. Carter said, as he did in all of his meetings, "I have no authority from my government," but he added that although the sanctions issue was a "political matter" that possibly went beyond both their arenas, he knew China had "some doubts about the sanctions vote." He said, "My own hope is that my government will hold in abeyance any decision on a sanctions resolution until we can discuss things some more." Carter said that as a private citizen, he was "willing to publicly say that if all the things we have discussed are agreed upon, then the sanctions resolution should be withdrawn." The U.S. government had been pursuing sanctions to support the work of the IAEA to preserve the continuity of nuclear surveillance. "So our role here is to try to remove uncertainty, and let the world know that today your President and I have made good progress."

Carter wanted to wrap up the meeting quickly so that he could call Washington. But Kang had his written instructions before him and insisted on going through all his points, promising to be brief—which he was not. Carter listened, appearing patient, although he regularly tried—without success—to get Kang to abbreviate his remarks. I thought he must be frustrated; I certainly was.

Kang said that North Korea had been disappointed that the United States, after the collapse of the Soviet Union, had not moderated its view about North Korea but rather continued its hostility, determined to change his country's unique system of government. The United States had caused the current nuclear crisis by encouraging the IAEA to insist on "special inspections, threatening another Team Spirit military exercise, and ignoring North Korea's technical proposal for segregating and measuring the spent fuel rods," a procedure that could still be used, he asserted, with the evidence that the North Koreans had preserved. The United States had also criticized North Korea for removing the spent fuel rods from their reactor even though the discharge was overdue and some of the rods had become misshapen. It had encouraged the IAEA's "notorious Hans Blix" to send the nuclear issue to the UN Security Council. Carter disputed many of Kang's false assertions, including that the United States had accepted North Korea's "unique status" in the NPT.

The first vice foreign minister said that the crisis could be solved only through new bilateral talks between North Korea and the United States. The solution was to agree on a package arrangement in which both countries would obtain benefits and undertake obligations simultaneously. He held up for emulation the North Korean package proposal of the previous fall that consisted of four elements: the United States would suspend Team Spirit '94; North Korea would accept IAEA inspections to ensure continuity of safeguards; North-South working level contacts would continue seeking agreement on an exchange of special envoys; and the United States and North Korea would announce a date for the third round of talks. He insisted that North Korea had done its part to implement the package proposal, whereas the United States had insisted on "special inspections," criticized North Korea even though the South had derailed the North-South discussions, backed out of the third round of talks, and led the push in the Security Council against North Korea.

Having blamed the United States for all the problems to date, Kang, his voice rising, tried to draw back some of Kim Il Sung's earlier commitments. He said that the continued insistence by the United States on "special inspections" returned the situation to square one because that was the issue that had forced North Korea to consider withdrawing from the NPT. The inspection of the two sites was "wholly unthinkable, even in a dream," he insisted. "It would be like showing our bedroom to the IAEA."

Carter intervened firmly. He said that Kang had contradicted what Kim Il Sung had said earlier in the day. The North Korean leader had affirmed that if a third round of talks were convened, the discussion could take place concerning the denuclearization of the peninsula and mutual inspections of both North and South, "leading to full transparency of the North Korean program." Repeating, Carter stated that Kim Il Sung had said this transparency (involving inspection of all North Korean nuclear related facilities) "would be part of the total package."

An interesting diplomatic dance followed. Doing a 180-degree turn, Kang said, almost breathlessly, "Yes, that is how we can proceed." But he quickly tried to regain some of what he had lost. He said the North Koreans thought the U.S. aim was to make them reveal how much plutonium had been extracted in the past.

Carter asked why he objected; what did he fear?

Kang replied, "We will not allow ourselves to be treated like criminals."

Carter responded, calmly, "If you have nothing to hide, why do you object to the kind of transparency your president assented to this morning?"

Kang, his voice tense, replied,

What our President said is that once a third round takes place, and if we reach agreement on a package, and after diplomatic relations are normalized, then we can go on to the matter of transparency. Perhaps we cannot wait until after diplomatic relations are established, but we can move forward with this kind of transparency only after both sides have reached a certain point of confidence in each other. We are still very hostile toward each other, and so neither of us is yet comfortable showing the other our inner thinking.

Carter persisted: "Kim Il Sung said the whole North Korean nuclear program would be made transparent."

Kang admitted, reluctantly, "That is true."

Kang continued to push, and Carter to counter. Kang sought to condition progress on an improved relationship between North Korea and the IAEA, but Carter said he had no authority with Hans Blix. He did say he would make an effort with the IAEA even though that had not been part of his agreement with Kim Il Sung. Carter emphasized that he would report to Washington only what he and Kim Il Sung had agreed.

The discussion then moved to how North Korea would handle the fuel rods discharged from the 5 MWe graphite reactor. Vice Foreign Minister Choi asserted that the discharged fuel rods could remain safely in the cooling ponds for three months only. Carter said that he understood that reprocessing under IAEA safeguards was permitted under the NPT. (This was the point mentioned earlier where Christenson whispered to Carter that the U.S. position opposed North Korea's reprocessing even with IAEA inspectors monitoring the procedure.) Carter did not pursue the issue further at this meeting, and neither did the North Koreans.

Finally, the discussion turned to Carter's upcoming CNN interview to announce his agreement with Kim Il Sung. Kang urged Carter to say only that North Korea had agreed to keep the inspectors and equipment in place and that the United States had agreed to the third round of talks with no preconditions. To stop Kang's continued haggling, Carter cut off further discussion. He said he would talk with Washington, write down what he and Kim Il Sung had agreed upon and go over it with Kang, and then appear on CNN. He thought but did not say that he would use the interview to pin down Kim Il Sung's commitments.[22] He rejected Kang's request that the interview be delayed until the morning so that he and his colleagues could have the evening to study the Carter text. Facing a still smiling but firm Jimmy Carter, Kang suggested that they proceed to the cultural program being presented in honor of the Carters. In the hallway outside the meeting room, Carter, with a grin, told Kang he now knew why he had a reputation for being a "tough negotiator." Kang grinned, as did his North Korean colleagues.

En route to the cultural performance, we stopped in the center of the shopping district and walked through a couple of department stores. Many well-dressed North Koreans were walking on the sidewalks and strolling through the stores, and many were making purchases from shelves that seemed well stocked. The following day, when I mentioned to Li Gun that I should like to buy a CD of popular North Korean music, he took me to the music section of one of the department stores; I made my purchase (with U.S. dollars) and, while I was there, several other shoppers appeared to buy CDs with North Korean currency. All members of our group were aware that we were seeing only what our North Korean escorts wanted us to see, and we had no opportunity to wander the streets on our own. Consequently, we could not say definitively whether what we were witnessing was a normal occurrence or an elaborately staged performance. If it were the latter, however, the large cast of shoppers performed flawlessly. At the time, President and Mrs. Carter and I did not think we were witnessing a charade. Nancy Konigsmark was more skeptical, and Eason Jordan told me later that he thought there were more people on the street than he had seen during his visit to Pyongyang two months earlier. I became more confident of my own earlier assessment when I spoke recently with Ken Quinones, who had visited Pyongyang and this shopping area a number of times between December 1992 and August 2002. In his view, since we were there in June, when the weather was pleasant, and late in the afternoon, when most of the offices were closed, he thought it highly likely that we were observing a normal scene on the streets and in the shops, and that the business transactions we saw were the real thing.

As we walked along the streets, we were somewhat removed from our North Korean handlers and their electronic bugs. I took this opportunity to tell Carter about Ambassador Laney's anxiety about decisions that would be taken that day in Washington to augment U.S. military forces on the peninsula and how that increase in personnel and equipment might increase the risk of military confrontation. Carter grasped immediately the seriousness of the White House meeting and the strong likelihood that the decisions taken would escalate the crisis. But he thought that his interview on CNN later that evening would have a positive influence on the outcome of that White House meeting.

Foreign Minister Kim Yong Nam welcomed Carter and his party as we arrived at the Cultural Palace. We were escorted to the first row of a large auditorium filled with people. In the few minutes before the performance, the foreign minister told Carter that his meeting earlier in the day with Kim Il Sung was an "important thing for our lives." Then he gave his version of the paean we repeatedly heard in North Korea. He said there was no field in which the "Great Leader" did not excel, and the "Dear Leader" followed the cause pioneered by his father.[23] Mrs. Carter noticed that the 60,000-square-meter Cultural Palace featured a plaque announcing that it had been designed and engineered by the "Dear Leader."

The cultural program proved to be spectacular. A gigantic cast of singers and dancers, dressed in elaborate costumes, often twirling flags, put on one extraordinary number after another. Some depicted the historic victories of their nation; others, the strong national resolve; still others, folk dances and songs from various parts of the country. On a few occasions, the performers broke into traditional American folk melodies and encouraged the Carter entourage to join in. Our North Korean hosts were most hospitable, and everyone in our group enjoyed the evening. But we were all keenly aware, as Mrs. Carter would record in her notes of the trip, that in that evening's performance, and the others we witnessed the next day, many of the songs and dances praised the "Great Leader and 'our country, which is the best.'" She wrote: "The people have a reverence for The Great Leader that is unsurpassed. It is like a religious commitment to honor him and spend their lives working for him and their country. . . . They—the society, the leaders—are self-contained and seemingly neither need nor want any outside help or interference."[24]

The curtain fell too soon, and it was back to work. Carter wrote out his agreement with Kim Il Sung. He then placed his call to Washington on the open telephone line, knowing well, as would Bob Gallucci when he took the call in the anteroom of the White House's West Wing Office, that the conversation would be overheard and taped. Carter's notes, which he had written down for his conversation with Gallucci, follow:

Agreement with Kim Il Sung:

Inspectors will remain at nuclear site and all surveillance equipment will be maintained in operation until U.S.-N.K. bilateral talks can take place to resolve the nuclear issue, including transparency of the entire nuclear program. What NK wants is US support for the acquisition of light water reactor and assurance that NK will not be subject to nuclear threat in this area. If this is done, NK will stay in NPT, and unique status can be removed. I made it plain that U.S. would support this light water reactor, but it and financing would have to come from other countries or international organizations. Third round talks will be designed to resolve total transparency issue.

Kang Sok Ju said that until this morning, decision had been made to expel all observers and turn off surveillance equipment. Activities of US and IAEA had made this necessary. Now, would comply with commitments of Kim Il Sung.

With Kang, made clear that this included the program since its inception. Only two provisos are that US will support light water reactor with financing and acquisition from other sources and that adequate assurance of denuclearization is forged, based on the N-S declaration and right of mutual inspection of military bases. NK also requested that US assist in working out mutual arrangement with IAEA. They have some compromise proposals to assure that assessment of 5 MW[e] fuel rods can be done satisfactorily.

NK wants simultaneous steps of cooperation, as discussed earlier: U.S. suspend Team Spirit '94; continuity of safeguards; N-S Korea resume talks at the working level, with special envoys; a date set for the third round. Inspection of two sites unthinkable except as part of package, including some assurance re light reactor and removal of nuclear threat against NK.

I need U.S. willingness to discuss these items with NK.[25]

On the back of his paper, Carter had listed key points related to his meeting with Kim Il Sung for possible reference during the conversation: "My Status; Inspectors Surveillance; Total Transparent; US: Light

H2O [light water reactor], No Nuclear Use; Freeze Nuke Program during Good Faith Talks; No Commit re Permanent except with Lt H2O; If Terms Honored, Sanctions in Abeyance; Not Auth. to Speak for US."[26]

Carter's call went through to Washington at 10:20 P.M. Pyongyang time (9:20 A.M. Washington time). After a short time, Bob Gallucci came on the phone. Using the notes he had prepared, Carter briefed him on his conversation. He emphasized that Kim Il Sung had agreed to freeze the North Korean nuclear program for the duration of the third round of talks, the purpose of which would be to resolve the outstanding nuclear questions. He elaborated that the North Koreans believed they could be subject to a nuclear attack from the United States and South Korea. He said that Kim Il Sung was pleased that the United States might work out a denuclearization of the peninsula. Carter told Gallucci that he was going to announce his agreement with Kim Il Sung to "help calm hysteria."[27] Carter later would write that after he was told that the high-level meeting underway in the White House would consider his report, he notified Gallucci of his plan to give CNN an interview, but to refrain from speaking for the U.S. government, and Gallucci raised no objection.[28]

Although Carter did not know it at the time, his report, when conveyed by Gallucci to President Clinton and his senior foreign policy advisers, set off an uproar. The president, vice president, and top officials from the NSC, State, and Defense had been meeting in the West Wing of the White House for over an hour to decide on next steps for dealing with the North Korean crisis. Clinton had agreed with his advisers to intensify the U.S. campaign to get the UN Security Council to adopt economic sanctions against North Korea. The officials had begun discussing options for augmenting U.S. military forces and equipment in South Korea, up to 50,000 troops, as a complement to the sanctions effort, aware that General Luck and Ambassador Laney had strong concerns that augmentation would be interpreted by North Korea as a build-up to a possible attack.[29] They were, in effect, contemplating possible military action.

The Carter message quickly shifted the conversation, first to expressions of disbelief and then to condemnation of the former president's audacity, which at least one participant suggested approached treason. Gallucci suffered silently the dismaying looks of his colleagues when he admitted that he had not tried to talk Carter out of appearing on CNN. Dejected, irritated, and curious, the disgruntled group gathered around the television screen to watch the Carter pronouncements from Pyongyang.[30]

CHAPTER 9

Raising the Ante

aving received no indication from his talk with Gallucci of how Washington might react to his agreement with Kim Il Sung, Carter proceeded with the interview on CNN. He knew that in doing so, he would be handing Washington, Pyongyang, and Seoul, as well as the IAEA and the UN, a fait accompli. Although each government would still have the option of rejecting the points out of hand, CNN's world-wide audience would ensure that public pressure would not allow the various responsible parties to ignore or give short shrift to his agreement with the North Korean dictator.[1]

Decision made, Carter closeted with Kang Sok Ju at 11:40 P.M. He showed Kang the notes he had made for the presentation on CNN, which closely paralleled what he had read to Gallucci. Despite his appeals to Kang Sok Ju to join him in the television interview, the North Korean official declined. The two men rehashed some of the same issues they had discussed during the afternoon meeting. Kang tried to limit the timeframe for which the IAEA inspectors would be permitted to remain in Yongbyon. Carter overruled him by asserting that Kim Il Sung had not put a time limit on the inspectors' stay in the country; they would remain throughout the good faith effort to resolve the nuclear issues. Kang tried again to get Carter to postpone his presentation until the next morning. Carter refused; there was no reason to wait because he would merely be repeating what Kim Il Sung and he had agreed upon.[2] At this moment, the bureaucrats in Washington and Pyongyang were united on one point. They would have preferred for Carter's public press conference to be delayed until their respective experts could have vetted and probably modified his remarks.[3]

Throughout the day, Mike Chinoy had reported to CNN's global audience about Carter's meetings. He had used and commented on the film clips shot at the beginning of the session with Kim Il Sung and those shot when Carter left the conference room and chatted briefly with Eason Jordan. But the big moment would be the Carter interview; this is when he would inform the world about the contents of his conversation with the North Korean leader. Eason and Mitch Farkas had converted a large room in the guest house where we were staying into a makeshift recording studio. Shortly before midnight in Pyongyang, Carter took his seat on a yellow-cushioned chair in the middle of the room facing Eason, who would ask the questions, and Mitch, who was manning the camera. The CNN crew intended to rush the videotape of the interview to the North Korean television studio, where it would be transmitted around the world by satellite.

Asked whether he had anything to report, Carter said that after his conversation with President Kim Il Sung, he understood more clearly the North Korean position and their proposals for alleviating the current crisis. The North Koreans had three key interests: to replace their graphite reactors with light water reactors, to get assurances against nuclear attack, and to engage in early talks with the United States, where Kim Il Sung promised that "North Korea would do everything possible to resolve all of the outstanding issues related to the nuclear question." With the promise of good faith talks with the United States, North Korea would allow the IAEA inspectors to stay on site and their surveillance equipment would not be interrupted. North Korea's withdrawal from the IAEA while remaining a member of the NPT should cause no problem since forty NPT nations were not members of the IAEA. Carter stated that he had relayed this information to Washington a few minutes earlier, and that he "hoped and expected" it would be considered seriously. He could not, of course, know what Washington's decision would be.

When the cameras shut down, Carter was all smiles. The North Korean officials who were there, including Kang Sok Ju, congratulated him, as did members of his team. When others moved away, I walked over to Carter, shook his hand, and said, "Great job." He beamed. "That killed the sanctions resolution," he said. "The Chinese will never permit it to get out of the Security Council now."

I knew that Carter was right. But I worried about his saying so out loud, relieved that I alone had heard what he said—or so I thought. I hoped that it did not become public. Carter had admitted to doing what his critics, both within and outside the administration, were accusing him of doing—encouraging actions as a civilian that contravened official tactics if not the policy itself. In Carter's mind, however, the U.S. policy—publicly stated as well as privately held—was to prevent North Korea from acquiring nuclear weapons and to resolve the current nuclear crisis peacefully. Sanctions were a tactic being used as a last resort—one that he was convinced would be highly detrimental to achieving the policy objectives. But that distinction could easily be lost in the heated atmosphere of Washington politics. At one point during the next week, when I was advising him not to criticize the administration in public interviews—despite oft repeated negative press stories about him that were sourced to "unnamed" administration officials, I told him that I had refrained from telling anyone what he had told me about his interview's impact on the Chinese attitude toward sanctions because his statement would be interpreted as his undercutting U.S. policy. He said he believed in being more open with the press than I did; but then he added that, perhaps on that issue, I might be right. My discretion actually made little difference. I would learn years later when reading Lee Sigal's book that Carter must have also told someone else the same thing.

As the CNN men packed away their equipment, we said goodnight to the North Korean officials and went to our respective rooms, hoping for several hours of deep sleep. President and Mrs. Carter, tired from the long day, quickly changed into their nightclothes. They were flossing their teeth when they were told that Eason Jordan was outside the door requesting to see President Carter. When admitted, Jordan, embarrassed, explained that he had just learned that the North Korean television station had closed for the night and the taped interview could not be transmitted until the morning. He urged Carter to do a phone interview, saying that CNN would be able to broadcast the oral interview immediately to its stations around the world. Carter was initially reluctant, and Jordan sensed that he was irritated. But after a few moments, Carter agreed, reasoning that if his deal with Kim Il Sung was not quickly made public, the subordinates of the North Korean president might try to persuade him to revise his position.

When Jordan received Carter's assent, he rousted Chinoy and Farkas from the hotel bar, where they had ordered a pizza, telling them to come immediately to the presidential guest house,[4] and then he called Atlanta. CNN was soon ready to roll. Donna Kelly, CNN anchor and moderator, moved before the cameras in the Atlanta studio. The questioners, Wolf Blitzer, Ralph Begleiter, and Judy Woodruff, did the same in Washington. Tom Johnson, president and CEO of CNN, stood in the editing room in Atlanta, earphones on and mike at his lips, prepared to orchestrate the interview, and Jimmy Carter came into the room where the CNN crew had established the telephone linkup by satellite, sat down, and cradled the phone against his chin. In the United States and around the world, the CNN interviewers would be shown asking their questions, and a picture of President Carter would appear on the screen as his answers came back by telephone.[5] This interview, which began at 12:27 A.M. on June 17 in Pyongyang (11:27 A.M. on June 16 in Washington) lasted much longer and contained much more information than the one done earlier before the camera; CNN never aired the previous interview.

Donna Kelley began by asking Carter whether he had progress to report. Replying yes, Carter set the context. He said that he had met with South Korean officials, including President Kim Young Sam, and then come to Pyongyang to meet with President Kim Il Sung, his foreign minister, and his chief nuclear negotiator. At the meeting this morning, he and Kim Il Sung had "resolved two or three major points." First, the North Korean president had agreed to keep the IAEA inspectors in place and to guarantee that the surveillance equipment would remain working, a commitment that would permit a "constant monitoring of the status of the fuel rods that [had] just recently been removed." This decision reversed the North Korean position to expel the inspectors. They would now stay as long as "good faith efforts" were being made "jointly between the United States and North Korea to resolve the entire nuclear problem."[6]

Carter said the North Koreans had two desires that were shared by the United States: First, they would like to shift their entire nuclear program to light water-moderated reactors. The fuel for these reactors would have "to be refined," and this could "only be done in another country."[7] Moreover, light water reactors did not produce as easily as graphite reactors the high-grade plutonium that was used in nuclear weapons. Second, the North Korean leaders wanted a denuclearized Korean peninsula and were seeking mutual, official declaration that no nuclear weapons would be "deployed or used against anyone in this entire Korean peninsula." Third, the peaceful resolution of these matters and other more technical ones depended on the resumption of talks between the United States and North Korea. Carter said that he had relayed this information to administration officials in Washington, and they would have to "make a decision about what to do." "I'm not authorized to speak for them, but I look upon this commitment of President Kim Il Sung as being a very important and very positive step toward the alleviation of the crisis."

Carter confirmed that he had also talked with North Korean officials about closer bilateral economic and diplomatic ties between the United States and North Korea, but he made clear that such ties were not a condition for North Korea's keeping the international inspectors in place and dealing with all nuclear issues in the context of resumed bilateral talks. If the nuclear issues could be resolved, he thought both countries would favor movement on the economic and diplomatic fronts. Despite World War II, the United States now considered Germany, Japan, and Italy among its best friends; it had even taken recent steps to begin normalizing relations with North Vietnam.

When asked whether North Korea would let the IAEA inspect the fuel rods discharged from its 5 MWe reactor, Carter said that North Korea had agreed that all aspects of its nuclear program would be discussed in "good faith talks" with the United States. The word being used in his talks on nuclear issues was "transparency"—"so that a full accounting can be made of all of the plutonium that might have been separated by North Korea." The North Koreans had never before agreed to such comprehensive discussions on their nuclear program.

Carter said that North Korea had not withdrawn from the NPT, but it was not currently in "full status" as a member. Its objective, however, was to return to full NPT status. He did not expect North Korea to rejoin the IAEA.

Ralph Begleiter, the CNN world affairs correspondent, asked whether there had been any discussion of the North Koreans freezing the operation of the reprocessing plant that was under construction, or the means that had been used earlier to reprocess some nuclear waste. This was critical to the consideration going on in Washington. Carter answered yes, and described the context for how North Korea looked at this issue. It could not afford to scrap its nuclear program without modernizing its plant; it was willing to dismantle its present graphite-moderated operation if it could get a light water reactor. Carter said that he had explained that the United States could neither fund nor supply equipment for such a reactor, but the technology was available from several other countries. The North Koreans would want the United States to help them "find a legitimate capability for shifting completely away from the graphite-moderated technology to the light water-moderated technology."

What next steps did Carter envisage, assuming some type of freeze took place? He said that the North Koreans wanted to resume their bilateral talks with the United States, that is, to begin the delayed third round of discussions, without any preconditions. But that decision, Carter emphasized again, would be made in Washington, not by him; he was making this trip as a private citizen representing The Carter Center. He hoped that higher-level discussions between the United States and North Korea might take place, but the issue now for Washington was whether to let the already constituted delegations commence their third round of talks.[8]

Carter said that the North Korean nuclear experts were convinced that they had a feasible plan for assessing the previous use of the fuel rods, which the IAEA disputed. They claimed to have identified every rod that had been discharged from the reactor and asserted that they could place it in the exact spot in the reactor core from which it was withdrawn. Carter, noting that he had earlier been a nuclear engineer under Admiral Hyman Rickover, said he could not personally make a judgment on the North Korean proposal since he had not studied those issues for more than forty years.

When asked whether the United States and its supporters in the United Nations should withdraw the economic sanctions against North Korea, Carter said he hoped they would:

> The reason I came over here was to try to prevent an irreconcilable mistake and one that would permanently isolate North Korea and prevent any resolution of this very important issue in peaceful terms. So my hope is that everyone will look on this development [the decisions of Kim Il Sung] in a positive way. Obviously, there's a great lack of trust and I think only through direct, good faith, sincere, sustained talks—primarily between the United States and North Korea—can we hope to have the success that made me come over here with an element of hope.

He expressed another hope toward the end of the interview—"that in the future, when we can eliminate the distrust and get over the [current] crisis stage that there would be, you know, normal visitations back and forth between private citizens and high officials and normal trade relations, those kinds of things, [that] will help to prevent this sort of crisis arising again."

Closing the interview, Carter said he looked forward to returning to the United States and sharing additional information and impressions with American officials. One matter on his mind, to which he alluded in his interview, was that Kim Il Sung made the key policy decisions in North Korea and, despite his age of eighty-two, he remained "extremely sharp and surprisingly well versed" on the issues raised. Carter wanted to be sure that Washington understood that the son, Kim Jong Il, was not in charge.

Carter was pleased with his CNN interview, but the senior national security officials in Washington were infuriated. Carter had told the world via CNN about his agreement with Kim Il Sung before he had personally briefed President Clinton and his advisers and given them time to reflect on its meaning and ramifications. Despite their insistence prior to the trip that Carter was not an administration emissary, they expected—correctly—that their political critics would have a field day and allege Clinton/Carter collusion when they wanted to attack the substance of Carter's mediation effort and a Carter foreign policy insurgency when they wanted to charge the Clinton administration with incompetence. They also recoiled at Carter's public criticism of UN sanctions, which undercut the administration's principal vehicle for trying to force North Korea to scrap its nuclear program.[9] Intemperate remarks could be expected, and they occurred—before President Clinton and Vice President Gore told the administration officials watching the Carter interview to focus on how to advance U.S. policy in light of the developments in Pyongyang.

Surprisingly, their general consensus was that Carter had achieved little, if anything, that was significant. One official groused that Carter had reported nothing new; another argued that Carter's restatement of old North Korean demands did not make them new ones. The group thought Carter's only useful comment had been his report that North Korea had agreed to keep the IAEA inspectors in place. Given the urgency Secretary of State Christopher had placed on this issue three days earlier in his call to Carter in Seoul, it was interesting that this matter did not seem particularly important now. An even more significant achievement by Carter had been Kim Il Sung's commitment to freeze the North Korean nuclear program for the duration of the third round of talks, subject, of course, to Washington's approval of the talks. How could this not be considered a new and potentially decisive development? The officials in the White House meeting must have recognized the importance of the freeze because they decided to "up the ante" and redefine the proffered freeze. The new administration position, formulated after the Carter interview, was that the North Korean "freeze of its nuclear program" must include specific commitments for "no reprocessing" and for "no refueling" of the 5 MWe reactor as preconditions for the third round of talks as well as a North Korean commitment to allow the IAEA inspectors and equipment to carry out their monitoring responsibilities. This condition of not refueling the reactor had been discussed among administration officials in the past, but it had never been raised with the North Koreans because it went beyond North Korea's obligations under the NPT and would, it had been thought in Washington, be rejected by Pyongyang. Stanley Roth, the NSC's senior official for Asian affairs, suggested adding the "no refueling" provision, and Gallucci, Poneman, and Leon Fuerth, foreign policy adviser to Vice President Gore, closeted to draft the press release and the guidance that would subsequently be called to Carter. Through these actions, the administration thought it could "pocket the good elements in Carter's CNN interview," put a Clinton stamp on the outcome by requiring North Korea to neither produce nor separate plutonium with its more stringent definition of the freeze, and gain international support for the UN sanctions resolution if the gambit failed.[10]

Because of his past personal relationship with Carter, Tony Lake was chosen to deliver the tough message to the former president that the administration had "upped the ante" for agreeing to the third round of bilateral talks. Lake contacted CNN and asked that its team in Pyongyang tell Carter to call him. Eason Jordan notified Carter of Lake's message after his telephone interview ended. Shortly thereafter, Nancy Konigsmark began trying to place the call. She encountered problems in getting the call to go through even though it was on an open—and certainly tapped—line. Finally, the connection was made. Carter and Lake talked briefly. Lake told Carter that the administration was studying what he had said in the CNN interview and asked him to call again in an hour. Washington wanted to get its reaction to him before his second meeting with Kim Il Sung. Carter hung up and went to bed.

During the intervening period, the Washington officials worked and reworked the talking points Lake would use when he spoke the second time with Carter. After two hours, the talking point paper was generally ready, but then it was decided that South Korea, Japan, and some European allies needed to be consulted before the official response was communicated.[11]

Nancy placed a second call around 3:00 A.M. Korean time and woke Carter when she was told that Lake was coming to the phone. A sleepy Carter waited for several minutes on the phone before a secretary informed him that Lake had passed word to call again in two more hours. Carter stomped back to his room, disgusted with being wakened with no one in Washington ready to talk with him. Around 5:30 A.M. the White House's pivotal call shattered the stillness. Nancy tapped on the former president's bedroom door. Carter emerged almost instantly and took the phone.

Not surprisingly, the conversation quickly became testy. Lake read to Carter the administration's carefully crafted position, including the explicit conditions that the North Korean nuclear freeze would have to contain commitments not to reprocess the nuclear fuel and not to refuel the 5 MWe reactor. Even though he assumed the line was tapped, Carter argued that these provisions were not included in his Washington briefings, nor in the talking point paper that he read to Gallucci before leaving Plains. In his own mind, Carter thought Kim Il Sung's agreement to freeze the North Korean nuclear program probably included reprocessing, despite his having said that reprocessing under IAEA safeguards was permitted under the NPT. Carter was much less certain about whether Kim Il Sung had meant to include refueling in his freeze. Moreover, with the afternoon meeting with Kang Sok Ju and his colleagues still fresh on his mind, Carter did not want to reopen the nuclear issue with Kim Il Sung and give the North Korean leader's subordinates a new opportunity to urge him to take a tougher position. Carter also objected to the U.S. position on continuing the campaign for sanctions. He thought Lake had agreed to reconsider some of the wording on points he raised, but Lake apparently did not come away with the same impression. In any event, the substance of the points was not revised. Both Carter and Lake were angry when they hung up their phones.[12]

More than a decade later, reflecting back on the conversation, Lake told me that his firm position on the phone had reflected two primary considerations: to make clear to Carter that he had not gone as far with Kim Il Sung as the administration's current position demanded, and, since he assumed the North Koreans were listening in on the conversation, to ensure that the Pyongyang leadership understood three conditions the United States insisted upon for restarting bilateral talks.[13] For his part, Carter was convinced that he had accurately conveyed to Kim Il Sung the U.S. position as explained to him in Plains and Washington and that his agreement with Kim Il Sung provided the administration with a means to end the nuclear crisis peacefully. He resented the toughening of the U.S. position and worried that it might cause the deal he had negotiated to come unstuck.

Shortly after Lake's phone call with Carter, President Clinton met with the White House press corps to explain the administration's position on the nuclear freeze (without saying that it was raising the bar), and after he left, Bob Gallucci elaborated further for the reporters. Neither the president nor his negotiator with North Korea directly criticized Carter. They instead insisted that the U.S. government must receive a full explanation of the North Korean position through diplomatic channels before it could take a definitive view.

Clinton read the statement crafted by his subordinates. His administration had been consulting with its allies and friends about imposing sanctions on North Korea because of its refusal to allow "full inspection of its nuclear program." Today, in discussions with Carter, the North Koreans may have offered new steps to "resolve the international community's concerns." He said that North Korea had agreed to allow the IAEA inspectors and equipment to remain in place and had indicated its desire to replace its graphite-moderated reactors with "light water technology that is more resistant to nuclear proliferation." If North Korea was "genuinely and verifiably prepared to freeze its nuclear program while [bilateral] talks go on," Clinton said, "then we [United States] would be willing to resume high-level talks." But until such assurances had been received, the United States would continue its consultations on sanctions.[14] Gallucci's statement tracked closely that of the president except he defined explicitly the administration's new definition of the North Korean freeze.[15]

Clinton and Gallucci deftly handled the reporters' questions. Clinton said that the administration would be able to determine whether North Korea froze its nuclear program while new talks were being conducted— if such talks were authorized after Carter's additional talks in Pyongyang and a subsequent diplomatic exchange between the two governments. If the North Koreans had changed their position to one on which "we can honorably resume negotiations," the president said, then undertaking such talks would not be an "inappropriate delay." Gallucci said that the U.S. objective was not to seek sanctions; seeking sanctions was a means to get the North Koreans to the table to resolve the issue. If the North Koreans spelled out in a diplomatic message that it would suspend reprocessing, suspend refueling, and maintain safeguards, an adequate basis for resuming the bilateral dialogue would be established.

Both officials faced questions about why the administration was keeping considerable distance between Carter and itself. Clinton said that he

intended to debrief Carter upon his return, noting that he had talked with
him before he departed. Carter was invited to North Korea as a private
citizen representing The Carter Center, and during his visit they had
"gotten some information there that might not have otherwise been the
case." Yet the official position of the United States can be put forward
only by the people "who are ultimately in charge of doing that." Clinton
said that he believed Carter would agree with the way he had characterized the former president's role. Gallucci, when chided about why he was
not happier about what Carter had accomplished, said he wanted to have
more definitive information before responding "with any more joy." Gallucci admitted that the North Korean commitment to allow the inspectors to stay in place was a *new* (author's emphasis) development. Gallucci
confirmed that the issue of substituting light water reactors for North
Korea's graphite-moderated reactors had been discussed at the U.S.-
North Korean talks in July 1993, and that the United States had committed itself to helping bring that about as part of an ultimate settlement.
Gallucci dodged the question of whether the administration had raised
the bar for the negotiations by saying that the United States was now stating what would be required for the bilateral dialogue to resume.[16]

Back in Pyongyang, not long after Carter had spoken with Lake, Nancy
Konigsmark received a call from her North Korean contact inviting the
Carter party to accompany Kim Il Sung and his wife for a cruise on the
official yacht down the Taedong River, which flowed south from Pyongyang to the sea. Carter quickly assented to the invitation. Nancy mentioned the cruise to Dick Christenson and me as we breakfasted together.
This invitation could only be interpreted as a demonstration of Kim Il
Sung's satisfaction with the Carter visit. It would mean that the Carters
and the North Korean president and his wife would spend several hours
together in an informal and relaxed atmosphere. Since the invitation came
after the Carter-Lake call, we assumed that the North Korean leader had
reviewed a transcript of the taped call and had not been upset by it.

Shortly before 9:00 A.M., the Carter team left the guesthouse and were
driven to the pier where the presidential yacht was anchored. We were
greeted by Kim Il Sung and his wife, Kim Song Ae, who seldom appeared

in public.[17] The second wife of the North Korean leader, she reportedly was an active party member who had considerable influence on her husband. He had married her in 1962. His first wife, Kim Chong Suk, the mother of Kim Jong Il, had been a revolutionary colleague during the war with the Japanese, and a strong supporter and adviser until her death during childbirth in 1949.

While the rest of us were directed to the rear of the yacht, the Carters and the Kims went to the office at the front for a brief conversation and refreshments. Eason Jordan and his cameraman, along with North Korean media representatives, were permitted to shoot a small amount of footage before they were escorted off the yacht to allow the Kims and the Carters to chat privately. The CNN film recorded Carter telling Kim Il Sung that the U.S. government had stopped the sanction activities at the UN. He also said the United States would be prepared to schedule the third round of bilateral talks at an early time and would discuss, among other things, U.S. support for helping North Korea obtain a light water reactor and a declaration against the use of nuclear weapons on the Korean Peninsula. After the media personnel had left, Carter made sure the North Korean president understood that his earlier remarks about sanctions and the convening of new bilateral talks represented his personal view of what he thought would happen, but he could not speak for the U.S. government. He also clarified that he expected the sanctions move in New York to be held in abeyance (and defined abeyance for the North Korean interpreter) rather than terminated. Unfortunately, the CNN tape did not contain these elaborations, and subsequently Carter would regret his careless use of words in the filmed portion of the conversation.

When CNN broadcast the Carter comments on its global network, the already disgruntled administration officials in Washington reacted vehemently. Twelve hours earlier, Carter had embarrassed the Clinton team by announcing his deal with Kim Il Sung without prior approval from Washington; now he seemed to be pronouncing unilaterally a change in U.S. foreign policy. Matters were made worse by press attacks that criticized the administration for vacillation and timidity on the matter of sanctions.[18] In a private conversation several years later, Bob Gallucci would refer to Carter's having put Clinton in a "box," a position, he said, no sitting president could find acceptable.[19] In response to the CNN report, the White House press secretary said that the effort to reach UN agreement on sanctions was continuing, and an irritated President Clinton made the same point a few hours later.[20] But the White House press statement also repeated its earlier point about the U.S. government's willingness to engage in the third round of talks if North Korea confirmed in diplomatic channels that its announced nuclear freeze included no reprocessing and no refueling.[21]

Neither Carter nor his team members learned of this diplomatic faux pas and the intense administration reaction until we crossed back over the DMZ the following day.

Following their short conversation, the Kims and the Carters joined the rest of us. Then the cruise began, and we relaxed, talked, and enjoyed the scenery. The flat land of the city with its towering buildings and monuments gave way to rolling hills as we motored south toward the sea. The fields were green, and the crops looked healthy, probably the result of the extensive irrigation channels from the river. Mrs. Kim took particular pride in explaining to Mrs. Carter how her husband had masterminded the agricultural advances that we were viewing. According to Mrs. Kim, her commitment to *Juche* frequently announcing itself, the entire country had been remade. They (referring at times to the party, the Workers' Party; at times to the North Korean people) planned and built the cities; the soldiers did all of the construction. She insisted that the soldiers "worked for peace, not war." She claimed they could construct the houses required for workers in a community within days. She was not bothered by consistency. On one occasion, Mrs. Carter commented on the "planted" trees along the roadsides that were visible from the yacht; Mrs. Kim said that their country was "so great" that the trees were growing naturally. Later, Mrs. Carter remarked that the plants up a steep bank were beautiful, "growing naturally." Mrs. Kim instead said that they had "planned and designed the hillside"![22]

Sailing alongside of us at a respectable distance was a rented cruiser containing the CNN crew. They waved to us, and as we suspected, they were filming.

During the relaxed sailing, I snapped a number of photographs; no one complained or suggested that I not do so. I took several of Kim Il Sung, who posed without inhibition or apparent concern that my photos might show the large benign tumor on the back right side of his neck. The official North Korean photographers clearly had different marching orders. They chose their camera angles carefully to ensure that the tumor was not revealed in their photos—as the photos later presented to the Carters demonstrated.

After about an hour, the Carters and the Kims moved up to the second-floor suite for further conversations. I did not think others would be allowed in the room, but Dick Christenson, who had been blocked at the door, prodded me to try to get in. I asked to join the two couples, seeing at the same time that Kang Sok Ju was in the suite along with a North Korean interpreter. When he saw me, Carter intervened with the North Korean sailors guarding the access into the suite and invited me in.

The conversation was animated and friendly. Carter said that he had talked with Washington, knowing that Kim Il Sung knew of the conversation. Kim expressed appreciation that President Clinton had announced that high-level talks between the United States and North Korea would take place and said that he was indebted to President Carter for his efforts; Carter expressed gratitude for Kim's desire to resolve the nuclear problem in a peaceful way. Carter said that there would be difficult arguments ahead on the issues, and he invited Kim to call on him, if he were needed, to help resolve future problems. Kim said he would keep Carter informed, and Carter said he would make a personal report to President Clinton and other U.S. leaders.[23]

Kim told Carter that he had looked forward to meeting him; had they met sooner, bilateral relations would have improved much earlier. Some people on both sides opposed improved relations and purposefully distorted the issues. He had changed his schedule today so that he could get to know Carter better.

Carter asked permission to raise two items of business. He said he had not explicitly mentioned reprocessing the previous day. If the bilateral talks went well and arrangements were worked out for the light water reactors, he would urge that North Korea not reprocess its spent fuel rods. He asked for an answer from President Kim after the latter had had time to consult with his ministers. Kim promised to provide the answer later, noting that he was not an expert on nuclear matters.

Subsequently, shortly before the group disembarked, Carter pressed Kang strongly on this issue, emphasizing that reprocessing could cause major problems and was not necessary. Kang said he understood the seriousness of this matter and promised not to reprocess for as long as possible. He repeated what he had told us the day before—that his experts were insisting that reprocessing had to be done within three months because of the corrosion of the rods. Carter told him that there were alternatives to reprocessing, such as burying the rods, and Kang admitted that he did not know that alternatives existed. When Carter left to rejoin the Kims, I remained with Kang and urged that he and Gallucci get their technical experts together because U.S. experts maintained that the fuel rods could remain in the cooling ponds for as long as twelve months. He said he would do so.

Returning to the Kim-Carter conversation, Carter raised his second item of business—the recovery of the remains of American personnel killed during the Korean War and buried in North Korea. Carter requested Kim to allow joint U.S.-North Korean teams to search for the remains so that they could be returned to their families. Kim said that North Korean personnel had already handed over the remains of a hundred Americans. Carter said that the U.S. government knew where the remains of many U.S. troops were located; a joint team should go to these sites together. Kim said he would study Carter's proposal, but Carter persisted. He explained that U.S. maps depicted the locations where thousands of Americans were buried. "In the spirit of cooperation and friendship, let our people join the search. We would pay all of the expenses," he urged. The American people would greatly appreciate this "fine good-will gesture." Kim admitted that the U.S. maps would be helpful. He consulted briefly with Kang in Korean and said that if relations between the United States and North Korea improved, he would consider permitting joint survey teams. Carter did not let up. He urged Kim to take the initiative—as a unilateral voluntary act of friendship. Mrs. Carter added that this gesture would be positively received in the United States. Throughout the conversation, Mrs. Kim pressed her husband to accede to the request; she made clear her displeasure when he, after consulting with

Kang, had tied his approval to an improvement of bilateral relations. Cornered from three sides, Kim finally assented. "We will go together and unearth them together." Mrs. Kim beamed.

The growing rapport between the Carters and the Kims was evident. Carter told Kim Il Sung to let him know if problems arose with the Gallucci team in interpreting what they had agreed. Kim replied that if the relationship could create mutual confidence, all matters could be solved; everything could be settled by human effort. Carter said that they both wanted to build good will and trust.

The four felt comfortable enough to joke with each other. Carter mentioned that he had hoped to visit the nuclear reactor site at Yongbyon, but had been told that it was too far away to work into his schedule. Kim Il Sung, his eyes twinkling, bantered that he had never been there. When Carter said that he had been trained as a nuclear engineer, Kim Il Sung responded that his knowledge of nuclear matters was "zero." Smiling, Carter said he had told President Clinton [via his telephone conversation with Gallucci] that the North Korean president knew a great deal about graphite and light water reactors; hence, President Clinton thought Kim Il Sung was a nuclear expert. Mrs. Kim interjected into the light-hearted discussion that she and Kang Sok Ju assisted her husband on nuclear matters. All chuckled when Carter said that perhaps Kim Il Sung could talk of birds and fish and Kang Sok Ju could talk about nuclear matters. Instead, Kim Il Sung suggested that his guests sample his green-bean jelly, which was delicious.

Since the Carters had revealed their interest in fishing, Kim Il Sung suggested that on their next visit they would be taken to a good fishing place. "Now we are turning to serious matters," Carter observed. Mrs. Carter said that she had been told that trout was found in North Korea's cold mountain streams and the North Korean president said rainbow trout and char were quite plentiful. Carter said that sport fishing could offer an excellent economic opportunity for North Korea; many American fishermen, who now go to New Zealand, Argentina, and Australia to fish for trout, could be persuaded to come to North Korea. When Mikhail Gorbachev became friendly with the United States, Carter had organized an expedition to assess Russia's streams for fishing. Kim said the American fishermen should come to North Korea. He then provided an interesting bit of history. He said that prior to the Japanese occupation, Americans had developed Korean gold mines, and they had brought rainbow trout species with them. After World War II, when the Japanese were forced off of the Korean Peninsula, North Koreans began to kill the trout, associating them incorrectly with the Japanese. He had stopped the destruction of the fish and had instructed the people to breed the fish so that they would multiply. Carter said he had heard that when people complained about the trout, which had been released into North Korean streams, only to swim away to the south, Kim Il Sung had said that the trout would still be in Korea and would be caught by Koreans. Kim Il Sung nodded approvingly.

Mr. and Mrs. Kim said that they both liked to hunt. She had recently shot a boar; he had bagged two bears. They joked about each other, with her suggesting that she was the better shot and that he was reluctant to allow her to follow him on a hunt. Carter, whose repeated requests to other North Korean officials to meet Kim Jong Il had been greeted with silence, asked whether Kim Jong Il had time to fish and hunt. Kim Il Sung replied that his son's work with the party and military left little time for such activities. He had handed over responsibility for the military to his son two years before, when Kim Jong Il was fifty years old. But the father made it clear that he expected to remain as president for several years before passing on that responsibility to his son.

Carter then shifted the conversation to relations between the two Koreas and the possibility of a Korean summit meeting. Kim Il Sung, mentioning that Kim Young Sam had said in his inauguration address that he would like to meet the North Korean president, told Carter he would be prepared to meet his southern counterpart anytime and anywhere. It was time, Kim Il Sung said, "to let bygones be bygones." He asked Carter to try to arrange such a meeting, and Carter promised to raise the matter with Kim Young Sam. The North Korean leader also asked Carter to tell Kim Young Sam that he desired to see reunification as quickly as possible. The problems could be resolved only by the two of them meeting together; they should not be left to lower-ranking officials on both sides. He asked Carter to serve as a go-between with North and South Korea because Carter had achieved considerable success with his current visit.

Carter agreed that progress had been made, but emphasized that more needed to be done. He concurred that a mediator could play a key role in an inter-Korean dialogue, going back and forth between the two parties and talking with them in moderation. He mentioned that he had successfully applied this technique at the Camp David meeting between Israel and Egypt. Kim Il Sung said that Koreans wanted to see improved relations between North and South achieved in their lifetime. He told Carter to give Kim Young Sam a message: "Let us meet and shake hands together. All issues can be dealt with. Tell him I am waiting for him to meet me, and I am keeping my fingers crossed."

Kim, as he had the previous day, said his concept for reunification envisioned one nation and one people, two governments and two systems. The two governments would collaborate and build mutual confidence, and then all other issues could be solved. There would be a central chairman or rotating chairmanship between the two governments. However, if early implementation of these ideas seemed too fast to the other side, they could start by permitting an exchange of older people to see their families. Carter told Kim Il Sung that South Korea lacked confidence and trust in him and his proposals. When the North Korean president talked of reunification without outside interference, the South Korean leaders believed that his real intent was to force U.S. troops to leave the peninsula so that North Korea could attack South Korea with superior military forces. Kim Il Sung said that at a later stage, proportional reductions could gradually occur so that each army could eventually be reduced to 100,000 troops. Then the U.S. troops could also withdraw proportionally. He said this idea was on the agenda when Park Chung Hee (South Korea's ruler from 1961–1979) was in power. Carter suggested that because of South Korean suspicions, other things should probably be done before moving to Kim's ambitious idea of reducing troops on both sides. An example: Even though neither side was supposed to have weapons in the DMZ, both sides did. A first step might be to remove these weapons, and the next step might be to move troops on both sides back five to ten miles from the DMZ. Kim said he could agree to both of these proposals.

After about an hour, Kim Il Sung announced that it was time for a meal. Kang Sok Ju and I were ushered downstairs to eat with the other passengers. The Carters and the Kims remained in the stateroom for their meal.

Once the presidential yacht had docked, the gangplank was lowered to the pier, and the Americans and North Koreans disembarked. We walked in small groups up to the top of a small hill where we could view a five-mile-long dam, with sea locks, called the "West Sea Barrage," that had been constructed across the Taedong River to control flooding of crop land and to prevent the salt water of the Yellow Sea from flowing into the river water and spoiling the fresh water used for irrigation and industry. Kim Il Sung told the Carters that civilian engineers and officials had doubted that such a large dam could be built, but Kim Jong Il had put the military to work and the project was finished in record time. He cited statistics as to how many hectares could be irrigated, and how much electricity could be generated. Kim Il Sung, clearly proud of this accomplishment, insisted that the military had made it happen.

In this and in other conversations on the boat, the Carters were told that about half of North Korea's reputed army of a million people was used for civilian construction projects. President and Mrs. Kim insisted that the military was more efficient and more disciplined than civilian construction workers. Its duty included building as well as protecting the homeland. We had no way to evaluate the truth of these statements.

The observation building on the hill overlooking the barrage served also as a visitors' center. Like the other buildings we visited in North Korea, this one was also ornate and large, yet light and airy; it, too, was decorated with enormous murals depicting idealized scenes of nature and large statues of Kim Il Sung and Kim Jong Il. After a brief stop for refreshments, Carter presented to Kim Il Sung a copy of his book, *Talking Peace,* and the North Korean president gave the Carters a large picture, in which two pheasants amid green foliage were constructed from tiny colored shells, and an intricately carved silver dish. We were then escorted to cars that would drive us back to Pyongyang.

The return trip was desultory. There was little to say to our North Korean car companions other than to praise the dam and comment on how enjoyable the cruise had been. Many of them expressed amazement that Kim Il Sung had allocated so much time for his meetings with Carter.

Two separate meetings was very unusual, and one involving a cruise and several hours of association and conversation was extraordinary.

Later that afternoon, Foreign Minister Kim Yong Nam, Vice Foreign Minister Song Ho Kyong, and Vice Chairman of the Central Committee Ham Un Kon escorted the Carters and their team to the Mangyongdae School Children's Palace, which contained 2 million square feet of floor space. We were told that about 5,000 children came there each day after their regular school classes for instructions in such activities as swimming, music, and sewing. We first entered a room with an Olympic-sized swimming pool and witnessed small children engaged simultaneously in swimming races and diving from high towers. Mrs. Carter would later write that seeing "six-year-olds diving from ten meter towers in perfect form was breathtaking . . . and a little scary!" We also visited an accordion class, an embroidery class, and a musical performance where children ranging from five to fourteen years of age sang, danced, and played musical instruments like professionals. I think all of us agreed with Carter's assessment: It was "one of the most remarkable performances of young people's skill and talent of our lives."[24]

After returning to the guest house for a short rest, most of us joined Mrs. Carter to go shopping. We were taken to a government emporium where I purchased a beautiful celadon vase painted with storks frolicking among clouds, a gift for Linda.

After our shopping expedition, we requested a ride on the subway. We had heard that Pyongyang's subway system was the deepest in the world.[25] Even to a layman's eye, the North Korean expertise in tunneling was evident. The escalators to the subway train descended to great depths. We were told that some of the subway lines lay as deep as three hundred feet under the street surface. The subway cars looked new and well-maintained. We rode for several stops. We saw North Korean passengers, but there were plenty of empty seats on the car we entered. Even though it was around 5:30 P.M. on Friday evening, there was no sense of rush-hour traffic either on the subway or on the streets above. Yet the subway manager told Mrs. Carter that 500,000 people rode the subway every day. When Mrs. Carter raised the apparent disparity between what the subway manager had said and what we were witnessing, her interpreter, Choe Sonhee, said that masses of people going to work in the morning packed on the subway. The crowds were so large that a person got caught up in the swell and had to move with the crowd.[26] She did not explain how those masses got home at night.

The subway walls were also painted with large murals that glorified nature or the "Great Leader" and the "Dear Leader." Not only did these murals reinforce the almost God-like quality attached to Kim Il Sung and his son, they reinforced other government propaganda concerning the beauty of the country and the purported "superiority of North Korea over all other countries." The incessant message was that North Koreans enjoyed the most wonderful life in the world, thanks to the energy and commitment of the people and particularly to the wisdom and leadership of Kim Il Sung.

After we emerged from the underground caverns of the subway, our North Korean–supplied vehicles took us back to the guest house. We were exhausted. When Nancy Konigsmark and I neared our rooms in the guesthouse, we were told that North Korean doctors had just examined Dick Christenson, who had experienced heart palpitations. He proved to be okay, but overly tired. He had slept even less than I during the past seventy-two hours.

Members of our delegation found gifts from the North Korean government in their respective bedrooms. Each of us received a collage composed of numerous tiny colored shells arranged to create colorful scenes of nature in North Korea; mine showed a small river rambling through sheer bluffs. Additionally, a set of books allegedly written by Kim Il Sung, and a coffee table book showing stunning photographs of North Korea awaited each of us. Getting home with the items proved to be a challenge, but I, and I assume the others, managed.

After crawling into bed, I fell asleep immediately. It was a good thing. I knew the next day would start early and would be another full one. But I had no inkling of how shocking and frustrating it would prove to be.

At the DMZ in July 1993, President Clinton threatened to destroy North Korea if it developed nuclear weapons. (The Clinton Presidential Library)

President Carter and President Clinton discussed several times how to handle the growing nuclear crisis with North Korea, although they did not agree on an approach. (The Carter Center)

On June 15, 1994, President Carter received his last briefing before crossing into North Korea. The DMZ lies just beyond the "Freedom Pagoda," shown here. The Carter team would be the first group of non-Koreans to cross the DMZ from south to north and north to south since the Korean War. (Author's photo)

Prior to crossing, President Carter talks with U.S. troops stationed on the DMZ, the most heavily armed frontier in the world. (Author's photo)

President and Mrs. Carter pose for photographers with Ambassador James T. Laney (left) and Col. Forest Chilton (right) moments before crossing the DMZ. Within the Clinton administration, Laney had strongly urged negotiations with North Korea. (Author's photo)

The DMZ viewed from south to north. President Carter described stepping across that military barrier as a "bizarre and disturbing experience." (Author's photo)

President and Mrs. Carter received by Foreign Minister Kim Yong Nam in a reception room of the Mansudae Assembly Hall. The rooms in all the public buildings were enormous, decorated with large paintings depicting dramatic views of nature, and dwarfed any people in the room. (Author's photo)

President and Mrs. Carter with North Korean diplomat, Choe Sonhee, who served as Mrs. Carter's private interpreter during the trip. Carter had his own unofficial interpreter, U.S. diplomat Dick Christenson, who ensured that the official North Korean interpreters translated correctly. (Author's photo)

The North Korean government's guest house where the Carter party stayed during their three days in Pyongyang. (Author's photo)

President Carter and President Kim Il Sung greeting each other for the first time, prior to their historic June 16, 1994, meeting. (The Carter Center)

Photo-op of the Carter and Kim Il Sung delegations before the meeting. (l to r) Foreign Minister Kim Yong Nam, Dick Christenson, President Carter, President Kim Il Sung, Mrs. Carter, Nancy Konigsmark, and First Vice Foreign Minister Kang Sok Ju. (The Carter Center)

The meeting where President Carter and President Kim Il Sung negotiated the agreement that made possible the subsequent Agreed Framework that ended the 1994 nuclear crisis. The atmosphere was businesslike but not tense. It soon became apparent that President Kim Il Sung shared President Carter's desire to resolve the nuclear crisis peacefully and begin improving bilateral relations. (The Carter Center)

President Kim Il Sung's luncheon honoring the Carters following the June 16, 1994, breakthrough meeting. This meal, as with all of our official meals in Pyongyang, featured many courses of delicious food and elegant silverware, beyond the reach—and probably the imagination—of ordinary North Korean citizens. (The Carter Center)

A few hours later, Vice President Al Gore and senior national security officials of the Clinton administration watched on television Carter's CNN interview from Pyongyang. They were furious that he had told the world about his agreement with Kim Il Sung before personally briefing President Clinton and that he had indicated his personal opposition to U.N. sanctions against North Korea, for which the U.S. government was pressing in New York. (The Clinton Presidential Library)

President Clinton and other administration officials discuss how to respond to the Carter interview. (l to r) Dan Poneman, Bob Gallucci, Vice President Al Gore, President Clinton, and National Security Adviser Tony Lake (from rear). (The Clinton Presidential Library)

President Kim Il Sung welcomes President Carter aboard his presidential yacht, June 17, 1994, for a cruise down the Taedong River. (The Carter Center)

President Carter and President Kim relaxing on the North Korean presidential yacht. The photo captures the conviviality and rapport between the two men that Carter's detractors at home would later sharply criticize. (The Carter Center)

Mrs. Carter and Mrs. Kim on the presidential yacht. On this trip as in other Carter Center endeavors, Mrs. Carter served as her husband's closest adviser and confidant. (The Carter Center)

President Kim Il Sung and the author in discussion on the presidential yacht. As did others, I found him self-assured, interesting, and animated whether he was discussing affairs of state or his love of hunting. (The Carter Center)

The Carters and the Kims at the observation point of the five-mile dam ("barrage") that separates the Taedong River from the Yellow Sea. Both Kims relished talking about major construction achievements, which they credited to the military. (The Carter Center)

President and Mrs. Carter greet young North Korean musicians at the Mangyondae School Children's Palace after they and other children had performed. Throughout the trip, the North Korean hosts provided spectacular artistic performances and lavish receptions for the American visitors. (Author's photo)

President Carter and President Kim Il Sung exchange gifts before saying good-bye. Despite his negotiated agreement with the North Korean president, Carter would initially face considerable criticism when he returned to the United States. (The Carter Center)

President Carter and author. (The Carter Center)

CHAPTER 10

Back Across the DMZ

The alarm shattered the stillness. It was Saturday, June 18, 1994. I dressed quickly, ate breakfast, and along with other Carter team members lugged my suitcase, laptop computer, and gifts outside to the waiting cars. It was 6:00 A.M.

This time the two Carters rode together, Dick and Nancy rode in another car, and I was in the third. My regular escort, Li Gun, accompanied me, as did Choe Sonhee.

I questioned the two foreign office officials about themselves and about normal life in North Korea. Although they were guarded in their replies, they provided some information.

I learned that both had been intensively trained in the English language. After studying English in school, they had later spent considerable time in their government's language institute as part of their diplomatic training. Most of their official assignments had required them to use and improve their English.

They told me, as I had heard before, that North Koreans generally worked a six-day week. They said that they spent Sundays with their spouses and children, usually on picnics in public parks when the weather was nice. Both gave the impression of being close to their children and of putting a high value on family life.

Earlier, Choe Sonhee had told Mrs. Carter an interesting story. She said that her husband liked to go out at night and on Sunday to drink beer "with the boys." One night after dinner, she slammed a beer bottle on the kitchen table and said, "I'll drink beer with you; you don't need to go out." Since then, she and her husband have remained at the kitchen table after the evening meal and enjoyed their beer; their three-year-old son drinks juice. She told Mrs. Carter that this was "one of her best times." When Mrs. Carter asked her whether people had any say about what kind of work they would do, she said they could request specific kinds of jobs, but if such jobs were not available, they were required to do other things. She said, after a moment of hesitation, that she thought "most people [were] happy in their work."[1]

She explained that the two main religions in North Korea were Buddhism and Christianity. Men were the primary participants in worship services. With a six-day work week, the women usually stayed busy at home on Sundays. She volunteered that all men ought to be Christians so they would be better to their wives.[2]

As we sped along toward the DMZ and talked about family life, we largely avoided political subjects. However, my companions occasionally seemed to find it necessary to mention the greatness of the "Great Leader" and what he had done to make their lives more pleasant.

After stopping at the restaurant above the expressway for tea and coffee, we arrived at the North Korean side of the DMZ. We again climbed the steps of the Tongil House (Unification Hut), took refreshments, and Carter faced the North Korean press for the last time. The ubiquitous CNN crew was also there. Carter expressed appreciation to Kim Il Sung and the North Koreans for their hospitality. He said that he believed the agreement he and Kim Il Sung had reached, if honored and accepted by both sides, would open a new and more productive relationship between the two countries. To questions about whether the sanctions move would stop and new bilateral talks would begin, Carter said that he personally did not think sanctions were effective or necessary, but President Clinton would make the decision for the U.S. government. As correctly reported by the Pyongyang Korean Central

Broadcasting Network, he expressed the personal hope that his government would agree "that the crisis is over and the sanctions are no more necessary for consideration."[3] Carter praised the children's performance we had witnessed, and he expressed his and his wife's desire to return to North Korea in the future.

We said our good-byes to our North Korean hosts. Having earlier been admonished for delaying his departure from an event because I was talking with someone else, this time I quickly broke off my conversation when Carter moved toward the door.

The next few moments were exhilarating. The Carter party shook hands again outside the reception center as the cameras rolled. Then we all turned and faced the south. A North Korean military official took up his position beside Carter, and we walked together to the concrete stones that marked the DMZ. The North Korean military officer stopped when he was directly across from his American counterpart. He then in firm tones said that he was returning President Carter and his entourage to the custody of the American forces. After those words, we stepped across the concrete markers to where Ambassador Jim Laney was waiting with an outstretched hand. News networks from around the world recorded the historic scene. The Carter party became the first non-Koreans to cross the DMZ markers from both sides. It was 8:35 A.M. (Korean time).

Colonel Chilton escorted us into the U.S.-South Korean reception building. Carter explained the general outline of his agreement with Kim Il Sung, Kim Il Sung's strong interest in a Korean summit meeting, and his commitment to allow U.S. and North Korean teams to search for the remains of the American soldiers killed in the Korean War, news that Chilton particularly welcomed. Carter told Chilton to let him know if problems arose with the joint recovery effort.[4]

As Dick Christenson, Nancy Konigsmark, and I rode to Laney's residence, we talked about Carter's success. We were convinced that he had prevented a new Korean war. Since we had been able to say little while in North Korea, we used this time for rejoicing.

Our enthusiasm would have been much more restrained had we known what was taking place in the car in which Carter and Laney were riding. The standard Carter grin, projected so prominently as we stepped across the DMZ, had been replaced by a grim, irate face. Laney had told him that rather than celebrating his accomplishments, Washington was fuming. The White House's embarrassment over Carter's interview on Thursday night (Pyongyang time) had turned to white-hot anger when the CNN sound-bite, in which Carter had said that the sanctions effort had ended, hit the airwaves on Friday. According to Laney, some administration officials were more concerned with embarrassing Carter than with evaluating his agreement with Kim Il Sung, and some thought the agreement was nothing more than a ruse that had suckered a gullible do-gooder. Fortunately, the Washington clearance process had softened the language of the press release so that although it reaffirmed that consultations were continuing on sanctions, it also expressed the hope that the Carter-Kim Il Sung agreement, if confirmed in diplomatic channels, would prove to be constructive.[5]

Carter was caught off-guard when Laney told him of Washington's reaction. Although confident that his agreement with Kim Il Sung would make sanctions unnecessary, he had not realized how categorical he had been in his remarks filmed by CNN on Kim Il Sung's yacht. In his private discussions in North Korea, as well as in his CNN interview on Thursday evening, he had carefully said that President Clinton would have to make the official decision about sanctions. His personal expectation was that the administration would decide to hold the sanctions effort in abeyance until the conclusion of the third round of bilateral talks. On more than one occasion in North Korea he had defined, when asked, what "abeyance" meant. Although he was irritated that his sound-bite was being exaggerated into a question of who was in charge of American foreign policy, Carter told Laney that he would correct the record if he had, indeed, said that the sanctions effort had stopped.

Carter knew that there was one potential substantive problem with the North Korean freeze commitment after the administration added the requirements of no reprocessing and no refueling. Refueling was a new subject that had not been addressed during the Thursday talks. Carter thought that Kim Il Sung would regard no refueling of the reactor as part of his nuclear freeze, but he had not found the appropriate occasion to go into this subject on the yacht. He did not want to give Kim Il Sung's subordinates an opportunity to try to convince their "Great Leader" to pull back from his freeze agreement. Carter decided to raise this matter in a communication with Kim Il Sung after he returned to the United States. He knew that the North Korean president would watch closely what happened in Washington over the next days and that, in any event, their agreement would have to be confirmed through diplomatic channels.

Laney swallowed hard before conveying the remainder of his instructions to his friend. He told Carter that the administration had decided that he should not come to Washington to report the results of his North Korean trip. Instead, he should return to Plains, and someone from Washington, probably Gallucci, would visit him in a few days to collect his trip report. Carter was first incredulous and then furious.

I found it incredible that after President Clinton had acquiesced to the trip, Carter would now be told that he would not be welcomed in Washington. I thought Carter had handed the Clinton administration a major foreign policy victory. He deserved the opportunity to give a first-hand report to the president and his advisers. Yet he was being shunned and told to go home. According to Laney, who had known Carter well for the past decade, he had never seen him so angry.

Laney also told Carter that Vice President Gore wanted him to call on the secure phone as soon as they reached the residence. Once there, Carter went to the small closet area where the secure phone was located. I followed him and sat close enough to hear his part of the conversation. I declined Laney's suggestion that I be available to talk with the foreign minister, who was expected momentarily, and said that I would come into the living room as soon as the telephone call concluded.[6]

The conversation was tense. Carter attempted to be calm. He knew that Gore was his best friend in the administration. But at times he grew testy, particularly when talking about his Pyongyang telephone conversation with Lake. Carter explained his understanding with Kim Il Sung. He said that the North Korean leader had committed 1) to keeping the IAEA inspectors on site and to keeping intact the surveillance equipment, and 2) to seeking during the formal talks to resolve all nuclear problems with "full transparency of its nuclear program from its inception." He expected the sanctions to "be held in abeyance" during these bilateral talks.

Shifting to the conversation with Lake, Carter pointed out that he had not demanded "no reprocessing" and "no reloading" of fuel in the 5 MWe reactor in his first talk with Kim Il Sung. During his Washington briefing, he had understood that under the NPT, North Korea could reprocess as long as it was under IAEA safeguards. He had talked to Kim Il Sung, with Kang Sok Ju present, after his telephone conversation with Lake, and told him that it was important not to reprocess the spent fuel even though that point had not been mentioned in their earlier conversation. The North Korean position was that if the country could shift to light water reactors, it would have no need to reprocess. Carter told Gore that he believed reprocessing would be delayed until Kang Sok Ju and Gallucci had completed the new round of bilateral talks, but he had no specific North Korean commitment to that effect. In fact, Carter insisted, if they have no alternative, they have a right to reprocess under IAEA safeguards.

Carter said he would clarify his misstatement about sanctions at his press conference scheduled shortly before he departed South Korea. He asked that Gore send him a statement of clarification to read at the press conference. (No statement was later sent from Washington.)

Gore intervened at this point. Regarding the reprocessing issue, he said that North Korea "was not in a situation of a normal NPT party" and that "it was out of compliance and was launching a major plutonium production program." He added that North Korea "could not be considered 'entitled' to reprocess under the NPT."

Gore said firmly that the administration had not stopped its campaign to get a sanctions resolution passed by the UN Security Council, labeling as "unfortunate" Carter's CNN comment. Carter responded that he had made clear that morning to his North Korean hosts that the U.S. government had not withdrawn consideration of sanctions. But he added that the agreement with Kim Il Sung should form the basis for the third round of talks and an end to punitive action. Carter said the North Koreans thought they could keep the spent fuel rods in the cooling pond for only three months, but he had told them that the rods could remain in the pond for twelve months. He then told Gore that it would be a serious mistake to issue a harsh ultimatum to North Korea about reprocessing; the point should be made instead in a "mutually respectful way." North Korea needed an alternative nuclear program in the form of light water reactors, and Carter said he would continue to work with the North Koreans on this issue if Washington agreed.

Some confusion arose as to how long Washington was demanding that North Korea halt reprocessing—for the duration of the third round of talks or permanently as a precondition for talks. Carter had the impression that Lake was insisting on the latter position, and he said he differed with Lake on this point. The North Koreans would not reprocess during the time frame of the talks, but neither would they give up reprocessing forever without an alternative. Gore then called Lake, and, with a phone in each ear, he confirmed that both Carter and Lake understood that the "no reprocessing" commitment would apply only until the end of the talks. Carter stated confidently that the North Koreans would freeze their entire nuclear program during the U.S.-North Korean talks, but they would have to go back to the graphite reactor if they failed to get light water reactors. On the other hand, if the talks were successful, their no reprocessing commitment would "obviously be permanent."

To avoid misunderstanding, Gore said that the United States needed the North Koreans to say three things to Carter before Washington would commit to restarting the bilateral dialogue. They would have to agree to "no reprocessing of plutonium from spent fuel, no restarting of the 5-megawatt reactor, and the continued presence of IAEA inspectors at Yongbyon." This was "the heart of the matter." If these commitments were obtained, we would have a "breakthrough." Carter responded quickly: "I already have that commitment; it is not necessary to talk with them again. I can speak for them. We can make these points clear through their office in New York [the North Korean mission to the UN through which messages were passed to Pyongyang]." Gore repeated that the third round of talks would take place if the North Koreans did not refuel, did not reprocess, and kept the inspectors in place; this would be "extremely significant." The next step would be to nail down this understanding.

With the tension eased, Carter told Gore he would like to come directly to Washington from Seoul for a debriefing on Sunday. He had found some of the information provided to him by the intelligence agencies in Washington prior to his trip to have been "disturbingly incorrect." The actual circumstances in the country of North Korea were different from what the Washington experts on North Korea had said they were. Gore agreed to his proceeding to Washington to brief administration officials directly.

When the telephone conversation was over, I went to meet Foreign Minister Han Sung Joo, who was engaged in a conversation with Ambassador Laney, Deputy Chief of Mission Charles Kartman, political officers Danny Russel and Jim Pierce, and Dick Christenson. Carter joined us a few minutes later. Han's main interest was to get a general overview that he could share with President Kim Young Sam to facilitate a more in-depth discussion when Carter and his team arrived at the Blue House for lunch.

In the manner that I had observed so often, Carter concisely summarized the events of the trip, the elements of the agreements reached, who had been his principal interlocutors, and his views of how best to build on what had been achieved. He emphasized that Kim Il Sung wanted to resolve the nuclear issues through bilateral talks, but he expected South Korea to be involved in discussions that dealt with the Korean Peninsula. Carter answered the foreign minister's questions about Kim Il Sung's proposal for a North-South summit and how the nuclear past would be clarified in the new round of U.S.-North Korean talks. He said the Clinton administration would probably decide to hold the sanctions issue in abeyance to test Kim Il Sung's commitments. Its current principal concern was preventing reprocessing by North Korea, and Pyongyang would not reprocess during its talks with the United States. Kim Il Sung was the decisionmaker in North Korea on key issues. He had reversed on the spot the decision of others to expel the IAEA inspectors. Carter believed that the nuclear and other issues could be solved through serious negotiations, but that belief would be tested by future events.

Foreign Minister Han excused himself and left for the Blue House. The Carters, Laney, and I followed a few minutes later for the luncheon scheduled at noon. Before I left, Dick and I were able to watch the controversial CNN interview with Carter on Kim Il Sung's yacht, which someone at the embassy had taped for Laney. There was no doubt. Carter had said that the sanctions effort had been stopped. He had misspoken.

At the Blue House, President Kim Young Sam greeted Carter more warmly than on the previous occasion. We proceeded almost immediately to the elegantly decorated table for lunch because there was to be a press conference back at the Laney residence afterwards and then an afternoon flight. The meal must have been superb, although with listening, taking notes, and reflecting, I ate little and tasted less.[7]

Carter reported on his trip to the north. He said his interlocutors had spoken positively about Kim Young Sam; they had not criticized any South Korean official. Kim Il Sung had expressed disappointment that the two leaders and people could not resolve their differences—for which both sides bore responsibility; he deplored the lack of communication between the two countries. He said he had been excited by Kim Young Sam's mention of a summit meeting in his inaugural message; he regretted that their respective subordinates had been unable to agree on an agenda for such a meeting, which, he said, was typical of how relations had been conducted between the two countries for the past forty years. Kim Il Sung had said he wanted to meet Kim Young Sam without preconditions, without extensive preparations; it could be no more than an exchange of greetings and a handshake and a pledge by both of them to begin implementing the 1991 agreements. After this symbolic meeting, their respective ministers could pursue specific items.

Carter summarized his discussion with Kim Il Sung about possible joint actions the North and South could take to reduce tensions and perhaps facilitate reunification: allowing older Koreans to cross the DMZ to visit their families; pulling back the military personnel and equipment of both countries several miles from the DMZ; and proportionally reducing the troop strength of the two Koreas and the United States. The North Korean leader had said that progress on denuclearization of the peninsula required cooperation between the North and South, and he favored negotiation of a regional denuclearization agreement by the two Koreas, the United States, China, Russia, and perhaps others.

Kim Young Sam expressed appreciation for Carter's comprehensive report and then picked up the line of argument that he had used before Carter left for North Korea—that Kim Il Sung was responsible for all the problems and could not be trusted. He had spoken to many people who had met the North Korean leader; Kim Il Sung always claimed to be a pacifist, but his propaganda sought to instigate student uprisings against the South Korean government and the United States. His North Korea wanted to talk only to the United States and ignore South Korea. He was not sincere about reducing the troops in both countries to 100,000 each. Such a proposal revealed his anxiety about sanctions; Carter disagreed. Kim Young Sam insisted that Kim Il Sung was the one who had prevented a summit meeting from taking place. His explanation that his nuclear program, even if it had a nuclear bomb or two, could not stand against that of the United States with its thousands of nuclear weapons was deceptive. His target was not the United States; his goal was to conquer South Korea.

On several occasions, Carter said he could not vouch for Kim Il Sung's integrity or sincerity, but his actions could be tested. His control was clear. He made the basic decisions for his country. He was intelligent, vigorous, well-informed, and apparently in good health. He was virtually venerated by his people.

Twice during the conversation, Carter pitched for The Carter Center, "a non-official, academic organization," to play a mediating role in facilitating a North-South dialogue. Kim Il Sung favored its doing so. Carter said he was willing if South Korea also thought it useful. He asked Kim Young Sam to communicate his decision through his ambassador in Washington.

The South Korean president said he would announce that he had received a message from Kim Il Sung about a summit meeting and he accepted such a meeting without preconditions and preparations. He hoped Carter would not reveal publicly that he doubted Kim Il Sung's sincerity and would not portray the North Korean leader as a "lover of peace." Carter agreed. He would simply say that the time had arrived for good faith talks between the two Koreas, and that the leaders of both countries had proposed such talks.

The luncheon ended with some camaraderie, a very different scene from the conclusion of the Kim Young Sam dinner for Carter less than ninety-six hours earlier.

Upon arrival at the Laney residence, Carter mounted quickly a makeshift speaker's dais to speak to the large contingent of Korean and international media assembled on the spacious front lawn. Concerned that differing interpretations of his trip were being aired in Seoul and in Washington, including charges that he was subverting U.S. policy on North Korea, he wanted to get his version and his personal conclusions on the public record.

Carter said that he had traveled to North Korea because of his "assessment of the seriousness of the confrontation concerning the nuclear issue and the lack of apparent direct communication with the leaders of North Korea." In his meetings, Kim Il Sung had agreed to permit the IAEA inspectors to remain at the reactor and the surveillance equipment to continue operating. He had also agreed to freeze the nuclear program of North Korea if assured that the third round of bilateral talks with the United States would take place.[8]

Turning to his controversial statement about sanctions, Carter said he had told Kim Il Sung that, in his personal opinion, if the terms of their agreement were implemented, the sanctions matter would be held "in abeyance" and the third round of talks could take place soon to "resolve all of the issues relating to the nuclear issue." He said Kim Il Sung understood that he was speaking as a private citizen and not as a U.S. government official.

Carter said Kim Il Sung had asked him to convey to President Kim Young Sam his hope that a direct meeting between the two Korean leaders could be arranged without extensive delays caused by arguments among subordinate officials. A few minutes later, a reporter shouted that Kim Young Sam's office had just announced his acceptance of the North Korean president's invitation for a summit.

During the question period, Carter said he knew discussions about sanctions were continuing in the Security Council, but he hoped that "the final decision on these matters" would await his debriefing in Washington. He found Kim Il Sung to be "quite reasonable in his response to [Carter's] proposals on the nuclear issue," but his "degree of reasonableness [would] be tested in the future" when the United States tried to "implement what has been agreed," Carter said.

Carter also used this forum to explain publicly what he had been emphasizing in his private discussions with U.S. and South Korean officials—that the adoption of sanctions against North Korea would prove counterproductive. Sanctions would not damage North Korea's society or economy, but North Koreans would consider them an affront to their nation and a "personal insult to their so-called Great Leader, branding him as a liar and a criminal," Carter said. "This is something, in my opinion, which it would be impossible for them to accept. I thought this before I went to North Korea and that's why I went. Now after observing their psyche and their societal structure and the reverence with which they look upon their leader, I'm even more convinced that what I've just said to you is true."

After a quick good-bye to Dick Christenson, who would stay a day or two longer in Seoul before returning to Japan, and to Chuck Kartman, Danny Russel, and other embassy officers, we departed for the airport with Ambassador Laney and the Carters in the lead car. The passengers spontaneously applauded the former president as he appeared in the cabin of the plane. Because of the intensive CNN coverage, virtually everyone on the aircraft knew of the Carter visit to North Korea. Following his standard procedure, Carter moved down the aisles of the plane and shook hands with the passengers. The many expressions of appreciation deeply affected the former president. His eyes were watery when he took his seat, strapped on his seatbelt, and squeezed Rosalynn's hand. On schedule, the Delta flight departed Seoul at 4:15 P.M.

THE CRISIS ENDS—
PEACEFULLY
Part III

CHAPTER 11

The Homecoming

The plane raced down the runway, took to the sky, and assumed the flight course that would take it first to Portland, Oregon, and then to Atlanta, Georgia, where Jimmy Carter would board a domestic carrier for Washington. Twelve hours earlier, before he had crossed the DMZ, he would have expected an enthusiastic and welcoming homecoming in Washington. Now he knew he would face a skeptical group of administration officials. Carter understood that he had to confront a new challenge: to convince the Clinton administration that he was reporting accurately the commitments made by Kim Il Sung and that he had negotiated a deal that was beneficial, that could be converted through diplomatic negotiations into a peaceful solution of the nuclear crisis with North Korea, and that could gain support domestically despite its requiring the administration to modify its hard-line approach to Pyongyang. As he pondered the impending events, Jimmy Carter thought his Washington foray might prove more difficult than had his venture to Pyongyang.

As always, after he had relaxed for a while on the plane, Carter took out his laptop computer and composed his trip report. Whenever he traveled on a Carter Center mission, on the way home he recorded the events and his reflections on what had transpired in his terse, personal, and informative style. The day after he returned to Atlanta or Plains, his report of that trip was sent to the U.S. president, the secretary of state and other officials, the Carter Center staff, and friends whom he thought would be interested. It went later—perhaps as an abridged version, depending on the sensitivity of the mission—to a list of Carter Center patrons and to members of the Center's board of counselors.

When we arrived in Portland, Oregon, Carter asked Nancy to run off copies for him, his wife, and me. A succinct and accurate account of the trip, Carter's report also reflected in several places his irritation with the Washington administration. A couple of examples: He said that his briefing by Eason Jordan of CNN proved far more helpful than his briefings in Washington and that dealing with Kim Il Sung had been easier than dealing with administration officials. I understood his frustrations. But I thought that inclusion of these and other references would be politically unwise, particularly since Carter had told me that he intended to make this report available to the press in addition to the regular circulation mentioned above. After I had had time to peruse the document, he asked for my reaction. I was honest. I told him it was a good report, but I would suggest deleting or revising a few sentences; if he publicly chastised the administration, he would hamper moving forward on the agreement he had achieved. He told me to write my suggested language changes on a draft, which he would consider before circulating the report. I spent considerable time trying to figure out how to excise the most objectionable passages with the fewest changes of Carter's words.

In Portland we went to the small meeting room reserved for us by Delta. Carter was handed a message to call Tom Johnson, president and CEO of CNN. The Johnson call rekindled Carter's irritation. Tom told him that the Washington newspapers, particularly the *Washington Post*, had carried articles that morning critical of the Carter effort. He faxed Carter the *Washington Post* article written by R. Jeffrey Smith and Bradley Graham, which confirmed Johnson's assessment. Terry Adamson, an influential Washington lawyer who had served in the Carter administration and acted as counsel for The Carter Center, had a similar reaction; independent of Johnson, he faxed a copy of the article to the Center for delivery to Carter. In his accompanying memo, Adamson advised the former president to develop a media strategy to get his version of the story to the public.[1]

The Smith and Graham article,[2] headlined "Carter Faulted by White House on North Korea: Policy Statements Cause Confusion on Sanctions," reported that the Clinton administration had disowned statements made by Carter in North Korea because the former president had misrepresented administration policy despite his earlier briefings in Washington. Administration officials could not understand why Carter had said that the United States had dropped its sanctions proposal the day after Clinton had stated that the drive for sanctions would continue: "'We have no way of knowing why he [Carter] thought what he thought, or why he said what he said," one unnamed "senior administration official" was quoted as saying. Only President Clinton had reportedly left open the possibility that Carter's statement about sanctions could have been misinterpreted.

The article elaborated on the Washington reaction as follows: "While publicly welcoming the unexpected North Korean concession to Carter on Thursday—in which North Korea promised not to eject international inspectors from a sensitive nuclear site—the officials had been privately scathing that the former Democratic president would so embarrass his successor by challenging his policy at a highly sensitive moment." An unidentified "senior U.S. official" was quoted as saying, "Carter is hearing what he wants to hear, both from Kim Il Sung and from the administration. He is creating his own reality." Another "senior official," when asked whether the scrambled signals would reflect poorly on Clinton, allegedly retorted: "The implications are for Carter and what does it say about Jimmy Carter, not what does it say about Bill Clinton."

Carter called his office in Atlanta and instructed the Center's public information director, Carrie Harmon, to arrange a press conference for him in Washington after his meeting on Sunday with the White

House. Since Mrs. Carter had appointments planned for the following week for which she needed to prepare, she and her husband decided that she should not go to Washington, although they would talk by phone later that evening to strategize on the meeting at the White House. Carter came to me and asked whether I would go with him to Washington. I quickly said yes. I was not about to drop out at this point, even though I knew the visit would probably not be pleasant; I had friends and former colleagues who would be the "adversary" on this fateful visit.

When the Delta plane landed in Atlanta, arrangements were in place. Somehow the Delta crew found all our bags, and we were able, on the runway, to take out what we would need for Washington and leave the rest of our luggage with Carter Center personnel. We then boarded another plane for Washington. Carrie Harmon also boarded the plane, as did Beth Kurylo, a correspondent from the *Atlanta Journal Constitution.* Carrie, who had worked in public relations in a publishing company before taking her senior position at the Center, enjoyed the confidence of both President and Mrs. Carter. Beth had been the local correspondent who had covered Carter's activities at the Carter Center for a number of years. She had traveled to many of Carter's destinations, sometimes on the same private plane he was using. (On various Carter Center initiatives, particularly to places where commercial flights were infrequent, wealthy supporters of the Center loaned Carter their private planes.)

Once the plane was airborne, I huddled with Carrie. She explained that, after consulting with Adamson and Jody Powell, a Washington consultant who had served as Carter's press spokesman during his presidency, she had arranged for a select group of media representatives to meet with Carter in the hotel after his session with administration officials in the White House. The purpose: to give Carter the opportunity, as Adamson had recommended, "to diffuse the import of these kind of stories and put the focus back on the real accomplishments" of the former president's trip.[3] I showed Carrie Carter's trip report, and my suggested revisions, with which she agreed. She said she would have access to computers and printers in the office space that had been reserved for us in the hotel.

After arriving at our Washington hotel, Carter, Carrie, and I had an early dinner. During the meal, Carrie and I raised with Carter the desirability of revising his trip report before he passed it out to journalists the next day. We suggested that the reporters, as the press stories were already demonstrating, would likely emphasize more the differences between him and the administration than his achievements in Pyongyang. He did not want to reinforce this viewpoint. Carter took the copy of his report with our recommendations and said he would get back to us.

We went to bed, but I could not sleep. For several hours I tossed and turned. I was anxious about the meeting on Sunday. We had heard that Carter would be received in the White House by Tony Lake and other officials working on the Korean issue. Clinton would not be there. He had gone to Camp David for the weekend, reportedly an earlier planned trip, but one that he did not change in order to meet with Carter. Neither Gore nor Christopher would attend. I thought that Carter, given his own past record of showing respect to former presidents while he was in the White House and the importance of what he had achieved, would be upset at what was clearly a serious slight. I feared he might be tempted to vent his rage, and that if a blow-up occurred, it might destroy the breakthrough he had achieved in North Korea.

Around 3:00 A.M., I decided to put my concerns on paper, not knowing whether I would share them with Carter. I knew I would not be able to sleep until I had done so. I organized the memo as follows: First, I listed Carter's achievements with his trip, namely, he had averted the possibility of immediate war; created a new opportunity for the United States and North Korea to begin to move their relationship in a more peaceful and productive manner; and provided a new chance for South Korea and North Korea to reduce animosities and gradually improve relations. Second, I listed the "costs of the trip": the embarrassment to the Clinton administration because it had "put all of its policy eggs in the sanction basket" and was conducting a

high-profile campaign to get the required votes for sanctions; the reinforcement of "right wing criticism that the administration was in-
decisive and wimpish"; and further embarrassment to the administration
by South Korea's initial complaints about the trip, although Seoul's
concerns had been largely neutralized after Carter's second meeting
with President Kim Young Sam. Then under "Future Prospects," I
pointed out that the accomplishments of the trip must be nurtured
and sustained and that a future role that Carter might play would require the "support, or at least the acquiescence" of the Clinton administration, North Korea, and South Korea. Finally, I drew the
"Bottom Line": Even though the administration "has treated you
shabbily, you need to try to reconcile differences." Further: "You will
probably need to allow it to save 'face'—as you did with North Korea
and even South Korea. This could best be done by narrowing the
publicly perceived disagreements between you and the administration, and allowing it to take . . . some of the credit for your achievements." I then suggested specific things Carter might wish to consider
in his meeting later that day with administration officials and subsequently with the press:

> "Acknowledge that many of the elements of the package proposal
> accepted by Kim Il Sung had been devised by the administration.
> You pulled them together and sold them to Kim Il Sung, some-
> thing an administration official could not have done because of
> the lack of diplomatic relations and mutual suspicions of the two
> governments."
> "Admit [as at the Seoul press conference] that the sound byte on
> sanctions was unfortunate, but affirm that North Koreans clearly
> understood that immediate reaction on sanctions is being held in
> abeyance pending U.S.-North Korean efforts to resolve all aspects
> of the nuclear problem and move toward improved relations."
> "Reaffirm your willingness to assist the processes in the future."
> "If White House meeting goes well, extract most of the critical re-
> marks of the administration in press handout."[4]

After drafting and revising the memo, I rewrote it (lacking a printer, I could not use my computer) and slid it under Carter's hotel room door around 5:00 A.M. After that, sleep came easily. But soon, the alarm sounded to start the day.

I do not know whether the memo influenced Carter's behavior at the White House meeting and subsequently with the press. He never mentioned it to me. I was surprised to find my handwritten memo in the papers Faye Dill had filed in the Carter Presidential Library; Carter passed on to her most papers, other than his personal diaries, for filing. What I do know is that, despite his irritation with the treatment he had received during the past two days and the thick tension in the air, he remained temperate, composed, and pragmatic at the White House meeting. Only once did his irritation boil over. When one of the participants suggested that Carter limit the distribution of his trip report to President Clinton and cabinet members, Carter—his eyes narrow and locked on the official—snapped sharply that he would decide who received his report.

At breakfast before the White House meeting, Carter told Carrie to make the modifications we had suggested on his trip report so that he could provide Tony Lake with a revised copy and that additional revised copies should be available for his session with journalists after the White House meeting. Carrie left us at the breakfast table to produce the modified report and make final arrangements for the media meeting.

A few minutes before 10:00 A.M., Carter and I arrived at the White House. We went in the front entrance on Pennsylvania Avenue. No official greeted us. Carter spoke to a couple of the female receptionists whom he knew, and we took seats in the reception area to wait for Tony Lake to call for us. Carter, who since his student days at the U.S. Naval Academy has rigorously followed a daily schedule and put a premium on punctuality, squirmed as the minutes ticked by beyond the scheduled time of the appointment. Being kept waiting only added to his frustration about the level of the participants with whom he would be meeting.

Many administration officials thought Carter had gone too far both in claiming credit for a diplomatic breakthrough and in publicly criticizing sanctions.[5] Nevertheless, those waiting in Lake's office saw the purpose of the meeting to be to try to mend fences as well as to get Carter's direct impressions of his discussions in Pyongyang. They would share my assessment that at the outset of the meeting, the tension was palpable.[6] Dan Poneman, one of the participants, described the atmosphere as "so cold you could cut it with a knife."[7]

About fifteen minutes after the appointed hour, one of the receptionists escorted us to Tony's office. A desk opposite the entrance fronted the windows looking out on the Old Executive Office Building. A sofa lined the wall to the left as we entered. A small table with a phone sat at the far end of the sofa; next to it was a large government-issue leather chair in which Lake usually sat. Other chairs from elsewhere in the room were drawn up to parallel the sofa.

Lake met Carter at the door, shook hands, acknowledged the others in the room, and motioned to Carter to sit on the sofa next to the chair that Lake would take. I sat next to Carter on the sofa. Also in attendance were Bob Gallucci; Sandy Berger, the deputy national security adviser; Winston Lord, the assistant secretary of state for East Asia and the Pacific; and Poneman.

Tony welcomed Carter back; said he and his colleagues wanted to learn more about his trip and its results; and told him that President Clinton, who was at Camp David for the weekend as previously planned, would like to talk with him by phone after the meeting. That evening, Carter would record in his personal diary his pique that neither the president nor vice president had attended the meeting at the White House and that no one had met him when he arrived at the airport or at the White House.[8] Nevertheless, Carter thanked the participants for making the meeting on Sunday morning and said he would be happy to talk with Clinton. He apologized for any embarrassment he might have caused the administration by his inadvertent remark about sanctions on CNN on Friday morning. He said that he had corrected the record at the large press conference at Ambassador Laney's residence following his final meeting with President Kim Young Sam. He said that he was loyal and not naïve; he hoped that he and the administration officials could sort out any problems between them at this meeting so that they could move forward together. An opportunity existed to solve the critical nuclear problem with North Korea, but articles, such as the recent one in the *Washington Post* quoting unnamed administration officials, could be detrimental to this process.[9] Lake quickly insisted that no one in the administration had authorized press leaks. He agreed that a single voice should be the goal.[10]

Carter spent a lengthy period reading most of the revised trip report that explained the background to his trip. (The text of the final trip report is found in Appendix F.) When he concluded his presentation, he mentioned his intention to share the report with his mailing list of supporters (but he did not say that he would provide the paper to the reporters waiting for him in the hotel).[11]

In the report Carter had included language containing the assessment General Luck had given him about the likely cost of a new Korean war and his hope that such a conflict could be avoided. Lake insisted on revising the language about Luck, saying that Carter's text suggested that the "highly decorated commander of U.S. Forces, Korea . . . quailed before the prospect of military conflict."[12] That was not Carter's intent nor was it our reading of the language he had penned. But he readily agreed to the following revised language: "U.S. General Luck, Commander of all military forces in South Korea, was deeply concerned about the consequences of a Korean war. He estimated that the costs would far exceed those of the 1950s."[13]

The tenor of the conversation then turned to trying to reconcile the views of Carter and the administration and to present a more united public front. Carter said that he thought his actions had been consistent with administration policy and that he had obtained from the North Koreans an agreement that met the administration's objectives. But he said again that he firmly believed that the talk of sanctions was counterproductive. He said that in his telephone conversation with Lake he thought Washington had agreed to the proposals that he and Kim Il

Sung had framed. He was extremely surprised when he returned to Seoul and learned of the dispute about sanctions. He had explained to the North Korean interpreter the meaning of sanctions being held in "abeyance" after CNN filmed his remarks to Kim Il Sung on the boat. He said Kim Il Sung certainly understood what "held in abeyance" meant. Nevertheless, Carter apologized for the confusion his recorded remark had caused.

Lake responded that that was "water under the bridge." The United States was not now pushing hard for sanctions. All administration statements included a sentence saying that the United States continued to talk about sanctions, and reporters "jump on this point." Lake said what was needed was to shift the public attention to the idea that the United States was exploring points discussed with Carter in Pyongyang "through diplomatic channels."

Carter volunteered that he intended to send a letter to Kim Il Sung and offer his services. Should deadlocks arise in the impending discussions between Gallucci and Kang Sok Ju, Carter would be able to communicate with Kim Il Sung, as they had agreed. He said that he had made the same offer to Kim Young Sam. Answering Lake's question, Carter emphasized that Kim Il Sung offered the nuclear freeze before their telephone conversation. His subsequent meeting with Kang Sok Ju had as its primary purpose to work out the details of the freeze.

Lake asked for more details about the "freeze." Carter said that in his discussion he had stressed "total transparency from inception." This process would drag on for some time. He said that Kim Il Sung had "two hang-ups": conversion of the North Korean graphite reactor to light water reactor technology and the denuclearization of the peninsula in order to avoid a nuclear attack on his country. Carter then took issue with those who belittled Kim Il Sung's role in North Korea. He said North Korea was a "unique society" with a "homogeneous attitude." Kim Il Sung was the person in charge of the country and made all the important decisions. No one was going to attempt a coup against Kim Il Sung. Kim Jong Il was always reported to be out working in the

countryside; he was never seen by anyone; he might be an embarrassment to his father.

Lake returned the conversation to the subject of light water reactors
and the North Korean overall nuclear program. Carter said these were
the subjects for the third round of talks. He had told Kim Il Sung that
the United States supported North Korea's acquiring light water reactors but the U.S. government could neither furnish nor finance this
equipment. Gallucci asked what message would he need to convey to
the North Koreans to persuade them to meet Washington's three conditions (no reprocessing, no refueling, keeping IAEA inspectors and
monitoring equipment in place). Carter said that Gallucci should tell
them that the United States supported their desire to obtain light water
reactors; he said that this statement should represent a genuine U.S.
commitment to help the North Koreans find others to supply the
equipment and financing. They should also be reassured that the United
States would not attack North Korea with nuclear weapons. The North
Korean leaders feared a nuclear attack. Elaborating, Carter pointed out
that a few months earlier President Clinton had said publicly at the
DMZ that North Korea could be obliterated if it persisted with its nuclear weapons development. Senator John McCain was currently using
language that suggested the possibility of a nuclear strike. The North
Koreans believed these statements. Kim Il Sung had indicated willingness to proceed with the denuclearization of the peninsula. Carter said
that he had repeated U.S. and South Korean official statements suggesting that there were no nuclear weapons in South Korea or at sea.
He had told his North Korean interlocutors that the United States
would be willing to join others in a nuclear free zone for the peninsula.
Poneman and Gallucci suggested that North Korea benefited from negative assurances against attack, as do all NPT members. Carter said that
this point should be reaffirmed to them.

Gallucci asked how he could make the point about the three U.S. requirements without saying they were conditions. Carter said that he
would frame language in his letter to Kim Il Sung that defined the
freeze to include the provisions on "no reprocessing" and "no refueling"—

even though he had not explicitly discussed "no refueling" with Kim Il Sung—as well as the need to reaffirm that the IAEA inspectors and equipment would remain in place. He would send a copy of his letter to President Clinton and make his language available to Gallucci for his use. Then on the basis of these assurances, Kang could be invited to a meeting in July. Carter emphasized two points. First, the United States should look positively on the new developments unless the North Koreans betrayed Kim Il Sung's commitments. Second, the U.S. negotiators should remember that Carter's agreement was with Kim Il Sung, not Kang Sok Ju (the implication being that Kang Sok Ju could be overruled if he tried to deviate from Kim Il Sung's agreement with Carter).

At this time, Lake asked all the participants to step out of his office so that President Carter and President Clinton could have a private telephone conversation. Lake and Carter remained as the rest of us filed out. Poneman and I moved to the small office of Lake's special assistant to revise the language in Carter's report on the points he and Lake had discussed.

In his diary, Carter recorded that President Clinton expressed gratitude for the trip and appreciation for its results. Carter told Clinton that he was the "first person in the government who had said this." He spent about twenty minutes briefing the president on a secure phone. Although Carter would later talk publicly about Clinton's congratulating him, he did not reveal that after the telephone conversation he and Lake had a sharp discussion about the alleged administration-sourced criticisms in the press about the Carter trip and the general attitude of the Clinton administration against having The Carter Center involved in an important issue. Carter also expressed the resentment he felt when he was initially advised not to come to Washington for debriefing; he also said that higher-level officials (in addition to Lake) should have been present for his report. According to Carter, Lake stressed his friendship with the former president, said he had favored his trip, and denied any responsibility for the criticisms directed toward Carter. Years later, Lake confirmed that he had supported the Carter trip, and he rejected strongly any responsibility for the leaks to the press. He said that no leaks had been authorized because that was not the way he did business and, moreover, the leaks were not in the administration's interest.[14] Gallucci and Poneman took a similar position in separate conversations. All suggested that the leaks must have come from political appointees who incorrectly thought they were protecting President Clinton.[15]

After the telephone conversation, we gathered again in Lake's office. Responding to Winston Lord's question, Carter said that no official in North Korea had talked abusively about South Korea or its leaders. He drew a contrast with his conversations in Seoul, where all his interlocutors, except Unification Minister Lee, had made vituperative comments about North Korean leaders.

Carter added a few comments about the North Korean father and son. He said that Kim Il Sung wanted a summit meeting to take place and had asked Carter to be an emissary. He was eighty-two but still active; he envisioned leading his country for ten more years. Carter explained that Kim Jong Il held an exalted place in North Korea, but he did not make fundamental decisions. Not even the Japanese Socialist Party, which was sympathetic toward North Korea, had been able to meet the son during a visit to Pyongyang.

Carter said that Kang Sok Ju had initially thought that the spent fuel rods could only remain in the cooling pond for three months, but he had told Kang they could stay there for twelve months. Gallucci said that a year was possible with some technical adjustments. Gallucci confirmed the North Koreans' claim to have an alternative methodology for determining the history of the fuel rods, but the U.S. government's technical people had two problems with the North Korean proposal: First, the North Koreans did not seem to be technically able to discharge the rods from specific channels in the core into specific baskets in the cooling pond, as required by their proposal; and second, their operators did not always do what they said they would do. From the IAEA's viewpoint, North Korea had crossed the Rubicon on the history issue. Carter said that Kang had not seemed very concerned about the discharge of the fuel rods and the inspectors. He had been led to believe that North Korea had decided to discharge the spent fuel rods when Washington and Seoul had insisted that the North-South talks had to precede the U.S.-North Korean discussions.

Gallucci asked whether Carter saw special inspections as part of the final package. Carter said yes. Both Kim Il Sung and Kang Sok Ju knew that his use of the term "transparency from inception" meant inspection of the two disputed sites. But the United States must avoid putting out ultimatums. Kim Il Sung was not going to admit that he had misled the world by lying. Carter urged the administration to let him discuss with Kim Il Sung any issue that threatened to become a problem. Additionally, the United States should not insist that North Korea must do something before Washington would do anything but rather agree to do things more or less together. He also suggested that Team Spirit exercises not be held if denuclearization talks between the two Koreas were resumed.

The participants concurred that Carter and Lake should talk briefly with the press after the meeting and that Gallucci should have a more extensive press conference during the afternoon. It was agreed that Carter would again make the point that he traveled as a private citizen, explain the context of his public remarks in North Korea on sanctions, and indicate that the next step involved a confirmation of his agreement with Kim Il Sung through diplomatic channels. Lake would say that pending this diplomatic exchange, the United States would continue its consultations on sanctions in New York. However, these consultations could be suspended if the third round of talks commenced.

Around noon, Carter and Lake went outside the north entrance to the White House where ten or twelve reporters were waiting in the hot sunshine. In the ten or so minutes that the session lasted, the two men followed the agreed guidance. Carter told the reporters that he had had a "fine meeting" with Lake, Gallucci, and others; he had shared with them what had happened on his trip, and he had spoken by phone with President Clinton for about half an hour. He had relayed to the White House Kim Il Sung's proposals. The next step would be for the administration to confirm officially in writing his understandings with Kim Il Sung. Carter said he personally believed the crisis was over if the North

Koreans followed through on the assurances made to him.[16] The remark that "the crisis is over" (ignoring the dependent clause that followed these words) was one of the tag lines that reporters and critics would use in the next few days as evidence of a continuing split between the Clinton administration and Carter as well as a reflection of the former president's naïveté. After this brief press exchange, Lake went back into the White House, and Carter and I returned to the hotel.

I thought Carter had largely achieved his purpose for the White House meeting. He had shared in detail the encouraging developments that had occurred during his Pyongyang visit with the key administration officials working on the North Korean issue. Despite past disagreements, he and they had agreed to work together in the days ahead to turn his breakthrough with Kim Il Sung into a peaceful resolution of the nuclear problem. His next challenge was to counter the efforts of those who rejected an agreement with North Korea as a solution to the nuclear crisis and were using the media to try to torpedo the U.S.-North Korean negotiations before they began. He did not talk on the way to the hotel. His mind was focused on the task ahead.

Carrie Harmon and Jody Powell had assembled the media representatives invited to the roundtable discussion with Carter. When we arrived, I gave Carrie the amended trip report, which she had copied and then passed out to the attendees. Carter sat down with his back to the hotel room window, and the journalists sat and stood around the room. Carter said he had had a "long and pleasant talk" at the White House and that in the course of it, he had spoken by phone with President Clinton. He then summarized the main points in his trip report and responded to questions.

Many of the questions focused on the reports of sharp differences between Carter and the Clinton administration. Carter's answers sought to close that gap. He minimized his disagreements with Lake during their telephone conversation when he was in Pyongyang. He admitted that he had made a mistake on his statement on CNN about sanctions being stopped even though Kim Il Sung knew he had been expressing his personal view and was not speaking for the U.S. government. He acknowledged, however, that he differed with the administration about the utility of sanctions and explained why he thought the voting of sanctions could possibly lead to war.

Reminded that he had said in the earlier press appearance with Lake that he believed the crisis to be over, Carter repeated his earlier statement that again made the resolution contingent on North Korea actions. His words: "I think the crisis is over provided that . . . the assurances I have from North Korea are carried out."

Carter left the meeting satisfied that he had explained as well as he could why he had gone to North Korea and what he had achieved. He also thought he had avoided saying anything that would help the media participants embellish on differences between him and the administration except for the sanctions issue, on which they disagreed. Carter's view on sanctions would lead some administration officials to charge Carter with undermining U.S. government policy. If by the time of his trip, U.S. policy was to get UN Security Council endorsement of sanctions regardless of the cost, then Carter had indeed sought to undermine policy. But if the policy was to stop North Korea's nuclear program from advancing further and to get it dismantled over time—as the Agreed Framework of October 1994 called for—then sanctions were a tactic that Carter believed would prevent the achievement of the policy objective.[17]

While Carter was still in his discussion with the media representatives, Bob Gallucci, as agreed at the Carter-Lake meeting, walked into the briefing room in the White House shortly after 1:00 P.M. to discuss the morning meeting. On the key points, his views and those of Carter largely coincided. Gallucci refused to be baited into talking about differences between the administration and Carter except to note that they disagreed on the utility of sanctions.

He said both agreed that the next step was to receive diplomatic confirmation of the North Korean position. If Pyongyang met the U.S.'s three conditions, the sanctions effort would be suspended and the third round of the U.S.-North Korean talks started. Gallucci's characterization: "I think we are all on the same sheet of music." When asked whether he viewed Carter's trip "as an assist rather than as something negative," Gallucci responded, "I would like to answer that unambiguously and clearly—yes, we welcome President Carter's efforts, and we intend on following up on them immediately."[18]

Back at the hotel, after Carter had concluded his session with the media representatives and said goodbye to Jody Powell and Carrie Harmon, he and I departed, heading, I thought, for the airport. It was only then that he told me of his intention to stop by the CNN studio for a live interview before he left Washington. I learned years later that Eason Jordan had passed him a handwritten note before he left Pyongyang urging him to permit a CNN interview after he had been to his White House briefing.[19]

During the CNN interview, Carter reiterated much of what he had said in his press conference in Seoul on Saturday and with the Washington media representatives a short time before. He said his meeting at the White House and his telephone conversation with President Clinton were "completely satisfactory." He rejected the charge of his critics that the North Koreans were using him to stall for more time to develop a nuclear bomb by pointing out that the international inspectors on the site would quickly detect any effort by North Korea to use the fuel rods to make a nuclear weapon.

When *Late Edition* aired later, the taped Carter interview was shown, and then a live interview took place with Congressman Lee Hamilton, chairman of the House Foreign Affairs Committee, and Lawrence Eagleburger, former secretary of state under President George H. W. Bush. Both were skeptical about the Carter intervention and supported continuing the sanctions effort and strengthening the U.S. military in South Korea. Hamilton did say that the former president deserved credit for creating an "opening," but the "crisis was not over." Eagleburger saw nothing positive in the Carter trip. He said Carter should have stayed home; he had confused the situation. He had been "horrified," Eagleburger emphasized, to hear "Selig Harrison, and to a degree even a former president, taking the word of this murderer who runs North Korea."[20]

When we left the CNN studio for the airport. Carter, though tired, was in good spirits. I asked him whether he would like to be the U.S. president again. He surprised me by saying no. He explained that he found the work he could do and his independent position at The Carter Center to be extremely satisfying at this time. I knew that was true, but I was less than sanguine that, if given the chance to be in the White House again, he would turn it down.

We dozed during the trip back to Atlanta and parted at the airport. A vehicle picked Carter up on the tarmac and transported him to Plains. I walked to the parking lot, found my car, and drove home.

CHAPTER 12

The Deal Holds

When I arrived at The Carter Center the next morning, Monday, June 20, at around 8:00 A.M., Faye Dill handed me a copy of a letter to Kim Il Sung that Carter had written after returning to Plains the preceding evening. She had already faxed it to the North Korean Mission at the United Nations. It read:

To President Kim Il Sung

I want to express my deep appreciation to you for the wonderful hospitality extended to us during our visit to Pyongyang this week. We had many fine experiences, which we will never forget, and we look forward to returning to your country. One of the most remarkable events of our lives was the performance of the Korean children at their palace. I wish the entire world could witness this amazing talent.

Because of your wisdom and leadership we were able to resolve the international crisis that had materialized from misunderstandings and lack of communication concerning the nuclear issue. The fact is that the agreements reached will, if implemented, be beneficial both to your country and to others. Your willingness to permit international inspectors and surveillance equipment to continue operating; to freeze your nuclear program, foregoing reloading and reprocessing during the conduct of good faith talks; to acquire light water reactor technology to replace those moderated by graphite; and to pursue a common effort to insure the absence of any nuclear threat on the Korean peninsula comprise a wonderful and constructive package.

In order to insure that there are no misunderstandings in the future about our discussions, I am sending a copy of this letter to President Bill Clinton, whom I have briefed about our visit to North Korea.

Also, I presume you have noticed that President Kim Young Sam has announced acceptance of your offer for a summit meeting. I have offered my services to you if there are any future problems concerning any of these matters, and trust that you and I can continue to exchange ideas about the future relationships among your nation, South Korea, and the United States.

My hope now is that your ultimate goal of a peaceful and united Korea can be realized. As you requested, we at The Carter Center will be prepared to assist whenever there are problems in sustaining mutually beneficial talks between North and South Korea. I made this same offer to President Kim Young Sam. I wish you and him every success in this effort.

Please extend our best wishes to your wife and family.

Sincerely,

Jimmy Carter (signed)[1]

Faye had also sent a copy of the message to President Clinton through Tony Lake along with a request to make it available to Bob Gallucci. (Carter also provided me authorization for Dick Christenson to send his notes on Carter's first conversation with Kim Il Sung to Gallucci in an "Eyes Only" format, meaning that only Gallucci should see it.[2] Believing the key opponents to his trip to be senior State Department officials, Carter did not want copies of the message distributed through normal State communications channels.)

Later that morning, one of Bob Gallucci's deputies, Gary Samore, called me to express appreciation for the copy of Carter's letter to Kim Il Sung. He said that the Gallucci letter to Kang Sok Ju would track closely with Carter's letter. Gary also confirmed what officers from the U.S. embassy in Seoul had already communicated to us directly: that South Korea had proposed a ministerial-level meeting for the following week to plan for the Korean summit; that Unification Minister Lee Hong Koo would head the South Korean delegation to that meeting; and that the Kim Young Sam government was now pleased with the Carter visit since he had not ignored their interests. Samore told me that the South Korean embassy had asked Gallucci's office for a copy of Carter's letter to Kim Il Sung, but had been told that the embassy must deal directly with Carter on that matter. After the phone call, with Carter's permission, I summarized information from our conversations in North Korea that I thought would be useful to Seoul in planning the summit and sent that paper to Jim Laney to be passed to the South Korean government[3]

Gallucci's fully cleared letter to Kang Sok Ju left Washington late that same evening. It framed the message to the North Korean official as seeking official confirmation of the language below:

My government has received the message that former President Carter has conveyed at the request of President Kim Il Sung regarding the DPRK's [North Korea's] willingness to return to full compliance with the NPT and IAEA safeguards and its desire to replace its gas graphite reactors and related technology with light-water reactors as part of an overall settlement of the nuclear issue. . . . Former President Carter has also conveyed President Kim's assurances that the DPRK will permit IAEA inspectors and IAEA surveillance equipment to remain in place at the nuclear sites at Yongbyon and will freeze the major element of the DPRK's nuclear program while US-DPRK talks are under way. On the basis of these assurances, we understand that your willingness to freeze the nuclear program means that the DPRK will not refuel the 5-MW[e] reactor nor reprocess spent fuel while U.S.-DPRK talks continue. We also assume that the DPRK will permit IAEA inspections necessary to maintain continuity of safeguards at the declared sites.

Gallucci's message concluded by saying that with North Korea's confirmation, the United States would be prepared to begin bilateral talks in Geneva as early as July 6.[4]

Operating out of his home office in Plains, but staying in close touch with The Carter Center in Atlanta by fax, phone, and e-mail, Carter worked to keep the nuclear understandings on track and to advance the Korean summit concept. The first task was to restrain the political rhetoric of the North Korean mission in New York. According to an article in *USA Today* on June 21, the North Korean diplomat Han Song Ryol had told the press that his country would neither freeze its nuclear program nor allow nuclear inspectors and surveillance cameras to remain as long as the United States engaged in sanctions discussions with other members of the Security Council. The newspaper article contrasted Han's statement with the U.S. government's position, articulated again the previous day by President Clinton, that discussions on sanctions would continue until North Korea kept its promise to freeze its nuclear program.[5]

After a short telephone conversation with President Clinton, Carter sent a stern letter to Minister Counselor Han. He told Han that he had a firm commitment from Kim Il Sung that the North Korean nuclear program would be frozen during "good faith talks" with the United States and that he had reiterated that point in the letter he sent to President Kim Il Sung the previous day; he concluded: "Any statement from you to the contrary creates serious problems in the White House and among the American public." President Clinton had already expressed concern about his statement. The U.S. president had also said that he would publicly state that there would be no further need for sanctions if Pyongyang confirmed through diplomatic channels the agreement reached between Carter and Kim Il Sung. Carter also told Han that he should emphasize in his diplomatic reports to his capital that personal attacks against the South Korean president, Kim Young Sam, were counterproductive and would strengthen those seeking to undermine the desires of his president, Kim Il Sung.[6]

The same day, the South Korean consul general in Atlanta faxed me the copy of a letter to Carter from President Kim Young Sam, which was transmitted immediately to Carter in Plains. The South Korean leader's view of the trip had changed dramatically. He said that he had long been impressed with Carter's ability to translate his principles and beliefs into action; recalled how President Carter's support for human rights and democracy while in the White House had helped "fertilize the blossoming Korean democracy"; and emphasized that their candid consultations prior to and after Carter's visit to Pyongyang had been "consistent with the common efforts of the U.S. and Korean governments to reach a peaceful solution of the North Korean nuclear problem through negotiations." He admitted that in the months leading up to the Carter trip, tensions on the peninsula had heightened, and the chances for successfully solving the nuclear issue had almost vanished. "I think it is very fortunate that your visit improved the chances for peaceful resolution of the North Korean nuclear problem by inducing North Korea to promise to freeze its nuclear development program." His administration was following up quickly on "the proposal" Carter had delivered to him from President Kim Il Sung "for South-North summit talks"; a deputy prime ministerial–level preparatory meeting would be held on June 28 at Panmunjom. His government would pursue the summit talks in a "fair and open manner" and maintain "close and continuous consultations" with Carter.[7]

Carter had talked by phone with the South Korean ambassador to the United States, Han Seung Soo, on Sunday and Monday. The ambassador had first requested that Carter urge Kim Il Sung to accept Kim Young Sam's proposal for the June 28 meeting, but later called to report that the North Korean leader had accepted the meeting. In a new letter to Kim Il Sung, Carter said he was pleased to learn of Kim Il Sung's positive decision for the preparatory meeting. He asked to be kept informed should problems arise in arranging the meeting and said that he would be glad to be of assistance on this or other issues.[8] He had made the same point in his ongoing discussions with Ambassador Han Seung Soo.

On June 22, Ambassador Han wrote to add his own praises for Carter's achievement. He said that Carter's "fine efforts" had "provided new momentum to resolving the North Korean nuclear issues and to improving relations between South and North Korea." He said that his government would continue to solicit Carter's support and expressed the hope that Carter's "valiant efforts will be ultimately and justly rewarded."[9]

Tom Lantos, the Democratic chairman of a subcommittee of the House Committee on Foreign Affairs, called to invite Carter to testify before his subcommittee. He asked me to tell Carter that he was impressed by what he had achieved and thought that he was being unfairly criticized. After talking with Carter, I told the congressman that although Carter appreciated his offer, his policy was not to testify in Washington. Once the "dust had settled," he would be glad to talk with the subcommittee if its members came to Atlanta.[10]

In Plains, Carter followed closely the reporting on his trip and his White House meeting. Carrie Harmon, Phil Wise, and I did the same thing in Atlanta. Newspapers covered the Carter trip extensively in their Monday, June 20, editions. Most articles correctly reported the basics: that Carter and administration officials had had a good meeting at the White House, that a new diplomatic "opening" might result from the Carter trip, that the next step was to receive an official North Korean confirmation of Kim Il Sung's agreement with Carter, and that President Clinton had complimented Carter during their telephone conversation. The reports also mentioned Carter's explanation of his misspoken remark in Pyongyang about UN sanctions. They recorded as well that Carter and the administration continued to differ on the use of UN sanctions in influencing North Korea's decisions on its nuclear weapons program.

On the other hand, the editorials and individual commentaries on that day and the next two days—before the North Koreans had responded to the U.S. government through diplomatic channels—were less positive than Carrie, Phil, and I had expected. We were disappointed.

A few writers praised Carter's efforts, but more criticized him. *USA Today* editorialized that Carter's "promising breakthrough . . . provides Kim [Il Sung] and Clinton with an honorable, face-saving way out."[11] The *New York Times*'s June 21 editorial said that if the North Koreans confirmed their agreement with Carter, "it offers a promising route toward a deal." Kim Il Sung's pledge that the inspectors could remain at Yongbyon would ensure against diversion of an additional five bombs' worth of plutonium; another way must be found to ascertain the history of previous diversion.[12]

Carter's critics attacked on two fronts: censoring him for being gullible, naïve, or an appeaser; and for weakening Clinton and perhaps torpedoing U.S. policy toward North Korea.

The *Washington Post* led the national newspapers in disparaging Carter. Its June 20 editorial charged that Carter had been "duped." Irritated about Carter's positive references to Kim Il Sung, the editorial writer emphasized that the North Korean leader was a "dictator, aggressor, and terrorist"; his country was "a chronic cheater on its anti-proliferation vows."[13] Lally Weymouth, a *Washington Post* columnist and a consistent hard-liner on North Korea, lambasted Carter as a "virtual apologist" for "the brutal dictator who [had] launched the Korean War" and who was using the former president to buy more time to build its nuclear program." She said Clinton had been "blindsided by Carter" and should now send North Korea a message that if it starts a war over the nuclear issue, the United States will fight until the regime is destroyed.[14] Other commentators also berated Carter. The editorial in the *Atlanta Journal Constitution* said that "part of the rationale for the former president's visit seemed to be the care and feeding of Kim's [Kim Il Sung's] ego—a duty that Carter performed to excess."[15] Writing in *USA Today*, Harry Schwartz insisted that Carter's actions illustrated the wisdom of the maxim that "former presidents should be put out to pasture and kept there."[16]

R. Jeffrey Smith and his *Washington Post* colleagues continued to highlight differences between Carter and the Clinton administration.

One article pointed out that Gallucci had declined to endorse Carter's assertion that "the crisis is over," while Carter in his hotel press conference had said that the administration's sanctions proposal could have been a "direct cause of a potential war."[17] Another held that Carter's visit had derailed the administration's drive for UN sanctions and quoted an unnamed high-ranking diplomat who said that Carter had been "very effectively used by Kim Il Sung to dissipate the pressure for sanctions and split the coalition."[18] A third reported that administration officials had "voiced irritation, and in some cases direct anger with Carter over his traveling to North Korea and seemingly misstating the administration's position on sanctions."[19]

Two Republican senators, John McCain of Arizona and Phil Graham of Texas, who had just returned from a trip to Seoul, said in an NBC interview that they saw nothing new in Kim Il Sung's offer to Carter. McCain said that he could not believe "a former president of the United States would go to a foreign country and repudiate the policy of a standing president." The senator called for a reinforcement of U.S. forces in South Korea to "strengthen its ability to launch a preemptive nuclear attack in case diplomatic efforts and sanctions failed to persuade North Korea to abandon its nuclear weapons program."[20]

Perhaps no one posed the issue of how the Carter trip embarrassed the administration as sharply as Jay Leno on his June 21 late-night television program. Leno joked, "I think we've finally got a president with a foreign policy, willing to stand up on principle and confront the North Koreans. I think that's great. But enough about Jimmy Carter."[21]

Appreciating that the administration was encountering considerable political flack because of his trip, Carter composed and sent a lengthy letter to President Clinton. Acknowledging the political attacks on the administration, Carter sought to explain why he thought it so important for him to go to North Korea and why he was convinced that he had correctly represented the administration's views in dealing with the

North Koreans. He did not try to gloss over his views on the sanctions campaign, but instead tried to articulate clearly why he opposed it. In Carter's mind, his letter represented an attempt to heal his rift with the Clinton administration. The letter takes on increasing interest since it was written and transmitted before the diplomatic response came from the North Korean government. Much of the letter is quoted below.

> *I appreciated our brief conversation this morning, and your willingness to make a statement that there will be no need for sanctions if the commitments of President Kim Il Sung to me are honored. I have asked the North Koreans to be patient, to make only positive statements for a few days, and to refrain from criticisms of President Kim Young Sam.*

Carter then noted that he would like to supplement his trip report left for President Clinton with a "few personal reflections."

> *What I intended to be a mission designed to help implement your policy and demonstrate my unity with you in a common effort has, unfortunately, created some difficulties for your administration. In retrospect, and perhaps too subjectively, I consider my effort to have been completely successful—provided the North Koreans honor the commitments made to me by President Kim Il Sung. I attempted to be as thoroughly briefed as possible by your assistants on the nuclear issue. Bob Gallucci and quite a number of others gave me a good picture of the technical aspects of the situation, so that when I prepared my talking points before leaving home and checked them with Bob, I was confident I was on the right track. However, as you know, I had no instructions, authority, or insight into strategy or diplomacy.*

> *Realizing when I left home that there was opposition to my trip both in Washington and in South Korea, I attempted at least to assuage the concerns in Seoul. I believe I succeeded, as their crisis atmosphere dissipated, and now they are probing toward a summit conference. Their top officials, by the way, have called and written to thank me profusely.*

However, something like a comedy of errors has kept the pot brewing at home. I regret this very much, and have explained thoroughly the quick sound bite on CNN that caused the basic problem. It was plain to the North Koreans that I was giving my personal opinion of what the results would be, predicated on a full implementation of Kim Il Sung's previous commitment to me. It was basically the same statement that you and I discussed this morning. Also, I went on to explain my comment as applying to the sanctions resolution being held in abeyance— and had to define the word for the interpreter.

I realized when I arrived at the White House that all was not well when none of the cabinet officers or their superiors were there for my briefing. I can say, however, that Tony and Bob helped us to relieve the strain, and your phone call was very welcome. As I remarked, yours were the first affirmative or complimentary words I had heard.

Our only possible difference, which is not insignificant, is that I did not agree that sanctions should be pursued without giving some chance for direct communication with Kim Il Sung, the only person who could make a decision that could end the impasse. I still feel that a war was imminent if official international condemnation were imposed on a leader treated almost as a deity.

Maybe you and I can talk over some basic international matters sometime in the future, after we all have had a chance to observe how well the North Korean nuclear agreements are implemented. I do not wish to intrude or to be a problem to you. I have been eager to help when given an opportunity with NAFTA, the Aidid problem [in Somalia], MFN [Most Favored Nation treatment on trade issues, particularly related to China] and a few less significant matters.

My life and Rosalynn's are in work of The Carter Center, and we have a surprisingly broad agenda. In most cases, we go our own way in parts of the world where few others want to be involved, and we prefer little or no publicity. This week, for instance, I'll be in Nicaragua in a Carter Center effort at reconciliation of the fragmented parties, in preparation for what I hope will be a successful election. Only rarely do we inject ourselves into something in the front pages or the evening news. The North Korean case, I believe, will be a rare if not unique occurrence.

My hope and expectation is to work with you as a loyal and admiring friend.

The letter was signed, *"Sincerely, Jimmy."*[22]

Once Carrie, Phil, and I had reviewed the press, we prepared guidance that The Carter Center would use in responding to the deluge of press inquiries that were descending on Carrie's office. Despite our irritation with the continuing criticisms sourced to unnamed administration officials, we decided that the Center should avoid any comments to the press that could facilitate efforts to focus more on the alleged feud between Carter and the administration than on Carter's efforts in North Korea. We decided to stick to the line that Carter had gone to North Korea because he feared war was imminent; that Clinton had agreed that he could go as a private citizen representing The Carter Center; that Carter had been well briefed and had discussed issues with Kim Il Sung consistent with the thinking in Washington; and that Carter believed the agreement he had reached with Kim Il Sung met the administration's policy requirements, but that the administration would have to make the final determination on this point. We would also insist that when Carter had said that the crisis was over, he had conditioned his statement on the North Koreans living up to the promises made to him by Kim Il Sung. Carter approved this approach.

We also decided that Carrie and her colleagues would handle all the press questions except those from reporters insisting on talking with someone who had traveled with Carter. Those calls would be referred to me. I spoke with Jeffrey Smith of the *Washington Post* on two or three occasions during that first week we were back at the Carter Center. A skilled questioner, he probed many aspects of the trip, and I tried to be helpful in giving a factual account of what had happened. But I refused to cooperate when he tried to ferret out the differences between Carter and the administration. I declined to say who had told us what prior to our departure and after our return and who attended which meetings. I reaffirmed what Carter had already said publicly— that he had received an extensive briefing in Washington and that the views he represented to Kim Il Sung and other North Korean officials were fully consistent with the briefings he had received. After a couple of conversations, I had the distinct impression that Smith found me unresponsive. In any event, if he continued to call the Center, he stopped asking to talk with me.

In Washington with editors whom he knew personally, Terry Adamson followed a more proactive approach. On June 21, he wrote to Howell Raines, the editorial page editor of the *New York Times,* to praise its generally positive editorial. However, most of his letter was devoted to underlining the caveat that Carter had attached to his statement about the crisis being over, that is, "based on the condition that Kim Il Sung delivered on his commitments." Adamson went on to say that should Kim Il Sung not fulfill his commitments, "the U.S.'s hand for rallying world opinion for a more forceful response would have been immeasurably strengthened, again by the Carter trip."[23] He made the same point about the "crisis is over" remark in a separate letter to Meg Greenfield, the editor of the editorial page of the *Washington Post,* but this letter did not praise the paper's editorial, which, as noted earlier, took a negative line toward the Carter actions.[24]

The debate over the value of the Carter trip would not stop after Wednesday, June 22, 1994, but the issue about whether Carter had misinterpreted his conversation with Kim Il Sung would.

Around 9:30 A.M. on Wednesday, June 22, 1994, Faye called me to her office to review a fax just received from the North Korean ambassador to the United Nations. The ambassador's cover note said that the attached message was being delivered at the same time to Bob Gallucci in the State Department. It was the reply of Kang Sok Ju to Gallucci's diplomatic note based on the letter Carter had sent to Kim Il Sung. The ambassador said in his cover message that Kim Il Sung wanted Carter to have a copy at the same time that it went to the administration and that he was sure that Carter would be pleased with the message. Indeed he was.

As I read the message, Carter was en route from Plains to Atlanta. I reached him on the car phone. "Mr. President," I said, "Kim Il Sung has sent you the North Korean reply to Gallucci's diplomatic note. It looks very good."

"Read it to me," Carter responded.

"Should I, on an open phone line?"

"Read it," he repeated firmly.

I read him the following letter to "Ambassador Robert L. Gallucci, Head of the USA Delegation to the DPRK-USA Talks" from "Kang Sok Ju, Head of the DPRK Delegation to the DPRK-USA Talks:"

Dear Ambassador Gallucci:

I acknowledge my receipt of your message dated June 20.

We are pleased to see that, during [the] recent significant meeting between the great leader of our people President KIM IL SUNG and Mr. Carter, the basis has been established that will enable a resolution of the outstanding issues between the DPRK and the United States.

The great leader told former President Mr. Carter that the process of building confidence between the DPRK and the United States is the key to the resolution of the nuclear issue, and he has made a momentous proposal aimed at to [sic] breaking the current DPRK-USA impasse and resolving the nuclear issue at its root once and for all.

In this connection, we would like to make it clear that we are willing, within the framework of the DPRK-USA confidence-building process and also of our proposed package solution to the nuclear issue, to fully implement the Nuclear Non-Proliferation Treaty and the safeguards agreement with the International Atomic Energy Agency (IAEA/Agency), to replace the existing graphite-moderated reactors

with light–water reactors and to freeze the major elements of our nu-
clear program while the DPRK-USA talks go underway.

For the immediate future, we would like to assure you that, for the sake
of the third round of the DPRK-USA talks, we are prepared neither to
reload the five-megawatt experimental reactor with new fuel nor to re-
process the spent fuel, and to permit the inspections for the continuity of
safeguards including the maintenance of the presence of IAEA inspectors
and of the Agency's surveillance equipment in place at the Yongbyon
nuclear facilities. Issues after that stage will be subject to the discussion
at the third round of talks.

We would have no objection to your suggestion of holding a third round
of DPRK-USA talks in Geneva on July 6, but we would like to propose
to begin the proposed third round of talks on July 8, for the reason of
convenience of air route connections. The specific scheduling of the talks
for final confirmation of date could soon be agreed upon through work-
ing-level contacts in New York.

I would like to take this opportunity to note the arguments by some of-
ficials within the US Administration for the "sanctions" against the
DPRK, and also to reiterate, in no uncertain terms, our position that
the "sanctions" and dialogue are absolutely incompatible.

It is my hope that the third round of talks will certainly take place on an
equal and unprejudiced basis, that will bring me to another meeting
with you soon in Geneva.[25]

When I had finished reading the Kang Sok Ju letter, Carter exclaimed, "Well, that sounds great! It has everything in it that's needed."

His voice was exuberant. He had every reason to be. Few would have
dared to take so great a political risk. He had placed his reputation on
the line, and he had suffered sharp criticism for the past few days. He
would now have the satisfaction of having it publicly revealed that he
had, indeed, cut the deal that "experts" said could not be cut with the
North Koreans. He must have relished the victory of proving his critics

wrong. But primarily he relished, and probably gave thanks to his God, that his actions had stopped a dangerous spiral toward war.

When Carter arrived at the Center, he quickly prepared and dispatched a new letter to Kim Il Sung. He said he was "most gratified to learn of Minister Kang's positive response to Ambassador Gallucci's letter," which had officially confirmed the agreement that they had framed together in Pyongyang. Carter wrote: "I am confident that the bilateral talks will go forward, and I hope that they will, as you suggested, resolve 'the nuclear issue at its root once and for all.'" Carter also reiterated his firm support for the quick move to a summit meeting. He said he shared Kim Il Sung's conviction that in building trust between his government and the U.S. government and between the people of both countries, both nations would gain. He said he would follow the upcoming talks between North Korea and the United States and between North and South Korea with "great interest," and would stand ready to be of help if his assistance was needed.[26]

Four days later, Carter would receive a faxed copy of Kim Il Sung's reply to Carter's letter of June 22. The North Korean leader recalled his "significant meeting" with Carter in Pyongyang and their "open-hearted exchange of views and agreements that we reached on a number of important matters related to the improvement of relations between our two countries and to the resolution of the nuclear issue based on mutual confidence." He said the changes in Seoul and Washington since the Carter trip showed that his visit and their meetings had "marked an event of paramount importance." He then said that his competent officials would notify Washington officials of North Korea's position through diplomatic channels and "work hard to translate them into practice." He said he anticipated that the agreements he and Carter reached would lead to an improvement in the relations between the two countries. He also said he expected Carter to be involved in this process in the future.[27]

Tom Johnson asked Carter to come to the CNN studio for a live interview that afternoon. CNN scheduled the Carter interview to follow immediately after President Clinton had announced the North Korean response on television. En route to the CNN interview, Carter received a phone call from Clinton. I could hear only Carter's side of the conversation. Carter advised Clinton that he had received a copy of the Kang Sok Ju letter that had repeated back the key elements that were in the letter he sent to Kim Il Sung on Monday. Then, for a lengthy period, Carter listened, nodding occasionally. He later told me that the president had expressed his appreciation and that of the nation to Carter. Clinton had also told the former president that he would stop the sanctions initiative and that the administration would schedule early commencement of the third round of bilateral talks between the United States and North Korea. Carter thanked the president for the call, expressed appreciation for his comments and future actions, and told him that he and the Center would be available to help in the future if called upon.

Tom Johnson was waiting at the door when we arrived at the CNN studios a few minutes before the Clinton press conference in Washington would begin. Carter went quickly into the make-up room to prepare for his subsequent interview. Then the three of us watched President Clinton's press conference on the CNN monitors.

President Clinton looked pleased as he announced that the United States had received "formal confirmation from North Korea that it will freeze the major elements of its nuclear program while a new round of talks between our nations proceeds." Characterizing this development as "an important step forward," he said that North Korea had assured the U.S. government that its freeze would include not reloading its reactor and not reprocessing its spent fuel and that the IAEA inspectors and monitoring equipment would be allowed to remain in place, thereby permitting verification of the freeze. Clinton said that these assurances restored the basis of talks between the two countries. Consequently, the United States was informing the North Koreans that it was prepared to participate in a new round of talks in Geneva early the next month (July). The president also said that the United States, in addition to the nuclear issue, would be prepared to "discuss a full range of security, political, and economic issues that affect North Korea's relationship with the international community." He went on: "During these discussions we will suspend our efforts to pursue a sanctions resolution in the United Nations Security Council." Clinton also welcomed the agreement of South Korea and North Korea to arrange a summit meeting. He then thanked President Carter "for the important role he played in helping to achieve this step [relating to the above-mentioned developments]." He said that although these developments did not mark a solution to the problem, they did mark "a new opportunity to find a solution."[28]

He then invited questions. Asked whether the "other guy [North Korea] blinked," Clinton said that such a characterization was not useful. For the past eighteen months, the United States had followed a two-pronged policy: to be firm and bring its allies—South Korea, Japan, Russia, and China—closer together, but to keep the door open to North Korea to become "part of the international community."[29] The world would be the winner if the nuclear issue could be resolved. When reminded that critics would charge that the North Koreans were using new talks as a ploy to continue to develop their nuclear program clandestinely, Clinton said that the presence of IAEA inspectors and equipment on the ground would verify the agreement. He emphasized that if the United States could not verify the North Korean freeze, "you and I wouldn't be having this conversation at this moment."

Most of the questions to Clinton focused on why the administration up to now had been leery about the Carter mission and why he personally had not met with Carter when he returned from Pyongyang. Clinton said that when Carter was invited to visit North Korea and expressed willingness to do so, he thought it gave the United States the opportunity to have a distinguished private citizen communicate the administration's position to the DPRK leaders. "The very fact that he went, I think, was a gesture of the importance that we placed on resolving this matter, and not just for ourselves but for the world." Asked whether Carter, before the trip, had perceived something that Clinton had not seen, Clinton said that he would not use that characterization. Carter had called him, and they had talked about the problem. He had ensured that Carter received adequate briefings. Clinton affirmed that he thought Carter had faithfully articulated the policy of the U.S. government and that provided a "forum in which the North Korean leader, Kim Il Sung, could respond as he did." He added: "And I am pleased about it." As to why he did not meet Carter in Washington, Clinton said that he already had plans to go to Camp David, and he did not want Carter to have to "come all the way up to Camp David." He and Carter had known each other for twenty years, and they had decided instead to talk by phone. He said he had told Carter how glad he was that he went, that he thought it was "a trip worth taking, a risk worth taking," and that he was very pleased.[30]

Almost immediately after the Clinton interview in Washington, Carter faced the CNN cameras in Atlanta. Bernard Shaw, the CNN anchor, introduced Carter but then asked Wolf Blitzer, in the CNN studio in Washington, whether one could say this was "vindication for all of the speculation and the distance that was put between this White House and the former president." Blitzer responded, "Absolutely." Shaw asked Carter, "What did it?" Carter replied, "Opening up . . . direct communication with Kim Il Sung." He elaborated: "None of his subordinates [could] make any sort of concessions or [put] new ideas into effect [on their own]."

Judy Woodruff raised the riff between Carter and the administration. "I think it's all roses now," he said. He admitted that he had known for more than a year that some top officials, particularly in the State Department, had not wanted him to make the trip. But after he notified President Clinton of his inclination to travel to the peninsula, the president "came back almost immediately and, in effect, authorized [the] trip." "I feel that I got adequate approval and support from President Clinton, and I appreciate his faith in me, even under very difficult circumstances." Vice President Gore had been supportive from the beginning.

Then Carter, while expressing his true belief, made a statement that would give ammunition to his critics. Referring to his talks with the

North Korean leader, Carter said: "It was kind of like a miracle and almost an incredible statement Kim Il Sung gave me in response to my proposals," and for those in Washington who had never talked with the North Korean leader "it was hard to believe." Summing up, Carter said he had "no criticism of anyone."[31]

I stood with Johnson in the editing room during the interview. He was talking nonstop with CNN correspondents in Atlanta and Washington about questions to be asked Carter when the individual correspondents were brought on camera. As the interview neared its end, Johnson turned to me and asked: "Anything important we have missed?" I replied that I could not think of anything. Tom then signaled to the interviewing reporters to wrap up the session. They did. The camera faded on a smiling Carter, the same smile on a somewhat older face that had been his trademark during his days of active political campaigning.

After the CNN cameras stopped rolling, the CNN people in the studio gathered around Carter to talk with him and praise his achievement. Carter allowed the celebration to continue only for a few minutes. Then it was back to the Center, where much work awaited—most of it about Center issues in Africa and Latin America. But when we arrived at the Center, the staff had gathered at the front door to welcome their boss. They were good people, hard-working people, people who labored to assist the Carters in trying to resolve conflicts, promote democracy, advance human rights, improve health care in poor countries, and help poor farmers increase their crop yields. They felt, as they congratulated him, that they, too, shared in this moment of triumph. They sought at great personal sacrifice to make the world better by their work at The Carter Center. It was exhilarating when, on rare occasions such as this one, it was clear that their efforts could make a difference. And they rejoiced.

That afternoon the Carter Center issued as a press release the following:

STATEMENT FROM FORMER PRESIDENT JIMMY CARTER ON KOREA
I have been informed by the North Koreans that they have reconfirmed to the Clinton Administration the proposals President Kim Il Sung

agreed to in my discussions with him last week. Specifically, the North Korean government has affirmed that they will freeze their nuclear program—including refraining from either refueling their nuclear reactor or reprocessing the spent fuel during the conduct of U.S.-North Korean talks, and that they will permit IAEA inspectors and the agency's surveillance equipment to remain in place at the Yongbyon nuclear facilities, all within the framework of North Korea's shifting from existing graphite-moderated reactors to light-water reactors.[32]

After North Korea confirmed the Carter-Kim Il Sung understandings in diplomatic channels, the media's evaluation of the Carter initiative swung dramatically into the positive column. Many editorial writers extolled Carter. The *Washington Post*, earlier skeptical, commended Carter for creating an opening for a peaceful resolution of the nuclear crisis, and Clinton for accepting it.[33] The *New York Times* editorialized that "Mr. Carter [had] helped Mr. Clinton regain his footing"; the president should cut through "the bickering in his own Administration" and "put together a persuasive diplomatic package to coax North Korea to become truly nuclear-free."[34] The *Christian Science Monitor* credited Carter with brokering a chance for a peaceful settlement. To charges of some "conservative commentators" that Carter was a "meddling and naïve do-gooder," the editorial writer gave this answer: "Would that we had more naïve do-gooders like him."[35]

Several columnists contrasted Carter's insight and actions with his critics' words. Carl Rowan wrote: "Americans have begun to see beyond the snide insults of the bellicose right-wingers and understand that Jimmy Carter did a great service for his country and for mankind. He at least temporarily defused a mindless crisis that could have ended up in a new Korean war far more terrible than the 1950–53 conflict."[36] In the *Denver Post*, Sandy Grady said Carter's critics who had called Carter "a patsy and pushover" should line up to apologize to him.[37] Closer to Carter's home, Randall Ashley, foreign editor of the *Atlanta Journal Constitution*, expressed amazement that "both the State Department and the South Korean government [had] been stunned since Carter's visit by the swiftness of the positive responses from North Korea. "To Carter, it's a simple matter: Somebody had to talk to the man who can get things done, and in North Korea that man is Kim Il-sung."[38]

Statements critical of Carter and sourced to unnamed administration officials stopped appearing in the media. Several administration officials insisted, however, that Clinton's firm policy had made possible Carter's successful trip.[39] At the time and later, Tony Lake, the NSC adviser, expressed the view that the combination of the threat of sanctions, the offer of future concessions, and the Carter trip had produced the breakthrough.[40]

The generally positive evaluation of Carter's intervention into the nuclear crisis did not dampen the ardor or cool the rhetoric of the hardliners. George Will's op-ed, printed in many newspapers, said that Carter was "either a modern Merlin or a megalomaniac." He elaborated: "Either [Carter] has convinced Kim Il Sung to mind his manners and mend his ways, or he has convinced himself that the world has no hurt that cannot be cured by applying to it the poultice of his personality." Will also said, "It would be nice if Carter's cameo appearance in the geopolitics of the 1990s would remind Clinton, who came to power demonizing the 1980s, how dangerous the 1970s were because of Carter and people like him." Will concluded that if Carter and the Clinton administration were "on the same sheet of music," as Gallucci had recently noted, "the future [was] in jeopardy."[41] Charles Krauthammer slammed Carter for thinking that all that stood between war and peace was "dining with a dictator" and for undercutting the U.S. sanctions policy that Clinton had "belatedly and tepidly" begun to press.[42] William Safire accused Carter of misrepresenting the U.S. view on sanctions, of usurping presidential authority, and of betting "on the contagion of his own indisputable goodness." Mocking Carter's declaration that the accomplishments of his trip were "kind of like a miracle," Safire concluded: "With no basis for trust, we're trusting North Korea with precious time. It is kind of like a miracle."[43]

The hard-liners would continue to criticize efforts at reconciliation toward North Korea throughout the 1990s and early 2000s. Many influential politicians would subscribe to their views. But for the moment their ideas did not have the resonance of those extolling Carter and his approach. Carter received many commendations—from thankful citizens and public figures—praising his mission. Three letters stand out because they were from U.S. government officials who understood how close the United States had come to war.

Ambassador Jim Laney, whose advice and assistance had been indispensable to Carter, wrote:

> *You have made many trips, ones which have accomplished great good. But none can compare to your recent trip to Korea. There is no question but what we were on a collision course and you averted virtually certain war. As a result, people are talking across the DMZ in a different tone and spirit, and there is rekindled hope for this tortured peninsula. . . . Although [South Korean] people are holding their breath somewhat pending the outcome—having been disappointed so many times—their gratitude for what you have made possible is overwhelming. I wish you could hear some of the people that speak to me from such heartfelt appreciation.*[44]

Dick Christenson, who accompanied Carter to Pyongyang and who would return to Washington to back up the U.S. delegation in Geneva that negotiated the Agreed Framework, wrote:

> *I continue to think about your achievement in Pyongyang, and I am proud to have been able to assist you. You brought us a providential new chance to resolve issues peaceably with North Korea, and the world is in your debt. . . . I will bear fully in mind your gift to us of another chance. We have a heavy responsibility to make good use of that chance.*[45]

One of the most poignant letters came from Danny Russel, Political Unit Chief at the embassy in Seoul, whose briefing paper had been helpful to Carter as he prepared his thoughts for his meetings in Pyongyang. Russel assured Carter that the U.S. was assembling a strong team for the Geneva discussions, that it "was set to make serious progress," and that he would be a member of that team. Russel's conclusion:

You, Mr. President, are personally responsible for this turn of events. Your absolute determination in the face of official discouragement, the condescension of experts, and the formidable substantive obstacles of the issues—your resolve and faith, along with your skill and insight, are in my opinion directly responsible for saving the lives. . . of countless thousands of people in Korea, likely myself included. Your visit was the fulcrum on which the inexorable but stupid slide towards war was turned back, enabling a frightened and sobered set of officials to scramble back toward dialogue and compromise. . . . I flatter myself that I can imagine that you must have asked yourself at some point whether it was possible that nearly everyone else was right and you were wrong. I myself was afraid to hope that your mission could do more than to stabilize a degenerating situation. The confidence that fortified you against doubt during your mission must now serve to insulate you against the insulting slights that I am reading in the U.S. press. You were right, you did right, and it is the source of immense personal satisfaction to me that I was able—encouraged and guided by Ambassador Laney—to help.[46]

CHAPTER 13

The Agreed Framework and Aftermath

After June 22, 1994, when President Clinton announced confirmation of the Carter-Kim Il Sung understandings, the primary action on the nuclear issue shifted to Washington, Pyongyang, and Geneva. The key actors in the Geneva talks were Ambassador Robert Gallucci and First Vice Foreign Minister Kang Sok Ju and their colleagues, along with their superiors, to whom they reported in their respective capitals. Kim Young Sam and his government in South Korea and their North Korean counterparts controlled the action related to the inter-Korean summit.

His mission achieved, Jimmy Carter moved out of the limelight on Korea and focused on other Carter Center business. In September he negotiated the departure of Haiti's military dictator and the return of its earlier democratically elected president; in doing so, he staved off a U.S. military invasion of which planes and paratroopers were already in the air en route to that country. In December, again with Clinton's support, Carter intervened in the Bosnian imbroglio, mediating a four-month cease-fire between the Muslim and Serb forces.

Despite these and other Carter Center activities, the former president followed intently the negotiations in Geneva and developments on the Korean peninsula. He periodically gave advice to the U.S. negotiators, spoke out publicly in support of the administration's pursuit of a peaceful resolution for the North Korean nuclear problem, and urged the leaders of both countries to reconcile their differences.

On July 8, Kim Il Sung, reportedly while at a retreat up-country preparing for the summit, suffered a massive heart attack and died. Less than three weeks earlier, President Carter had left North Korea. In Seoul on his way home, Carter had told journalists that Kim Il Sung had appeared in good health. I came away with a similar impression. In her trip report, Mrs. Carter described Kim Il Sung as "vigorous and active." In describing his April visit to Pyongyang, Eason Jordan told Carter in June that Kim Il Sung seemed healthy, and Mike Chinoy would later write that in June 1994 the North Korean president "looked terrific—alert, vigorous, and bursting with energy."[1] Some of Carter's critics later scorned his description of Kim Il Sung, suggesting that if Carter could not tell that an overweight, eighty-two-year-old man was in bad health, how could he interpret the more subtle workings of the man's mind when he promised to freeze the North Korean nuclear program? It was true that Kim Il Sung did not walk up the narrow, steep ladder from the deck of the yacht to his office suite on the second level, using instead a personal elevator. On the other hand, when we reached the disembarkation point at the "West Sea Barrage," Kim Il Sung strolled off the yacht and walked up a hill, along with Carter and the rest of us, to the observation building where refreshments were waiting. He did not seem more winded than anyone else, nor did he have difficulty after the walk in explaining to the Carters how the dam was built and the purpose it served. He did have a slight shuffle in his walk, quite common with older people, but his appearance did not in any way hint that he would be dead twenty days after we left his country.

Kim Il Sung's sudden and unexpected death, and the reaction of the United States and South Korea to his demise, profoundly influenced the outcomes on the Korean Peninsula and in Geneva. The Korean summit initiative floundered, and the meeting of the presidents of the two Koreas would not take place until 2000. In contrast, the United States and North

Korea built on the Jimmy Carter-Kim Il Sung deal of June 1994 and four months later concluded the bilateral Agreed Framework that halted the North Korean plutonium-based nuclear program and placed it under constant international surveillance. It stayed that way for eight years.

Events related to the Korean Peninsula moved quickly in late June and early July 1994 as the three involved governments sought to take advantage of the "openings" created by Jimmy Carter. Before June ended, North and South Korea had held a productive ministerial-level meeting that selected July 25–27 as the dates for the summit meeting and Pyongyang as the venue. On July 8, the United States and North Korean delegations met for the first day of their "third round" of talks in Geneva.

North Korea did not release the news of the death of its "Great Leader" until thirty-six hours later. Consequently, the first session of the U.S.-North Korean talks had already taken place before the North Korean delegation learned that Kim Il Sung had died. At its request, the U.S. delegation agreed to suspend the talks. Shortly thereafter, Pyongyang announced that the summit meeting would need to be postponed as well. For a couple of weeks, no one outside North Korea knew how the death of the country's only leader since independence would affect its attitude toward the Geneva talks and the summit.

The United States government and the South Korean government treated Kim Il Sung's death differently, and their respective behaviors affected significantly the ultimate North Korean decision on these two sets of negotiations. President Clinton, despite sharp criticism by Republican leaders and U.S. hard-liners on Korea, issued a condolence statement "expressing sympathy for the Korean people"; when Bob Gallucci signed the condolence book at the North Korean mission in Geneva, he wrote: "Words cannot express the feeling of sympathy I have for the Korean people."[2] Publicly and privately, the North Korean government communicated to Washington its appreciation for the U.S. actions. The suspended Geneva talks would be resumed in early August.

The government of President Kim Young Sam agonized for several days about whether to send an official condolence. In an early public statement, the Seoul government used a Korean formulation of "he will be missed" *("ashipta")* that was "a notch above 'too bad' but less personal than 'regret.'" Receiving indirect messages that the North intended to continue the inter-Korean dialogue, Foreign Minister Han made a public statement: "We sincerely hope that the new leadership in Pyongyang will keep alive the recently created momentum for dialogue, resolve the nuclear issue and pursue peaceful coexistence and prosperity between North and South Korea." But within days, the official position changed. In internal consultations, Kim Young Sam and his colleagues debated whether the South Korean president should meet with Kim Jong Il, who had neither the titles nor the experience of his father and had not yet demonstrated that he could control the levers of power in his country. Outside the Blue House, conservative forces condemned those urging that an official condolence be sent to Pyongyang. In the end, the South Korean government decided against an official expression of sympathy, sought to prevent South Korean citizens from going to Pyongyang to express their personal sympathies, cracked down on "dissident" students who allegedly were found with pro–North Korean material, and released documents recently given to the Korean government by the Russian government that proved that Kim Il Sung had started the Korean War. The North Korean rhetoric rose to caustic levels in response to these South Korean actions, which Seoul quickly matched with its frequency, if not with its venom.[3] As the end of the month came and went, the two Koreas, rather than engaging in their first summit talks ever, spent their energies condemning each other for torpedoing the meeting.

In September, with the Geneva talks restarted and making substantial progress, Carter decided to try to revive the languishing summit idea. He wrote to Kim Young Sam and expressed the hope that new preparatory talks for the summit could be initiated soon. He said that he intended to encourage the North Koreans to propose a resumption of the talks, and he urged the South Korean president to respond positively should they do so.[4] On September 18, Ambassador Laney advised Carter that Kim Young Sam's response, which would be delivered to Carter by the South Korean ambassador two days later, would affirm Seoul's commitment to reopening the dialogue with Pyongyang, express its pleasure that Carter was willing to press for the resumption of the inter-Korean talks, and invite President and Mrs. Carter to revisit Korea in the near future.[5] In Laney's view, the invitation marked a major turning point for the South Korean government; it now wished to pursue the dialogue with the North.[6]

The next day, the North Korean ambassador, Pak Gil Yon, traveled to the Carter Center from New York to present Carter with the signed original (and English translation) of Kim Il Sung's letter to him dated June 25, 1994. During their lengthy meeting, Carter expressed his disappointment that it had not been possible to "carry on Kim Il Sung's dream for reconciliation with the South." Hoping to induce the ambassador's superiors in Pyongyang to reinvigorate the summit initiative, Carter said that he believed Kim Il Sung had entrusted him with trying to improve inter-Korean relations, and he offered the services of The Carter Center and himself "to promote reconciliation, peace, and friendship on the peninsula." Unmoved by Carter's entreaties, the ambassador responded that the North Korean people "will not forgive forever" the behavior of the South Korean government at the time of the death of Kim Il Sung. Carter said that he, too, had been upset with Seoul's actions at the time, but he told the ambassador he hoped that North Korea, even if it could not forget what had happened, would forgive the South. Mixing his diplomacy and his religion, Carter said his own experience had taught him that forgiveness was the only path to progress. He mentioned that the South Korean president had invited him to visit Korea again and to continue his efforts toward reconciliation. He asked Ambassador Pak to convey to President Kim Jong Il his willingness to explore ways toward mutual forgiveness and for carrying out his father's wishes through a return visit to the peninsula; he also said, however, that he would not come unless there was a possibility for progress. He told Pak that he would wait for Kim Jong Il's reply before responding to Kim Young Sam.[7]

The North Korean response was not long in coming. On September 25, North Korean Ambassador Pak called me and asked me to come to New York to receive Pyongyang's answer to Carter's appeal. I flew to New York the next day where I received a firm rejection by North Korea for moving forward on the summit conference unless South Korean

President Kim Young Sam took actions that Pyongyang knew would be politically impossible for him to take.[8]

I reminded the ambassador that Carter now had an official invitation to visit Seoul and asked about his visiting Pyongyang. He said Carter should make his own decision about going to Seoul. The timing was "not yet appropriate" for Carter to return to Pyongyang because of the continued mourning of the North Korean people for the death of Kim Il Sung.[9]

Carter continued trying to induce the two Koreas to reopen talks and to allow him to assist in the process throughout the last part of 1994. But separate communications from Mike Chinoy (via Eason Jordan) in late September, Steve Linton in late October, and Tony Namkung in mid-November, all of whom had recently visited Pyongyang and talked with North Korean officials, confirmed Carter's suspicions that North Korea had no intention of agreeing to a summit meeting during Kim Young Sam's presidency. Their reports also underlined that North Korean officials did not favor a new Carter mediation effort at that time because they believed that Seoul, to quote Chinoy, hoped to use Carter to "help them recover some of the diplomatic ground they have lost by their clumsy anti-Pyongyang behavior of recent months."[10] Although Carter had communications with Kim Jong Il in late 1994 and early 1995 about various subjects, one of which was always the possibility of his visiting North Korea again, the consistent reply from Pyongyang was that a future visit would be welcomed but that the present was not the appropriate time.[11] Consequently, Carter decided to stand down on pushing the summit initiative with North Korea.

The South Korean government apparently decided in mid-June 1995 not only to stop seeking to revive the summit proposal but also to stop encouraging Carter's efforts to promote it. Reacting to a report in a South Korean newspaper of Carter's interest in the North-South dialogue, the consul general in Atlanta, upon instructions from his government, advised Carter that no summit could be held until Kim Jong Il had officially become "head of state," that the two Korean governments should handle preparations for the North-South dialogue, and that "third party assistance" would not be helpful.

The Korean summit did not take place until more than two years after Kim Dae Jung succeeded Kim Young Sam as president of South Korea. Carter had periodic conversations with the new South Korean president in which the subject of Korean reconciliation figured prominently. But the former U.S. president was not personally involved in planning for the historic inter-Korean summit in 2000.

If the summit concept stalled during the mid-1990s, the Geneva talks transformed and expanded the Carter-Kim Il Sung agreement in June into the formal bilateral Agreed Framework of October 1994 that resolved peacefully the nuclear crisis. In their arduous bilateral talks, Bob Gallucci and his talented team would often experience tough brinksmanship by their North Korean negotiating partners. On more than one occasion, the latter's intransigence seriously threatened to break up the talks. But such tactics did not cow Gallucci and his colleagues. They matched toughness with toughness and a willingness to find mutually advantageous compromises when their North Korean counterparts took a similar posture.

While negotiating with the North Koreans, the United States also had to undertake a series of major consultations with other international partners involved in aspects of the agreement. The most important of these, and the most difficult, was South Korea, the country that would eventually commit to providing the expensive light water reactors to North Korea as called for by the Agreed Framework and pay for most of their cost. President Kim Young Sam feared that Pyongyang would use the negotiations with the United States to drive a wedge between Washington and Seoul, and he worried about alienating the politically conservative groups at home upon whom his government depended for support. Consequently, Seoul, never as concerned as Washington about the North Korean nuclear threat, tried to get the United States to stiffen its negotiating demands, or even scrap its efforts to frame an agreement with Pyongyang. However, the Clinton administration after June 1994 decided not to let itself get so enmeshed in meeting South Korean domestic political objectives that it failed to deal effectively with what it perceived to be the serious North Korean nuclear threat. This new approach resulted from

Washington's assessment that South Korea's policy flip-flops in the months before June 1994, and the repeated attempts of the United States to accommodate the Kim Young Sam government, had played a major role in creating the gridlock that had produced the June 1994 nuclear crisis. This time, the Clinton team—while continuing to consult frequently with Seoul—kept control of the process as it conducted its negotiations with North Korea during the summer and fall. Washington also kept close contact with the IAEA, but here, too, it stayed in the driver's seat rather than allow the Vienna energy agency to dictate its negotiating position.[12]

Carter would occasionally provide advice to Washington, and he would try to use the relationship he had established with Kim Il Sung to move the negotiating process forward. As the Principals Committee was completing its instructions for the opening session of the Geneva talks (prior to the death of Kim Il Sung), the *New York Times* carried a lengthy article on June 30 saying that the U.S. delegation would demand that North Korea agree to ship its spent fuel rods out of the country, probably to Russia or China, or bury them indefinitely in a "concrete sarcophagus" under IAEA inspection.[13] When Gallucci called Carter to brief the former president on the U.S. delegation's instructions for the upcoming talks, Carter raised the article and urged Gallucci to handle with care the issue of North Korea's ultimate disposal of the fuel rods. In a letter to Gallucci (with a copy to Tony Lake) the following day, he elaborated his view on this matter and provided additional information based on his own experience and that of others who had dealt with North Koreans. He called counterproductive the article's characterization of the United States as *demanding* that the spent fuel rods be sent outside the country or buried. The North Koreans should be given credit for positive moves they made during the negotiations, not be made to look as though they subserviently caved to U.S. demands. Moreover, the United States should not allow the IAEA to determine the conditions that the North Koreans must meet in order to solve the nuclear issue. He said that there was a struggle going on between the IAEA and North Korea and the Vienna agency's technical demands "may go beyond practicality." The North Koreans had told him several times that the nuclear problem was a political rather than a technical matter. Although the North Korean leaders were "extremely proud and self-reliant," they could be "accommodating and flexible if the negotiations are on the basis of a package deal of equal give and take." As an example, he said that in his discussions in Pyongyang, they had seemed amenable to inspections of the prohibited waste sites if the inspections were combined with their being able to inspect military sites in South Korea, to which neither General Luck nor President Kim Young Sam had objections. Carter emphasized that, given past U.S. negotiating tactics, the North Koreans did not look on diplomatic relations or trade openings as a "gift, reward, or punishment if withheld." "To the North Koreans, these issues should be considered on the basis of mutual benefit, being resolved on an equal basis between two sovereign nations." Carter also gave specific advice on dealing with Gallucci's negotiating counterpart, Kang Sok Ju. He said that Kang was "something of a tough guy, less flexible than Kim Il Sung." Gallucci should always reserve the right to go "directly to the top if a deadlock seems imminent." This tactic should not involve threatening Kang Sok Ju or minimizing his stature, yet he should be aware that going over his head was an alternative that could be used. Carter concluded the letter with praise for Gallucci, saying that he knew of no one who could better handle the responsibility of the Geneva talks.[14]

President Carter was visiting Japan on Carter Center business when he learned of Kim Il Sung's death. We spoke by phone, and he was deeply disappointed. He had been convinced that with Kim Il Sung in charge in Pyongyang the U.S.-North Korean negotiations, although difficult, would end successfully. He also had thought that the summit meeting could lead to a breakthrough in Korean relations and improve long-term prospects for peace. Now the situation was less clear.

Carter acted immediately to try to discourage the new Pyongyang leadership from revising Kim Il Sung's decisions. He penned the following public statement for release by the Carter Center:

Rosalynn and I deeply regret the unexpected death of President Kim Il Sung. We extend our sincerest sympathy to his family and the people of

North Korea. We hope and trust that as Kim Jong Il and other officials of North Korea honor the memory of their country's "Great Leader" of nearly 50 years, they will also honor him by maintaining the commitment toward peace that President Kim Il Sung made two-and-a-half weeks ago.[15]

The Carters then wrote condolence notes, he to Kim Jong Il and she to Kim Song Ae. Carter's letter, in addition to expressing his condolences, urged Kim Jong Il to uphold the commitments Kim Il Sung had made to him. Emphasizing the high value he had placed on the opportunity to meet and talk with Kim Il Sung, Carter wrote, "I believe we shared the view that problems between our countries, including the nuclear issues, could be resolved to the mutual satisfaction of both nations, that relations between our two countries could be significantly improved, and that a peaceful and productive Korean Peninsula would serve the interests of your country, the Republic of Korea, the region, and the world." Saying he trusted that Kim Jong Il shared that vision, he said he was confident that Kim Jong Il and his countrymen would "honor the commitment to peace and the desire for friendship that your father expressed to me."[16]

North Korean politics immediately became apparent. When Faye Dill sent the letters to the North Korean mission in New York with the request that President Carter's be sent to Kim Jong Il and Mrs. Carter's to Kim Song Ae, the mission advised that both letters must be sent to Kim Jong Il. Acting on Carter's instructions, Faye protested, saying that Mrs. Carter had visited with Kim Song Ae, and she wanted to express her sympathy directly to her. The North Korean official clearly had a problem. Kim Song Ae was not Kim Jong Il's mother. His mother had died in 1949. Kim Song Ae's elder son, Kim Pyong Il, was the North Korean ambassador in Poland; he was regarded as a skilled and sophisticated diplomat by his diplomatic colleagues in Warsaw. (He may have been viewed by Kim Jong Il as a potential rival for power.)[17] This diplomatic stand-off came to an end on July 12 when the North Korean mission in New York gave assurances that Mrs. Carter's letter to Kim Song Ae would reach Kim Song Ae if both letters were sent under cover of a message to Kim Jong Il. Faye followed this procedure.[18]

Kim Jong Il's response was historically significant. On July 25, 1994, Carter received a faxed message from Ambassador Pak Gil Yon saying he had been authorized to convey a message to Carter from "Comrade Kim Jong Il." Not only did the son of Kim Il Sung thank Carter for his condolences, *he also pledged that he would carry out all the understandings that Carter had reached with his father* (my italics). Kim Jong Il also expressed the hope that Carter would again visit North Korea at a "reciprocally convenient time."[19] Carter immediately sent a note to President Clinton: "Kim Jong Il of North Korea has given me his personal assurance that the commitments made by Kim Il Sung will be honored." He asked that his note also be shown to Bob Gallucci.[20]

The Kim Jong Il message provided encouragement to President Clinton and his negotiating team, who were facing a new onslaught by the hardliners toward North Korea. When Kim Il Sung died, the earlier critics of the Carter-Kim Il Sung agreement, in Washington, as in Seoul, had renewed their attacks with claims that Carter's agreement with him had become null and void. They insisted that the United States should return to its earlier tough posture toward the Communist regime in North Korea. The critics, seconding the complaints by South Korean officials, disparaged Kim Jong Il; they questioned his mental balance, his masculinity, and his ability to be more than a stooge or front for the North Korean military.

President Clinton wrote to President Carter on August 1; he welcomed Kim Jong Il's having given Carter his "personal assurances that the commitments made by Kim Il Sung [would] be honored." He added: "We attach great importance to these commitments and will seek to build on them in the third round of U.S.-DPRK talks beginning next week." The president went on to tell Carter that he would be kept "fully briefed on the progress of the third round," and that he valued Carter's "continuing counsel" and believed that the "unexpected events of recent weeks only increase[d] the importance of the commitments North Korea made before the death of Kim Il Sung."[21]

The U.S.-North Korean delegations met again in Geneva on August 5 to continue their negotiations that had been suspended after Kim Il

Sung's death. After intense bargaining in Geneva, the two delegations released on August 12 an Agreed Statement that would later serve as an outline for the October Agreed Framework. The Agreed Statement nailed down several important issues, but it contained language less rigorous than would be needed in a final agreement on the question of refueling of the 5 MWe reactor after the third round of talks had been completed; on how to ensure that the North-South Korean dialogue would be resumed; and on how to deal with special inspections. A few days after the August session ended, Carter authorized a press statement expressing his support for the Agreed Statement. It said that the results achieved so far were consistent with Kim Il Sung's commitments to him, recognized that difficult issues remained to be resolved, and indicated Carter's willingness to help if appropriate. He also declined a reporter's request for an interview so soon after Geneva to avoid the possibility that the interviewer might try to restart the debate about Carter's achievements versus that of the administration.[22]

About the same time, R. Jeffrey Smith of the *Washington Post* interviewed Kang Sok Ju in Geneva. Smith wrote that Kang had emphasized that Carter had been instrumental in achieving the breakthrough that had enabled the Geneva talks to resume. Kang reportedly said that North Korea's "willingness to work toward a nuclear accord was a legacy of the decisions and statements made by Kim Il Sung during former president Jimmy Carter's visit to the North Korean capital of Pyongyang in June." Kang explained that "a deal became possible after Carter's visit because Washington dropped its campaign of 'pressure and offensive' action toward North Korea."[23]

Eleven days later, Han Vriens filed a story from Pyongyang in the *Far Eastern Economic Review* after a two-week visit to North Korea. In addition to observations about the North Korean perception of the nuclear crisis, he reported that in North Korea Carter was viewed as a national hero. "He is seen as the first American statesman who understood Kim Il Sung. The official palace for foreign heads of state in Pyongyang has recently changed names: it's now called the Carter Palace."[24]

As the United States prepared for the September session of the talks with North Korea, Carter instructed his Center staff to submit to him a comprehensive strategy document with recommendations as to how he could influence positively the Geneva negotiations (and seek to effect a reconciliation between the two Koreas so that the summit planning could restart.) In preparing the document, Center personnel consulted with NGO experts on Korea, Bob Gallucci and his colleagues at the State Department, Ambassador Jim Laney, the South Korean consul general in Atlanta, and a senior official of the North Korean mission in New York.[25] It also drew on the conclusions reached at a one-day meeting composed largely of nongovernmental experts on Korea, most of whom had been supportive of the Carter trip, held at the Carter Center on August 22.[26] After perusing the document, Carter concurred in some of its recommendations. In a letter to President Clinton, he commented favorably on the U.S. negotiating strategy for the September meeting with North Korea in Geneva. He advised that, among other things, he would urge continued progress at the Geneva talks during his upcoming meeting with Pak Gil Yon on September 19. As noted earlier, Carter also wrote a letter to the South Korean president, Kim Young Sam, in which he focused primarily on the summit issue, but he also expressed the hope that the Geneva talks would resolve all the nuclear problems, including that special inspections would be part of the final agreement.[27] Given the general progress in the negotiations in Geneva, Carter decided not to write an article for publication in a journal, such as *Foreign Affairs,* explaining why negotiations were preferable to intransigence in dealing with North Korea.

Through Center conversations with State Department officials, Carter was able to follow closely the Geneva talks that commenced on September 23. The talks stymied on September 26 and 27 when serious differences arose over special inspections and continued construction of the two new reactors and the reprocessing facilities. The two delegations temporarily adjourned the discussions in order to return to their respective capitals for consultation.[28]

Gallucci called Carter from Washington on Saturday evening, October 1. Noting that the United States had a commitment from South Korea and Japan for a $4 billion package for the light water reactors, he said, according to Carter's notes, that the remaining issues were complicated and boiled down to these two: "1) Special inspections re the two dump sites and 2) the freeze on existing facilities (not refueling the 5 MWe reactor, shipping the spent fuel out of the country, and IAEA inspection of the reprocessing plant)." Although Carter did not think the special inspections issue was important enough to sabotage the talks, particularly since the IAEA had never exercised this option, Gallucci said that South Korea and Japan were insisting on IAEA inspection of the two disputed sites; the issue was the timing when the inspections would occur. Carter told Gallucci that Kim Il Sung had promised him "total transparency," and that this was "kind of an ultimate fallback position" should the Geneva talks break down. According to Carter, Gallucci agreed that the North Koreans would want to avoid an allegation that they had "welshed on a deal, and particularly one made by the 'Great Leader.'"[29]

The Geneva talks recommenced on Wednesday, October 5. After six days, having resolved the controversial issues in substance, the two delegations turned to drafting the final language of the agreement for submission to their respective capitals.[30] On Tuesday, October 18, the Principals Committee voted to recommend that President Clinton approve the Agreed Framework. The NSC memo submitted to the president summarized its terms: It "would freeze and lead to the dismantlement of North Korea's nuclear program [all of its graphite reactors and reprocessing facilities, including those under construction or expansion], bring Pyongyang into compliance with nonproliferation obligations, promote stability on the peninsula, commit the United States to oversee the construction of the two new reactors financed largely by South Korea and Japan, and provide interim energy to Pyongyang."[31]

As part of the agreement, the United States committed to sending 500,000 tons of heavy fuel oil annually (at an estimated annual cost of $35–50 million) to North Korea to replace the energy that the shut-down 5 MWe graphite reactor and other reactors (when completed) would have provided; this obligation would continue until the two new light water reactors were operational. The United States also undertook to reduce some of its export restrictions against North Korea and to open discussions for liaison offices and perhaps eventual diplomatic relations. The IAEA inspectors would remain in North Korea and monitor North Korea's compliance with all the relevant provisions of the Agreed Framework.

President Clinton gave his approval for the United States to sign the Agreed Framework.[32] Carter would later affirm that the Agreed Framework was everything that he and Kim Il Sung had envisioned.

Gallucci then flew to Geneva and along with Kang Sok Ju signed the agreement on Friday, October 21. Two hours after the Agreed Framework was signed, Gallucci briefed a packed room of reporters at the U.S. mission. Faced repeatedly with questions about North Korea's not permitting special inspections before it began receiving benefits from the agreement, Gallucci explained the situation candidly, forthrightly, and what should have been convincingly. He said that Washington's priority had been to prevent North Korea from being able to produce hundreds of kilograms of plutonium over the next five years with which it could have produced many nuclear weapons. "What had happened in the past was important but not urgent, since it did not present the same threat."[33]

The signing of the Agreed Framework officially ended the 1994 nuclear crisis, but the Clinton team still faced numerous hurdles to secure necessary support for the agreement and to keep it from becoming unstuck. Hard-liners on Capitol Hill and in the think tanks attacked the agreement as a sellout. When the congressional elections of November 1994 produced a sharp shift to the right, giving the Republican Party control of both houses of Congress for the first time in forty years, the administration's job of maintaining the minimal necessary support on the Hill—particularly for supplying annually heavy fuel oil to North Korea—proved to be extremely difficult and time-consuming. Then, in December, an American military helicopter inadvertently strayed across the DMZ into North Korea and was shot down; the North Koreans proved tough in negotiating the release of the one crewmember who had survived the crash. During the spring, North Korea threatened to wreck the Agreed Framework by rejecting light water reactors manufactured in South Korea as replacements for their graphite reactors and insisting that if other reactors were not substituted, North Korea would not be bound by the October agreement. In the end, however, after going to the brink, Pyongyang accepted ambiguous diplomatic language that did not mention the South Korean reactors but allowed the U.S.-led Korean Peninsula Energy Development Organization

(KEDO) to select the reactors; KEDO, whose head was an American, Stephen Bosworth,[34] simultaneously issued a statement saying that it would use South Korean reactors.

While the administration did the heavy lifting in garnering political support for the Agreed Framework and keeping the agreement intact, President Carter tried to be helpful. He communicated to several senators and congressmen his endorsement of and rationale for supporting the Agreed Framework. When the final round of talks on the source of the light water reactors began in Kuala Lumpur on May 19, Carter sent a letter to Kim Jong Il urging his government to conclude an agreement on the issues under discussion.[35] Six days later, under authorization from Kim Jong Il, the North Korean foreign minister, Kim Yong Nam, replied and reported that the talks in Malaysia had resolved the sensitive issues about which Carter had been concerned, and that the breakthrough opened the prospects for the "smooth implementation of the DPRK-U.S. Agreed Framework." He expressed appreciation for Carter's efforts in improving U.S.-North Korean relations and resolving the nuclear issue.[36]

At the conclusion of the Kuala Lumpur negotiations, Carter issued a press statement: "Today's understandings are an important step on the road toward full implementation of the U.S.-DPRK Agreed Framework, which provides the international community with assurance against a North Korean nuclear threat and North Korea with the opportunity to rejoin the community of nations."

As he had when the Agreed Framework had been signed, Carter again contacted key people on Capitol Hill to urge their support of the administration's efforts toward North and South Korea. On June 17, for instance, he sent a handwritten note to Newt Gingrich, the Republican Speaker of the House and a Georgia congressman.[37] Although they disagreed on many issues, Carter and Gingrich found it possible to work collaboratively on areas of mutual interest, and their personal relationship remained cordial.

From October 1994 to December 2002, the Agreed Framework remained in force. During that period North Korea's plutonium-based nuclear facilities remained frozen and under international surveillance. The spent fuel, sealed in safe canisters and stored with the assistance of outside experts, was continuously monitored by IAEA inspectors. The North Korean regime no longer claimed special status within the NPT, and it rejoined the IAEA with a commitment to permit inspection of its two disputed sites in a timeframe tied to the delivery of the first light water reactor.

Slightly more than a year after the agreement had been signed, Dan Poneman, the NSC senior director for Nonproliferation and Export Controls in the Clinton White House, summed up for the press the differences between the situation in June 1994 and that at the time of his interview on December 15, 1995. He said that in the middle of the preceding year, North Korea had an active 5 MWe nuclear reactor and possessed some plutonium that the United States believed had been extracted from that reactor. North Korea appeared to be on the verge of restarting that reactor, and was building two larger reactors. These three reactors "together would have been able to have produced enough plutonium for literally dozens of nuclear weapons." In addition, North Korea had a large reprocessing plant that it was expanding, and the spent fuel rods in the cooling pond could support the separation of five to six more bombs-worth of plutonium. The October 1994 Agreed Framework shut this nuclear program down and "stopped it in its tracks under international monitoring." It froze all these nuclear facilities, enabled international inspectors to ensure that the freeze continued indefinitely, and tied their dismantlement and the shipment of the spent fuel out of North Korea to the delivery of the light water reactors.[38]

When Poneman was asked whether the administration could say with confidence that North Korea did not have any nuclear weapons, he replied:

We have never said with confidence that North Korea does not have any nuclear weapons. We do not know what we do not know. Based on the information that we've had now for a long time, we believe that North Korea may have separated enough plutonium before we got the agreed framework in place for perhaps one or two nuclear weapons. We have no knowledge beyond that as to what use they have made of that. But what we do know is that since the agreed framework has been in place, *they have not been able to separate one additional nanogram of plutonium* [my italics].[39]

That situation would hold until December 2002 when, as a result of a serious dispute between a new George W. Bush U.S. administration and the old Kim Jong Il North Korean administration, the Agreed Framework of 1994 collapsed.

When viewed through the prism of what could have been realistically achieved in 1994 (in contrast to the unrealistic insistence of hard-liners that North Korea could be intimidated into acceding to all U.S. demands, including those that they believed undercut their country's security and their governing regime's existence), the Clinton administration correctly proclaimed the Agreed Framework to be a major success. Jimmy Carter shared that assessment. During the coming years, the Clinton administration would herald the agreement and the peaceful solution to the North Korean nuclear crisis of 1994 as one of the most significant foreign policy achievements of its terms in office. Seldom, however, would its official statements after 1994 refer to Jimmy Carter's contribution to that achievement.

When the George W. Bush administration came to power in January 2001, it took a much tougher position toward North Korea than had the outgoing Clinton administration. The latter had engaged during its last two years in office in discussions with Pyongyang focused on threat reduction and cooperation that Washington hoped would, among other things, constrain North Korea's production, testing, and sale of ballistic missiles. It left for the new administration the "rough outline of a prospective missile deal."[40] The Bush administration, with hard-liners in strong positions, had little inclination to build on its predecessor's missile negotiations with North Korea. In fact, the new team in Washington, even before assuming power, had identified North Korea as one of those states toward which it would take a confrontational stand and use as a justification for its envisaged national defense shield. Early in his administration, President Bush embarrassed the visiting South Korean president, Kim Dae Jung, who had won the Nobel Peace Prize for his efforts to improve relations with North Korea, by publicly declaring his animosity toward the Pyongyang leadership. In a comprehensive policy review on relations with North Korea completed in June 2001, the administration, while calling for a "serious dialogue" and holding out prospects of economic assistance, demanded that North Korea accelerate safeguard compliance with the IAEA, terminate its mid- and long-range missile programs, adopt a less-threatening conventional military posture, improve its human rights performance, and take tangible efforts toward economic reforms. It put these terms to the North Koreans on an all-or-nothing basis, and the North Koreans balked at negotiating under such conditions. Following the September 11, 2001, attack on the United States and the declaration of the "War on Terrorism," President Bush named North Korea as part of the "Axis of Evil" in his State of the Union message in January 2002. Two months later, the *U.S. Nuclear Posture Review,* which listed North Korea as one of the countries against which the United States might consider launching a preemptive attack employing small nuclear weapons, was leaked to the press. In September, the administration put forward its National Security Strategy, which included a justification for preemptive attack against "rogue states" that possessed weapons of mass destruction; North Korea was listed as a prominent example.[41]

During the same timeframe, the State Department insisted that it would hold talks with North Korea "any time, any place, without preconditions." In April 2002, the North Koreans finally agreed. Initially set for July, the talks were rescheduled for October.[42] U.S. intelligence on North Korean actions during the previous four years would dominate that meeting.

The 1994 Agreed Framework had an important omission, one that was fully recognized and discussed by the Clinton administration at the time and after the signing of the Agreed Framework. Its inspection procedures could not prevent North Korea from later seeking surreptitiously to acquire the capacity to enrich uranium. This means for making nuclear weapons, though much slower than the plutonium-based process, was suspected of being used by Pakistan, and perhaps a few other countries as well. From a strictly legal point of view, the development of a highly enriched uranium (HEU) program by North Korea would violate the

Agreed Framework because that document committed North Korea to observe the provisions of the 1992 Joint Declaration of the Denuclearization of the Korean Peninsula that prohibited the manufacture and production of nuclear weapons. (Both Koreas had signed this bilateral agreement, but neither had begun to implement it; in fact, implementation discussions broke down in January 1993.) In defending publicly the Agreed Framework before the Congress, as well as in private conversations with senators and congressmen, Bob Gallucci specifically raised and addressed this uranium-enrichment problem and pointed out that the United States could not persuade the North Koreans to accept an explicit prohibition against the enriched uranium process in the Agreed Framework. However, the administration had viewed the North Korean proven plutonium-producing nuclear capacity, which the Agreed Framework froze, as the principal danger. As Gallucci testified in 1995, the United States and others would have to depend on their intelligence capabilities to find out whether North Korea tried surreptitiously to develop a uranium-enrichment program in the future.[43]

In the late 1990s, U.S. intelligence obtained evidence that North Korea was pursuing a uranium-enrichment program. Whereas its research program may have started earlier, North Korea's acquisition of actual capabilities appears to have come after it began complaining to the Clinton administration in 1998 and 1999 that the United States was failing to move forward on normalization in violation of the Agreed Framework. The U.S. intelligence community estimated that North Korea had been "assembling actual HEU [highly enriched uranium] capabilities since 2000 and 'seeking centrifuge related materials in large quantities' since 2001."[44] In 2003, an independent study by the Council on Foreign Relations made this assessment: "It is entirely possible that Pyongyang's HEU program followed its own schedule and logic, and was unrelated to U.S. actions. But the apparent timing of key events also makes it possible that the speed at which the North pursued its HEU program, as well as Pyongyang's changing negotiating position since October 2002, may be partly explained by its increasing fear of the United States."[45] North Korea may also have been influenced by how relatively quickly the United States removed its sanctions imposed on India and Pakistan after their nuclear tests in 1998.

The United States went to Pyongyang for the October 2002 talks with the intention of confronting North Korea with its evidence of Pyongyang's HEU program. According to U.S. sources, the North Koreans, surprised by the information provided by the United States, confirmed its HEU program and asserted that it was a reaction to U.S. actions that had effectively destroyed the Agreed Framework. When the United States revealed this exchange publicly a couple of weeks later, the North Koreans denied the U.S. report and claimed that their country did not have an HEU program. Following through with its threat at the October 3 meeting to cut off the delivery of heavy fuel oil pledged under the Agreed Framework until the North Koreans came clean on the HEU program, the United States ensured that the KEDO suspended heavy oil shipments to North Korea in November. The next month, North Korea announced that it would restart its nuclear facilities at Yongbyon, which had been frozen since 1994. Subsequently, it expelled the IAEA inspectors, removed the agency's monitoring devices, reactivated its 5 MWe reactor, said it would resume construction on the other two larger reactors, withdrew the canisters containing the spent fuel rods from the place they had previously been stored under international surveillance, and withdrew from the NPT. The October 1994 Agreed Framework collapsed.

With these developments, Pyongyang regained immediate and unilateral possession of the spent fuel, capable of producing five to six bombs-worth of plutonium, and it claims that it has reprocessed it. Washington assumes that some or all of this reprocessing has taken place. In addition, North Korea's current plutonium inventory would also include whatever plutonium it had separated prior to 1994, estimated now, as then, as between 0 and 2 bombs-worth. With its 5 MWe reactor refueled and running, it will accumulate additional irradiated fuel rods from which plutonium can be manufactured. Moreover, as Poneman stated in 1995, should North Korea complete its additional reactors and expand its reprocessing facility, it could produce "enough plutonium for literally dozens of nuclear weapons."[46]

Since early 2003, North Korea has consistently said that it was willing to negotiate—while continuing to deny that it had an HEU program. The Bush administration refused to meet again bilaterally with North Korea, insisting instead on multilateral talks. One round of three-power talks (United States, North Korea, and China) and four rounds of six-power talks (in which South Korea, Japan, and Russia also participated) took place in Beijing between the spring of 2003 and the fall of 2005. During these talks, the United States insisted on the complete, verifiable, and irreversible dismantlement (CVID) by North Korea of its nuclear programs before substantive discussions of North Korea's security, political, and economic needs could be undertaken. In June 2004, the George W. Bush administration put a negotiating proposal on the table for the first time. This proposal fell well below North Korea's minimum demands. Pyongyang's opening position greatly exceeded anything Washington seemed likely to negotiate. It was unclear at the time whether Washington's June offer represented an opening position in what likely would be a long and difficult set of negotiations or was merely a stalling tactic to mollify the other non–North Korean participants who had urged the United States to be more forthcoming. The next round of six-power talks, tentatively scheduled for September 2004, was postponed because North Korea refused to attend—probably wanting to see the results of the U.S. presidential elections before resuming negotiations.

Throughout the first half of 2005, Washington appealed to South Korea, Japan, Russia, and particularly China to pressure North Korea to return to the negotiating table, which they apparently did, and these countries also pressed the United States to take a more accommodating position toward North Korea. These six countries met again in September 2005, and, after a difficult set of negotiations, signed a joint statement that sets forth mutually agreed upon guidelines for a possible resolution of the North Korean nuclear problem.[47]

Additional negotiating rounds will be required. Contentious issues of timing and implementation remain. A larger sticking point is whether and when North Korea would obtain light water reactor(s). It is insisting that it must receive them before it will dismantle its nuclear program, a position the United States firmly rejected. Pyongyang's specific demand that the United States provide it with at least one light water reactor as compensation for its accepting the complete, verifiable, and irreversible dismantlement of its current nuclear program rallied the hard-liners within the George W. Bush administration to oppose strongly the joint statement despite the signature of the United States on it. An additional concern, particularly within the Defense Department and the U.S.-led United Nations Command in South Korea, is the statement calling for the negotiation of a permanent peace agreement to replace the Korean War Armistice. The U.S. Treasury Department's imposition in September 2005 of USA PATRIOT Act Section 311 economic sanctions on North Korea's international financial transactions further complicates the situation. In early December, North Korea announced that it would not return to the six-party talks until the United States lifted its new sanctions. The United States held that the sanctions had nothing to do with these talks. There were also reports of growing strains between Washington and Seoul over the appropriate policies to pursue toward North Korea. In mid-February 2006, when this book was being completed, no new six-power talks had been announced, even though China, as chairman, had expected the September round to be followed by another round in November 2005. If such talks resume, they must overcome formidable impediments if they are to achieve a diplomatic settlement that will ensure the peaceful dismantlement of North Korea's nuclear weapons programs.[48]

For more than twenty years, Jimmy and Rosalynn Carter have used their Carter Center to promote democracy, advance human rights, expand health care, encourage economic development, and prevent or resolve conflicts around the world. President Carter's quest for a peaceful resolution of the nuclear crisis on the Korean Peninsula probably has been his most momentous and certainly his most high-profile post-presidential endeavor.

Carter's intervention in the 1994 nuclear crisis built on his previous experiences in dealing with conflicts, but it introduced new elements as well. Like the George H. W. Bush and Bill Clinton administrations, Carter wished to prevent North Korea from developing nuclear weapons. But he rejected as counterproductive the confrontational approach pushed by hard-liners within and outside of these administrations. Based on personal study and analysis as well as on advice from Chinese contacts, Japanese acquaintances with North Korean connections, and several NGOs with direct experience in North Korea, he concluded that the North Korean leadership, no longer able to count on security and economic support from the Soviet Union and China, sought to bargain its nuclear weapons program for security guarantees and economic and political concessions. Unlike the current and previous administration, Carter held the strong conviction that coercion via sanctions or other forceful measures would not result in the dismantling of North Korea's nuclear weapons program. In fact, he was convinced of the opposite—that such measures would increase Pyongyang's intransigence and could well lead to war. Carter did not know for sure that he was right, but he did believe strongly that his proposition, shared by others outside the U.S. government, should be tested through good-faith negotiations before steps were taken that could lead to a military showdown. Certainly, sanctions should not be risked until someone—preferably a senior administration official, but if that was not politically possible, then Carter himself—had communicated directly with the one person in North Korea who would decide whether that country would cut a deal or take further actions that could end in conflict. Consequently, Carter decided to go to North Korea, if necessary without White House agreement. He did not lightly set aside his personal policy not to undertake delicate international missions without the permission or acquiescence of the administration in power. But when he became convinced that war would likely result if he did not go to North Korea and that a peaceful resolution might be possible if he did, he made the irrevocable decision. He would have traveled even in the face of administration disapproval. But he was pleased and relieved when President Clinton endorsed his making the trip as a private citizen representing The Carter Center. In Pyongyang, he found that his analysis had been correct, that Kim Il Sung was ready to deal, and that the North Korean president would and could hold his own hard-liners at bay. To its credit, the Clinton national security team, once the Carter-Kim Il Sung agreement had been confirmed in diplomatic channels, moved swiftly and adroitly to negotiate the Agreed Framework that stopped cold North Korea's plutonium-based nuclear weapons program for eight years.

This book has attempted to tell the Carter story in a comprehensive manner. It has sought to explain what Carter did and why his intervention succeeded. Also, using the North Korean situation as an example, it has tried to describe how Carter thinks about conflict situations in general and how he relies on certain approaches that his long experience has convinced him hold the best prospects for ameliorating and hopefully resolving disputes peacefully. He believes firmly that a potential mediator must seek to gain the confidence of all key parties to the conflict before he agrees to undertake that role. For almost three years, Carter parried the appeals of Pyongyang for his involvement in the face of opposition from Washington and ambiguous responses from Seoul. Only when he thought that war was imminent if the three governments did not revise their strategies and that he might be able to bring about those revisions did he decide to insert himself into the process. As he always does, he prepared himself thoroughly, ensuring that he fully understood both the technical complexities of the nuclear issues and the political imperatives of the involved nations. Typically, he focused on the fundamental interests of the disputants, not on their stated negotiating positions. Before he left the United States, he put on paper a potential settlement that he believed met the necessary conditions of each side, and he had devised talking points to sell his proposed settlement, or one close to it. His paper prepared in Plains turned out to be remarkably close to the deal to which Kim Il Sung agreed in Pyongyang. He rigorously assembled and absorbed material that provided relevant background to his mission. Cognizant of information that he still needed after perusing what he had obtained from private sources, staff memos, and submissions from other nongovernmental sources, he compiled a series of questions for which he sought answers during his briefings in Washington and Seoul and through his discussions and observations in Pyongyang. He crafted his interventions carefully, trying to anticipate difficulties and devise scenarios that would advance his purposes. In Washington, he set out to convince administration officials that he and they were on the same team while simultaneously trying to get them to think more flexibly about their strategy and the intelligence upon which it was based. In South Korea, he sought to allay the apprehensions of Kim Young Sam and his associates that the North Korean leaders would exploit his visit as a propaganda coup while not retreating from his view about what would be needed to resolve the crisis peacefully. In Pyongyang, as he does wherever he becomes involved in trying to resolve a conflict, he consciously demonstrated respect and friendship for his interlocutors. In doing so, he was not engaging in a charade. Carter typically looked for the good in those with whom he negotiated. But he was oblivious neither to their faults nor to their responsibility for the horrific consequences that had resulted from some of their earlier decisions in Pyongyang. He knew that a peaceful outcome that met his necessary conditions was far more likely to be achieved in an atmosphere of mutual respect than in one of disdain and/or hostility. Coercive pressure, including military hostility, could sometimes compel an adversary to retreat, but that result was never a sure thing. If a nation in a crisis threatened force, it must be prepared to follow through should its adversary prove intractable. Otherwise, its credibility would be seriously damaged and its influence internationally would be greatly weakened. In Carter's view, the coercive route should be the last alternative employed because it could lead to war. Finally, Carter appreciated the value of international and national public opinion in bringing a crisis to resolution. He has often used his access to the media to induce a reluctant disputant to take action it would prefer not to take or to extol and strengthen a disputant willing to compromise. In the 1994 nuclear crisis, he took advantage of the CNN interview to compel the involved governments to deal with the agreement he had negotiated with Kim Il Sung. This maneuver, followed by his press conferences in Seoul and Washington, precluded the leaders in the three governments from ignoring or misinterpreting (although some tried) the breakthrough that he had achieved. They not only had to react; they also had to explain to their respective publics and to world opinion how and why they had done so.

Despite his intense preparation, the subsequent demonstration of the correctness of his perceptions about the intentions of the North Koreans, and the final outcome of his trip, his critics, before he traveled and after he returned, insisted that he undertook the venture unprepared. They claimed that he lacked sufficient knowledge about the peninsula, its people, its leaders, and the strategic issues involved. However one views his proposal as U.S. president to reduce American troops in Korea in the late 1970s, it is hard to accord credence to pundits' assertion that Jimmy Carter did not know a great deal about Korea. Whatever one held to be the desired outcome of the 1994 nuclear crisis, it tests credibility to argue that Carter, a nuclear engineer by training and someone who had ensured that he was highly informed about the technical aspects of the North Korean nuclear issue, did not understand the problem. Given the role Carter played in fashioning the Camp David Accord in 1978, the provisions of which still hold today, one must wonder at charges made in 1994 that Carter was a diplomatic dilettante. Yet these charges were trumpeted by his critics on the Hill and in think tanks, and quietly encouraged by his detractors within the administration.

These accusations probably took on such polemical tones because the critics and Carter had profoundly differing views of the crisis and how to resolve it. The critics believed that the North Koreans were stalling for time to develop their nuclear weapons, and perhaps to make this weaponry available to others, thereby raising the level of danger in the world. Carter was convinced that unrelenting pressure without the assurance of concrete benefits to be gained from cooperation would make North Korea more intractable and more likely to proceed with the actual manufacture of nuclear weapons. He also believed that an approach based on mutual gains negotiated in an atmosphere of mutual respect could resolve the immediate crisis, make the Korean peninsula and the world safer immediately, and provide a new opportunity for the Koreas, the United States, and the international community to fashion a long-term peaceful arrangement.

Although the Carter trip and the subsequent negotiations of the Clinton administration produced the Agreed Framework in 1994, many of its critics, and even some of its supporters in the United States and South Korea, never expected it to be implemented. Incorrectly, they anticipated an early demise of the Pyongyang regime, caused either by an economic collapse or an internal uprising as Kim Jong Il tried to replace his father. This projection proved far off the mark. North Korea survived a leadership transition and a devastating famine without credible evidence that its populace would rise against the current regime. In fact, there is little support today in other countries in the region for an early termination of the Pyongyang leadership. Most experts on North Korea and most senior officials in South Korea and China fear that an implosion of the North Korean regime would lead to internal chaos, floods of refugees, and major instabilities on the heavily armed Korean Peninsula. This assessment should give pause to policymakers in Washington as they plan and implement their policies toward North Korea, particularly in view of the recent experience the United States has had with regime removal in another part of the world.

The 1994 nuclear crisis yielded general and Korea-specific lessons that might prove useful to current U.S. policymakers. They are especially valuable if the employment of the military weapon is to be regarded, as I firmly believe it should be, as the last resort for dealing with international disputes between countries. The "War on Terrorism" does not change the validity of this proposition.

First, the Carter intervention in 1994 demonstrated the essentiality for U.S. leaders to talk directly with the decisionmakers in countries that might involve the U.S. in military confrontation. Since the United States had no embassy in Pyongyang and since Washington did not know whether its messages delivered to the North Korean mission in New York reached the Pyongyang leadership in an unabridged form, the Clinton administration should have tried to send a high-level emissary to talk with Kim Il Sung before undertaking actions, such as seeking UN sanctions, that could have ended in war. The decision to use Senators Nunn and Lugar was the correct one, but it should have been tried earlier, before the situation had become so confrontational. Fortunately, the North Koreans welcomed a visit by Carter shortly after they denied visas to Nunn and Lugar. They probably expected Carter to be more sympathetic to their views than two senators with whom they had had even less experience. Because of their limited knowledge of the United States, the North Korean leaders may have thought that Carter, as a former U.S. president with a Democratic administration, would have greater influence on the Clinton team than a bipartisan senatorial delegation. It would not be surprising that, with its New York mission as its only listening post, Pyongyang did not appreciate the reticence of the Clinton administration to involve Carter in sensitive international problems. Once in North Korea, Carter was not hemmed in with rigid negotiating instructions because he was not an official emissary. Nevertheless, his negotiating flexibility was severely constrained by what he could get the North Koreans to accept, what he could sell to Washington, and what Washington would be able to get the South Koreans to acquiesce to.

Given the importance of direct communication with potential adversaries, the U.S. national security community should rethink the advantages and disadvantages of denying diplomatic recognition to countries labeled as "rogue states." The United States, unlike many other nations, has long used diplomatic nonrecognition to show disdain for countries that, in its judgment, fail to meet their international obligations, and to induce them to change their policies. Other than using persuasion and diplomatic nonrecognition, the methods the United States uses for challenging perceived adversaries consist of financial, economic, and trade restraints (made more potent with participation by other countries and/or international organizations) and military force, and each of these options carries costs to the United States—sometimes substantial costs. Breaking off diplomatic recognition or refusing to grant it is considered less costly and less risky politically than sanctions or military action. But a major negative effect of withholding diplomatic recognition is to make much more difficult clear communication with the targeted country. A case could be made that it is as important, if not more so, to talk directly with potential enemies as with friends. Unfiltered communication will not prevent war if one or both sides desire it, but it will reduce the odds substantially that one or both sides will stumble into confrontation because of inadequate knowledge or miscalculation. The concern of members of the Clinton administration in 1994 about possible parallels with the plight of European nations in 1914, which were unwittingly plunged into war, was perceptive and alarming. Additionally, without direct communication with decisionmakers, there is no assurance that messages sent through intermediaries will be conveyed accurately to leaders who may be more flexible. Nevertheless, if diplomatic recognition is to remain a reward the United States dispenses to countries that meet its unilaterally established criteria for international citizenship, then U.S. administrations should ensure that they have the means (be it with emissaries or through other methods) to consult directly with the leadership of countries they view with hostility.

Second, as the 1994 nuclear imbroglio demonstrated, the U.S. government (and presumably other governments as well) sometimes finds it difficult to reach consensus on how to deal with serious national security issues that could become major crises. Frequently, disagreement arises over the exact nature of the danger and/or what policies and actions should be adopted to deal with it. In their internal debates, policymakers often hold conflicting views, sometimes but not always reflecting their particular positions and responsibilities within the bureaucracy, and they argue their views forcefully, intelligently, and with conviction. Such competition of ideas is healthy and much more likely to occur in a democratic than in an authoritarian government; this exchange forces the decisionmakers to assess a broader range of policy possibilities and a wider variety of likely repercussions. The downside is that often the internal disagreements are not resolved, and decisions are not taken in favor of one view or another. Instead, the matter is kept under review while events play out on the ground. If a negotiation with a potential adversary is an integral part of grappling with an evolving crisis, the result can be that the U.S. negotiating team's instructions force it to protect all the positions that have not been resolved at home. As a consequence, the negotiators have little flexibility either in formal or informal sessions to work with their counterparts on the other side to define fundamental interests and seek mutually acceptable solutions. At best, the negotiation process is dragged out; at worst, it can become gridlocked, and then it will be abandoned.

The policymakers in the George H. W. Bush administration and in the Bill Clinton administration agreed that North Korea's nuclear program represented a danger to the world and that that program should be terminated. Most of the individuals involved probably appreciated that if North Korea acceded to U.S. demands, the United States would need subsequently to undertake some constructive actions to assist

North Korea deal with its economic difficulties and reduce its political isolation. Yet in both cases, policymakers could not agree on how to define this connection. When the Bush team decided to hold the first U.S. bilateral meeting with North Korean officials since the Korean War, its internal policy debates centered on whether at that meeting to give any concrete indication of the concessions that might be forthcoming if the North Koreans changed their nuclear policies. The bureaucratic battle was joined but not resolved between those who insisted that North Korea must be forced to meet U.S. conditions as a prerequisite to changes in future relations and those who thought the odds of getting what the United States sought would be improved if a clear indication was given to the North Koreans of subsequent actions the United States would probably be prepared to take. As a result, the U.S. team went to the bilateral talks with a negotiating brief that virtually guaranteed that the consultations would be a substantive failure. In the first six months of 1994, the Clinton administration failed to follow a consistent policy, swinging back and forth between insisting on an approach that demanded prior action by the DPRK and a package approach that sought to negotiate simultaneous quid pro quos. It failed as well to decide whether preventing North Korea from developing future nuclear weapons capacity was more important, less important, or equal in importance to learning the details of how much plutonium it had processed in the past. As late as June 10, 1994, when Carter was briefed in Washington before leaving for his Korean journey, the lack of agreement on priorities related to past and future North Korean nuclear weapons actions became manifest, to what appeared to be the discomfort of the administration participants. On the other hand, once the Carter trip had broken the gridlock, the Clinton team established the needed priorities, gave the U.S. negotiating team considerable flexibility, pursued a negotiating strategy based on the concept of a package approach, and concluded the Agreed Framework in about three months.

The nuclear crisis of 1994 suggests that on extremely sensitive national security issues that might end in a military conflict, decision-makers should avoid papering over conflicting policy views. They should instead frame the differences clearly and force the controversial issue(s) as high up the bureaucratic ladder as necessary to get an unequivocal decision. In 1994, before pushing for UN sanctions, the U.S. government should have taken clear policy decisions about 1) whether to try to negotiate the termination of the North Korean plutonium-based nuclear weapons program with a package proposal, or to force Pyongyang to meet preconditions with the understanding that doing so could well lead to military conflict; and 2) whether to give higher priority to preventing future North Korean nuclear actions than to learning about previous ones.

Third, closer cooperation between governments, nongovernmental organizations, and scholars could enhance policymaking and implementation. During the past decades, NGO personnel have accumulated a wealth of experience and knowledge through their extensive and extended endeavors in countries. Their activities include collaborating with national government officials on projects having country-wide impact and working at the grassroots level on locally targeted activities. Through their endeavors, they have gained considerable appreciation of these countries and of the attitudes and priorities of their leaders and their populace. Their understanding, particularly at the local level, often varies with that obtained by intelligence officials and diplomats from their own sources of information. The same is true of scholars who spend years working in and on particular countries or areas of those countries. They have their own assessments on the local situations, and their views sometimes provide critical nuances that may be missed by government officials. Persons preparing the intelligence information for policymakers should make a concerted effort to include NGO and scholarly analyses and to ensure that those responsible for policy formulation are alerted when the conclusions of outside sources differ from those of the bureaucratic consensus. In 1994, the assessments of nongovernmental groups and scholars who had traveled to North Korea and interacted with North Koreans proved much closer to the mark as to the likely Pyongyang reaction to U.S. actions than did those of South Korean and U.S. intelligence officials. Although NGOs and scholars insist correctly on keeping sufficient distance between themselves and government policy, they will usually welcome the opportunity to provide their understanding of the situations and conditions in the area in which they work.

Administration officials should also consider using NGO leaders more frequently as unofficial emissaries, particularly when their organizations are engaged in work in a country with which the United States has a serious political problem. Although the approached NGO leader would have to decide whether such cooperation would endanger his organization's independent status, he would also factor into his calculations the degree to which the resolution of the problem would benefit his organization and its mission. In most cases, there would be no issue regarding conflict of interest in his conveying U.S. policy positions and rationales to his collaborators abroad and then passing back to Washington their reactions to its proposals and their argumentation for their own. Additionally, the NGO go-between might be able to offer fresh ideas that would facilitate the dialogue. For instance, even though the Clinton administration wanted to send Kim Il Sung a tough message in January 1994, it probably could have benefited from the recommendations of the Reverend Billy Graham and his adviser, Steve Linton, about how to frame the message to enhance its prospects of eliciting a constructive response. Instead, Graham had no input except to include the administration's oral message in his own longer letter. When Kim Il Sung read the terse Clinton message, the North Korean dictator interpreted it as a threat, and he countered with one of his own.[1] When Carter conveyed much of the same substance in different words five months later, the North Korean president responded positively and worked out with Carter the deal that led to the Agreed Framework. Another advantage of soliciting the help of NGO leaders is that with their commitment to trying to resolve problems peacefully, they are not afraid of failure or criticism. In contrast, governments cannot fail very often and remain in office, and they are strongly adverse to criticism. Finally, governments can largely control the politics of using an NGO leader as an unofficial emissary, even one as independently minded as Jimmy Carter. Should the emissary succeed, an administration with its formidable communication resources could easily appropriate the emissary's achievements and claim them as its own.

That is what the Clinton administration did after it confirmed in diplomatic channels that Kim Il Sung had agreed to what Carter had reported.
Should the unofficial emissary fail, the administration could largely deflect most of the criticism away from itself and toward the NGO, as the
Clinton team had positioned itself to do had Carter's gamble not succeeded. Although I initially resented that Carter did not get as much
public credit as I thought he should, I later had to acknowledge that such
was the way the political game was played. In fact, in urging Bob Gallucci
to seek an administration decision supporting Carter's involvement as we
drove from Plains to Atlanta after his briefing of Carter on June 5, 1994,
I had made the argument that the Clinton administration could reap the
credit if Carter succeeded and divorce itself from his initiative if he failed.
In retrospect, I should have been neither surprised nor disgruntled when
the administration acted as it did.

The Carter intervention in North Korea raises an important question:
Could any NGO, other than The Carter Center, have successfully intervened in the 1994 nuclear crisis, or in any other serious government-to-
government crisis that could spiral into war? The Carter Center brought
certain advantages to the North Korean crisis. First, as a former U.S. president who had considerable experience with Korean issues, Carter was
particularly well qualified for the role. Moreover, he had communicated
intermittently with Kim Il Sung beginning in 1976, and for three years
prior to his visit, Pyongyang had been urging him to come to North
Korea. It is doubtful that any other head of an NGO could have matched
Carter's high-level entrée to key officials within the "Hermit Kingdom,"
or be thought by the North Korean leadership as having sufficient influence to persuade the Washington administration to rethink its strategic
policy toward North Korea. Carter was well informed about Korean developments. He had his own private sources of information, particularly
from knowledgeable Chinese officials whom he thought better understood the North Korean leadership than did Washington. The former director of his Conflict Resolution Program had made an advance trip to
both Koreas in 1992 and had consulted with senior-level officials in both

Koreas. His staff had followed the Korean situation closely for several years and had provided him with extensive reporting based on their own analyses and their good contacts with North and South Korean diplomats, scholars on the Koreas, and administration officials. Carter also had consulted regularly with nongovernmental experts on North Korea who had traveled to North Korea on several occasions and had met there with senior North Korean officials. Finally, because of his long-standing ties with CNN leaders, he was able to benefit both from Eason Jordan's insights garnered from his trip to North Korea in April 1994 as well as CNN's coverage of his trip, including his interview from Pyongyang.

Given these considerations, it is doubtful that some NGO leader other than Carter could have achieved what he did on his trip to Pyongyang. But the 1994 Korean crisis was unique, as are all crises. Other persons or groups might well be able to intervene successfully in other crises. It would be necessary for the individual and his organization to have access to the top officials involved, extensive contacts with lower-level officials, solid information about the pertinent issues and the personalities involved, honed negotiating skills, and political clout relevant to the particular crisis. For each, the NGO mediator would need to gain the trust of the disputing parties and be able to help them fashion the outlines of an agreement that would meet their fundamental interests. A Norwegian social science group with close ties with officials in Norway's foreign office took the first critical steps in mediating the Israeli-Palestinian agreement of 1993. The Community of Sant'Egidio, a Catholic lay society, whose work was financed by the Italian government, played an essential facilitative role in structuring the agreement that ended the civil war in Mozambique in the early 1990s.

In addition to the general lessons above, I believe that the 1994 nuclear crisis and its resolution provided specific lessons that are relevant for dealing with North Korea in the future. Having never worked directly on Northeast Asia during my diplomatic career, I do not pretend to be an expert on the Koreas. Nor have I had access to classified information on this or other subjects since I left The Carter Center in 1996. Yet in writing this book and following developments generally on the Korean Peninsula, I am struck by some important similarities between the past and the present. For whatever they are worth, I offer the observations below.

The United States' Vital Interests and North Korea

In dealing with North Korea, the United States should decide with precision how that country relates to its vital interests. As a nuclear power, North Korea represents a real danger to the United States and to the rest of the world for two reasons. First, with its legions of hungry people and its faltering economy, which can earn little foreign exchange from legitimate, nonmilitary trade, the Pyongyang leadership may be tempted to defy international norms and sell its plutonium or bombs— if it has manufactured them—to others, perhaps even to terrorist groups. A second, longer-term danger is that Japan and South Korea could decide that because North Korea has nuclear arms, their own security requires them to develop nuclear weapons. Should North Korea, South Korea, and Japan join China and Russia in possessing nuclear weapons, Northeast Asia would become a far less stable and less secure place than it is today. This ratcheting up of the region's nuclear capacities would make peace substantially more tenuous in this area of critical interest to the United States. Unlike these two real threats, the idea of North Korea's shooting a nuclear weapon at the United States does not constitute a realistic hazard—the rhetoric of the supporters of a national defense shield to the contrary. The North Korean leaders know that any intimation they might be considering such an action, or any activity suggesting that they were moving in this direction, would be swiftly answered by a preemptive and devastating U.S. attack that would destroy them and their country.

Does the existence of the current North Korean regime constitute a compelling danger to the United States? By international standards, the regime has a terrible record in how it treats its people and how it operates within the international community. It abuses its citizens by imprisoning those who complain about its policies and by permitting large numbers to starve rather than deprive its military of food and military equipment. It brainwashes its citizen to believe that their problems result from callous action by other countries, particularly the United States and South Korea, and not from their own incompetent policies. However, there is no credible evidence that a large-scale internal uprising is likely to occur in the forseeable future.

Although the United States and other countries would like to see a different government and political system, a North Korean regime change does not constitute a vital interest of the United States. The world has lived with North Korea for more than fifty years. That country has committed despicable terrorist acts in the past, and the United States and other countries must remain vigilant. A new act of terrorism might well call for a forceful response. But military action now to bring down a regime for its behavior almost two decades earlier is neither appropriate nor justifiable—not by our own terms nor by those of most countries. Moreover, the countries of the region do not desire a sudden destruction or implosion of North Korea because they appreciate the costs that would be involved and the instabilities that would be produced.

U.S. Understanding of North Korea

U.S. leaders must learn as much as possible about the fundamental attitudes and motivations of the North Korean adversary. But they must recognize that, despite their efforts, their understanding will be incomplete. They must continually test their assumptions and revise them as appropriate. The North Korean rulers pursue a political and economic set of policies that cannot survive over time. But that time horizon cannot be predicted with any accuracy. During the next years, they will try to balance the application of essential reforms with maintaining strict political control. They have made small changes in their economic approach with free-trade zones, some limited involvement with South Korean firms, and appeals for food and other forms of aid from abroad, although recent developments suggest a retreat in some of these areas. The Chinese are and will continue to urge the North Koreans to adopt more economic openness; they point to their own experience to show that liberal economic policies can be effected for a sustained period without significantly undermining political control by the ruling party. If the North Korean leaders press forward with cautious economic reforms, political attitudes in the country may evolve. But if this evolution does not occur, North Korea would be a danger to the region and the world only if it continues to have and to expand its nuclear weapons capacity.

The North Korean leaders may be ruthless, but they are not stupid. There is no evidence that they would knowingly commit suicide by threatening the United States. Nor would they likely launch a new Korean war without what they regarded as extreme provocation. Even though their point of view encompasses years of indoctrination about the superiority of their system and its victimization by others, as well as excessive concerns about face, they must suspect that the likely outcome of a new Korean war would be their own demise and that of the system that had produced and nurtured them and given them the elite status that they hold in their society. Nevertheless, if their only alternatives are to surrender all they possess in terms of self-esteem, position, and material goods or to launch a perhaps futile but—from their view—honorable, preemptive military strike on South Korea that causes much death and destruction to their South Korean and U.S. adversaries, they may well choose the latter. To reject the possibility that the North Korean leaders could ever undertake such an action, as some hard-liners do, carries risks, perhaps enormous risks. Our recent experience in Iraq should make us less sanguine about our ability to project accurately future actions by our adversaries and the populations over whom they rule.

It is likely that the North Korean leaders believe—as do strategic thinkers in Israel, India, and Pakistan—that nuclear weapons enhance their security by deterring attacks on their country. They may envision using their nuclear capacity to intimidate their perceived adversaries and/or to gain foreign exchange by selling them, as many hawks assert. They may intend, as the bargainers project, to use this capacity as negotiating leverage for concessions to mitigate their strategic and economic weaknesses because they can no longer rely on others to serve as their international protectors, as China and the Soviet Union once did. We do not know enough about the bottom-line thinking of the rulers of the "Hermit Kingdom" to judge definitively whether either or both of these views drive them. They have given many indications that they genuinely fear that the United States contemplates a military operation against them, and U.S. official statements in recent years have surely reinforced these concerns. The challenge to the United States is to find a way to achieve our objectives—the dismantling and destruction of North Korea's nuclear weapons program in its entirety—without having to engage in a highly destructive war followed by a dangerous and expensive peace-making and peace-building effort on the Korean peninsula and a large-scale, difficult, and perhaps explosive endeavor to restore regional stability and security. China's current efforts to be helpful in dealing with North Korea might be reversed if the United States massively increases its military presence in Northeast Asia.

Negotiations First

Consequently, U.S. policy toward North Korea should be based on two propositions. First, U.S. vital interests include getting North Korea to dismantle and destroy its nuclear weapons program, but not to bringing about an early regime change in Pyongyang. Without nuclear weapons, that regime can continue to control North Korea without endangering the United States, South Korea, or Japan, or obstructing the major objectives of any of the countries in the region. As noted earlier, none of the regional states desires an early implosion of North Korea, and Seoul does not want to be forced to follow the German example of massively bankrolling reunification. The issues of human rights within North Korea, its missile program, its illegal shipment of goods, its counterfeiting, and the size of its conventional military can and should be dealt with separately from the more urgent nuclear weapons issue. Second, constructive nuclear action by North Korea should be something for which the United States and others would be willing to pay, particularly since the price of a guarantee not to attack North Korea, to provide some economic assistance, and to talk about future diplomatic relations would be far less than the cost of the increased security measures that will have to be put in place if North Korea keeps and expands its nuclear weapons program. To postulate that the United States will not "surrender to blackmail" or become an "appeaser," as

some loudly proclaim, is neither a security strategy nor a meaningful tactic; it is instead a subterfuge for a more forceful or coercive policy that
could require military action to implement it. Seeking to achieve a specific
national interest by employing first a relative low-cost option before moving to higher-cost courses of action that might entail military hostilities
represents astuteness, not weakness.

No one can say with certainty that North Korea would ultimately be
willing to bargain away its nuclear weapons program for security guarantees, economic aid, and political concessions. But we should test them
with a serious and sustained set of negotiations that accept that each
side must protect its fundamental interests. The negotiations should be
sincere, designed to try to reach a mutually acceptable arrangement;
they must not be political theater designed to win public relations con-
tests while ensuring negotiating failure. If the United States does engage in such negotiations, and if, despite its good faith effort, these
negotiations founder, the other key regional actors—South Korea,
Japan, China, and Russia—will be much more likely to join us in more
forceful actions toward North Korea than has been the case up to now.

Is a Deal Negotiable?

As the United Staes participates in negotiations with North Korea in
2006 and subsequently, it should heed two specific lessons from the
Carter trip in 1994 and the subsequent negotiations of the Agreed
Framework. First, as in 1994, the question of priority is important. The
priority issue now relates not to the earlier question about plutonium
reprocessed before 1992 and North Korea's capacity for reprocessing
plutonium after 1994 had the Agreed Framework not been negotiated;
it concerns instead the urgency of refreezing the plutonium-based program and of dealing with the plutonium that has been reprocessed since
December 2002 and the important but much less urgent matter of ensuring that North Korea does not succeed in the future in bringing
onstream a capacity to enrich uranium. A process that has the effect of letting North Korea continue to reprocess plutonium and hide its disposi-

tion while negotiators struggle to arrive at a mutually acceptable formula that verifiably ensures that North Korea will never be able indigenously to enrich uranium to weapons grade fails the priority test.

The second lesson concerns North Korean negotiating behavior. In talks with North Korean officials, U.S. participants should expect the North Koreans to be tough, recalcitrant, and irritable negotiating partners throughout the entire process. Such is the standard North Korean negotiating style. It also reflects the ever-present concern of North Korean negotiators that they must be able to convince their superiors in Pyongyang that they achieved the best possible result from the negotiations. Consequently, U.S. negotiators must match toughness with toughness and be ready to compromise when the persons across the negotiating table indicate a similar disposition. In addition, a U.S. administration that cuts a deal with North Korea must expect and be able to deal with the inevitable criticisms from hawks at home that it had surrendered to blackmail and prolonged the life of North Korea's Communist regime.

Should current or future negotiations with North Korea fail, the United States would likely pursue one of three courses of action. If it could not build support among other key countries for stronger measures against Pyongyang, it might continue with the position that it has followed since the end of 2002 of demanding that North Korea completely, verifiably, and irreversibly dismantle its nuclear programs before resuming negotiations, coupled, perhaps, with threats that would seem credible. With this position, the administration in power could not be accused by hard-liners or others of surrendering to blackmail. The cost, however, is that North Korea would continue to use its one reactor, which will produce enough plutonium for one or two bombs a year, and would probably complete the construction of its other reactors and reprocessing facilities and so be able to produce much more plutonium. It would also likely continue its efforts to produce highly enriched uranium.

A second course, if negotiations fail, would be for the United States and other key countries in the region to mount UN sanctions against North Korea, establish an effective naval blockade around North Korea to prevent Pyongyang from selling its technology and perhaps bombs to others, and/or use military force to bring down the Kim Jong Il regime. However, without a dramatic change in the positions of China, South Korea, Russia, and Japan, their willingness to support such actions would likely hinge on whether they concluded that in the six-power talks the United States had made a serious, good-faith effort to resolve peacefully the nuclear problem. The September 2005 joint statement is an encouraging development, but despite Washington's public explanations, it is unlikely that the participating countries are lined up five to one on the undecided issues.

The third course would be for the United States to decide to go it alone. It is the world's one great superpower. It could threaten and, if necessary, use military force to change North Korea's nuclear weapons policy and/or bring down the Kim Jong Il regime. Should the United States pursue this unilateral route, it would have to anticipate a very large number of U.S., South Korean, and North Korean casualties as well as tremendous property damage. Moreover, in contemplating a military engagement on the Korean Peninsula, a Washington administration could probably not count on significant reductions of U.S. troop levels in Iraq and Afghanistan, at least for the next several years, to provide resources for a conflict on the peninsula. Additionally, the United States would have to devise realistic plans not only for defeating the North Korean forces but also for stabilizing and rebuilding the country and the region after the military phase ended—and it would need to do a better job on this latter aspect than the United States has been doing in Iraq.

Despite differences, the North Korean nuclear situation in 2006 shares some similarities with that in 1994. As earlier, the U.S. policy is grounded on getting the North Korean government to give up its nuclear weapons program, and North Korea is insisting on major quid pro quos before doing so. The North Korean demands aim at strengthening the country's security and economy and likely lengthening the life of its ruling regime. Threats have generally dominated the rhetoric of Pyongyang and Washington over the past several years. At least until September 2005, the respective policies of the two governments seemed to be gridlocked, and the public statements from Washington and Pyongyang since then raise questions about how much was actually achieved last fall. In 1994, a former U.S. president, Jimmy Carter, believed that the nuclear crisis with North Korea could be resolved satisfactorily and peacefully through good-faith negotiations. Though pilloried by the hawks and hard-liners as idealistic, naïve, and gullible, he put his historical reputation on the line, went to North Korea, talked directly with its leader, and reached an agreement that the Clinton administration converted into the Agreed Framework. While critics railed then and subsequently about the Agreed Framework, it closed down the North Korean plutonium-based nuclear weapons program and kept it under close international surveillance for eight years.

Jimmy Carter's advice for the future would not be that different from his view in 1994. Just as he would have urged the Clinton administration, had he been asked, to avoid a push for sanctions before ascertaining directly the views of the decisionmaker in Pyongyang, he would have also advised the George W. Bush administration, had he been asked, not to take a confrontational approach at the October 2002 bilateral meeting but to find a means to discuss directly and respectfully with key North Korean policymakers in Pyongyang (not the negotiators who came to the Beijing meeting) U.S. evidence about its development of a uranium enrichment facility and the need for North Korea to disprove the evidence or terminate this program. His focus would have been on preserving the constraints on North Korea's plutonium-based weapons program while seeking quietly but persistently for North Korea to forego uranium enrichment. Given the public attitude of Washington toward Pyongyang at the time, an outside emissary would probably have been necessary, but finding a talented emissary who was trusted by the George W. Bush administration should not have been difficult. (Carter would have known that it was unlikely the Bush administration would ask him to go.) If the emissary's mission proved unsuccessful, the administration could have then arranged a more public display of its displeasure with Pyongyang, although it should have considered carefully the benefits and costs of losing the international control over North Korea's plutonium-based program in order to denounce publicly Pyongyang's uranium-enrichment program. Since the collapse of the Agreed Framework in late 2002, Carter would have advised that the administration seek to negotiate a package arrangements of quid pro quos rather than to demand, as Washington had done since late 2002, that Pyongyang completely, verifiably, and irreversibly dismantle and destroy its nuclear weapons program before the United States would talk seriously about North Korea's security, economic, and political concerns. Neither Carter nor anyone else can know in 2006, when this book is being written, how the follow-up negotiations to the September 2005 joint statement of the six-power talks will progress. He would certainly hope that all the parties, and particularly Washington, would develop firm priorities; establish realistic positions that give serious attention to the fundamental needs of others as well as their own; make a concerted, if laborious, effort to reach mutually acceptable outcomes peacefully; and conduct the negotiations in a way that suggest equality and mutual respect for each of the participating countries and their respective representatives.

I have written this book because of my conviction that Jimmy Carter's quest for peace in 1994 made the world safer and probably prevented a war that was neither necessary nor desired. It is my hope that those dealing in the future with North Korea will reflect seriously on his experiences and approach, even if their political philosophy differs significantly with his. A serious, sustained U.S. effort to work out mutually acceptable arrangements with North Korea that protects the basic interests of all the relevant countries, first on the nuclear-related issues and then on other important matters such as missiles, conventional forces, human rights, and regional cooperation for enhanced stability and security, will garner for the United States strong support from our regional partners. It will increase the likelihood that others will join with us should more forceful measures prove necessary. Last but not least, the current and future negotiations may succeed, and everyone—except those who seek to do us harm—would gain.

The Substance of the Official Answers to
Former President Jimmy Carter's Questions
that the Clinton Administration Provided
to Him on June 10, 1994

At most the North Koreans have separated enough plutonium to make one or two nuclear weapons; at least, they have the 72 grams they reported to the IAEA. By suspending their announced withdrawal from the NPT on June 11, 1993, North Korea maintained that it had "special status" in the NPT—a claim the United States did not accept. The North Koreans defined this special status as providing that existing safeguard measures would be maintained, but that other obligations, such as routine and special inspections, were not in effect. The principal facilities at the Yongbyon nuclear research center were an 8 MWt research reactor supplied earlier by the Soviet Union, a 25 MWt (5 MWe) reactor built by the North Koreans, and a reprocessing plant, a fuel fabricating plant, and a nuclear waste storage site along with additional laboratory and support equipment. A 200 MWt gas graphite reactor was under construction. Using the recently discharged fuel, they could—in the absence of NPT safeguards—build from six to eight nuclear weapons; they could build weapons at a faster pace once the 200 MWt reactor was completed, and the estimated date for this reactor's going critical was 1995. IAEA inspectors were currently in Yongbyon observing the final stages of the unloading of the fuel rods.

Normally the IAEA would request another inspection in a few months to obtain readouts from the safeguards cameras and maintain safeguards equipment.

Full compliance with IAEA safeguards required that North Korea "accurately declare all of its nuclear facilities and material and permit unimpeded access to them by IAEA inspectors, including the use of instruments and the taking of samples." The IAEA invoked a *"special inspection* provision of the safeguards agreement" to inspect undeclared sites because of its belief that these sites contained nuclear material subject to safeguards. Samples taken from these sites could provide evidence as to whether North Korea had separated more plutonium than the amount it declared to the IAEA. With regard to the recently unloaded fuel, North Korea must store it in a safeguarded location and allow periodic IAEA inspection of it. It must declare any new reactors, and the IAEA would install safeguards equipment; nuclear material used in the reactors would be subject to safeguards.

The United States had told the North Koreans that it supported its "stated intention" to replace graphite-moderated reactors with light water reactors, and in the context of resolving the nuclear issue, the United States would be prepared to help North Korea obtain the light water reactors. U.S. law made it unlikely that the United States would directly supply such reactors to North Korea. Light water reactors typically produce a higher percentage of Pu-40, which is less desirable for producing nuclear weapons, than the graphite reactors. Moreover, light water reactors are easier to safeguard and its fuel is harder to reprocess than that used in graphite-moderated reactors.

North Korea had been told that U.S. bases in the South could be inspected as part of the implementation of the bilateral Korean denuclearization agreement; that the '94 Team Spirit exercises could be suspended if North Korea resumed a direct dialogue with South Korea; that total suspension of these exercises could be discussed as part of a broad dialogue; and that in addition to statements already provided by the presidents of the United States and South Korea regarding the absence of nuclear weapons in South Korea, the United States was prepared to propose in the "broad and thorough" discussion, a formal agreement "committing the nuclear weapons states to respect a nuclear-free zone on the Korean Peninsula."

Regarding other countries' commitments to UN sanctions, the United Kingdom, France, and Japan supported sanctions, although the Japanese would prefer a gradual approach toward sanctions. China opposed sanctions on the grounds that they would be counterproductive. If China did not approve sanctions, Japan might be willing to limit its trade with North Korea, and Russia might be willing to participate in voluntary sanctions. The United States already had a total trade embargo on Pyongyang.

The current position of the United States was that it was willing to hold high-level official talks with North Korea if progress was made on the nuclear issue. Previously, such talks had been at the under secretary level, but the United States could be flexible as to the level. Bilateral U.S.-North Korean talks on the nuclear issue was acceptable, but South Korea must be a full participant in broader discussions of the peninsula's future. The "broad and thorough package" of the United States "included progressive steps toward full diplomatic relations, linked to North Korean action on security and other issues. The U.S. would also be willing to lift existing U.S. restrictions on trade, again in return for corresponding North Korean action." Although direct U.S. assistance was "unlikely," South Korea, Japan, and the Asian Development Bank and other international financial institutions were potential aid donors.

The paper also provided the total number of North Korean, South Korean, and U.S. troops, and discussed briefly the strengths and weaknesses of the North Korean military, its chemical weapons and missile capacities, and its ability to attack with little warning.

Accompanying the written answers were slide charts on some of the points. These charts carried a "Secret" classification. The paper Carter received did not answer his question about the views of specific senior administration officials on how best to deal with the North Koreans.

Talking Points for Resolution of
the North Korean Issues

Prepared by President Carter and Read to
Bob Gallucci on the Phone on June 11, 1994

The United States and South Korea desire to live in peace and harmony with North Korea. As agreed through definitive discussions, this includes mutual respect for the cultural and political commitments of the three nations, and the promotion of common economic progress through increased trade and commerce, economic investments, normal services of international financial institutions, visitation of citizens, and free and normal diplomatic exchanges among political leaders.

A crucial issue for the United States and all other nations is the integrity of the international nuclear non-proliferation issue. This means that in all participating nations there must be full compliance with all Non-Proliferation Treaty safeguards. I know that this is a commitment made and reconfirmed by North Korea. Inspectors in all countries must be given access to all nuclear facilities and materials. This includes non-diversion of spent fuel and transparency of the nuclear program. Downloaded fuel should be inspected as removed, and must be stored in a safeguarded location. Surveillance equipment must remain intact. Inspectors must have the right to verify that spent fuel rods are not being diverted to use for explosives. Reprossessing [sic] is not prohibited, but must be subject to inspection. The design of new nuclear reactors must be shared with inspectors, cameras and other safeguard equipment installed, and nuclear materials used must be subject to unimpeded inspection.

There are no nuclear weapons in South Korea, and President George Bush has stated officially on behalf of the United States that there would be no nuclear weapons on U.S. ships in the area. As part of a broad agreement, the United States is prepared to propose a formal agreement committing nuclear weapons states to respect a nuclear-free zone in the Korean peninsula area.

As part of the implementation of the North-South Denuclearization Agreement, the United States is prepared to permit inspection of U.S. military bases in South Korea.

The United States and South Korea are ready to suspend Team Spirit '94 exercises when North and South Korea resume dialogue through the Joint Nuclear Control Commission or another established channel. These military exercises would be permanently suspended as part of a broad and thorough dialogue.

The United States is prepared to hold high-level official talks with North Korea as part of the discussion of political and economic issues that would follow resolution of the nuclear issue. Any talks that involve the political future of the peninsula would, of course, have to include South Korea as a full participant.

As part of an overall settlement of issues, the United States is prepared to lift existing trade restrictions in return for corresponding action by North Korea.

The United States is prepared to work with North Korea toward full diplomatic relations.

In my present capacity representing The Carter Center, with the knowledge and approval of the United States and South Korea, I would be glad to continue as requested to assist in the accomplishment of the goals described above.[1]

Optimum Commitment of North Korea—
Prepared in Advance of Trip

North Korea has never had and does not intend to develop a nuclear weapons program. As is permitted under Non-Proliferation Treaty terms, we have removed and reprocessed damaged fuel rods, and have accumulated a small quantity of plutonium. Under terms of the Non-Proliferation Treaty, our pledge is that no spent fuel will be diverted to plutonium without full transparency. Inspectors will continue to have full access to the 8010 fuel rods recently removed and the integrity and continuity of surveillance equipment will be maintained. Under mutually acceptable conditions, in accordance with the Non-Proliferation Treaty terms, full transparency of the entire nuclear program of North Korea from its inception will be provided. In order to enhance the effectiveness of the nuclear program of North Korea and to minimize the need for reprocessing in the future, it is desired to obtain light water reactor technology to replace graphite reactors now operating or being constructed.[2]

Questions President Carter Hoped to
Answer on Trip to the Korean Peninsula

QUESTIONS FOR THE SOUTH KOREAN LEADERS:

What is your concern about my visit to North Korea?

Where are the IAEA inspectors?

What can be done to implement the N-S Denuclearization agreement?

Are you willing to permit unlimited IAEA inspections?

Would you be willing to assist NK in shifting from graphite to light water reactors?

Under what conditions would you be willing to forego Team Spirit exercises?

What direct talks between the United States and North Korea are you willing to approve?

Under what conditions do you envision direct talks with NK Leaders? At what level? Where?

In which ones must South Korea be involved?

Why have most past discussions been fruitless?

What is the basic difference between NK and SK re reunification of the peninsula?

In what kinds of sanctions will SK participate?

What preconditions would permit full diplomatic relations between NK and SK?

How do you feel about diplomatic relations between US and NK?

What direct economic or trade relations to (sic-do) you envision with NK, and under what conditions?

You stated recently that NK was deploying new weapons systems near the DMZ. Please explain.

What is your advice to me for my talks with the NK leaders?

What is your assessment of NK attempt to have nuclear weapons? What would induce them to give this up?

QUESTIONS TO TRY TO ANSWER IN NORTH KOREA:

The questions for which Carter would seek answers in North Korea follow:

Describe the personal vigor, demeanor, habits, competence of the top leaders.

What is relative authority between Kim Il Sung and Kim Jong Il?

What other leaders seem to speak with authority? Describe them.

What is the NK attitude toward unification talks with SK?

Do they consider binding the Denuclearization agreement? What would it take to implement it?

What is the apparent economic situation?

How do N Koreans describe mandatory imports now, and in the future?

Is there any mobilization of military forces?

What about agriculture?

Do the people seem open, relaxed, friendly? Do we have unrestricted access to them?

Is there any family planning program? Are large families sought?

What is the condition of health care?

Describe the food markets and department stores.

What kind of entertainment is available?

What about the media coverage of events?

Describe the educational system. To what extent is English taught?

What is the aftermath of the Billy Graham crusade? Is religious freedom respected?

What are the main sources of electrical power?

Is there an interest in environmental quality? Reforestation?

What private control over land use is exerted by farm families? Are there private plots?

Is there an attempt to emulate China's privatization?

What is the relationship among the Supreme People's Assembly (655 members, the Standing Committee, the Administrative Council, and the Communist party, KWP, and its 39-member politburo. Is it all under Kim Il Sung's control?

*A Description of Some of the Key Passages
in the Paper, "Your Visit to North Korea,"
Provided to President Carter by Its Author,
Danny Russel, on June 14, 1994*

- There was "symmetry between the two sides in U.S.-DPRK negotiations: suspicion of motives; concern for toughness and credibility; zero-sum approach to each session; negotiators handcuffed by strong political doubts and intense public scrutiny; conservative establishments with prejudicial and non-disprovable assumptions about the other; reliance/abhorrence of deadlines; etc." The "national instincts of each side tend to lead away from settlement." The paper added: "We want to prove we can make North Korea do something; North Korea wants to prove we cannot." It stated that the North Korean negotiating brinkmanship tended to founder because of their poor timing, lack of credibility, and bad judgment. For its part, the United States deprived itself of "the most valuable tool for influencing DPRK behavior—face-to-face negotiation—by defining dialogue as a reward for good behavior." Moreover, the process was made more complicated by the involvement of South Korea and the IAEA with their own policy imperatives.
- North Korea is a caste system that has an elite of several thousand people, a privileged "core population" of about 4 million, and a peasantry of around 18 million. Although there are factions among the upper strata,

the nation and its people are "held together by the glue of nationalism, residual ideological fervor, worship of the father/liberator Kim Il-Sung, external threat, and nearly total social and security controls." According to the paper, "Life in North Korea is tough," though not likely that much different from the seventeenth and eighteenth centuries, "when famine, disease, weather, and royal displeasure were often fatal facts of life." It asserted that there was no known political resistance.

- Under the heading of "Where Are We Now?" the paper quoted President Clinton's remark that "the door is still open," but then asserted that the United States had "done little or nothing to show the North Koreans in practical terms where the door was located." "The protagonists seem locked into a cycle of mechanical escalation in the confrontation, with an increasing risk that the diplomatic conflict will become a military one." It held that the United States seemed to be "seized by the urge to punish North Korea; ostensibly for destroying important evidence about its past reactor operation, but in large part because we are frustrated and angry by its obduracy." "We know that this punishment is likely to cost us the significant controls now in place over DPRK plutonium. North Korea is poised to respond with steps that genuinely challenge us, which will form the basis for calls for tougher responses to new defiance."

- The paper stated: "North Korea, thus far, has avoided taking the kind of provocative countermeasures for which it is notorious, despite what surely looks to Pyongyang as belligerent affronts by it [sic] enemies. If a North Korean legislator made remarks such as U.S. congressmen are making on TV, if its military introduced a new weapons system like Apache attack helicopters [as the United States was doing], if (like the mayor of Seoul) Pyongyang authorities ordered citizens to stock up on staples 'against war,' or even if its civil defense system scheduled a 'war-exercise' (announced by the ROKG [Republic of Korea Government] last week), we would take the move as a clear and present danger. Neither side wants war, neither is sure of the other's intentions, neither is willing to appear to be deterred by the threat of war."

On sanctions, the paper emphasized that "the drive to adopt a sanctions resolution is almost unstoppable," yet "few people want to carry through with sanctions and fewer still with more extreme enforcement steps." "Although everyone hopes for a breakthrough that leads back to negotiations, there is no plan, no alternative to escalation, unless the North Koreans capitulate." The paper suggested two policy goals, the implication being that the first was preferable to the second, but both would restrain the escalation toward conflict. In its words: "One policy goal would be to end the DPRK nuclear threat through substantive negotiations, leading to an agreement whose terms are already largely understood. Another would be to contain it safely through some combination of deterrents, while leaving basic problems unsolved and tensions on the Korean Peninsula high." The paper urged Carter to review with Kim Il Sung the political constraints on the U.S.'s "already limited options," making sure the North Korean leader understood how the issue was perceived outside of Pyongyang, and discouraging him from taking any action that would "magnify the risk of conflict." Kim Il Sung "faces a crisis of immense gravity, and is considering how to respond. You [Carter] can affect those calculations to some degree."[3]

Report on Our Trip to Korea,
June 1994, by Jimmy Carter

About an hour before President Clinton departed for Europe to participate in the Normandy landing ceremonies, I called to tell him how concerned I was about the developing crisis with North Korea. We agreed that I would receive a definitive briefing, which later resulted in Assistant Secretary Robert Gallucci's visit to my home on Sunday afternoon, June 5. I was impressed with the seriousness of the situation and the apparent lack of an avenue of communication with the top leader of North Korea, who was the only one who could make the decisions to alleviate the crisis and avoid another Korean war.

The following day the North Koreans reconfirmed my standing invitation to visit Pyongyang, with assurances that it was from President Kim Il Sung. I called Vice President Al Gore and informed him of my strong inclination to accept. The next morning he called back to report that President Clinton and his top advisors approved my visit. While still in Atlanta, conducting our annual budget hearings, I received a number of briefings, including one from a Georgia Tech nuclear engineer and information from the CNN crew who had recently been to North Korea. On Friday afternoon, June 10, Rosalynn, Marion Creekmore, and I went to Washington for additional briefings on the subject. (We were to find some of the assessments of our North Korea experts sharply different from our later observations.) Saturday, I reviewed all the information, wrote out my talking points for the trip, and read them to Gal-lucci. He had no suggestions for changes.

We left home on Sunday, June 12, as well briefed as possible but without any clear instructions or official endorsement. In effect, we were on our own. While in Seoul, we had talks with President Kim Young Sam and his top ad-visors. They seemed somewhat troubled about our planned visit to Pyongyang. Minister Li, in charge of reunification talks, was more positive and helpful, and seemed to have more objective views toward North Korea. United States Gen-eral Luck, commander of all military forces in South Korea, was deeply con-cerned about the consequences of a Korean war. He estimated that the costs would far exceed those of the 1950s.

The crossing at Panmunjom was a bizarre and disturbing experience, evi-dence of an incredible lack of communication and understanding. For more than forty years, the Koreans and Americans have stared across the demilita-rized zone with total suspicion and often hatred and fear. We were the first persons permitted to cross the DMZ to and from Pyongyang—since the armistice was signed in 1953! One current problem that was explained to me by United States Colonel Chilton was that they could not work out an agree-ment for the joint United States and North Korean teams to find and recover the remains of Americans killed in the Korean War. He believes our people know precisely where three thousand bodies were buried while our troops oc-cupied the territory.

We were turned over from United States authorities to the care of Vice For-eign Minister Song Ho Kyong. His high rank was an indication of the impor-tance they attached to the visit. We had a pleasant two-hour drive over an almost empty four-lane highway. He explained that they did not produce lux-ury cars, but only buses, trains, subways, and trucks. We were to find a superb mass transit system in Pyongyang, with an especially beautiful subway system more than three hundred feet under ground.

Throughout our visit, our hosts were open, friendly, and remarkably reticent about making abusive or critical comments against the South Koreans. The North Koreans expressed concern about misunderstandings and lack of progress on the peninsula, but would acknowledge that these had been caused by mutual mistakes.

Our first meeting was with Foreign Minister Kim Yong Nam. The re-sponses to my proposal on how to end the impasse were quite hard-line, with an apparent fixation on beginning a third round of talks with the

United States as a prerequisite to any affirmative actions. It was obvious that the threat of sanctions had no effect on them whatsoever, except as a pending insult, branding North Korea as an outlaw nation and their revered leader as a liar and criminal. This was something they could not accept. Economic sanctions had no meaning for them, since their basic philosophy—almost a religion—is "Ju-che," meaning self-reliance. In a practical sense, what was being proposed in the United Nations Security Council would not be damaging since their trade with the United States and its allies was almost nonexistent and United Nations agencies provide them with little benefit. They seemed totally uninterested in the specifics. Although the foreign minister's comments were moderate in tone, it seemed quite likely that they would go to war rather than yield to international condemnation and economic pressure.

I was distressed, and woke up at 3:00 A.M. the following morning to decide what to do. I realized that I had no instructions or authority. In desperation, I finally decided that Marion Creekmore should drive down to Panmunjom to send a secure message from South Korea, to inform Washington of the situation and seek authorization from President Clinton to propose a third round of talks to defuse the crisis. In addition, I included a suggestion that Bob Gallucci might consider a visit to Korea. Marion was to refrain from sending my message until I could meet that morning with President Kim Il Sung.

When this meeting took place at his palace the next morning, Foreign Minister Kim, Vice Foreign Minister Song Ho Kyong, and First Vice Minister Kang Sok Chu also attended. The latter is Bob Gallucci's counterpart, responsible for negotiating with the United States on the nuclear issue.

President Kim Il Sung is eighty-two years old, but we found him to be vigorous, alert, intelligent, and remarkably familiar with the issues. He consulted frequently with his advisors, each of whom bounced up and stood erect while speaking to "The Great Leader." There is no doubt that Kim Il Sung was in full command and could make the final decisions. After thanking me for accepting his three-year-old invitation, he asked me to speak first.

I described my unofficial role, my briefings, my visit with South Korean President Kim Young Sam, and then made the presentation that I had prepared before leaving home. I outlined the entire situation to be sure that he was fully aware of all the concerns about North Korean nuclear policies. On occasion, he would nod or ask me to pause while he talked to his advisers. Dick Christenson, our state department interpreter, later reported that he was obviously not thoroughly briefed on one important problem: IAEA inspectors being expelled.

Finally, in effect, he accepted all my proposals, with two major requests. One was that the United Sates support their acquisition of light water reactor technology, realizing that the funding and equipment could not come directly from America. (He had been promised a 2,000 megawatt reactor by President Brezhnev in the late 1970s, but the Soviets later defaulted on this after Chernyenko became leader.) This is something we want the North Koreans to have, because the enriched fuel will have to be acquired from foreign sources, and the production of weapons-grade plutonium is not so easy as in their old graphite-moderated reactor that can use refined uranium directly from their own mines. His second request was that the United States guarantee that there will be no nuclear attack against his country. He wanted the third round of United States-North Korea talks to be resumed to resolve all the outstanding nuclear issues. He was willing to freeze their nuclear program during the talks, and to consider a permanent freeze if their aged reactors could be replaced with modern and safer ones. I was surprised to find him familiar with these detailed issues.

I assured him that there were no nuclear weapons in South Korea or tactical weapons in the waters surrounding the peninsula, and that my understanding is that the United States desires to see North Korea acquire light water reactors. He agreed with me that the entire Korean peninsula should be nuclear-free. Since I now felt that I had gotten everything we needed, Dick called Marion to tell him to return to Pyongyang without any message to Washington.

After lunch, we moved to talks with First Vice Minister Kang Sok Chu, their chief negotiator on nuclear questions. He went through the history of the nuclear issue from their point of view, which seemed reasonable on some respects. He was meticulous in his description of what had happened, and I could understand the correlation of events from totally disparate perspectives. On occasion, he tended to deviate in his position from what Kim Il Sung has committed to do, but when I asked him each time if he had a different policy from his "Great Leader," he would back down.

He claimed that they had delayed unloading their reactor more than six months after the normal date, and had been surprised by the IAEA's announcement to the United Nations Security Council, backed by the United States, that they had violated their agreement and passed the point where inspectors could confirm the history of their reactor's operation. He claimed they had made a reasonable proposal, to which they never received any response.

Vice Minister Kang informed me that when I arrived they had already decided to expel the inspectors and disconnect surveillance equipment as a response to the abusive sanctions language announced by United Nations Ambassador Madeleine Albright and Bob Gallucci. Also, he said, "All the people in this country and our military are gearing up now to respond to those sanctions. If the sanctions pass, all the work you have done here will go down the drain." He said they are convinced that the spent fuel rods can still be assessed by the IAEA, and are willing to be flexible if this conviction is proven wrong. He maintained that noted physicists in Europe and the United States agreed with their position. We discussed a number of other points of a somewhat technical nature. I saw no reason to argue with him on these points, but just to protect the agreement I had reached with his president.

After supper, I called Bob Gallucci on an open line to report the apparent agreement with President Kim Il Sung. He said they were having a high level meeting in the White House and would consider my report. I notified him of my plan to give CNN an interview, but to refrain from speaking for the United States government, and he had no objection. During the end of my interview, I was informed that National Security Advisor Tony Lake wanted to talk with me, and we finally got him on the phone. After I answered a few questions, he asked me to call him back in an hour for the United States decision. I did this, and he asked for three more hours to consult with other nations. This brought us to 5:30 A.M., and I understood that they would accept the terms I had worked out. He then went over a statement that they proposed to make. He agreed to a few changes. It was understood the North Koreans would freeze their nuclear program through the new good faith talks. It will be several months before the rods are cooled down enough for reprocessing, and President Kim Il Sung had agreed to "freeze" their nuclear program during good faith talks.

Later that morning (Friday in Korea, Thursday at home) we were invited to go on a long boat ride with President Kim, from Pyongyang to the "barricade," a remarkable five-mile dam, built by North Korean soldiers, that separates the river from the sea. I advised him that in my opinion the implementation of our agreement would mean that the sanctions effort would be stopped, or held in abeyance. I explained to the interpreter the meaning of "abeyance." We discussed the issue of removing the remains of United States soldiers buried during the war, and when I explained that this would avoid later arguments and be a significant goodwill gesture to the American people, the president finally listened to comments of his wife and then agreed to permit joint teams to find and return these bodies to the United States. I urged him not to let this joint effort become bogged down in debates. On the boat ride I had a more thorough talk with Vice Minister Kang concerning no reprocessing of spent fuel rods. And I explained that a permanent commitment could be predicated on approval of light water reactor technology. He is not a nuclear expert, and did not seem to understand that once rods are removed there are alternatives to reprocessing.

During the trip, President Kim and I had a long discussion about future relations between North and South Korea. He described several North-South discussions that had been held, but stated that no good results had ever materialized. He stated that fault for lack of progress lay on both sides, and responsibility for mistakes had to be shared. He expressed pleasure that President Kim Young Sam had proposed a summit meeting during his political campaign, and President Kim Il Sung said it should be done without preconditions or extended preparatory talks. He also expressed willingness to work on the issue of reciprocal military site inspections to implement the 1991 Joint North-South Declaration on Denuclearization of the Peninsula; to follow up on general principles adopted in 1992 regarding reunification; to a step-by-step reduction of Korean armed forces to 100,000 men on each side, with the United States forces to be reduced by the same proportions; to remove weapons from within the DMZ; to permit cross border visitation, etc. He said that for forty years no progress had been made, and he asked if The Carter Center would be willing to provide our good services to bridge the existing gaps and to help insure success of North-South talks in the future. I promised to mention all these things to President Kim Young Sam on my return to Seoul.

He is very friendly toward Christianity, having been saved from a Japanese prison in China by Christian pastors. Also, he is an avid hunter (killed two bears and two hundred boar this past year), and quite interested in fishing. He said that after the Japanese were expelled in 1945, the families along the rivers tried to kill all the "Japanese fish." He knew there were rainbow trout introduced before 1910 by American miners, and has had a large program since then to stock the streams from several nurseries. We agreed that I would send in some biologists and fly fishermen to analyze North Korea's fishing opportunities.

After visiting the children's palace and seeing one of the most remarkable performances of young people's skill and talent of our lives, I finally went back to the guesthouse for some sleep. The next morning we returned to the DMZ, where we had a press conference and answered questions from CNN, the North Korean news media, and those from China and Russia. Then we traveled with Ambassador Jim Laney to Seoul, where we were amazed to discover that our actions in North Korea had been met with criticism and partial rejection in Washington. I discussed this on a secure telephone line with Vice President Al Gore, and told him I would like to go to Washington before going home to explain the results of my trip in more detail. I considered all my actions to have been in accord with the policies of the administration.

I met with the South Korean president and his ministers, relayed the messages from Pyongyang, and found them to be very interested and supportive. Then I held an extensive press conference, during which I was informed that President Kim had agreed to the summit meeting. I explained the nuclear situation to the best of my ability, answered questions, and made it plain that I was still speaking as a private citizen representing The Carter Center.

Marion Creekmore and I returned to Washington via Atlanta, while Rosalynn went on home to Plains.

Jimmy Carter
The Carter Center
19 June 1994
Atlanta, Georgia

PROLOGUE

1. This opening scene drew on the following sources: Jimmy Carter, "Report on Our Trip to Korea, June 1994," Carter's Post-Presidential Papers (hereafter cited as Post-Presidential Papers), "Korea—June '94," specific file: "Korea—trip report," (all files from Carter's Post-Presidential Papers are from box 109, 1 of 2, unless otherwise specified); conversations with President and Mrs. Carter, Ambassador James Laney, and Nancy Konigsmark; the author's notes, recollections, and photographs; CNN camera footage made available to the author; and descriptions in Don Oberdorfer, *The Two Koreas: A Contemporary History* (Reading, Mass.: Addison-Wesley, 1997), xii, 1–3, 68, 322; Mike Chinoy, *China Live: Two Decades in the Heart of the Dragon* (Atlanta: Turner Publishing, 1997), 348; Joel S. Wit, Daniel B. Poneman, and Robert L. Gallucci, *Going Critical: The First North Korean Nuclear Crisis* (Washington, D.C.: Brookings Institution Press, 2004), 204, 214–215; Nancy Soderberg, *The Superpower Myth, The Use and Misuse of American Might* (Hoboken, N.J.: John Wiley, 2005), 262; Bradley K. Martin, *Under the Loving Care of the Fatherly Leader: North Korea and the Kim Dynasty* (New York: Thomas Dunne Books, St. Martin's Press, 2004), 87; Samuel S. Kim and Tai Hwan Lee, *North Korea and Northeast Asia* (Lanham, Md.: Rowman and Littlefield, 2002), 5; Daniel R. Russel, "Letter to President Carter," June 28, 1994, Post-Presidential Papers, "Korea—June

'94," specific file: "Korea-follow-up communication non-official." Mr. Russel enclosed with his letter copies of two FBIS (Foreign Broadcast Information Service) reports: FBIS, serial no. SK1506055994, source: Seoul Yonhap in English, 0539 GMT, June 15, 1994; and FBIS, serial no. WS2106124594, source: Warsaw Rzeczpospolita, June 21, 1994.

2. Jimmy Carter's Nobel Lecture, Oslo, Norway, December 10, 2002, http://nobelprize.org/peace/laureates/2002/carter-lecture.html.

3. In 1960, two men, either South Korean agitators working for Pyongyang or North Korean infiltrators into South Korea, broke into the house of Kim Young Sam's parents and killed his mother when she discovered them. See Bradley K. Martin, *Under the Loving Care of the Fatherly Leader: North Korea and the Kim Dynasty,* 99, and Oberdorfer, *The Two Koreas,* 175.

CHAPTER 1

1. Victor D. Cha, "Assessing the North Korean Threat: The Logic of Pre-emption, Prevention, and Engagement," in Samuel S. Kim and Tai Hwan Lee, eds., *North Korea and Northeast Asia* (Lanham, Md.: Rowman and Littlefield, 2002), 222. According to the statistical archives of South Korea's Bank of Korea, the gross national product for South Korea in 1993 amounted to $362.1 billion, and the gross national income of North Korea was $20.5 billion, making the South Korean economy almost eighteen times larger than that of North Korea. See http://ecos.bok.or.kr/Eindex__en.jsp, accessed December 12, 2005.

2. According to Samuel S. Kim, between 1948–1984, Moscow provided $2.2 billion in aid to North Korea, and Beijing provided $900 million. With the collapse of the Soviet Union, its aid to Pyongyang ceased and its concessional trade dropped from 56.3 percent in 1990 to 5.3 percent in 2000. Samuel S. Kim, "North Korea and Northeast Asia in World Politics," Samuel S. Kim and Tai Hwan Lee, *North Korea and Northeast Asia* (Lanham, Md.: Rowman and Littlefield, 2002), 41.

3. In addition to the loss of economic support from the Soviet Union and China, Pyongyang's massive expenditures on its military played a key role in creating North Korea's serious economic problems in the 1990s. Kim, "North Korea and Northeast Asia in World Politics," 42.

4. Leon V. Sigal, *Disarming Strangers: Nuclear Diplomacy with North Korea* (Princeton: Princeton University Press, 1998), 21–22.

5. A 5 MWe means that the reactor produces 5 megawatts of electricity. One U.S. government official, when talking about this reactor, referred to it as a 25 MWt (the "t" standing for thermal.) "According to nuclear experts in Washington, D.C., 5 MWe and 25 MWt refer to the same reactor at Yongbyon. The different numbers reflect two different units of heat measurement and methods to rate a nuclear reactor's capacity. The preferred rating for the nuclear reactor at Yongbyon is "5 MWe." (Language provided by C. Kenneth Quinones on February 16, 2006, after consulting with nuclear experts he knew in Washington.) A few days earlier, Charles Pennington, a nuclear expert and senior official with NAC International, a nuclear services company in Norcross, Georgia, told me that although the conversion factor seemed somewhat low, there were a variety of explanations that could make the numbers 25 MWt and 5 MWe roughly equivalent. (Telephone conversation with Charles Pennington, February 13, 2006.) In this publication, I will state the size of nuclear reactors in terms of MWe unless I am quoting or paraphrasing a person who explicitly used the MWt designation.

6. Light water reactors are less of a proliferation danger than graphite moderated reactors. The former require enriched uranium as its fuel, which North Korea would have had to import, and no country would supply the enriched uranium if North Korea were not in good standing with the NPT. Moreover, suppliers of enriched uranium require that the spent fuel from these reactors be returned to the original supplier for reprocessing or disposal. Finally, with reprocessing, the spent fuel of the light water reactors will produce less nuclear weapons-grade plutonium (plutonium-239) than that produced by spent fuel in a graphite-moderated reactor having the same burn time. Sigal, *Disarming Strangers*, 21–22.

7. Telephone conversation with C. Kenneth Quinones on December 31, 2005; Sigal, *Disarming Strangers*, 5, 21–22; Don Oberdorfer, *The Two Koreas: A Contemporary History* (Reading, Mass.: Addison-Wesley, 1997), 252–255; C. Kenneth Quinones, "North Korea: From Containment to Engagement," in Dae-Sook Suh and Chae-Jin Lee, eds., *North Korea After Kim Il Sung* (Boulder: Lynne Rienner, 1998), 107–108. There are slight variations in the description by these three sources as to when North Korea built its first nuclear reactor and the number of light water reactors the Soviet Union promised but did not deliver in 1985. Where the accounts differ, I have used Quinones's information since he was working on North Korea in the State Department before and during the 1994 nuclear crisis.

8. Sigal, *Disarming Strangers*, 25–26; Oberdorfer, *The Two Koreas*, 255–257.

9. Quinones, "North Korea," 104–105.

10. The Bush administration made the decision to take this worldwide action after completing a global strategic analysis of the future role of nuclear weapons in its defense posture primarily vis-à-vis the Soviet Union. According to Robert A. Manning, the August 1991 attempted coup in the Soviet Union and Washington's new concerns about "loose nukes" motivated the Bush administration to announce its unilateral withdrawal of tactical nuclear weapons worldwide. Mikhail Gorbachev, the Soviet president, would subsequently reciprocate, and then the Bush administration announced that it would remove all air-launched nuclear weapons overseas. With this initiative, the Bush administration took a step toward negative security assurances in that it removed what Pyongyang had frequently railed against as a nuclear threat to North Korea. Robert A. Manning, "United States-North Korean Relations: From Welfare to Workfare?" in Samuel S. Kim and Tai Hwan Lee, eds., *North Korea and Northeast Asia* (Lanham, Maryland: Rowman and Littlefield, 2002), 70; also see Quinones, "North Korea," 109, 111.

11. Subsequently, it was learned that in 1990 the dictator in North Korea, Kim Il Sung, had taken three important decisions: to open up partially the country's autarkic economy to the outside world, to try to normalize relations with the United States, and to accept coexistence with South Korea. Sigal, *Disarming Strangers*, 24. Moreover, some scholars believe that from the late 1980s North Korea viewed its nuclear weapons program partly as a "political bargaining chip to achieve the key goal of regime survival," to be employed principally toward the United States. Manning, "United States-North Korean Relations," 65, 70–71.

12. Sigal, *Disarming Strangers*, 24–32; Oberdorfer, *The Two Koreas*, 219–223, 231–232, 255–257; Joel S. Wit, Daniel B. Poneman, and Robert L. Gallucci, *Going Critical: The First North Korean Nuclear Crisis* (Washington, D.C.: Brookings Institution Press, 2004), 210. Manning, "United States-North Korean Relations," 71.

13. Quinones, "North Korea," 110.

14. Oberdorfer, *The Two Koreas*, 266.

15. Ibid., 267.

16. Wit, Poneman, and Gallucci, *Going Critical*, 12–13; Sigal, *Disarming Strangers*, 32, 39; Oberdorfer, *The Two Koreas*, 269. Wit, Poneman, and Gallucci, as well as Oberdorfer, said that the North Koreans admitted to repro-

cessing 90 grams of plutonium; Sigal mentioned 100 grams. Later, the IAEA learned by taking swabs from inside of the steel tubes used to process the plutonium in a waste storage pipe that the North Koreans had also shut down the reactor in 1989 and 1991. No one outside of North Korea knew how much plutonium had been reprocessed during these shutdown periods, and Sigal, whose book was published in 1998, said that U.S. intelligence resources had affirmed that the North Koreans had not resumed reprocessing after 1991. Sigal, *Disarming Strangers*, 22, 43; Oberdorfer, *The Two Koreas*, 270–271.

17. In September 1992, the IAEA, using chemical analysis, assessed that three separate batches of plutonium had been reprocessed over a three-year period rather than one batch on one single occasion. Manning, "United States-North Korean Relations," 72.

18. These large-scale joint military maneuvers had been held in most years since 1976. In 1991, to encourage the improving relations between the two Koreas, a decision had been taken not to hold Team Spirit in 1992. North Korea had consistently and severely condemned these military exercises in the past, asserting that they were designed to prepare for a U.S.-South Korean invasion of North Korea. During the exercises, North Korea put its military on its highest alert status.

19. The IAEA took a more assertive position with North Korea than had earlier been agency policy. This new approach, encouraged by the United States and others, reflected the Vienna agency's reaction to widespread criticisms that it had failed to detect Iraqi violations of the NPT before the 1991 Gulf War. Its leaders were determined that the agency not be accused of laxity a second time, which they feared would undermine global nonproliferation efforts and make much more difficult the negotiations for a permanent extension of the NPT. The insistence of its right to inspect undeclared nuclear sites was one of the existing but never-before-used measures that the IAEA declared to be part of its mandate in the post–Gulf War period. Oberdorfer, *The Two Koreas*, 271, 275–280; Sigal, *Disarming Strangers*, 19, 42, 49–50; Wit, Poneman, and Gallucci, *Going Critical*, 14; Scott Snyder, *Negotiating on the Edge: North Korean Negotiating Behavior* (Washington, D.C.: United States Institute of Peace, 1999), 69.

20. Manning, "United States-North Korean Relations," 72–73; Oberdorfer, *The Two Koreas*, 271.

21. Sigal, *Disarming Strangers*, 28–29; Manning, "United States-North Korean Relations," 73.

22. Oberdorfer, *The Two Koreas*, 280.

23. Ibid., 281–283.

24. Even though the North Koreans agreed to maintain "full-scope safe-guards," implementation proved difficult because of ambiguity in precisely defining such safeguards. Telephone conversation with C. Kenneth Quinones, February 10, 2006.

25. Wit, Poneman, and Gallucci, *Going Critical*, 51–60, 63; Oberdorfer, *The Two Koreas*, 285, 287; Sigal, *Disarming Strangers*, 64–65; Manning, "United States-North Korean Relations," 73.

26. Wit, Poneman, and Gallucci, *Going Critical*, 63–69; Oberdorfer, *The Two Koreas*, 287.

27. Acceding to the South Korean request that no joint statement be issued after this round of talks, the two delegations issued separate though generally similar statements when the talks concluded. Oberdorfer, *The Two Koreas*, 291.

28. The LWR idea was not really new. In 1992, North Korean representatives had discussed it with Hans Blix, the IAEA's director general, and the North Korean delegation had briefly alluded to the idea during the June 1993 talks in New York, where other issues had dominated the discussions. Wit, Poneman, and Gallucci, *Going Critical*, 54.

29. Oberdorfer, *The Two Koreas*, 291; Sigal, *Disarming Strangers*, 70–72.

30. Wit, Poneman, and Gallucci, *Going Critical*, 69–77; Oberdorfer, *The Two Koreas*, 291; Sigal, *Disarming Strangers*, 70–72.

31. To try to help work out the problems between North Korea and the IAEA, the State Department started working level talks on this matter with the North Korean mission to the UN in August 1993. C. Kenneth Quinones, in the Bureau for East Asia, and Gary Samore, in the Bureau for Political and Military Affairs, held regular discussions with their North Korean counterparts on this issue throughout the fall and in January 1994. The next month, the talks shifted to trying to restart the U.S.-North Korean negotiations, and the level of the two delegations was raised. Tom Hubbard, the deputy assistant secretary for East Asia, led the U.S. delegation, which also included Quinones and Samore; the North Korean deputy ambassador to the UN, Ho Jong, headed the North Korean team. Telephone conversation with C. Kenneth Quinones, February 10, 2006.

32. Mike Chinoy, *China Live: Two Decades in the Heart of the Dragon* (Atlanta: Turner, 1997), 333–334; Oberdorfer, *The Two Koreas*, 294–295.

33. Sigal, *Disarming Strangers,* 73–76. The events in Somalia and Haiti for which the critics excoriated the administration were the killing of American soldiers and their bodies being dragged through the streets in Somalia and the retreat of the U.S. military ship when faced by Haitian toughs on the dock in Port-au-Prince.

34. Wit, Poneman, and Gallucci, *Going Critical,* 100–101.

35. Ibid., 95–96. C. Kenneth Quinones, the State Department official who accompanied Congressman Ackerman, was given by the North Koreans new informal (handwritten) proposals for what they described as a "small package" and a "big package" for dealing with the nuclear issue. The "small package" linked expanded IAEA inspections with the suspension of Team Spirit, a confirmation that Washington would not threaten North Korea with nuclear weapons, and a date for the next round of Gallucci-Kang talks. The provisions of the "big package" called for North Korea to remain a member of the NPT, comply fully with safeguards, and commit to implementing the North-South denuclearization agreement; the United States would "conclude a peace agreement, including legally binding assurances on the nonuse of force against the North, take responsibility for providing the North with light water reactors, fully normalize diplomatic relations, and commit itself to a balanced policy in its relations with the North and South." The "big package" also seemed to accept the idea of "special inspections." Wit, Poneman, and Gallucci, *Going Critical,* 96.

36. Ibid., 107–113.

37. Sigal, *Disarming Strangers,* 88–89.

38. Conversation with C. Kenneth Quinones, December 31, 2005.

39. Wit, Poneman, and Gallucci, *Going Critical,* 137–139; Sigal, *Disarming Strangers,* 105; Oberdorfer, *The Two Koreas,* 303.

40. Wit, Poneman, and Gallucci, *Going Critical,* 141–143.

41. Oberdorfer, *The Two Koreas,* 299.

42. Sigal, *Disarming Strangers,* 93–95.

43. Oberdorfer, *The Two Koreas,* 302; Sigal, *Disarming Strangers,* 95; Conversation with James Laney, January 28, 2005; Wit, Poneman, and Gallucci, *Going Critical,* 165–166.

44. Wit, Poneman, and Gallucci, *Going Critical,* 147, 156–159; letter from C. Kenneth Quinones, January 25, 2006.

45. Oberdorfer, *The Two Koreas,* 268–270, 299, 301, 304, 312–313; Sigal, *Disarming Strangers,* 40–41, 94–95, 107–108; Wit, Poneman, and Gallucci,

Going Critical, 149–150. Nancy Soderberg, the number three official in the NSC at the time, revealed in her recent book that the Clinton administration considered war with North Korea a "real possibility" in early 1994. According to Soderberg, the North Koreans were digging trenches in the demilitarized zone (DMZ) and using fishing vessels to lay mines, their intent being to show the United States that North Korea was prepared to go to war. Nancy Soderberg, *The Superpower Myth: The Use and Misuse of American Might* (Hoboken, N.J.: John Wiley, 2005), 261.

46. The Vienna agency believed that with these specifically identified rods it would be able to reconstruct the past history of the reactor and ascertain with considerable accuracy the amount of plutonium North Korea had reprocessed in the past.

47. Wit, Poneman, and Gallucci, *Going Critical,* 125–127, 170–175, 190; Oberdorfer, *The Two Koreas,* 306–311; Sigal, *Disarming Strangers,* 111, 113–115, 117.

48. Oberdorfer, *The Two Koreas,* 306; Wit, Poneman, and Gallucci, *Going Critical,* 126, 160.

49. Wit, Poneman, and Gallucci, *Going Critical,* 193, 206, 210. Soderberg, *The Superpower Myth,* 261.

50. Oberdorfer, *The Two Koreas,* 315. By mid-June, when the military drew up specific options to augment U.S. military strength in South Korea, Luck had raised his cost estimates, stating that a new war in Korea would kill as many as a million people, including from 80,000 to 100,000 Americans; its out-of-pocket costs to the United States would exceed $100 billion, and "destruction of property and interruption of business activity would cost more that $1,000 billion (one trillion) to countries involved and their immediate neighbors." Oberdorfer, *The Two Koreas,* 324.

51. Ibid., 316. As late as May 27, 1994, the members of the Principals Committee reportedly concluded that sanctions would not cause North Korea to meet its nonproliferation obligations, stop its nuclear activities, or reveal them to others. But they nonetheless "supported the imposition of sanctions as the least bad option," reportedly believing that the risk of North Korea converting more spent fuel into plutonium and carrying through on its threat to view sanctions as an act of war was less than having the credibility of the nonproliferation regime undermined and compromising long-standing U.S. policy. Wit, Poneman, and Gallucci, *Going Critical,* 186–187.

52. About 600,000 pro-Pyongyang Koreans lived in Japan, and their organization, the Chosen Soren, sent large though poorly monitored cash contribu-

tions to North Korea. The amounts were thought to be between $200 and $600 million annually. Wit, Poneman, and Gallucci, *Going Critical*, 194. In 1994, at the Carter Center, we thought the amount involved was toward the high end of that range. David E. Brown, director of the Office of Korean Affairs in the State Department in 1994, estimated the annual amount to be $500 million or more. David E. Brown, "No Thanks Expected: America's Effort to Nurture a 'Soft Landing,'" in Wonmo Dong, ed., *The Two Koreas and the United States: Issues of Peace, Security, and Economic Cooperation* (Armonk, N.Y.: M. E. Sharpe, 2000), 196.

53. Oberdorfer, *The Two Koreas*, 318–320.

54. Wit, Poneman, and Gallucci, *Going Critical*, 159; Oberdorfer, *The Two Koreas*, 320–321. The South Korean foreign minister, Han Sung Joo, advised President Carter of a Chinese demarche along these lines the morning before he crossed the DMZ. Marion Creekmore, "Personal Notes: Korea Trip, June, 1994," 39.

55. Oberdorfer, *The Two Koreas*, 321. Also see Sigal, *Disarming Strangers*, 121, and Wit, Poneman, and Gallucci, *Going Critical*, 210.

56. Oberdorfer, *The Two Koreas*, 323.

57. Sigal, *Disarming Strangers*, 118, 131.

58. Oberdorfer, *The Two Koreas*, 323.

59. Ibid., 324–325.

60. Wit, Poneman, and Gallucci, *Going Critical*, 179.

61. Oberdorfer, *The Two Koreas*, 325.

62. Ibid., 326.

63. Ibid., 323. Brent Scowcroft and Arnold Kanter, "Korea: Time for Action," *Washington Post*, June 15, 1994.

64. Oberdorfer, *The Two Koreas*, 323.

CHAPTER 2

1. Douglas Brinkley, *The Unfinished Presidency: Jimmy Carter's Journey Beyond the White House* (New York: Viking, 1998), 388.

2. Ibid., 389; Don Oberdorfer, *The Two Koreas: A Contemporary History* (Reading, Mass.: Addison-Wesley, 1997), 87–108. In running for U.S. president in 1976, Carter made clear that he did not equate U.S. national interest with the projection of American military power around the globe. In that context, he advocated withdrawing U.S. troops and nuclear weapons from Korea.

As president, he faced strong opposition at home and in Seoul to reducing U.S. military presence in South Korea. He finally accepted a small symbolic reduction of troops, coupled with a South Korean government pledge on human rights that included releasing eighty-seven dissidents from prison.

3. Oberdorfer, *The Two Koreas*, 104–105; Bradley K. Martin, *Under the Loving Care of the Fatherly Leader: North Korea and the Kim Dynasty* (New York: Thomas Dunne Books, St. Martin's Press, 2004), 130.

4. Oberdorfer, *The Two Koreas*, 94–101.

5. The Carter administration had established formal diplomatic relations between the United States and the People's Republic of China.

6. This information is drawn from conversations the author had with President and Mrs. Carter between 1993 and 2003.

7. Powell would subsequently marry William (Bill) J. Spencer, a conflict resolution expert who owned his own consulting company; Bill would sometimes work on contract with The Carter Center. Hence, depending on the timeframe, the text and footnotes will refer either to Dayle Powell or to Dayle Spencer.

8. Dayle E. Spencer and William J. Spencer, "The International Negotiation Network: A New Method of Approaching Some Very Old Problems" (Occasional Paper Series, vol. 2, no. 2, The Carter Center, Atlanta, Georgia, January 1992). A version can be found on the Carter Center Web site. Interview with Steven Hochman, PhD, director of research and assistant to President Carter, one of the original staff appointees at The Carter Center, May 27, 2003.

9. John W. Lewis, "Letter to President Jimmy Carter," August 13, 1990, Post-Presidential Papers, "North Korea 8/90–4/93." Interestingly, Lewis mentioned that he was writing to Carter at the suggestion of William J. Perry, who had served as under secretary of defense for research and engineering during the Carter presidency and would be secretary of defense when Carter traveled to North and South Korea in 1994. Lewis, an arms control expert, wrote to Carter at a time when he and his colleagues at the Center for International Security and Arms Control were talking to counterparts in both Koreas about using confidence-building measures to reduce the danger of war between them. Bradley K. Martin, *Under the Loving Care of the Fatherly Leader*, 370.

10. At that time no non-Korean had crossed the DMZ since the 1950–1953 Korean War.

11. Jimmy Carter, "Confidential Memo," August 23, 1990, Post-Presidential Papers, "North Korea 8/90–4/93."

12. Dayle E. Powell, "Memo to President Carter," August 24, 1990, Post-Presidential Papers, "North Korea 8/90–4/93."

13. Ibid., September 4, 1990; Kathy Ward, "Memo to Sue Palmer" (forwarded to Carter), May 24, 1991; and Kathy Ward, "Memo to President Carter, June 6, 1991, Post-Presidential Papers, "North Korea 8/90–4/93."

14. North Korea and South Korea did not become official members of the United Nations until 1991.

15. Charles A. Wickham, "Letter to William Foege, Executive Director of The Carter Center," February 15, 1991, Post-Presidential Papers, "North Korea 8/90–4/93." The State Department had approved the travel of Dr. Han to expose him to a cross-section of popular opinion, according to a briefing memo prepared by Dayle Spencer, director of the Conflict Resolution Program, after discussions with the Korean Desk of the U.S. State Department. Dayle Spencer, "Memo to President Carter," June 10, 1991, Post-Presidential Papers, "North Korea 8/90–4/93."

16. Carter had been briefed by phone on Han and current Korean developments by the State Department assistant secretary for East Asia, Richard Solomon, the day before he met with Han. Carter always prepared extensively for meetings, such as the one with Han, that he thought might have potentially important follow-on consequences. Jimmy Carter, "Notes for the Record," June 6, 1991, Post-Presidential Papers, "North Korea 8/90–4/93."

17. Ibid.

18. Jimmy Carter, handwritten note dated October 1, 1991, of points made by Kim Yong Nam at meeting in New York on September 30, 1991. Post-Presidential Papers, "North Korea 8/90–4/93."

19. Song Ho Gyong (name Anglicized as Song Ho Kyong), "Letter to Mr. Jimmy Carter," September 10, 1991, Post-Presidential Papers, "North Korea 8/90–4/93."

20. Dayle Spencer, "Memorandum to President Carter," July 15, 1991, Post-Presidential Papers, "North Korea 8/90–4/93." Before he met with the South Korean ambassador, Powell had advised the State Department's Korean Office of Han Shi Hai's discussion with Carter about his visiting Pyongyang.

21. Hong-Choo Hyun, "Letter to Dr. Dayle E. Spencer," September 13, 1991, Post-Presidential Papers, Conflict Resolution Program of The Carter Center, "North Korea 8/90–4/93."

22. Dayle E. Spencer, "Memorandum to President Carter," October 13, 1991, and Carter's handwritten note on the front page of the memo that was returned to Spencer, Post-Presidential Papers, "North Korea 8/90–4/93."

23. Jimmy Carter, "MemCon" with Solomon that Carter instructed to be shared with Spencer, October 16, 1991; "Note to Files," October 24, 1991; "Note to Dayle Spencer," November 7, 1991, reporting on conversations with Solomon, Post-Presidential Papers, "North Korea 8/90–4/93." On several occasions Carter told me that Baker's request not to make the trip as tentatively planned in early 1992 figured prominently in his decisionmaking, a point he made in general terms in various public statements.

24. This paragraph is based on the paper produced by the rapporteur to the Korean panel, Pharis J. Harvey, titled "Summary of Discussion of the Korean Peninsula," Post-Presidential Papers, "Korean Peninsula" (box 109, 2 of 2). An abbreviated version is found in the final report of the INN Conference, *Resolving Intra-National Conflicts: A Strengthened Role for Non-Governmental Actors* (Occasional Paper Series, vol. 3, no. 2, The Carter Center, Atlanta, Georgia, January 1992). A version can be found on the Carter Center Web site.

25. Kim Dae Jung, "Letter to The Honorable Jimmy Carter," February 15, 1992, Post-Presidential Papers, "Korea—June '94," specific file: "Confidential—notes and transcripts of mtgs—No. & So."

26. Jimmy Carter, "Letter to Dr. Kim Dae Jung," February 28, 1992, Post-Presidential Papers, "Korea—June '94," specific file: "Confidential—notes and transcripts of mtgs—No. & So."

27. Information provided to me by former president Jimmy Carter.

28. Dayle E. Spencer and William J. Spencer, "The Role of the INN in the Korean Peninsula," a memo sent to President Carter on August 5, 1992, Post-Presidential Papers, "North Korea 8/90–4/93."

29. Ibid.

30. This information is drawn from several conversations I had with President Carter between October 1992 and December 1995.

31. Kim Yong Nam, "Letter to Mr. Jimmy Carter," November 13, 1992, Post-Presidential Papers, "North Korea 8/90–4/93."

32. Elizabeth Kurylo, "In Peace Work, Carter Careful Not to Step on Anyone's Toes," *Atlanta Journal Constitution*, February 19, 1993.

33. *Wall Street Journal*, February 17, 1993; Reuters, February 18, 1993; AFP, February 19, 1993. Reported in a summary of the Conflict Resolution Program of The Carter Center, February 26, 1993/vol. 3, no. 5, Office of Public Information, The Carter Center, Files on the Korean Trip 1994.

34. Dayle E. Spencer, "Memorandum to President Carter: Subject—Korean Peninsula," February 22, 1993; "Memorandum to President Carter: Subject—

Korean Peninsula," February 25, 1993, Post-Presidential Papers, "South Korea 1/92–2/93."

35. Laney had advised Spencer that Carter needed to craft a face-saving so-lution for the Seoul government because, after its public denial of a role for Carter, it might turn defensive toward Carter and begin backing away from its original invitation. In addition, Laney had just met with North Korea's deputy ambassador, Ho Jong, who advised Laney of the need to keep Pyongyang's in-vitation in strict confidence, suggesting that the North might also have some difficulty in light of the disclosure. Dayle E. Spencer, "Memorandum to Pres-ident Carter: Subject—Korean Peninsula," February 25, 1993, Post-Presiden-tial Papers, "South Korea 1/92–2/93."

36. Jimmy Carter, "Letter to His Excellency Kim Young-sam" and "Letter to His Excellency Kim Il Sung," both March 1, 1993, Post-Presidential Papers, "South Korea 1/92–2/93."

37. The Carter Center, in association with governmental and nongovern-mental groups in Atlanta, worked for eight years to help the city deal more ef-fectively with its urban ills and provide useful lessons for other cities in dealing with similar problems.

38. Conversation with Robert Pastor, the director of the Latin American Program at The Carter Center and a professor of political science at Emory University, shortly after Carter returned to Atlanta. Pastor, who had served as the Latin American expert in the National Security Council during the Carter presidency, accompanied Carter on his Washington appointments. Pastor had been on Clinton's foreign policy team during the election campaign, and he would subsequently be nominated to serve as the U.S. ambassador to Panama. Senator Jesse Helms used his position on the Senate Foreign Relations Com-mittee to prevent Pastor's nomination from coming to a vote on the Senate floor, thereby denying him the ambassadorship. Helms's action, at least in part, was taken to express disapproval for Pastor's role in negotiating and winning approval for the Panama Canal Treaty during the Carter presidency.

39. Later conversations suggested that my presumptions at the time were close to the mark. Dan Poneman, the nuclear nonproliferation expert in the NSC in 1994, said that Clinton, after facing problems with the military early in his administration, did not want to appear soft or too liberal. Too close an identification with Carter would undercut the image of toughness in interna-tional affairs that he was trying to project. Jim Laney's assessment was similar: Clinton, with his sensitive political antennae, regarded Carter as a loser and

did not want to appear to be close to him. Bob Pastor, a director of a Carter Center program who had good contacts within the Clinton administration, told me that Clinton was reluctant to get too close to Carter out of his fear of being categorized as "another failed Southern governor." Nancy Soderberg, the number three official in the NSC in 1994, and Poneman, in a recent conversation and in the book he wrote with Joel Wit and Bob Gallucci, both talked about the view in the administration that Carter did not follow instructions easily when they differed with his own views. Soderberg's language spells out the point this way: "With strong beliefs on his own and deeply skeptical of the use of force, Carter could also be a bit of a loose cannon, making his own policy." Nancy Soderberg, *The Superpower Myth: The Use and Misuse of American Might* (Hoboken, N.J.: John Wiley), 263. Telephone conversation with Robert Pastor, October 18, 2005; telephone conversation with James Laney, December 14, 2005; telephone conversation with Daniel Poneman, February 5, 2006; Joel S. Wit, Daniel B. Poneman, and Robert L. Gallucci, *Going Critical: The First North Korean Nuclear Crisis* (Washington, D.C.: Brookings Institution Press, 2004), 206.

40. Drawn from conversations I had with President Carter between 1993 and 1996. Carter's suspicions of the State Department were based on his own experiences. He found it difficult during his administration to talk to the individual experts on a subject in which he was interested. He complained that Secretary of State Vance insisted that communication be with him or his senior deputies to ensure that the president had the benefit of their broader analyses and interpretations rather than with a lower-ranking State officer, such as a desk officer, who would have a narrower mandate and focus. During the first Bush and Clinton administrations, it was usually senior State Department rather than White House officials who asked Carter not to undertake controversial missions abroad. Occasionally, he offered his own explanation—that because the State Department had the primary responsibility for coordinating foreign affairs, it was usually more resistant than other governmental institutions to Carter Center involvement in foreign policy issues.

41. Joyce Neu of Conflict Resolution, "Memorandum to President Carter on Travel to North and South Korea," April 21, 1993; Jimmy Carter, "Letter to Peter C. Goldmark," April 21, 1993, Post-Presidential Papers, "North Korea 8/90–4/93."

42. Sue Palmer of the Conflict Resolution Program, "Memorandum to President Carter: Subject—Meeting request from North Korean DCM at UN

Mission," July 9, 1993; Jimmy Carter, handwritten "Note to the Files, 9/23/93, Post-Presidential Papers, "Korea—June '94," specific file: "Korea (North and South), Files before visit planning."

43. R. Jeffrey Smith, "North Korea Deal Urged by State Department: Canceling Exercise Linked to Inspections," *Washington Post,* November 15, 1993. A more complete discussion of the developments involving the United States, North Korea, South Korea, and the IAEA during the period September–December 1993 is found in Wit, Poneman, and Gallucci, *Going Critical,* 78–117. Throughout this period, the IAEA and North Korea disputed how extensive inspections must be to meet the requirements of the language agreed to by the United States and North Korea in the July meeting in Geneva. Each side took rigid positions. One example of the intransigence of their interaction occurred in early August 1993. The IAEA cancelled an inspection trip to North Korea when the two sides could not agree about whether the IAEA inspectors must pick up their visas from the North Korean mission or have them brought by the North Korean diplomats to the inspectors. Telephone conversation with C. Kenneth Quinones, December 14, 2005.

44. Joyce Neu of Conflict Resolution, "Memorandum to President Carter: Subject—Update on Korean Peninsula," November 16, 1993; Sue Palmer of Conflict Resolution, "Memorandum to President Carter: Subject—Update on the North Korean-U.S. Negotiations," November 19, 1993, Post-Presidential Papers, "Korea—June '94," specific file: "Korea (North and South), Files before visit planning." On instructions from his boss, Charles Kartman, the director of the Office of Korean Affairs, Quinones maintained contact with Sue Palmer and her CRP colleagues and periodically talked with me about U.S. dealings with North Korea and the attitude of the administration about a possible visit of Carter to North Korea. Telephone conversation with C. Kenneth Quinones, December 14, 2005.

45. Jimmy Carter, "Memorandum of conversation with N. Korean Ambassador Ho Jong," November 19, 1993, Post-Presidential Papers, "Korea—June '94," specific file: "Korea (North and South), Files before visit planning."

46. Carter had met with the Editorial Board at CNN headquarters a few days earlier, as he did periodically, to review issues around the world. During their discussion, he had offered to try to help have CNN invited to North Korea to produce such a program—as recommended by the INN in January 1992. Tom Johnson, the president of CNN, welcomed the proposal, agreed with the desirability of a series of reports on North Korea, and noted

that the DPRK had rebuffed earlier CNN proposals to travel to and report on North Korea.

47. Jimmy Carter, "Memorandum of conversation with N. Korean Ambassador Ho Jong," November 19, 1993; Tom Johnson, "Letter to The Honorable Jimmy Carter," November 16, 1993, Post-Presidential Papers, "Korea—June '94," specific file: "Korea (North and South), Files before visit planning."

48. Joyce Neu (Contact Person: Sue Palmer) of Conflict Resolution, "Memorandum to President Carter: Subject—North Korea: Repeated pressures from non-Administration sources for emissary role," December 7, 1993, Post-Presidential Papers, "Korea—June '94," specific file: "Korea (North and South), Files before visit planning."

49. Ibid.

50. Han Park, "NEGOTIATING WITH NORTH KOREA IS THE BEST WAY TO AVERT A CRISIS," draft op-ed provided by the author to the Conflict Resolution Program of The Carter Center in early December, 1993, and sent to President Carter via Joyce Neu (Contact Person: Sue Palmer), "Memorandum to President Carter: North Korea: Repeated pressures from non-Administration sources for emissary role." Subsequently, Park provided to President Carter two longer papers that included additional information and analyses to support his major theses. One of the papers discussed Pyongyang's motivations and options; the other, the evolution of the *Juche* philosophy.

51. Years later, Kenneth Quinones explained that during this period the Clinton administration was seeking to deal with issues directly on a government-to-government basis. Almost weekly, U.S. officials were talking with North Korean officials in New York, and they did not think outside emissaries were required. Before telling Sue Palmer that a visit by Carter would not be useful at that time, Ken Quinones raised the matter with Tom Hubbard, deputy assistant secretary of state for East Asia, who discussed it with Bob Gallucci. An action memorandum on whether a trip by Carter to the Korean Peninsula in early 1994 would be desirable was sent to Secretary of State Warren Christopher. After a negative decision was taken, Quinones called the message to Palmer at the Center. Information contained in a letter dated December 14, 2005, that C. Kenneth Quinones sent me.

52. Jimmy Carter, handwritten note dated December 10, 1993, on returned memo from Sue Palmer titled "Memorandum for President Carter: Subject—North Korea: Repeated pressures from non-Administration sources for emis-

sary role," December 7, 1993, Post-Presidential Papers, "Korea—June '94," specific file: "Korea (North and South), Files before visit planning."

53. Marion Creekmore, "Memorandum to President Carter: Subject—U.S.-North Korean Discussions: Update," December 15, 1993, Post-Presidential Papers, "Korea—June '94," specific file: "Korea (North and South), Files before visit planning." Telephone conversation with C. Kenneth Quinones, December 23, 2005.

54. Creekmore, "Memorandum to President Carter: Subject—U.S.-North Korean Discussions: Update," December 15, 1993. David Brown told me in an e-mail letter dated January 1, 2006, that Bob Gallucci, Dan Poneman, and Tom Hubbard always regarded Carter as a "high-value card, to be played if and when the situation became appropriate." Brown added, "That was the case by June 1994, when North Korea's dogged intransigence had forced the U.S., Japan, and the Republic of Korea [South Korea] to up the ante by seeking sanctions at the UN." E-mail message from David E. Brown, January 1, 2006.

55. Jim Brasher, "Memo to President Carter and others: Subject: Trip to Seoul, KOREA," September 9, 1993, Post-Presidential Papers, "Korea—June '94," specific file: "Korea (North and South), Files before visit planning."

56. Hardman, a member of a prominent Georgia family and grandson of a former Georgia governor, is a medical doctor trained in psychiatry. He had served as the administrator of an Atlanta hospital, but decided in the late 1980s to make a career change. He joined The Carter Center in 1989 as head of its Initiative to Reduce Global Tobacco Use; a year later, he became the Center's representative to the World Health Organization's Tobacco and Health Program. He directed the Center's Mental Health Program from 1991 to 1993, became associate executive director in February 1992, and took up his current position as executive director in December 1992.

57. Kartman, who was the director of the Office of Korean Affairs until his assignment to Seoul in late 1993, would subsequently serve as deputy assistant secretary of state responsible for relations with the two Koreas, and then as head of the Korean Energy Development Organization (KEDO), which was charged with the responsibility of working with the two Koreas and other participating countries in implementing the 1994 U.S.-North Korean Agreed Framework.

58. John B. Hardman, "Memorandum to President Carter: Subject—Conversation with Ambassador Laney, December 15, 1993; "Faxed Letter to Ambassador James T. Laney," January 4, 1994, Post-Presidential Papers,

"Korea—June '94," specific file: "Korea (North and South), Files before visit planning."

59. State Department, "EAP Press Guidance," January 5, 1994; Joyce Neu (Contact Person-Sue Palmer), "Memorandum to President Carter: Subject— Update on the Korean Peninsula, January 11, 1994; "Memorandum to President Carter: Subject—Update on North Korea," January 25, 1994; "Memorandum to President Carter: Subject—Korean Peninsula—Agreement reached between IAEA and North Korea, February 16, 1994; "Memorandum to President Carter: Subject—Korean Peninsula—Update," March 7, 1994 (the latter memo contained the State Department press guidance: "Statement by Michael McCurry/Spokesman: RESUMPTION OF US-DPRK NEGO-TIATIONS ON NUCLEAR AND OTHER ISSUES," March 3, 1994, and a one-page statement, "ROK READOUT ON PANMUNJOM MEET-ING"), Post-Presidential Papers, "Korea—June '94," specific file: "Korea (North and South), Files before visit planning."

60. Marion Creekmore, "Memorandum to President Carter: Subject—Update on Korean Issue," April 12, 1994, Post-Presidential Papers, "Korea—June '94," specific file: "Korea (North and South), Files before visit planning."

61. Ibid.

62. Ibid.

63. This issue would become a critical one within days when North Korea suddenly began unloading the fuel rods.

64. Marion Creekmore, "Memorandum to President Carter: Subject—U.S.-North Korean Update," April 30, 1994, Post-Presidential Papers, "Korea—June '94," specific file: "Korea (North and South), Files before visit planning."

65. Ibid.

CHAPTER 3

1. At the time Oberdorfer, who had retired as diplomatic correspondent for the *Washington Post,* was based at the Johns Hopkins Nitze School of Advanced International Studies working on *The Two Koreas: A Contemporary History,* which was published in 1997. He filed the article referred to from Seoul.

2. Don Oberdorfer, "The Remilitarized Zone: In an Age of Diplomatic Tension, Korea Becomes the Toughest Test," *Washington Post Outlook: Commentary and Opinion,* May 1, 1994.

3. Don Oberdorfer, "Letter to President Carter, May 10, 1994, with Carter's handwritten "cc Jim Laney. In case you haven't seen Don's article. Jimmy C,"

Post-Presidential Papers, "Korea—June '94," specific file: "Korea (North and South), Files before visit planning."

4. Joel S. Wit, Daniel B. Poneman, and Robert Gallucci, *Going Critical: The First North Korean Nuclear Crisis* (Washington, D.C.: Brookings Institution Press, 2004), 206–207.

5. When President Clinton was touring the CNN facilities prior to his meeting with the reporters attending the CNN conference, Mike Chinoy seized a brief opportunity to describe his and his colleagues' conversation with Kim Il Sung a week before (while covering his birthday celebration). Chinoy told Clinton that the North Korean ruler had given the impression that his government would like to talk with President Clinton and that the North Koreans were interested in a negotiated solution to the nuclear problem. The president thanked Chinoy and said his administration was working hard on the problem. Mike Chinoy, *China Live: Two Decades in the Heart of the Dragon* (Atlanta: Turner Publishing, 1997), 343, 346–347.

6. This paragraph is based on Carter's notes of the meeting that were subsequently shared with me.

7. Interview with the former ambassador James Laney, Emory University, August 17, 2000.

8. Ibid.

9. Ibid. Aspin's trip took place in the same timeframe in which Washington policymakers were skeptically reviewing the unofficial North Korean proposal for a "package" deal; the IAEA director general, Hans Blix, had publicly suggested that the "continuity of safeguards" on North Korea's nuclear facilities would soon be lost; and South Korean defense minister Kwon Yong Hae had told a press conference of his concern about the North's nuclear program and indicated that military action might be required. Don Oberdorfer, *The Two Koreas: A Contemporary History* (Reading, Mass.: Addison-Wesley, 1997), 293–294.

10. Interview with the former ambassador James Laney, Emory University, August 17, 2000.

11. Ibid.

12. The paragraphs discussing this paper are based on the following document: U.S. Embassy, Seoul, "Reflections on the Korean Situation," 1–7, Post-Presidential Papers, "Korea—June '94," specific file: "Korea (North and South), Files before visit planning."

13. Ibid.

14. Ibid.

15. Interview with the former ambassador James Laney, Emory University, August 17, 2000. Laney would keep Nunn, a friend of many years, informed as the crisis continued to unfold.

16. James T. Laney, "Letter to The Honorable Jimmy Carter," January 26, 1994, Post-Presidential Papers, "Korea—June '94," specific file: "Korea (North and South), Files before visit planning."

17. Jimmy Carter, "Note to Ambassador Jim Laney," February 9, 1994, Post-Presidential Papers, "Korea—June '94," specific file: "Korea (North and South), Files before visit planning."

18. Leon V. Sigal, *Disarming Strangers: Nuclear Diplomacy with North Korea* (Princeton: Princeton University Press, 1998), 95.

19. Oberdorfer, *The Two Koreas*, 301–302.

20. Interview with the former ambassador James Laney, Emory University, August 17, 2000. According to Laney, Gallucci told him two months later how his appointment as point person for Korea had transpired. Oberdorfer reports that President Clinton and Vice President Gore found Laney's remarks sobering. Oberdorfer, *The Two Koreas*, 302.

21. Laney assessed Perry's replacement of Aspin to be a "godsend," but thought Christopher was inadequately interested in Korea. Interview with the former ambassador James Laney, Emory University, August 17, 2000. Oberdorfer pointed out that Gallucci was given a "charter to coordinate or at least rationalize the disparate views of the White House, State Department, Defense Department, CIA, and various officials and offices within them. Nonetheless, disagreements continued within the executive branch and also in the Congress and in the press." Oberdorfer, *The Two Koreas*, 302.

22. Interview with the former ambassador James Laney, Emory University, August 17, 2000.

23. A few days after Laney's arrival in Atlanta and his talk with Jimmy Carter, the North Koreans would suddenly begin to unload the fuel rods from their 5 MWe reactor, accelerating the pace of the crisis.

24. Laney later compared U.S.-North Korean communications as smoke signals from distant hills on a windy day.

25. Interview with the former ambassador James Laney, Emory University, August 17, 2000; Laney's April 13, 2005, lecture to the "Public Policy and Nongovernmental Organizations" class at Emory University, taught by Dr. Steven Hochman and me. Laney was not the only one in the administration seeing potential parallels between the situation on the peninsula and World

War I. Gallucci apparently thought, to quote Oberdorfer, that "the spring of 1994 had an eerie and disturbing resemblance to historian Barbara Tuchman's account of 'the guns of August,' when, in the summer of 1914, World War I began in cross-purposes, misunderstanding, and inadvertence." Gallucci said that the situation "had an escalatory quality, that could deteriorate not only into war but into a big war." Oberdorfer, *The Two Koreas*, 306. The idea must have been circulating widely within the administration. When Defense Secretary Perry briefed President Clinton on options for augmenting U.S. military forces in South Korea on June 16, he also likened the current situation to that which Barbara Tuchman had described in *The Guns of August*. Wit, Poneman, and Gallucci, *Going Critical*, 227.

26. Description of this conversation draws on notes provided to the author by President Carter in December 2004 and the author's interview with the former ambassador James Laney, Emory University, August 17, 2000.

27. Young Jack Lee, Special Assistant to the Chairman, Kim Dae Jung Peace Foundation for the Asia-Pacific Region, Washington Office, fax letter to Dr. John Hardman (executive director of The Carter Center), May 13, 1994, Post-Presidential Papers, "Korea—June '94," specific file: "Korea (North and South), Files before visit planning."

28. The description of Kim Dae Jung's speech comes from the copy sent to Carter by the author, "My Suggestions for U.S.-Asian Policies," speech to the National Press Club, Washington, D.C., May 12, 1994, 1–4, Post-Presidential Papers, "Korea—June '94," specific file: "Korea (North and South), Files before visit planning."

29. Ibid.

30. Young Jack Lee, "Letter to Dr. John Hardman" that accompanied Kim Dae Jung's remarks to the National Press Club and his policy paper elaborating the ideas in his speech, May 13, 1994, Post-Presidential Papers, "Korea—June '94," specific file: "Korea (North and South), Files before visit planning."

31. Faye Perdue grew up in Americus, Georgia a few miles from Plains. She went to work for Carter when he returned to Plains after his tenure in the White House. For more than two decades she has served as Carter's personal and executive assistant. The former president has high and justified confidence in her competence, loyalty, and discretion. On occasions she has traveled with President and Mrs. Carter on international initiatives, but usually she stays in Atlanta to "hold the fort" in their absence. At the time of the Korean crisis, she

was using her married name, Dill, but later she reclaimed her birth name, Perdue. Consequently, she is usually referred to in this narrative as Faye Dill rather than Faye Perdue.

32. In his frustration over the lateness of the proposed briefing, Carter apparently drew the conclusion that if Poneman's wife had just given birth, he must be too young to be the senior-level official he expected Clinton to send to Plains. I subsequently explained to President Carter that I had told Poneman that Monday was adequate, and that had I insisted, I was sure Poneman would have come to Plains on the weekend. I do not know whether Carter accepted that explanation or my description of Poneman as the senior NSC official dealing with the North Korean issue for NSC Adviser Tony Lake. I do know that he was pleased that Gallucci would be the one briefing him.

33. Conversation with Robert Gallucci, February 15, 2005.

34. Unless otherwise noted, the description of this conversation is drawn from Carter's handwritten notes of the meeting. Jimmy Carter, "Notes on Gallucci Briefing," June 5, 1994, 1–4, Post-Presidential Papers, "Korea—June '94," specific file: "Korea—Briefing info."

35. Marion Creekmore, "Office Diary: May 12–September 10, 1994," 32.

36. South Korean officials would later confirm to Carter that the bilateral nuclear declaration had been signed but not implemented since talks broke down before terms of implementation could be hammered out.

37. Creekmore, "Office Diary: May 12–September 10, 1994," 34.

38. This change in South Korea's position and its rationale for the change is described in Wit, Poneman, and Gallucci, *Going Critical,* 167–168.

39. Carter, "Notes on Gallucci Briefing," 2; Creekmore, "Office Diary: May 12–September 10, 1994," 36–39.

40. Creekmore, "Office Diary: May 12–September 10, 1994," 39.

41. Carter, "Notes on Gallucci Briefing," 2; Creekmore, "Office Diary: May 12–September 10, 1994," 40. Other sources placed U.S. troop levels at 37,000.

42. Carter, "Notes on Gallucci Briefing," 2; Creekmore, "Office Diary: May 12–September 10, 1994," 44.

43. Gallucci was referring to the CNN coverage of the North Korean ruler's eighty-second birthday celebration in April.

44. My memory and lack of mention in my and the Carters' note about a discussion on reprocession; conversation with Robert Gallucci, February 15, 2005. Also see Wit, Poneman, and Gallucci, *Going Critical,* page 202.

45. Chinoy, *China Live,* 338–339.

46. Conversation with Robert Gallucci, February 15, 2005.

47. Wit, Poneman, and Gallucci, *Going Critical*, 202.

CHAPTER 4

1. Jimmy Carter, "Letter to President Bill Clinton" (draft), June 6, 1994, Post-Presidential Papers, "Korea—June '94," specific file: "Korea—official communication w/US govt."

2. Because Han and I had some difficulty communicating over the phone, I then called Professor Han Park at the University of Georgia and asked that he contact the North Korean mission to ensure that my interpretation of the conversation coincided with that of Minister Counselor Han. Professor Park spoke frequently with the North Korean officials in New York, traveled periodically to North Korea where he had good access to senior North Korean officials, and kept the Center's conflict resolution officials informed of his discussions in Pyongyang and his views on developments within North Korea. Park reported back a short time later that my message had been correctly understood and that Pyongyang was being notified of Carter's request.

3. Jimmy Carter, "Letter to President Bill Clinton," June 8, 1994, Post-Presidential Papers, "Korea—June '94," specific file: "Korea—official communication w/US govt."

4. Joel Wit, Dan Poneman, and Robert Gallucci, *Going Critical: The First North Korean Nuclear Crisis* (Washington, D.C.: Brookings Institution Press, 2004), 203; conversation with Robert Gallucci, February 15, 2005. Lake later told the author that while he knew the Carter trip would complicate the situation, he gave greater weight to the possibility that it could have positive benefits. Conversation with Anthony Lake, February 15, 2005.

5. Jimmy Carter, handwritten notes of meeting with Professor Weston M. Stacey, Jr., June 9, 1994, Post-Presidential Papers, "Korea—June '94," specific file: "Korea—Briefing info."

6. Unless otherwise noted, the Jordan presentation in this and subsequent paragraphs is drawn from the written notes I made at the time (Marion Creekmore, "Personal Notes: Korea Trip, June, 1994," 1); and from Jordan's notes on his North Korean trip titled "Details re Our April 12–19 North Korean Trip," 1–2, which he placed in his CNN files on April 19, 1994. After his oral briefing, Jordan gave a copy of these notes to Carter. Post-Presidential Papers, "Korea—June '94," specific file: "Korea—Briefing info."

7. For more on the special lighting for Kim Il Sung, see Mike Chinoy, *China Live: Two Decades in the Heart of the Dragon* (Atlanta: Turner Publishing, 1997), 318.

8. Eason Jordan also described this incident in his lecture to the author's "Public Policy and Nongovernmental Organizations" course at Emory University, March 20, 2002.

9. Eason Jordan, "Detail re Our April 12–19 North Korean Trip," 2, Post-Presidential Papers, "Korea—June '94," specific file: "Korea—Briefing info."

10. Creekmore, "Personal Notes," 1. Subsequently, some Washington briefers would tell Carter that Kim Jong Il was effectively in charge, a proposition Carter would question at the time. In Pyongyang, it would become indisputably clear that Kim Il Sung, not his son, made the key policy decisions for his country.

11. Kim Yong Sun had headed the North Korean delegation that met with Under Secretary of State Arnold Kanter and the U.S. delegation in the first high-level bilateral exchange between the United States and North Korea during the George H. W. Bush administration in January 1992.

12. Jordan, "Details re Our April 12–19 North Korea Trip," 2.

13. Ibid.

14. None of the many U.S. officials who briefed Carter claimed that North Korea had such capacity or access to Russian and Chinese nuclear scientists.

15. The description by Tom Johnson of the Washington briefing is drawn from the author's written notes. Creekmore, "Personal Notes," 2.

16. Ibid.

17. Telephone conversation with Dick Christenson, February 8, 2006.

18. Information from his personal notes that former president Carter provided the author in December 2004, and Don Oberdorfer, *The Two Koreas: A Contemporary History* (Reading, Mass.: Addison-Wesley, 1997), 299.

19. "Statement of Dr. Billy Graham," Kim Il Sung Airport, Pyongyang, D.P.R.K., January 27, 1994; "Statement of Dr. Billy Graham" at the Welcome Banquet in his honor in Pyongyang, D.P.R.K. on January 27, 1994; "Speech by Dr. Billy Graham (U.S.A.)" at Kim Il Sung University, Pyongyang, D.P.R.K. on January 28, 1994, Post-Presidential Papers, "Korea—June '94," specific file: "Korea—Briefing info."

20. The description of the points in Linton's paper is drawn from Stephen W. Linton, PhD, "Approach and Style in Negotiating with the D.P.R.K.," 1–7, Center for Korean Research, Columbia University, no date shown, Post-Presidential Papers, "Korea—June '94," specific file: "Korea—Briefing info."

21. See Appendix A for the answers provided to President Carter. Jimmy Carter, "Questions re Korea," and Faye Dill, fax cover sheets to NSC Adviser Tony Lake and Secretary Bob Gallucci, June 10, 1994, Post-Presidential Papers, "Korea—June '94," specific file: "Confidential—notes and transcripts of mtgs—No. & So.," and also in "Robert Gallucci/Tony Lake."

22. News from The Carter Center, "Statement from Former U.S. President Jimmy Carter Announcing His Plans to Visit Korea," June 9, '94, Post-Presidential Papers, "Korea—June '94," specific file: "Korea—Briefing info."

23. "Carter Heads for Pyongyang as US Admits Chinese Sanction Vote in Doubt," Agence France Presse, June 10, 1994; "Former President to Visit North, South Korea as Private Citizen, Associated Press, June 9, 1994; "Carter to Make Private Visit to North Korea," Reuters, July 9, 1994; William Scally, "U.S. Policy on North Korea Comes Under Fire," Reuters, June 9, 1994; "Carter to Make Private Visit to North Korea," Reuters, June 9, 1994; "Carter to Visit North Korea," United Press International, June 9, 1994; "Carter to Make Private Visit to North Korea—CNN," Reuters, June 9, 1994.

24. Creekmore, "Personal Notes," 6.

25. Ibid.

26. Ibid.

27. Ibid.

CHAPTER 5

1. Anyone who works with President Jimmy Carter is quickly impressed with his phenomenal memory. Whatever his system, he recalls information better than anyone I have ever met. Bob Pastor once told me that, ten years after the fact, he witnessed Carter reeling off for a reporter the major arguments the Carter administration had used to support its signing of the Panama Canal treaty. Upon checking, Pastor found that Carter had accurately repeated virtually verbatim the official talking points used at the time.

2. Joel S. Wit, Daniel B. Poneman, and Robert L. Gallucci, *Going Critical: The First North Korean Nuclear Crisis* (Washington, D.C.: Brookings Institution Press, 2004): 202–203; Nancy Soderberg, *The Superpower Myth: The Use and Misuse of American Might* (Hoboken, N.J.: John Wiley, 2005), 263; conversation with Bob Gallucci, February 15, 2005.

3. Lake had headed the State Department Transition Team for the incoming Carter administration in 1976–1977 and served as director of the State Department's Policy Planning Staff during the Carter presidency.

4. Unless otherwise noted, the description of the airport conversation is drawn from my personal notes taken at the time. Marion Creekmore, "Personal Notes: Korea Trip, June, 1994," 7–9.

5. Wit, Poneman, and Gallucci, *Going Critical*, 197–198, 209.

6. "Carter Briefing Information: Briefing Schedule," handed to Carter when he and his team entered Gallucci's office, Post-Presidential Papers, "Korea— June '94," specific file: "Korea—Briefing info."

7. Unless otherwise noted, the discussion of this interagency meeting is drawn from my personal notes taken at the time. Creekmore, "Personal Notes," 9–24.

8. The Japanese decision was apparently not as firm as the administration officials insisted on June 10. According to a senior NSC official at the time, Nancy Soderberg, Prime Minister Tsumomu Hata of Japan was still wavering on June 13 when President Clinton entertained the Japanese emperor and empress at a White House dinner. During the dinner, NSC Adviser Lake pressed attending Japanese diplomats to agree with the U.S. sanctions strategy, and later that evening President Clinton called the Japanese prime minister to press the same message. These entreaties succeeded. According to Soderberg, "On June 14, the United States, Japan, and South Korea pledged sanctions against North Korea. The stage was set for war." Nancy Soderberg, *The Superpower Myth: The Use and Misuse of American Might* (Hoboken, N.J.: John Wiley, 2005), 262. Also see Wit, Poneman, and Gallucci, *Going Critical*, 209.

9. Deutch is the only official we encountered in the U.S., South Korea, and North Korea that referred to the North Korean reactor in operation as a 25 MWt rather than 5 MWe. C. Kenneth Quinones, a retired State Department official who still follows Korean developments, talked to nuclear experts in Washington and provided the following language: "According to a number of experts in Washington, 5 MWe and 25 MWt refer to the same reactor in Yongbyon. The different numbers reflect two different units of heat measurement and methods to rate a nuclear reactor's capacity." E-mail message from C. Kenneth Quinones, February 16, 2006. Charles Pennington, a nuclear expert and senior official with NAC International, a nuclear services company in Norcross, Georgia, told me that although the conversion factor seems somewhat low, there are a variety of explanations that could make the numbers of 25 MWt and 5 MWe roughly equivalent. Telephone conversation with Charles Pennington, February 13, 2006.

10. According to C. Kenneth Quinones, this reactor was about 80 to 90 percent complete in 1994. Another much larger reactor (200 MWe) was also in the initial stages of construction at that time. Telephone conversation with C. Kenneth Quinones, early February, 2006.

11. In their respective books, Sigal said North Korean officials told IAEA inspectors that they had reprocessed 100 grams of plutonium; Oberdorfer said the North Koreans admitted to reprocessing 90 grams. Leon V. Sigal, *Disarming Strangers: Nuclear Diplomacy with North Korea* (Princeton: Princeton University Press, 1998), 32, 39; Don Oberdorfer, *The Two Koreas: A Contemporary History* (Reading, Mass.: Addison-Wesley, 1997), 270–271.

12. The Carter team noted that Deutch's statement on mutual inspections was more forthcoming that it had heard at the airport meeting. The top U.S. military leader in South Korea would later take the same position as Deutch.

13. During this exchange, I sensed that Gallucci's firm rejection of the Deutch position might reflect his concern, as the administration's point man, with protecting the views of policymakers who did not share Deutch's views rather than his own personal view. I thought that in his briefing of Carter in Plains, Gallucci had implied, though not stated directly, that he favored focusing on the future rather than the past.

14. Armed with this information, Carter and I would subsequently tell Kang Sok Ju in Pyongyang that his advisors were overstating the case when they told him that the fuel rods could stay in the cooling ponds safely only for a maximum of three months before being reprocessed. We urged Kang Sok Ju to arrange to consult with American technical experts before making a policy decision based on what might be incomplete data.

15. This guidance would be revised by the time Carter arrived in South Korea on June 13. Secretary of State Christopher would call him and tell him that any chance of reaching an accommodation with North Korea would be squelched if the IAEA inspectors were forced to leave North Korea.

16. Creekmore, "Personal Notes," 14.

17. Ibid., 15.

18. Ken Quinones was an exception because he had accompanied Congressman Gary Ackerman and Senator Bob Smith to North Korea in 1993 and 1992, respectively.

19. The difference in views may not have been as far apart during that June 10 briefing as it seemed to those of us who were generally aware of the information on which Carter's views were based. Kim Il Sung probably left much of

the daily management of the North Korean government to his son. But on the fundamental questions of war and peace, Kim Il Sung made the decisions, as we witnessed first-hand on our trip and which this narrative later describes. Ken Quinones, after reading this chapter, believes that there was miscommunication at the interagency meeting more than a decade ago. He said that in 1994 the U.S. officials working on North Korea did not doubt Kim Il Sung's authority. On the other hand, Kim Jong Il, who had oversight of the military, probably did make the decision not to open the undeclared sites to IAEA inspection because the Yongbyon nuclear facility had been declared a top secret military facility under Kim Jong Il's direct authority. Letter from C. Kenneth Quinones, December 14, 2005. Perhaps we interpreted what the intelligence experts told us that day differently from what the other government participants understood them to say, but the Carters and I left the briefing convinced that we had been told that Kim Il Sung was not the final decisionmaker in North Korea. Carter disagreed, and, during our visit to North Korea, Kim Il Sung proved him right. Also see Sigal, *Disarming Strangers,* 152, and Wit, Poneman, and Gallucci, *Going Critical,* 207–208.

20. Creekmore, "Personal Notes," 18.

21. In 1991, North Korea announced the creation of a Special Economic Zone in the northeastern part of the country. U.S. Department of State, "Background Note: North Korea," Bureau of East Asian and Pacific Affairs, November 2005.

22. I took advantage of this advice and kept my camera with me throughout the trip.

23. Carter's interlocutors must not have focused on this point when the former president made it. The administration appeared very surprised later when it realized that CNN was in North Korea covering the Carter trip. The CNN interview of Carter after his first conversation with Kim Il Sung caused considerable consternation among senior administration officials meeting in the White House when the interview was aired live around the world. See later discussion.

24. This conversation is based on my personal notes. Creekmore, "Personal Notes," 26–27.

25. Carter frequently prepares for meetings in this way; in addition, he often goes into a negotiating situation having already put on paper for his own use the text of a potential final agreement, which he did before his first conversation with Kim Il Sung.

26. My conversations with President Carter before and during the trip to the Korean Peninsula. My personal interpretation at the time was that Gallucci would not have viewed his conversation with Carter as constituting a formal Washington clearance, but that he would have raised objections if he thought Carter's talking points contradicted U.S. policy. Years later, Gallucci said that his telephone conversation did not constitute a formal clearance. Conversation with Robert Gallucci, February 15, 2005. Also see Sigal, *Disarming Strangers*, 153.

27. Carter had obtained a clear understanding of the U.S. government's positions through the briefings he and other Carter Center members had received from administrative officials during the previous months, the discussions held in Washington on June 10, 1994, and the written answers to the questions he had sent Lake and Gallucci. The one issue that later proved to be difficult was whether North Korea could reprocess the discharged spent fuel rods under IAEA supervision. Carter knew that such action was normally permitted under the NPT. He did not know, and neither he nor I remember being briefed before arriving in North Korea, that the U.S. government could not accept such reprocessing because it had earlier prevented South Korea from constructing its own reprocessing facility. Carter's talking points for use with Kim Il Sung and read to Gallucci on June 11, 1994, stated that North Korea could reprocess under IAEA supervision, but Gallucci apparently did not focus on this sentence during his telephone conversation with Carter. The "reprocessing issue" would cause a short-term problem for a few days during and after the Carter trip, but it would not torpedo Carter's agreement with Kim Il Sung. Later chapters provide a fuller discussion of this issue.

CHAPTER 6

1. Joel S. Wit, Daniel B. Poneman, and Robert L. Gallucci, *Going Critical: The First North Korean Nuclear Crisis* (Washington, D.C.: Brookings Institution Press, 2004), 204.

2. From Athens, Linda would accompany her ailing parents on a trip to visit their families who lived near Des Moines, Iowa, where they had been born. I had planned to go on the trip with her to help with her mother who had to use a wheel chair and her father who was almost blind from glaucoma. The sudden trip to the Korean Peninsula meant that she had to handle both parents on her own. It turned out to be their last visit to Des Moines.

3. Phil Wise joined the Carter Center staff in early 1994 as John Hardman's executive assistant. He would later become the associate executive director for operations. Phil had grown up in Plains, Georgia, been a close friend of the Carter family, and at the age of twenty-five had managed the successful Carter campaign for president in Florida in 1976. He served as President Carter's appointment secretary in the White House.

4. Nancy Konigsmark, born and raised in Georgia, had worked for Jimmy Carter's presidential campaign, served in Washington as Rosalynn Carter's appointments secretary, and returned to Georgia to work with the Carters after they left the White House. For more than two decades, Nancy has served as Carter's efficient appointments secretary at The Carter Center, most of the time planning his international trips and traveling on them.

5. Jimmy Carter, "Report on Our Trip to Korea, June 1994," 1, Post-Presidential Papers, "Korea—June '94," specific file: "Korea—trip report."

6. Interview with Nancy Konigsmark, March 2, 2004.

7. Wit, Poneman, and Gallucci, *Going Critical*, 214; Leon V. Sigal, *Disarming Strangers: Nuclear Diplomacy with North Korea* (Princeton: Princeton University Press, 1998), 153.

8. Daniel R. Russel, "Letter to President Carter," June 28, 1994, Post-Presidential Papers, "Korea—June '94," specific file: "Korea—follow-up communication non-official"; Mr. Russel enclosed with his letter copies of two FBIS (Foreign Broadcast Information Service) reports: FBIS, serial no. SK1506055994, source: Seoul Yonhap in English, 0539 GMT, June 15, 1994; and FBIS, serial no. WS2106124594, source: Warsaw Rzeczpospolita, June 21, 1994; Xinhua News Agency, "South Korea Conducts Nation-Wide Civil Defense Exercise," item no. 0615136, June 15, 1994, Post-Presidential Papers, "Korea—June 1994," specific file: "Korea—follow-up communication non-official"; Wit, Poneman, and Gallucci, *Going Critical*, 214–215; Don Oberdorfer, *The Two Koreas: A Contemporary History* (Reading, Mass.: Addison-Wesley, 1997), 322; Nancy Soderberg, *The Superpower Myth: The Use and Misuse of American Might* (Hoboken, N.J.: John Wiley, 2005), 262.

9. Wit, Poneman, and Gallucci, *Going Critical*, 102.

10. Ibid., 150.

11. From several conversations I had with Ambassador James T. Laney, including one on August 17, 2000.

12. This paragraph is drawn from my conversations with Carter, Laney, and Luck, and all three have read and concurred with this description.

13. Ambassador Laney later confirmed to me the accuracy of this story.

14. The country team is an interagency group of the senior officers of the embassy. It is chaired by the ambassador or his/her designee.

15. This paragraph and the remainder of those describing the meeting of the country team, unless otherwise documented, are drawn from the author's notes taken during the meeting. Marion Creekmore, "Personal Notes: Korea Trip, June, 1994," 32–37.

16. At the time, Danny Russel was the political unit chief in the embassy's Political Section. He was responsible for following U.S.-South Korean relations, U.S.-North Korean relations, and North Korean-South Korean issues. Russel reminded me of his precise language in this and the following paragraph in an e-mail message of January 15, 2006, after he had reviewed my description of the meeting of the country team.

17. Fortunately, the Carter team avoided a major diplomatic faux pas later that day. Prior to Carter's meetings with South Korean officials, the author discovered that the Carter Center's development office, which did not follow internal Korean politics, had sent along as gifts copies of Carter's book *Talking Peace* translated into Korean. The translation had been produced by Kim Dae Jung's foundation and emblazoned on the back cover was a picture of Carter and Kim Dae Jung. The idea of gifts in Seoul was quickly scrapped, and the books returned to the United States with the Carter contingent a few days later.

18. Unless otherwise noted, the descriptions of the meetings with President Kim Young Sam are drawn from my personal notes of the trip. Creekmore, "Personal Notes," 48–52.

19. Whether these numbers were correct or not, the South Korean president was right in describing the North Korean regime as despotic.

20. Foreign Minister Han Sung Joo had illustrated his charge that Kim Il Sung could not be trusted by saying that he was "claiming falsely" that North Korea was genuinely trying to meet IAEA requirements.

21. Indeed, North Korea welcomed the aged and ill Lee to Pyongyang as a hero and broadcast his release as a triumph for the North. Wit, Poneman, and Gallucci, *Going Critical,* 23, 29–30.

22. During his inaugural address on February 24, 1994, Kim Young Sam had offered to meet Kim Il Sung "any time and any place"; he said dramatically that "no allied country can be greater than one nation." A private emissary from the North passed the message that Pyongyang had been pleased with that remark. Wit, Poneman, and Gallucci, *Going Critical,* 23.

23. FBIS, serial no. SK1406004094, 0649 GMT, June 14, 1994, Post-Presidential Papers, "Korea—June '94," specific file: "Korea—follow-up communication non-official."

24. "Questions Expected to Be Raised by Kim Il-Sung," a paper passed to President Carter by South Korean intelligence officials on June 15, 1994. Post-Presidential Papers, "Korea—June '94," specific file: "Korea—Briefing info."

25. This paragraph and the nine subsequent ones discussing the meeting with Lee Hong Koo are drawn from Creekmore, "Personal Notes," 52–65.

26. FBIS, serial no. SK1506055994, source: Seoul Yonhap in English, 0539 GMT, June 15, 1994, Post-Presidential Papers, "Korea—June '94," specific file: "Korea—follow-up communication non-official." Previously, U.S. Representative Gary Ackerman and UN Secretary-General Butros Butros-Ghali had flown into Pyongyang from Beijing, but they departed North Korea by walking across the DMZ at Panmunjom.

CHAPTER 7

1. Conversation with Nancy Konigsmark, March 2, 2004.

2. Kim Yong Sun told the CNN representatives that the North Korean Foreign Ministry had opposed giving visas to any journalist, that more than three hundred news organizations had applied to cover the Carter trip, and that Kim Jong Il had made the decision to allow CNN in because he was pleased with the impact of the CNN broadcasts at the time of Kim Il Sung's birthday in April 1994. Mike Chinoy, *China Live: Two Decades in the Heart of the Dragon* (Atlanta: Turner Publishing, 1997), 348–349.

3. Ibid.

4. Rosalynn Carter, "Report on Our Trip to North Korea, June 1994," 1; Jimmy Carter, "Report on Our Trip to Korea, June 1994," 2, Post-Presidential Papers, "Korea—June '94," specific file: "Korea—trip report."

5. Rosalynn Carter, "Report on Our Trip to North Korea, June 1994," 1.

6. Ibid.

7. President and Mrs. Carter had similar reactions as they described in their separate trip reports.

8. Rosalynn Carter, "Report on Our Trip to North Korea, June 1994," 2; Marion Creekmore's memory and personal photographs. Mike Chinoy described Pyongyang when he visited North Korea for CNN for the first time in

1989. Mike Chinoy, *China Live: Two Decades in the Heart of the Dragon* (Atlanta: Turner Publishing, 1997), 320–325. Chinoy said that as he and other reporters were driven around in official Mercedes cars, he saw many tall buildings, few people on the streets, and almost no shops or markets. He was unable to explore the streets near his hotel because he and the other reporters were not permitted to go more than a hundred yards from the hotel.

9. Rosalynn Carter, "Report on Our Trip to North Korea, June 1994," 2; Marion Creekmore's memory and personal photographs.

10. Ibid.

11. The description of the meeting with the foreign minister was drawn from the following: Marion Creekmore, Dick Christensen, "Memorandum to the Files," June 15, 1994, 1–8, Post-Presidential Papers, "Korea—June '94," specific file: "Confidential—notes and transcripts of mtgs—No. & So." In the typed memos of the Carter conversations in North Korea, Christenson's name as author was misspelled as "Christensen." The correct spelling is used in subsequent citations to avoid confusion.

12. Jimmy Carter's handwritten note, "Notes after mtg w Fmin.," Post-Presidential Papers, "Korea—June '94," specific file: "Confidential—notes and transcripts of mtgs—No. & So."

13. Rosalynn Carter, "Report on Our Trip to North Korea, June 1994."

14. From the toast of Foreign Minister Kim Yong Nam of North Korea, June 15, 1994, banquet in honor of the Carters, 2–3, Post-Presidential Papers, "Korea—June '94," specific file: "Confidential—notes and transcripts of mtgs—No. & So."

15. In their generally excellent book, *Going Critical: The First North Korean Nuclear Crisis* by Joel S. Wit, Daniel B. Poneman, and Robert L. Gallucci, the authors' short description of the foreign minister's dinner conveyed a misleading impression of the affair. One scene described in the book (page 222) simply did not occur: that in response to a reference in Carter's toast, the foreign minister responded harshly that sanctions would equal a declaration of war and that the "North Koreans and Americans momentarily froze in a motionless tableau, chopsticks and glasses suspended in mid-air as each guest took in this defiant gesture." As indicated earlier in this narrative, the foreign minister did threaten that sanctions would equal a declaration of war in the afternoon business session with Carter, but no threats were issued at the evening's dinner event, which was designed to project pleasantness and friendship.

16. Jimmy Carter, "Letter drafted to send to Wash after mtg with FM [foreign minister] and before KIS [Kim Il Sung]." It was not sent. Post-Presidential Papers, "Korea—June '94," specific file: "Confidential—notes and transcripts of mtgs—No. & So."

17. E-mail message from Danny Russel, January 15, 2006.

CHAPTER 8

1. In 1983, North Korean military officers detonated a bomb during the welcoming ceremony to Burma of the South Korean president, Chun Doo Hwan. The president, who was late for the affair, was not injured, but seventeen South Korean officials, including four cabinet members, were killed. In 1989, two North Korean espionage agents flew from Bagdad to Abu Dhabi on Korean Air Lines flight 858 and, when they deplaned, left in the overhead luggage rack a portable radio containing a bomb. The bomb exploded on the ongoing flight to Seoul, killing all 115 persons onboard. Don Oberdorfer, *The Two Koreas: A Contemporary History* (Reading, Mass.: Addison-Wesley, 1997), 140–141, 183–184.

2. In relating his coverage of Kim Il Sung's eighty-second birthday celebration for CNN in April 1994, Mike Chinoy reported that Kim Il Sung's "twinkle in his eyes gave him the air of a benevolent grandfather rather than a ruthless megalomaniac whose nuclear ambitions had raised fears of a second bloody conflict on the Korean Peninsula." Mike Chinoy, *China Live: Two Decades in the Heart of the Dragon* (Atlanta: Turner Publishing, 1997), 317.

3. Bradley K. Martin, *Under the Loving Care of the Fatherly Leader: North Korea and the Kim Dynasty* (New York: Thomas Dunne Books, St. Martin's Press, 2004), 15–16, 25–26.

4. Jimmy Carter, "Report on Our Trip to Korea, June 1994," 3, Post-Presidential Papers, "Korea—June '94," specific file: "Korea—trip report."

5. Congressman Gary Ackerman had other Americans on his team when they departed North Korea for South Korea via the DMZ in October 1993. Consequently, Carter was not literally the second American to cross the DMZ since the end of the Korean War. Instead, he and the members of his team were the second American group to cross it. They were also the first non-Koreans to cross the demilitarized zone both from south to north and north to south.

6. Unless otherwise noted, this Carter-Kim Il Sung conversation is drawn from the reporting memorandum that Dick Christenson prepared for Carter based on the notes he had taken at the meeting. Dick Christenson, "June 16 Meeting Between President Carter and Kim Il Sung," June 16, 1994, Post-Presidential Papers, "Korea—June '94," specific file: "Confidential—notes and transcripts of mtgs—No. & So."

7. Kim Il Sung had told Congressman Ackerman in October 1993 that he had quit smoking on the advice of his doctors. E-mail message from Ken Quinones to the author, January 25, 2006.

8. Joel S. Wit, Daniel B. Poneman, and Robert L. Gallucci, *Going Critical: The First North Korean Nuclear Crisis* (Washington, D.C.: Brookings Institution Press, 2004), 201–202. In our conversation on February 15, 2005, Gallucci reaffirmed his conviction that this issue was discussed during his meeting with Carter in Plains, Georgia on June 5, 1994.

9. These talking points are found in appendix B.

10. North Korea advised the United States in April that it would discharge the spent fuel rods from the reactor, and the unloading started in early May.

11. In his notes, Christenson used "DPRK" rather than "North Korea," a common tendency of notetakers, including myself. But in his oral presentation, Carter would have tended to use either "North Korea" or "Democratic People's Republic of Korea." Consequently, in descriptions of this presentation and other conversations that were drawn from his or my notes, I have substituted "North Korea" for "DPRK."

12. As noted in chapter 6, Harrison reportedly raised the idea of a freeze of North Korea's nuclear program until a comprehensive arrangement between the United States and North Korea could be negotiated. Harrison wrote about this conversation when he reached Beijing and later briefed officials in the State Department. Carter had no knowledge of Harrison's visit while he was in North Korea.

13. According to *Going Critical,* the U.S. administration officials dealing with the North Korean problem were aware of these remarks by the North Korean president as reported on CNN. Wit, Poneman, and Gallucci, *Going Critical,* 169.

14. He did not mention that the 5 MWe research reactor was not connected to the country's electric grid, but presumably the reactors sought earlier from the Soviet Union and the ones Kim Il Sung hoped to get in subsequent negotiations with the United States would have been tied into this grid. The 5

MWe reactor did supply the electricity for the research center and the housing provided for its more than 5,000 employees. (Phone conversation with C. Kenneth Quinones in early February 2006.)

15. Communication with author, December 2004.

16. Jimmy Carter's hand-written notes taken in meeting with Kim Il Sung, Post-Presidential Papers, "Korea—June '94," specific file: "Confidential—notes and transcripts of mtgs—No. & So."

17. CNN, "Jimmy Carter in Pyongyang, raw footage, June 15–16 [1994], video tape provided to the author by CNN shortly after Carter's return to the United States.

18. Telephone conversation with Dick Christenson, January 30, 2006.

19. For a comprehensive discussion of North Korean negotiating tactics, see Scott Snyder, *Negotiating on the Edge: North Korean Negotiating Behavior* (Washington, D.C.: United States Institute of Peace Press, 1999), 43–96.

20. Unless otherwise noted, the description of this meeting is drawn from the memorandum Dick Christenson and I prepared after the session from our respective notes. Dick Christenson and Marion Creekmore, "Meeting Between President Carter and 1st Vice Minister Kang Sok Ju, June 16 [1994], People's Cultural Palace, Pyongyang, 1–11, Post-Presidential Papers, "Korea—June '94," specific file: "Confidential—notes and transcripts of mtgs—No. & So."

21. Nancy Soderberg, *The Superpower Myth: The Use and Misuse of American Might* (Hoboken, N.J.: John Wiley, 2005), 263.

22. Communication from President Carter to the author, December 2005.

23. Marion Creekmore, "Personal Notes: Korea Trip, June, 1994," 90.

24. Rosalynn Carter, "Report on Our Trip to North Korea, June 1994," 4, Post-Presidential Papers, "Korea—June '94," specific file: "Korea—trip report."

25. Jimmy Carter's notes that he typed to use in conversation with Washington, Post-Presidential Papers, "Korea—June '94," specific file: "Confidential—notes and transcripts of mtgs—No. & So."

26. Jimmy Carter's handwritten note on back of typed notes for telephone conversation with Washington, Post-Presidential Papers, "Korea—June '94," specific file: "Confidential—notes and transcripts of mtgs—No. & So."

27. Creekmore, "Personal Notes," 91.

28. Jimmy Carter, "Report on Our Trip to Korea, June 1994," 4.

29. Wit, Poneman, and Gallucci, *Going Critical,* 226–227; Oberdorfer, *The Two Koreas,* 329–331; Sigal, *Disarming Strangers,* 157.

30. Wit, Poneman, and Gallucci, *Going Critical*, 226–227; Oberdorfer, *The Two Koreas*, 329–331; Sigal, *Disarming Strangers*, 157. In 2001, Bob Gallucci and I spoke informally about the Carter call, which Gallucci took on the morning of June 16, 1994, in Washington. Gallucci said that after Carter had told him the details of the agreement, Carter asked him what he thought. He said he did not give a reaction, nor did he try to convince Carter not to go on CNN. In Bob's mind, Carter had his course of action planned, and he could not be talked out of it. I told him he was right. Bob said that one of the most difficult moments of his career then ensued. He returned to the room to where he had been sitting. He looked across the room to Clinton, next to him Christopher, and next to him Lake. Bob reported what Carter had said. They could not believe that Carter was about to go on CNN. Lake asked him whether he (Gallucci) had stopped Carter from doing so. Gallucci said he hadn't. Then Lake said, impatiently, "You did try, didn't you?" "No," Bob admitted. On looking back years later, Bob said that he had "never felt lower in [his] life." Bob then mentioned the picture found in this book that shows administration officials watching the Carter interview. He said that he was the person sitting cross-legged on the floor with his eyes focused on the floor. Conversation with Robert Gallucci in New York, June 9, 2001.

CHAPTER 9

1. Carter found CNN interviews useful when he was engaged in conflict resolution interventions. With U.S. government approval, he had communicated in 1993 with the warlord Mohammed Aidid in Somalia in the aftermath of the "Black Hawk Down" incident through a CNN interview. In 1994, after he had convinced General Raoul Cedras to go into exile and permit Jean-Bertrand Aristide to return to power in Haiti, he gave CNN an exclusive interview before he had personally reported to President Clinton. A threatened interview with CNN convinced a reluctant President Al-Bashir of Sudan to establish a temporary cease-fire to permit the inoculation of Sudanese children in government- and rebel-held parts of the country in 1995. As noted earlier, Carter had a close relationship with Tom Johnson, CEO of CNN, and Carter and CNN editors periodically met for an off-the-record tour d'horizon on world developments. Both parties regarded these sessions as useful, and CNN saw benefit to its twenty-four-hour news coverage in tracking Carter in international forays not covered extensively by other networks. On the other hand,

CNN officials and journalists would react uncomfortably on those occasions when Carter suggested publicly that he viewed CNN as his "State Department" and their media rivals threw the quote back at them. In fact, CNN would not pull its punches in reporting Carter's activities. It would sometimes irritate him with unexpected questions or commentaries. Two examples: In the interview after Carter's intervention in Haiti, the CNN interviewer surprised Carter by asking about the contents of his private phone conversation from his departing plane with Bob Pastor, his Latin American expert on the ground in Haiti; the conversation had been electronically intercepted by a private citizen and forwarded to CNN. In 2002, during CNN's generally laudatory interview with Carter immediately following his receipt of the Nobel Peace Prize in Oslo, Norway, it used as an introductory clip to the years of the Carter presidency a summary that was less than flattering. Smiling but chagrined, Carter took direct issue with the film commentary, citing a number of positive achievements of his administration that the CNN clip had ignored.

2. Marion Creekmore, "Personal Notes: Korean Trip," June 1994," 91–93.

3. Dick Christenson also privately suggested to Carter that he delay going on CNN until after he had returned to Washington and discussed the results of his trip with the Clinton administration. Carter rejected his advice. Telephone conversation with Dick Christenson, January 30, 2006.

4. Mike Chinoy, *China Live: Two Decades in the Heart of the Dragon* (Atlanta: Turner Publishing, 1997), 351.

5. Ibid, 349–350. During their coverage of Kim Il Sung's birthday celebration in Pyongyang in April, the CNN team had discovered that by booking a special satellite communication link (called a four-wire) through Tokyo, their Japanese affiliate could patch the signal through to Atlanta. That gave CNN the ability to have two-way voice communication with the United States.

6. Unless otherwise noted, the discussion of the Carter interview on CNN was drawn from the CNN transcript. CNN, *News*, 11:27 A.M. (EST), June 16, 1994, transcript #637–616.

7. As a result, North Korea would have to obtain enriched fuel elsewhere, and, as was common, would have to agree in advance how the spent fuel rods would be disposed of—usually by shipping them back to the fuel supplier for reprocessing or storage.

8. When Carter suggested that at some future point it would likely be useful for the U.S. president or secretary of state to hold conversations with North Korean leaders, those watching in the White House winced, believing that

proposals in 1994 for higher-level bilateral talks would be viewed in the Washington political context as "appeasement." Nancy Soderberg, *The Superpower Myth: The Use and Misuse of American Might* (Hoboken, N.J.: John Wiley, 2005), 264.

9. Of all Carter's comments on the CNN interview, the one about sanctions probably infuriated the Washington officials the most. Ten years later, Tony Lake still bristled that Carter had publicly opposed sanctions while in North Korea. In Lake's view, Carter should have reserved his criticism of sanctions, for which the administration had expended considerable effort to gain international endorsement, to private discussions within the administration after he returned. He and his colleagues regarded Carter's statement on sanctions as "a direct slap at Clinton's policy." (Interview with Anthony Lake, a former NSC adviser, February 15, 2005.) Yet, "the main problem was that Carter did not support Clinton's policy of imposing sanctions against North Korea," as Soderberg correctly pointed out; he had "always believed that the North Koreans are incapable of accepting peacefully the insult of international sanctions." Soderberg, *The Superpower Myth*, 264–265.

10. For a fuller discussion of the White House meeting and the decision and formulation of the new U.S. definition of the North Korean nuclear freeze, see Joel S. Wit, Daniel B. Poneman, and Robert L. Gallucci, *Going Critical: The First North Korean Nuclear Crisis* (Washington, D.C.: Brookings Institution Press, 2004), 226–231. For an abbreviated discussion, see Don Oberdorfer, *The Two Koreas: A Contemporary History* (Reading, Mass.: Addison-Wesley, 1997), 331–332; see also Leon Sigal, *Disarming Strangers: Nuclear Diplomacy with North Korea* (Princeton: Princeton University Press, 1998), 159–160, whose descriptions are based on interviews with some of the participants.

11. Wit, Poneman, and Gallucci, *Going Critical*, 231; Sigal, *Disarming Strangers*, 159.

12. Although the author was not in the room when the call took place, this account accords with Carter's recollection and those of Dick Christenson who was in the room at the time. It has also been reviewed by Tony Lake. (Conversations at the time, written communication from Carter in December 2004, conversation with Anthony Lake on February 15, 2005, and telephone conversation with Dick Christenson on January 30, 2006.) It is also generally consistent with the reports in Sigal's *Disarming Strangers*, 159–160, and Wit, Poneman, and Gallucci's *Going Critical*, 231–232.

13. Conversation with Anthony Lake on February 15, 2005.

14. The White House, Office of the Press Secretary, "Remarks by the President in Press Availability," Briefing Room, 5:45 P.M. (EDT), June 16, 1994, 1–2.

15. The White House, Office of the Press Secretary, "Press Briefing by Assistant Secretary of State for Political and Military Affairs Robert Gallucci," Briefing Room, 4:52 P.M. (EDT), June 16, 1994, 1.

16. The White House, "Remarks by the President in Press Availability," 2–4; "Press Briefing by Assistant Secretary for Political and Military Affairs Robert Gallucci," 2–8. A shorter description of the press conference is provided in Wit, Poneman, and Gallucci, *Going Critical,* 229–231.

17. In his CNN report of the boat trip, Mike Chinoy stated that Mrs. Kim was not often seen in public. Videotape of CNN coverage of the Carter visit to North Korea given to the author after he returned from the Korean Peninsula in June 1994.

18. Wit, Poneman, and Gallucci, *Going Critical,* 233.

19. Author's conversation with Ambassador Robert Gallucci in New York on June 9, 2001.

20. Wit, Poneman, and Gallucci, *Going Critical,* 233.

21. The White House, "Statement by the Press Secretary," June 18, 1994.

22. Rosalynn Carter, "Report on Our Trip to North Korea, June 1994," 3, Post-Presidential Papers, "Korea—June '94," specific file: "Korea—trip report."

23. Unless otherwise noted, this discussion on the North Korean presidential yacht is drawn from the memorandum of conversation I prepared from my notes taken during the cruise. Marion Creekmore, "Note to the Files," June 17, 1994, 1, Post-Presidential Papers, "Korea—June '94," specific file: "Confidential—notes and transcripts of mtgs—No. & So."

24. Rosalynn Carter, "Report on Our Trip to North Korea," 4; Jimmy Carter, "Report on Our Trip to North Korea, June 1994," 6, Post-Presidential Papers, "Korea—June '94," specific file: "Korea—trip report."

25. The North Koreans had a reputation for tunnel building. In fact, in the 1970s the U.S. and South Korean soldiers had discovered the entrances to several tunnels on the South Korean side of the DMZ, which the North Koreans had dug undetected under the DMZ. The tunnels were extremely large and well-constructed. In the event of a military attack, the North Koreans were expected to try to use these tunnels to move tanks and other heavy military equipment surreptitiously into South Korea to follow up the initial bombardment of long-range artillery. The U.S.-South Korean allies assumed that the

North Koreans had dug many other tunnels that had not been discovered. This contingency had to be factored into their battle plans in case military hostilities arose between the two Koreas. Oberdorfer, *The Two Koreas,* 56–59.

26. Rosalynn Carter, "Report on Our Trip to North Korea, June 1994," 2.

CHAPTER 10

1. Rosalynn Carter, "Report on Our Trip to North Korea, June 1994," 2, Post-Presidential Papers, "Korea—June '94," specific file: "Korea—trip report." Choe Sonhee told Dick Christenson the same story about why she and her husband drink beer together after dinner. Telephone conversation with Christenson, January 30, 2006.

2. Rosalynn Carter, "Report on Our Trip to North Korea, June 1994," 3.

3. Pyongyang Korean Central Broadcasting Network, radio report on Carter's news conference in Panmunjom, 1736 GMT, 18 June, 1994, Post-Presidential Papers, "Korea—June 1994," specific file: "Korea—follow-up communications non-official."

4. Marion Creekmore, "Office Diary: May 12–September 10, 1994" (portion related to Korean trip), 1–2. In fact, problems did arise. After the death of Kim Il Sung on July 8, 1994, and the deterioration of relations between South and North Korea, Washington did not want to push ahead of its South Korean ally in dealing with the North. It delayed meetings related to recovering the MIA remains to accomplish this goal. I reported this fact to Carter a couple of months after we returned to the United States, and he made contact with the U.S. military officials charged with this responsibility. The matter dragged on for several months, but eventually the stalemate was broken and the cooperative effort got underway.

5. Office of the Press Secretary, the White House, "Statement by the Press Secretary," June 18, 1994, Office of Public Information, The Carter Center, file on the Korean Trip, 1994.

6. I was unable to hear much of the vice president's part of the conversation. Consequently, in describing this telephone conversation, I have relied on the discussion in Joel S. Wit, Daniel B. Poneman, and Robert L. Gallucci, *Going Critical: The First North Korean Nuclear Crisis* (Washington, D.C.: Brookings Institution Press, 2004), to give the Gore side of the conversation, although where their description as to the order of what was said differs from my notes, I have used my notes. (I have not seen the transcript prepared by

the notetaker in Washington.) Creekmore, "Office Diary" (portion related to Korean trip), 2–5; and Wit, Poneman, and Gallucci, *Going Critical*, 234.

7. The discussion of the luncheon at Blue House is drawn from my personal notes. Creekmore, "Office Diary" (portion related to Korean trip), 9–17.

8. The discussion of the press conference is based on the U.S. embassy's transcript: "Press Conference: President Jimmy Carter, June 18, 1994, Seoul, Korea." Located in the files of the Public Affairs Office, The Carter Center.

CHAPTER 11

1. Terry Adamson, "Memorandum to President Carter, Personal and Confidential," via telecopier, Saturday, 11:00 A.M. (EST), June 18, 1994, Office of Public Information, The Carter Center, file on the Korean Trip, 1994.

2. R. Jeffrey Smith and Bradley Graham, "Carter Faulted by White House on North Korea: Policy Statements Cause Confusion on Sanctions," *Washington Post*, June 18, 1994.

3. Terry Adamson, "Memorandum to President Carter: Personal and Confidential," via telecopier, Saturday, 11:00 A.M. (EST), June 18, 1994, 2, Office of Public Affairs, The Carter Center, file on the Korean Trip, 1994.

4. Marion Creekmore, handwritten note, "President Carter, —My suggestions. Marion," 6/19/94, 3:40 A.M., Post-Presidential Papers, "Korea—June '94," specific file: "Memorandums: In-house Marion Creekmore/Hardman."

5. Years later, Tony Lake explained the administration's reaction as follows: First, it had been surprised by CNN's presence in Pyongyang during the Carter visit (despite Carter's having mentioned the possibility during his briefing at the State Department on June 10). Second, the former president's remarks to CNN were not useful, and they "colored the purpose" of his trip. The interview put the matter much more into a public forum and raised the question, on which reporters were having a field day, as to whether Carter was trying to save the administration from itself. Third, by taking on the administration publicly on the issue of sanctions, Carter made it more difficult for the administration to get what was needed substantively and to make its policy viable in Washington. The interview made it look as though there was a conflict between Carter and Clinton rather than with North Korea and their common critics in Washington. (Conversation with Anthony Lake, February 15, 2005.) As has been discussed, Carter's reasons for giving the

CNN interview and his analysis of its impact differed significantly from the above view.

6. Joel S. Wit, Daniel B. Poneman, and Robert L. Gallucci, *Going Critical: The First North Korean Nuclear Crisis* (Washington, D.C.: Brookings Institution Press, 2004), 235. Robert Gallucci told me much later that the meeting was one of the most difficult in which he had ever been involved. It was "truly awful in all of its manifestations," Gallucci elaborated. "I felt I had a special relationship with President Carter, and I wanted to protect it." Conversation with Robert Gallucci, February 15, 2005.

7. Telephone conversation with Daniel B. Poneman, February 5, 2006.

8. Jimmy Carter, "Excerpts from Diary for June 1994," provided to the author September 24, 1996, in section under June 19, 1994.

9. Except as otherwise noted, the description of this meeting comes from Marion Creekmore, "Office Diary: May 12–September 10, 1994" (portion related to Korean trip), 25–34.

10. Wit, Poneman, and Gallucci, *Going Critical*, 235.

11. In *Going Critical*, Wit, Poneman, and Gallucci devote only three paragraphs to this meeting with Carter, who alone of present and past senior U.S. leaders had talked with and negotiated a deal with Kim Il Sung. Their description of the reaction of the administration participants to Carter's six-page, single-spaced report was that, in it, "Carter bore in on his disagreement with the administration over Lake's 'instructions' concerning plutonium reprocessing." The Carter report itself did not point out differences between Carter and Lake on reprocessing, although that issue was discussed after Carter had read his trip report, as described in this book. Apparently, some in the room interpreted Carter's report as being more sympathetic to North Korea than to South Korea. Wit, Poneman, and Gallucci, *Going Critical*, 235.

12. Ibid.

13. Jimmy Carter, "Report on Our Trip to Korea, June 1994," 1, Post-Presidential Papers, "Korea—June '94," specific file: "Korea—trip report."

14. Conversation with Anthony Lake, February 15, 2005.

15. Conversation with Robert Gallucci, February 15, 2005; telephone conversation with Daniel Poneman on February 5, 2006.

16. Creekmore, "Office Diary" (portion related to Korean trip), 33.

17. The study written by administration participants in the nuclear crisis comes close to endorsing the Carter position. In the concluding chapter, which explains why the Clinton administration acted as it did throughout the crisis

and why it came down on the side of engagement with North Korea leading to the Agreed Framework, the authors wrote: "Resort to the UN Security Council sanctions, however, was not an *independent* [their emphasis] option. Although the possibility of sanctions was central to U.S. policy, no one thought that exercising that option would have induced North Korea to surrender its nuclear program. Rather, the sanctions were intended *either* [their emphasis] to bring sufficient pressure to bear to induce North Korea to freeze its nuclear activities and return to the negotiating table or to serve as a justification for tougher coercive actions—including military measures—down the road, should North Korea choose to defy the UN Security Council. Thus the sanctions track was a potential element of the military and negotiating tracks, not an end in itself." Wit, Poneman, and Gallucci, *Going Critical,* 385.

18. This and the preceding paragraph are drawn from the Office of the Press Secretary, the White House, "Press Briefing by Assistant Secretary of State Robert Gallucci," June 19, 1994.

19. Eason Jordan, "Handwritten Letter to President Carter," June 18, 1994, Post-Presidential Papers, "Korea—June '94," specific file: "CNN."

20. The discussion of the CNN show was drawn from CNN *Late Edition* transcript, June 19, 1994, 5:00 P.M. (EST), 1–12, Post Presidential Papers, "Korea—June '94," specific file: "CNN."

CHAPTER 12

1. Jimmy Carter, "Letter to President Kim Il Sung," June 20, 1994, Post-Presidential Papers, "Korea—1994," specific file: "President Kim Il Sung."

2. Marion Creekmore, "Office Diary: May 12–September 10, 1994" (portion related to Korean trip), 42.

3. Marion Creekmore, "Eyes Only Memorandum to Ambassador Laney," June 23, 1994, Post-Presidential Papers, "Korea—June '94," specific file: "Confidential—notes and transcripts of mtgs—No. & So."

4. Joel S. Wit, Daniel B. Poneman, and Robert L. Gallucci, *Going Critical: The First North Korean Nuclear Crisis* (Washington, D.C.: Brookings Institution Press, 2004), 238–239.

5. Judy Keen and Lee Michael Katz, "North Korea Negotiations' 'Breakthrough' Short-Lived," *USA Today,* June 21, 1994.

6. Jimmy Carter, "Letter to Counselor Han Song Ryol," June 21, 1994, Post-Presidential Papers, "Korea—'94," specific file: "Korea—communications w/ No. Korea."

7. Kim Young Sam, President of the Republic of Korea, "Letter to the Honorable Jimmy Carter," June 20, 1994, Post-Presidential Papers, "Korea—1994," specific file: "Korea—communications with So. Korea."

8. Jimmy Carter, "Letter to President Kim Il Sung," June 21, 1994, Post-Presidential Papers, "Korea—1994," specific file: "President Kim Il Sung"; Seung-Soo Han, "Letter to the Honorable Jimmy Carter," June 22, 1994, Post-Presidential Papers, "Korea—1994," specific file: "Korea—communications with So. Korea."

9. Seung-Soo Han, "Letter to the Honorable Jimmy Carter," June 22, 1994, Post-Presidential Papers, "Korea—1994;" specific file: "Korea—communications with So. Korea."

10. Creekmore, "Office Diary" (portion related to Korean trip), 40, 44–45.

11. "Carter's Trip Brings Hope," *USA Today*, June 20, 1994.

12. "The Carter Opening," *New York Times*, June 21, 1994.

13. *Washington Post*, editorial, June 20, 1994.

14. Lally Weymouth, "What Good Did Carter Do?" *Washington Post*, June 21, 1994.

15. "Confusion Over Korea," *Atlanta Journal Constitution*, June 21, 1994.

16. Harry Schwartz, "Don't Fall on Korean Ploy," *USA Today*, June 20, 1994.

17. R. Jeffrey Smith and Ruth Marcus, "Carter Trip May Offer 'Opening': White House Wary of Ex-President's View N. Korea 'Crisis Is Over,'" *Washington Post*, June 20, 1994.

18. R. Jeffrey Smith and Ann Devroy, "U.S. Debate Shift on North Korea: Carter's Visit Derails Sanctions Drive," *Washington Post*, June 21, 1994.

19. Ann Devroy and T. R. Reid, "U.S. Awaits Word on North Korean Intentions: Pyongyang Extends Visas of Nuclear Inspectors, Sets Date for Summit with North Korea," *Washington Post*, June 22, 1994.

20. Michael R. Gordon, "Clinton Offers North Korea a Chance to Resume Talks," *New York Times*, June 22, 1994.

21. NBC, *The Tonight Show with Jay Leno*, "The White House Bulletin: Today's Briefing," June 21, 1994; Post-Presidential Papers, "Korea—1994," specific file: "Press—transcripts, etc."

22. Jimmy Carter, "Letter to President Bill Clinton: Personal and Confidential," June 21, 1994, Post-Presidential Papers, "Korea—1994," specific file: "Korea—official communication w/US govt."

23. Terrence B. Adamson, "Letter to Mr. Howell Raines," June 21, 1994, Post-Presidential Papers, "Korea—1994," specific file: "Korea—follow-up communication non-official."

24. Terrence B. Adamson, "Letter to Ms. Meg Greenfield," June 21, 1994, Post-Presidential Papers, "Korea—1994," specific file: "Korea—follow-up communication non-official."

25. Kang Sok Ju, head of the DPRK Delegation to the DPRK-U.S.A. Talks, First Vice Minister of Foreign Affairs, Democratic People's Republic of Korea, "Letter to Ambassador Robert L. Gallucci, Head of the U.S.A. Delegation to the DPRK-USA Talks, Assistant Secretary of State for Political-Military Affairs," June 22, 1994, faxed to "The Honorable President Jimmy Carter" by Counselor Han Song Ryol of the North Korean Mission to the United Nations, Post-Presidential Papers, "Korea—1994," specific file: "Korea—communication w/No. Korea."

26. Jimmy Carter, "Letter to President Kim Il Sung," June 22, 1994.

27. Kim Il Sung, "Letter to Former U.S. President, Mr. JIMMY CARTER," Pyongyang, June 25, 1994, Post-Presidential Papers, "Korea—1994," specific file: "President Kim Il Sung." The letter turned out to be the last one that President Kim Il Sung sent to a foreigner. The North Korean ambassador subsequently made a special trip to the Carter Center to present President Carter with the signed original of this letter and to express again his government's appreciation for Carter's efforts in June 1994 and thereafter.

28. The White House, "Press Conference of the President," Briefing Room, 5:34 P.M. (EDT), June 22, 1994, 1.

29. Later that afternoon, in a background press briefing at the White House, a "senior administration official," whom I surmised to be Tony Lake, elaborated on this two-pronged approach. He said the results of "three facts" had produced the basis for a new round of U.S.-North Korean talks. These facts were that the administration had pursued a steady course, that it had begun consultations on sanctions at the UN Security Council after the IAEA on June 3 said that North Korea had destroyed the evidence about past reprocessing, and that President Carter went to North Korea and offered its top leadership a means for reaching an agreement. The description of this White House briefing is drawn from the White House, "Background Briefing by Senior Administration Official," June 22, 1994, 1–7.

30. The White House, "Press Conference with the President," 1–5. Before his CNN interview, President Clinton mentioned to Dan Poneman that he had known that he would take political heat for letting Carter go to North Korea, but he thought a former president's trip to Pyongyang might give the leadership there a "way to climb down without losing face." E-mail message

from Dan Poneman, February 27, 2006; Wit, Poneman, and Gallucci, *Going Critical*, 240.

31. The discussion of the Carter interview is drawn from the CNN transcript of this event.

32. The Carter Center, "Statement from Former President Jimmy Carter on Korea," June 22, 1994, Post-Presidential Papers, "Korea—June '94," specific file: "Press—transcripts, etc."

33. "Cheaper Than Nuclear War," editorial, *Washington Post*, June 23, 1994.

34. "Finally, Talks with North Korea," editorial, *New York Times*, June 25, 1994, 22.

35. "Citizen Jimmy Carter," editorial, *Christian Science Monitor*, June 28, 1994.

36. Carl T. Rowan, "Carter Pulls U.S. Back from Brink," *Chicago Sun-Times*, June 24, 1994.

37. Sandy Grady, "Jimmy Carter in Korea: Did He Save the Day or Give Away the Store?" *Denver Post*, June 30, 1994.

38. Randal Ashley, "Carter Believes in Going to the Top," *Atlanta Journal Constitution*, June 24, 1994.

39. Ruth Marcus and R. Jeffrey Smith, "North Korea Confirms Freeze; U.S. Agrees to Resume Talks; Drive for Sanctions to Halt; Negotiations to Begin on July 8," *Washington Post*, June 23, 1994.

40. More than a decade later, looking back on the 1994 nuclear crisis with North Korea, Tony Lake's analysis was similar to what he articulated at the time. He believed that Carter played a useful role in making contact and offering the North Koreans a way out. However, Lake held that it was the combination of the threat of sanctions, the carrots the United States was prepared to offer in a final agreement (Agreed Framework of October 1994), and Carter's negotiated deal with Kim Il Sung that made possible the peaceful resolution of the crisis. (Conversation with Anthony Lake, February 15, 2005.) As the text has emphasized, Carter feared that the adoption of sanctions by the UN Security Council would have made a peaceful settlement impossible.

41. George F. Will, "Communing in Korea," *Washington Post*, June 23, 1994, and other newspapers.

42. Charles Krauthammer, "Peace in Our Time," *Washington Post*, June 24, 1994.

43. William Safire, "Jimmy Clinton," essay, *New York Times*, June 27, 1994.

44. James T. Laney, "Letter to President Jimmy Carter," June 30, 1994, Post-Presidential Papers, "Korea—1994," specific file: "Korea—official communication w/US govt." Without advising Carter that he had done so, Laney nominated the former president for the Nobel Peace Prize in March 1995.

45. Richard A. Christenson, "Letter to President Carter," July 4, 1994, Post-Presidential Papers, "Korea—1994," specific file: "Korea—follow-up communications non-official."

46. Daniel R. Russel, "Letter to President Carter," June 28, 1994, Post-Presidential Papers, "Korea—1994," specific file: "Korea—follow-up communication non-official."

CHAPTER 13

1. At the time, Chinoy said that he turned to Eason Jordan as they left the president's palace in Pyongyang and remarked, "Boy, the Great Leader seems in great shape. I bet he'll outlive Deng Xiaoping by a decade." Mike Chinoy, *China Live: Two Decades in the Heart of the Dragon* (Atlanta: Turner Publishing, 1997), 357.

2. Joel S. Wit, Daniel B. Poneman, and Robert L. Gallucci, *Going Critical: The First North Korean Nuclear Crisis* (Washington, D.C.: Brookings Institution Press, 2004), 259.

3. Ibid., 258–263; Don Oberdorfer, *The Two Koreas: A Contemporary History* (Reading, Mass.: Addison-Wesley, 1997), 344–345; and Leon V. Sigal, *Disarming Strangers: Nuclear Diplomacy with North Korea* (Princeton: Princeton University Press, 1998), 172.

4. Jimmy Carter, "Letter to President Kim Young Sam," September 16, 1994, Post-Presidential Papers, "So. Korea—Post Kim Il Sung: Kim Young Sam."

5. Summary of South Korean President Kim Young Sam's letter to President Carter: The letter began by praising Carter for his recent intervention in Haiti. Then the South Korean president wrote: "We in Korea are always grateful to you for the untiring efforts you have made to improve inter-Korean relations and to resolve the North Korean nuclear issue." He expressed particular appreciation for Carter's efforts to bring about a South-North Korean summit, which regrettably did not occur "due to an unexpected development." He said that it was heartening to learn of Carter's "reassured commitment to exert [himself] for the resumption of the inter-Korean talks," and added that he

hoped Carter would succeed. Affirming that the Republic of Korea was committed to reopening the dialogue, he extended an invitation to President and Mrs. Carter to visit Korea, he hoped in the near future, to "discuss extensively and frankly issues as the peace and security of the Korean Peninsula." Kim Young-sam, "Letter to President Carter," September 19, 1994, Post-Presidential Papers, "So. Korea—Post Kim Il Sung: Kim Young Sam."

6. Ambassador James T. Laney, "Fax Cover Note to the Honorable Marion Creekmore, enclosing the text of President Kim Young Sam's Letter to President Carter, September 19, 1994," Post-Presidential Papers, "So. Korea—Post Kim Il Sung: Kim Young Sam."

7. Harry Barnes, "Summary notes of conversation September 19, 1994 with North Korean Ambassador Pak Gil Yon," in Marion Creekmore, "Memorandum to President Carter: Memcons," September 21, 1994, Post-Presidential Papers, "Korea 9/94." Barnes had been an outstanding career U.S. diplomat who had served as the director general of the Foreign Service and U.S. ambassador to Romania; India, where I served as his deputy; and Chile. In 1993, shortly after I became director of programs, I asked Harry to become director of the Human Rights Program of the Carter Center with President Carter's and John Hardman's approval. The next year, Harry took over the Conflict Resolution Program as well. He held these two positions for several years, commuting between Atlanta and his home in Vermont.

8. The message contained the following language: The ambassador had been *authorized by the leadership of the Foreign Ministry* to tell President Carter that (1) the position on the North/South summit talks as clarified by President Kim Il Sung to President Carter remains North Korea's firm policy; (2) the points of agreement reached between North and South Korea in preparing for the summit remain valid; (3) the current "questions" are how to relieve the resentment, which is deeply rooted in the hearts of the North and South Korean people, caused by the antimoral, anti-North, and antireunification acts committed by the South Korean President, Kim Young Sam, during the period of mourning for President Kim Il Sung, and how forgiveness can be given; (4) for these purposes, President Kim Young Sam **at the least should** [their bold letters] apologize to the people of North and South Korea for his behavior, and show a willingness toward reconciliation and reunification by abolishing South Korea's National Security Law which prevents all contact with the North; (5) consequently, whether the North/South summit will be held will depend upon the behavior of the South Korean authorities; (6) therefore, in North Korea's

view, the U.S. should exert its influence on South Korea in this direction. Marion Creekmore, "Memorandum to President Carter: North Korean Reply to President Carter's Inquiries on September 19," September 26, 1994, Post-Presidential Papers, "Korea 9/94."

9. Ibid.

10. Eason Jordan, "Letter to Ambassador Marion Creekmore containing two page report of Mike Chinoy sent to CNN on September 26, 1994," September 27, 1994; Stephen W. Linton, PhD, "Letter to President Jimmy Carter," October 24, 1994, 1–4; Harry Barnes, "Memorandum to President Carter: The Koreas-Conversation with Jim Laney and Related Matters," November 17, 1994, and attached K. A. Namkung, "Letter to Ambassador Harry Barnes," November 15, 1994, Post-Presidential Papers, "Korea 9/94."

11. For example, the letter from North Korean Foreign Minister Kim Yong Nam responding primarily to Carter's letter to Kim Jong Il urging agreement on the reactor issues at the Kuala Lumpur meeting, had the following words about a future Carter trip to North Korea: "We look forward to your visit at an appropriate time in the future for our reunion, and hope that circumstances and conditions will be created in favor of such a visit." Kim Yong Nam, Vice Premier, Administrative Council, Minister of Foreign Affairs, Democratic People's Republic of Korea, "Letter to His Excellency Mr. Jimmy Carter, June 19, 1995; similar words are also found in Pak Gil Yon, "Letter to the Honorable Jimmy Carter," February 20, 1995, Post-Presidential Papers, "Korea 12/94–7/95."

12. Wit, Poneman, and Gallucci, *Going Critical,* 251, and discussion in chapters 9 and 10, 247–330.

13. Paul Lewis, "U.S. May Ask North Korea to Give Fuel Rods to a Third Nations," *New York Times,* June 30, 1994.

14. Jimmy Carter, "Letter to Bob Gallucci; copy to Tony Lake," July 1, 1994, Post-Presidential Papers, "Korea—June '94," specific file: "Robert Gallucci/Tony Lake." In late August, Gallucci told Ambassador Harry Barnes and me that he had used Carter's discussions in Pyongyang to move Kang Sok Ju away from some of his initial intransigent positions. Marion Creekmore and Harry Barnes, "Memorandum to President Carter: Meeting with Bob Gallucci on Korea," August 31, 1994, Post-Presidential Papers, specific file: "N. Korea—Post Kim Il Sung: Kim Jong Il."

15. The Carter Center, "Statement from Former President Jimmy Carter on the Death of Kim Il Sung," July 9, 1994, Post-Presidential Papers, "N. Korea—Post Kim Il Sung: Kim Jong Il."

16. Jimmy Carter, "Letter to the Honorable Kim Jong Il, July 11, 1994; Rosalynn Carter, "Letter to Kim Song Ae," July 11, 1994; Faye Dill, "Letter to Counselor Han Song Ryol," July 12, 1994, Post-Presidential Papers, "N. Korea—Post Kim Il Sung: Kim Jong Il."

17. Kim Song Ae probably hoped her own son, Kim Pyong Il, would succeed Kim Il Sung as North Korea's leader, and some reports at the time of Kim Il Sung's death suggested that Kim Pyong Il might be a rival to Kim Jong Il. However, according to Bradley K. Martin, Kim Jong Il had earlier brought disgrace to his stepbrother and assured that he would not have a shot at inheriting their father's mantle. In the late 1970s, while Kim Pyong Il was in a senior position in his father's military bodyguard corps, he reportedly engaged in extravagant living and drew around him a group of flatterers who used terms in referring to him that were reserved for Kim Il Sung. Kim Jong Il allegedly reported these activities to his father, who fired Kim Pyong Il; thereafter, this stepson drew assignments to overseas embassies from which he could exert little influence at home. Bradley K. Martin, *Under the Loving Care of the Fatherly Leader: North Korea and the Kim Dynasty* (New York: Thomas Dunne Books, St. Martin's Press, 2004), 280–282.

18. Marion Creekmore, "Memorandum to President Carter: Korean Update and Request for Action," July 13, 1994, 1, Post-Presidential Papers, specific file: "N. Korea—Post Kim Il Sung: Kim Jong Il."

19. Pak Gil Yon, "Letter to the Honorable President Jimmy Carter," July 25, 1994, Post-Presidential Papers, specific file: "N. Korea—Post Kim Il Sung: Kim Jong Il."

20. Jimmy Carter, "Letter to President Bill Clinton," July 26, 1994, and Faye Dill, "Fax Cover Note to the Honorable Tony Lake: Contact Wilma Hall," July 26, 1994, Post-Presidential Papers, "Korea—June '94," specific file: "Korea—official communication w/US govt."

21. President Bill Clinton, "Letter to The Honorable Jimmy Carter," August 1, 1994, Post-Presidential Papers, "Korea—June '94," specific file: "Korea—official communication w/US govt."

22. Marion Creekmore, "Memorandum to President Carter—Korea: Our Next Month's Agenda and Your Public Response to the Geneva Talks," August 18, 1994, 1–2, including Carter's marginal comments, August 22, 1994, Post-Presidential Papers, specific file: "N. Korea—Post Kim Il Sung: Kim Jong Il."

23. R. Jeffrey Smith, "Korean Diplomat Predicts New Era in U.S. Relations," *Washington Post,* August 14, 1994, in fax to President Carter from Terry Adamson, August 16, 1994, Post Presidential Papers, "Korea 9/94."

24. Hans Vriens, "North Korea: In the Dark: Ordinary Citizens Ignorant of Nuclear Confrontation," Far Eastern Economic Review, August 25, 1994, 15–16. Post Presidential Papers, "Korea 9/94."

25. Marion Creekmore, Harry Barnes, "Memorandum to President Carter: Suggested Strategy on Korea," September 11, 1994, Post-Presidential Papers, "Korea 9/94."

26. The attendees included Don Gregg, chairman of the Korean Society and former U.S. ambassador to South Korea; Herbert Behrstock, chief of the East Asia/Pacific Division of the Regional Bureau for Asia on the United Nations Development Program, who was last in Pyongyang immediately before the death of Kim Il Sung; Tom Graham, the Rockefeller Foundation's peace and security project; Selig Harrison, Carnegie Endowment for International Peace, who had been in North Korea during the previous month; Peter Hayes, head of the Nautilus Institute; Tomoyoshi Kaneko, head of a small foundation in Japan and close to former prime minister Takeshita; Steve Linton, a professor at Columbia University who helped arrange the Rev. Billy Graham's trips to the Korean Peninsula; Don Oberdorfer, a former correspondent with the *Washington Post* and an expert on Korea; George Perkovick of W. Alton Jones; and Scott Snyder, who was in charge of the Korean initiative at the United States Institute of Peace (USIP). Harry Barnes and Marion Creekmore, "Memorandum to President Carter: August 22 Meeting on the Korean Peninsula," dated August 17, 1994. Personal papers of Marion Creekmore.

27. Jimmy Carter, "Letter to President Clinton," September 16, 1994, Post-Presidential Papers, "Korea 9/94"; Jimmy Carter, "Letter to President Kim Young Sam," September 16, 1994, Post-Presidential Papers, "So. Korea—Post Kim Il Sung: Kim Young Sam."

28. Marion Creekmore, "Memorandum to President Carter: Geneva Talks Run into Problems," September 27, 1994; "Memorandum to President Carter: Geneva Talks Adjourn Temporarily," Post-Presidential Papers, "Korea 9/94."

29. Jimmy Carter, "Memcon of Conversation with Gallucci: 10/1/94," typed note dated October 1, 1994, Post-Presidential Papers, "Korea 9/94."

30. Marion Creekmore, "Memorandum to President Carter: Korea: Resumed Geneva Talks and Miscellaneous Points," October 6, 1994; "Memorandum to President Carter: Geneva Talks: Slow Progress Being Made," October 12, 1994, an attached *New York Times* article dated October 8, 1994; Harry Barnes, "Memorandum to President Carter: Geneva Talks—More Progress," October 13, 1994; Gordon Streeb, "Memorandum to President Carter: Update on Geneva

Talks," October 17, 1994, Post-Presidential Papers, "Korea 9/94." Gordon Streeb is a retired U.S. career diplomat who served as U.S. ambassador to Zambia before coming to the Carter Center initially as a diplomat-in-residence in 1994; he accepted an appointment as a permanent member of the Center staff in 1995. Although his primary responsibilities in 1994 were to develop and run the Center's Global Development Initiative, he pitched in as needed on the Korean issue. Both Streeb, who would replace me when I resigned from The Carter Center in 1996, and I had served as DCMs under Harry Barnes when he was the U.S. ambassador in India (1981–1985). We worked well as a team.

31. Wit, Poneman, and Gallucci, *Going Critical,* 329.

32. Ibid., 329.

33. Ibid., 330.

34. Bosworth had been an outstanding U.S. career diplomat who had served as U.S. ambassador to Tunisia and the Philippines before retiring in 1985. He was president of the U.S.-Japan Foundation when he was recruited to establish and manage KEDO. Subsequently, he would become U.S. ambassador to South Korea when Jim Laney departed his post in 1997.

35. Jimmy Carter, "Letter to President Kim Jong Il," May 19, 1995; Faye P. Dill, "Letter to His Excellency Pak Gil Yon," requesting transmittal of letter to Kim Jong Il, May 19, 1995, Post-Presidential Papers, "Korea 12/94–7/95."

36. Kim Yong Nam, Vice-Premier, Administrative Council, Minister of Foreign Affairs, Democratic People's Republic of Korea, "Letter to His Excellency Mr. Jimmy Carter," June 19, 1995, Post-Presidential Papers, "Korea 12/94–7/95."

37. Jimmy Carter, "Letter to Speaker Newt Gingrich," June 17, 1995, Post-Presidential Papers, "Korea 7/95."

38. The White House, "Press Briefing by Dan Poneman, Senior Director for Nonproliferation and Export Controls, National Security Council," December 15, 1995, Post-Presidential Papers, "Korea 12/95."

39. Ibid.

40. Morton I. Abramowitz, James T. Laney (co-chairs), and Robert A. Manning (project director), *Testing North Korea: The Next Stage in U.S. and ROK Policy: Report of an Independent Task Force Sponsored by the Council on Foreign Relations* (New York: Council on Foreign Relations, 2001), 13–17; Robert A. Manning, "United States-North Korean Relations: From Welfare to Workfare?" in Samuel S. Kim and Tai Hwan Lee, eds., *North Korea and Northeast Asia* (Lanham, Md.: Rowman and Littlefield, 2002), 79, 81.

41. Abramowitz, Morton I., James T. Laney, and Eric Heginbotham, *Meeting the North Korean Nuclear Challenge* (New York: Council on Foreign Relations, 2003), 12; C. S. Eliot Kang, "North Korean Security Policy: Swords into Plowshares?" in Samuel S. Kim and Tai Hwan Lee, eds., *North Korea and Northeast Asia* (Lanham, Md. Rowman and Littlefield, 2002), 208.

42. Abramowitz, Laney, and Heginbotham, *Meeting the North Korean Nuclear Challenge*, 12.

43. Robert Gallucci's presentation at the Center for Strategic and International Studies' roundtable "Nuclear Confrontation with North Korea: Lessons of the 1994 Crisis for Today," March 20, 2003. Reported as a Nautilus Institute Special Report in its *DPRK Briefing Book: Policy Area: Agreed Framework,* http://www.nautilus.org/DPRKBriefingBook/agreedFramework/1994Crisis.html.

44. Abramowitz, Laney, and Heginbotham, *Meeting the North Korean Nuclear Challenge*, 9, 19; Nancy Soderberg states that North Korea started its highly enriched uranium program in late 1997–early 1998 and probably accelerated it in 2001–2002, Nancy Soderberg, *The Superpower Myth: The Use and Misuse of American Might* (Hoboken, N.J.: John Wiley, 2005), 269.

45. Abramowitz, Laney, and Heginbotham, *Meeting the North Korean Nuclear Challenge*, 9, 19.

46. The White House, "Press Briefing by Dan Poneman, Senior Director for Nonproliferation and Export Controls, National Security Council," December 15, 1995, Post-Presidential Papers, "Korea 12/95."

47. The full text of the joint statement follows: "The six countries reaffirmed that the goal of their talks was the denuclearization of the Korean Peninsula. In this context, North Korea committed to abandoning nuclear weapons and existing nuclear programs and returning at an early date to the NPT and IAEA safeguards. The U.S. affirmed that it had no nuclear weapons on the Korean Peninsula and no intention to attack or invade the DPRK with nuclear or conventional weapons. South Korea reaffirmed that it would not receive or deploy nuclear weapons and that no nuclear weapons existed within its borders. The DPRK stated that it had the right to peaceful use of nuclear energy, and other parties agreed to discuss at the appropriate time provision of light water reactor(s) to the DPRK. The DPRK and the U.S. undertook to respect each other's sovereignty, exist peacefully together, and take steps to normalize relations. The DPRK and Japan undertook to respect each other's sovereignty and take steps to normalize relations. All six countries would seek to promote cooperation in the fields of energy, trade, and investment. China, Japan, South Korea, and the U.S. stated willingness to provide energy assistance to North

Korea. South Korea reaffirmed its offer of July 12, 2005, to provide 2 million kilowatts of electric power to the DPRK. The directly related parties will negotiate a permanent peace regime on the Korean Peninsula in an appropriate separate forum. They will also explore ways and means for promoting security cooperation. The parties will take coordinated steps to implement the aforementioned consensus in line with the principle, 'commitment for commitment, action for action.'" See http://www.nautilus.org/napsnet/sr/2005/0577Agreement.html.

48. This description of the current state of play (mid-February 2006) benefited significantly from communications with Ken Quinones.

EPILOGUE

1. Joel S. Wit, Daniel B. Poneman, and Robert L. Gallucci, *Going Critical: The First North Korean Nuclear Crisis* (Washington, D.C.: Brookings Institution Press, 2004), 132; Don Oberdorfer, *The Two Koreas: A Contemporary History* (Reading, Mass.: Addison-Wesley, 1997), 299.

APPENDICES

1. Jimmy Carter, "Talking Points for Resolution of the North Korean Issues," Post-Presidential Papers, "Korea—June '94," specific file: "Talking Points—for mtg in both No. and So. Korea."

2. Jimmy Carter, "Optimum Commitment of North Korea—Prepared in Advance of Trip," Post-Presidential Papers, "Korea—June '94," specific file: "Talking Points—for mtg in both No. and So. Korea." The sentence that refers to "full transparency of the entire nuclear program of North Korea from its inception" is the one that deals with clearing up the discrepancy between the amount of plutonium the North Koreans had reprocessed in the past. In his discussions in North Korea, Carter would raise frequently the need for full transparency of North Korea's nuclear program from its inception and explain what he meant by those terms.

3. POL:DRR, "Your Visit to North Korea," #22960, June 13, 1994, Carter's Post-Presidential Papers, "Korea: June '94," specific file: "Korea—Briefing Info."

BIBLIOGRAPHY

BIBLIOGRAPHICAL NOTE

The primary source material for this book was internal Carter Center documents. These included President Carter's letters and notes; analytical reports by Center staff; and letters and reports received from government officials, leaders of nongovernmental organizations, and private citizens. These documents are either archived in the Jimmy Carter Post-Presidential Papers or held in files of various offices within The Carter Center. Most have not been reviewed previously by researchers. I also drew extensively on my personal notes taken before, during, and after President Carter's historic trip to Pyongyang and on conversations I had at the time and later with governmental and non-governmental officials. President Carter's trip report and some of his diary entries were very useful, as was the trip report prepared by Mrs. Carter. The raw video footage provided by CNN helped clarify my memory when describing scenes that had occurred several years earlier. The extensive endnotes document the use of these materials.

I found three books particularly valuable in developing my narrative. Joel Wit, Dan Poneman, and Bob Gallucci's *Going Critical: The First North Korean Nuclear Crisis* (Washington, D.C.: The Brookings Institution, 2004) is an excellent insider account of the actors, competing views, and policy positions that dominated the Clinton administration's response to the North Korean nuclear challenge. Written by three U.S. officials who were deeply

involved, it concentrates on the actions of governments and international organizations. The book devotes a relatively small amount of space to the
Carter intervention in 1994 and, in my view, understates its significance. The
appearance of this book at the time I was writing mine enabled me to check,
and often refine, my own understanding of the relevant political developments
in Washington and elsewhere that set the context for the Carter initiative.
The studies of two outsiders, the respected journalists Don Oberdorfer and
Lee Sigal, who had long followed developments on the Korean Peninsula,
are also essential reading for comprehending the nuclear-related events of
1994. In *The Two Koreas: A Contemporary History* (Reading, Massachusetts:
Addison-Wesley, 1997), Don Oberdorfer paints on a large canvas, summa-
rizing the key political, economic, and security developments in South Korea
and North Korea during their first fifty years. His three chapters on the nuclear issues probe with historical perspective and insight the actions and motivations of the leaders of the two Koreas and the United States in dealing
with them. Lee Sigal's book, *Disarming Strangers: Nuclear Diplomacy with
North Korea* (Princeton: Princeton University Press, 1998), hones in more
narrowly on the 1994 nuclear crisis and its antecedents. He emphasizes how
miscommunication and misinterpretations among the involved governments,
as well as policy competition between the hard-liners and moderates, created
the gridlock that prompted the Carters' trip to Pyongyang. He deals at some
length with the campaign of the hard-liners to undermine not only Carter's
efforts but also the subsequent U.S.-North Korean Agreed Framework.
Oberdorfer and Sigal both credit Carter with playing an indispensable role
in the peaceful resolution of the crisis.

Three other books provided a baseline by which I could measure some of
the perceptions I gained from the trip. Scott Snyder's *Negotiating on the Edge:
North Korean Negotiating Behavior* (Washington, D.C.: United States Institute of Peace Press, 1999) allowed me to compare my conclusions about
North Korean negotiating styles and tactics, which were derived from Carter's
three days of diplomatic exchanges in Pyongyang, against Snyder's assessments, which were based on his study of several sets of negotiations with
North Korean diplomats by various parties. Mike Chinoy's *China Live: Two
Decades in the Heart of the Dragon* (Atlanta: Turner Publishing, 1997) has a
strong chapter on North Korea, including a discussion of June 15–June 18,
1994, when he and his CNN colleagues were in Pyongyang covering the
Carter visit. His descriptions often included an incident or insight that im-

proved my own narrative. Bradley Martin's *Under the Loving Care of the Fatherly Leader: North Korea and the Kim Dynasty* (New York: Thomas Dunne Books, St. Martin's Press, 2004) contains a wealth of material about Kim Il Sung, Kim Jong Il, and developments in North Korea over the past fifty years, and I consulted it with some frequency.

Because I have not been involved in Korean issues since I left The Carter Center in 1996, I relied on several secondary sources and conversations with governmental and nongovernmental sources for the information in chapter 13 on more recent developments involving the United States, North Korea, and South Korea. Three studies issued by the Council on Foreign Relations were particularly helpful:

Abramowitz, Morton I., and James T. Laney, Co-Chairs, and Eric Heginbotham, Project Director. *Meeting the North Korean Nuclear Challenge.* New York: Council on Foreign Relations, 2003.

Abramowitz, Morton I., and James T. Laney, Co-Chairs, and Robert A. Manning, Project Director. *Testing North Korea: The Next Stage in U.S. and ROK Policy.* New York: Council on Foreign Relations, 2001.

Abramowitz, Morton I., and James T. Laney, Co-Chairs, and Michael J. Green, Project Director. *Managing Change on the Korean Peninsula.* New York: Council on Foreign Relations, 1998.

I also found the essays and book chapters listed below to be useful:

Brown, David E. "No Thanks Expected: America's Effort to Nurture a 'Soft Landing.'" In *The Two Koreas and the United States: Issues of Peace, Security, and Economic Cooperation,* edited by Wonmo Dong. London: M. E. Sharpe, 2000.

The following essays appear in Samuel S. Kim and Tai Hwan Lee, eds., *North Korea and Northeast Asia* (Lanham, Md.: Rowman and Littlefield, 2000): Samuel S. Kim, "North Korea and Northeast Asia in World Politics"; Robert A. Manning, "United States-North Korean Relations: From Welfare to Workfare?"; C. S. Eliot Kang, "North Korea's Security Policy: Sword into Plowshares?"; Victor D. Cha, "Assessing the North Korean Threat: The Logic of Preemption, Prevention, and Engagement," and Samuel S. Kim and Tai Hwan Lee, "Chinese-North Korean Relations."

Quinones, C. Kenneth. "North Korea: From Containment to Engagement." In *North Korea: From Containment to Engagement,* edited by Dae-Sook Suh and Chae-Jin Lee. Boulder: Lynne Rienner, 1998.

_____. "North Korea Nuclear Talks: The View from Pyongyang." *Arms Control Today* 34, no. 7 (September 2004).

The reader who wishes to read more widely on U.S., South Korean, and North Korean relations might find useful the following selected bibliography:

SELECTED BIBLIOGRAPHY

Albright, David, and Kevin O'Neill, eds. *Solving the North Korean Nuclear Puzzle.* Washington, D.C.: The Institute for Science and International Security, 2000.

Albright, Madeleine, with Bill Woodward. *Madam Secretary.* New York: Miramax Books, 2003.

Bermudez, Joseph, Jr. *Shield of the Great Leader: The Armed Forces of North Korea.* Sydney, Australia: Allen & Unwin, 2001.

Breen, Michael. *Kim Jong-Il: North Korea's Dear Leader.* Singapore: John Wiley and Sons (Asia), Pte Ltd., 2004.

Brinkley, Douglas. *The Unfinished Presidency: Jimmy Carter's Journey Beyond the White House.* New York: Viking, 1998.

Cronin, Richard P. "North Korea: U.S. Policy and Negotiations to Halt Its Nuclear Program." *Congressional Research Service,* November 18, 1994.

Cumings, Bruce. *Korea's Place in the Sun: A Modern History.* New York: W. W. Norton and Company, 1997.

Downs, Chuck. *Over the Line: North Korea's Negotiating Strategy.* Washington, D.C.: The AEI Press, 1999.

Gibney, Frank. *Korea's Quiet Revolution.* Walker and Co., 1992.

Harrison, Selig S. *Korea Endgame: A Strategy for Reunification and U.S. Disengagement.* Princeton: Princeton University Press, 2002.

Kim, Hak Joon. *Unification Policies of North and South Korea 1945–1991.* Seoul: National University Press, 1992.

Koh, Byung Chul, ed. *North Korea and the World: Explaining Pyongyang's Foreign Policy.* Seoul: Kyungnam University Press, 2004.

Mansourov, Alexandre Y. "The Origins, Evolution, and Current Politics of the North Korean Nuclear Program." *Nonproliferation Review* (Spring-Summer 1995).

Mazar, Michael J. *North Korea and the Bomb.* London: St. Martin's Press, 1995.

Noland, Marcus. *Avoiding the Apocalypse: The Future of the Two Koreas.* Washington, D.C.: Institute for International Economics, 2000.

Park, Han S., ed., *North Korea: Ideology, Politics, Economy.* Englewood Cliffs, N.J.: Prentice-Hall, 1996.

Quinones, C. Kenneth. *Understanding North Korea.* New York: Penguin Alpha Books, 2004.

Suh, Dae-Sook, and Chae-Jin Lee. *North Korea after Kim Il Sung.* Boulder: Lynne Rienner, 1998.

ACKNOWLEDGMENTS

I think I knew from the time we boarded the plane for the Korean Peninsula on June 12, 1994, that I would someday write about the Carter intervention in the North Korean nuclear crisis. I knew I was witnessing a moment of historical importance: a former U.S. president interjecting himself into an international dispute with the reluctant acquiescence of the current U.S. president and the opposition of the South Korean president. The ultimate result, the peaceful resolution of a crisis that otherwise could have ended in war, justified Carter's actions and, in my opinion, provided important lessons that needed to be shared. For several years, work demands, first at The Carter Center and then at Emory University, prevented my devoting the necessary time and attention to the project. It was only after I had semiretired that I was able to complete the book.

I am indebted to many people for their assistance. First, of course, is President Carter, who offered me a position at The Carter Center, allowed me to coordinate many of his international initiatives, and invited me to accompany him and Mrs. Carter on his trip to the Korean Peninsula. Although he did not prompt me to write this book, he has been encouraging and very helpful throughout the process: reading an early draft and then the final draft, answering my questions on issues where my memory was hazy, letting me read portions of his personal diary, and checking—at my request—to ensure that my descriptions of what he was thinking at various times were correct. He did not try to influence me to change my analysis or my descriptions of him and his actions. Throughout my time at The Carter Center, and particularly on the

North Korean trip, I was impressed by Mrs. Carter's deep understanding of world affairs, her shared commitment with her husband to try to improve the conditions of the unfortunate, and her personal warmth. She was kind to me and generous with her counsel, which I greatly valued. Faye Perdue's friendship and professional competence were indispensable to the successful completion of this book. She facilitated my access to Carter Center documents, read the manuscript and provided astute advice about the substance and style of the book, and, in response to my innumerable questions, invariably steered me in the right direction. She was a close friend and professional colleague while I was employed at The Carter Center, and I am grateful that she remains so today. She is one of my favorite people. I value as well my friendship with Nancy Konigsmark, and I admire her insight and her tenacity. She serves President Carter with complete dedication, but she has always been most helpful and hospitable to me. She read the section of the book about our Korean trip and offered a number of comments that made the manuscript more accurate and, I believe, more interesting. In addition to Faye and Nancy, Carrie Harmon, the former director of public information at the Center, urged me to write up the Carter trip and gave me access to files in her office; Deanna Congileo, the Center's current director of public information, and her deputy, Jon Moor, have been generous with their time and advice on this project; Sara Williams has provided valuable assistance with the photographs used in this book; Tom Crick of the Center's conflict resolution program searched his office files for material relevant to my research; and Steven Hochman, the director of research, helped me locate and correctly cite a number of Center documents.

Several Atlanta friends have been particularly helpful. Jim Laney, former president of Emory University and former U.S. ambassador to South Korea (1993–1997), encouraged me to write the book, allowed me to interview him several times, read the manuscript, and made useful suggestions. I admire Jim greatly—as a scholar, a university administrator, a U.S. ambassador, and a man who lives his convictions. Tom Johnson and Eason Jordan, then CEO and president of CNN Newsgathering, respectively, reviewed the manuscript, clarified a number of points about CNN's role, and helped me gain access to CNN documentation of the trip. Tom Remington, chairman of the political science department and a highly respected professor at Emory University, perused an early draft and offered insightful suggestions on content and structure. Two former government colleagues now at Georgia Tech University, Dr. John Endicott, formerly a colonel in the U.S. Air Force, and Dr. William (Bill) Hoehn, who worked on nuclear and other issues on Capitol Hill and in the Defense Department, also reviewed the manuscript. At my request, they paid particular attention to my handling of technical nuclear questions and to my proposals in the epilogue, and they gave me good advice. I also consulted with John on bibliographical questions. In addition, Elizabeth Fricker of Emory tirelessly sent out copies of the manuscript for review; Angie Levin of Georgia Tech established contact for me with General Gary Luck; and Kathy Christenson, CNN's vice president for archives and research, and CNN's librarians, Priya Kamat and Jennifer Doaust, facilitated my access to CNN materials.

I am appreciative of the contributions of a number of previous and current U.S. government officials. Tony Lake, who served as national security adviser from 1993–1997; Bob Gallucci, the Clinton administration's point man for dealing with the North Korean nuclear crisis; and Dan Poneman, who was the senior NSC expert on nuclear nonproliferation, read portions of the manuscript and suggested useful revisions. General Gary Luck reviewed the portions on his involvement and helped me improve their accuracy. Several former State Department colleagues read and commented on my descriptions of The Carter Center's communication with the State Department in the year leading up to the trip, the briefings in Washington prior to our departure for the Korean Peninsula, and the discussion with the country team of the U.S. embassy in South Korea. These included David E. Brown, Lynn Turk, Ken Quinones, Chuck Kartman, and Danny Russel. I owe a particular debt of gratitude to Ken Quinones, who is a scholar (a Harvard PhD in East Asian history and language), a diplomat who worked on Northeast Asia (and particularly North Korea between 1981–1997), an author, and a consultant. Ken read my entire manuscript, made innumerable and invaluable suggestions, helped me obtain technical details on the North Korean nuclear program, and assisted me in the preparation of the bibliographical note. Dick Christenson, who also accompanied President Carter to Pyongyang and served as adviser and interpreter, read the chapters describing our time in South Korea and North Korea as well as the epilogue, and his memory and insight have strengthened those sections of the book. Mark Ramee deserves a special commendation. A retired U.S. diplomat now in the State Department's Office of Information Programs and Services, Mark shepherded my manuscript through the tedious clearance process in Washington to ensure that it did not contain material that was still classified. Since I had government clearances at the time of the trip, the separate reviews by State, Defense, NSC, CIA, and the U.S. Secret Service were necessary, and, thanks to Mark, the entire review was completed in record time. Yet the opinions and characterizations in this book are my own and they do not necessarily represent official positions of the U.S. government.

I have enjoyed working with a number of talented members of the Public Affairs team since Peter Osnos, then CEO, agreed to read my early draft and subsequently decided to publish my manuscript. David Patterson has been a superb editor; his facile pen and probing questions have ensured that the final product was a significant improvement over my original effort.

I am also grateful to Don Oberdorfer for locating and sending to me two photographs for possible use in my book.

Despite all this assistance, I am solely responsible for any errors of facts or judgments.

Finally, I wish to single out two personal friends and my family. On their own initiative, Dick and Paula Hornaday, friends of more than three decades, volunteered to read an early draft and suggest how it might be revised in order to appeal to the average informed reader in addition to the expert on international affairs. I hope the book comes close to meeting their expectations. My daughters, Catherine and Debra, and their husbands, Ted Decker and Dave Roesser, respectively, demonstrated continuing interest in the lengthy project and overlooked my impoliteness when I excused myself from family gatherings to get back to my laptop. Even my grandchildren, Collin and Sean Roesser and Nicole and Zoe Decker, asked frequently about the book, and only occasionally expressed their wonderment at why it took their grandfather so long to finish the thing. Most of all, I want to thank my wonderful wife, Linda, who has suffered my absences—both physical and mental—as I lived in my 1994 world. Her patience seldom cracked despite my many broken promises; every aspect of the conceiving, planning, writing, and ultimately completing the book took far longer than I had projected. For almost half a century, Linda has been my sweetheart, my wife, and my best friend. There was never any question in my mind to whom I would dedicate this, my first book; it could only be to Linda.

Spencer, William (Bill) J., 29, 336n7, 339n35

Stacey, Weston M., 72

State Department, 12, 69, 146, 340n40; bilateral talks and, 61; Carter Center and, 34, 269; Carter trip and, 32, 33, 36, 76, 250, 252; Gallucci and, 14; isolation and, 40; Kim Il Sung letter and, 234; Korea Desk of, 76; Laney and, 51, 53; Policy Planning Staff of, 351n3; Transition Team, 351n3; trip report and, 175

Streeb, Gordon, 379n30

Subways, in Pyongyang, described, 197–198

Summit Council, 72

Summit initiative, 258–259, 262, 263–264

"Sunshine Approach," 41

Supreme People's Assembly, 132

Surveillance, 141–142, 167, 259; international, 272, 273; maintaining, 149, 150, 156, 168

Surveillance equipment, 167, 236, 249; maintaining, 138, 140, 174, 178, 180, 204, 209, 225, 226, 246, 248, 252

Taedong River, 131, 188, 196

Takeshita, Prime Minister, 378n26

Talbott, Strobe, 42

Talking Peace (Carter), 196, 357n17

Talking points, 355n26, 355nn26, 27, 361n9; Gallucci and, 101, 137, 159, 186, 241

Tangun, tomb of, 100

Tapo Dung missiles, 64

Taylor, Bill, 160

Team Spirit, 11, 37, 87, 116, 169, 228; criticism of, 7, 168; rescheduling, 6, 14, 15; suspension of, 8, 12, 36, 39, 57, 174, 331n18, 333n35

Time magazine, on military action, 19

Tito, Marshall, 155

Tomoyoshi Kaneko, 378n26

Tongil House (Unification Hut), 129, 200

Track I/II diplomacy, 25

Trade, 119, 123, 138, 155

Transparency, 145, 156, 162, 204, 224, 228, 381n2; bilateral talks and, 174;

Gallucci and, 270; inspections and, 170; Kim Il Sung and, 270

Treasury Department, Patriot Act and, 279

Troop reductions, 23, 208, 336n2

Trout, story about, 193–194

Trust, building, 155, 158, 160, 193, 247

Tuchman, Barbara, 347n25

Tunnels, digging, 197, 366–367n25

Turk, Lynn, 89

"Understand[ing] the Sensibility of Asians" (Kim Dae Jung), 56

UNDP. *See* United Nations Development Program

Unification, 120, 121, 122, 136; achieving, 133; communication and, 119

Unification Church, 72

Unification Hut, 98, 129, 200

Unique status, 62, 141, 150, 169, 273; claiming, 93, 137; Gallucci and, 162; Kim Il Sung and, 162; removing, 174

United Nations, 8, 23, 27, 177, 337n14; Carter Center and, 24; sanctions and, 95, 100, 101, 105, 109, 113, 137, 139, 147, 166–167, 183, 184, 185, 240

United Nations Command, peace agreement and, 279

United Nations Development Program (UNDP), 64, 378n26

United Nations Military Affairs Committee, 151

United Nations Security Council (UNSC), 12, 17, 149, 169; Carter and, 139, 204–205; China and, 16; IAEA and, 15, 42, 63; inspections and, 43, 63, 141; nuclear crisis and, 14, 54, 140, 370n7; sanctions and, 48, 55, 65, 66, 70, 82, 87, 88, 89, 90, 95, 101, 102, 105, 109, 140, 158, 159, 167–168, 175, 179, 230, 236, 249

U.S. Air Force, 16, 17

USA PATRIOT Act (2005), 279

U.S.-Japan Foundation, 379n34

U.S. Marine Corps, 18

U.S. military, 5; reducing presence of, 22, 23

U.S. Navy, Carter and, 21–22

U.S. Nuclear Posture Review, 275